T0215574

IT Security Risk Control Management

An Audit Preparation Plan

Raymond Pompon

■ ■ ■

Apress®

IT Security Risk Control Management: An Audit Preparation Plan

Raymond Pompon
Seattle, Washington
USA

ISBN-13 (pbk): 978-1-4842-2139-6   ISBN-13 (electronic): 978-1-4842-2140-2
DOI 10.1007/978-1-4842-2140-2

Library of Congress Control Number: 2016952621

Managing Director: Welmoed Spahr
Acquisitions Editor: Susan McDermott
Developmental Editor: Laura Berendson
Technical Reviewer: Mike Simon, Dena Solt
Editorial Board: Steve Anglin, Pramila Balen, Laura Berendson, Aaron Black, Louise Corrigan, Jonathan Gennick, Robert Hutchinson, Celestin Suresh John, Nikhil Karkal, James Markham, Susan McDermott, Matthew Moodie, Natalie Pao, Gwenan Spearing
Coordinating Editor: Rita Fernando
Copy Editor: Kim Burton-Weisman
Compositor: SPi Global
Indexer: SPi Global

Distributed to the book trade worldwide by Springer Science+Business Media New York, 233 Spring Street, 6th Floor, New York, NY 10013. Phone 1-800-SPRINGER, fax (201) 348-4505, e-mail orders-ny@springer-sbm.com, or visit www.springer.com. Apress Media, LLC is a California LLC and the sole member (owner) is Springer Science + Business Media Finance Inc (SSBM Finance Inc). SSBM Finance Inc is a Delaware corporation.

For information on translations, please e-mail rights@apress.com, or visit www.apress.com.

Apress and friends of ED books may be purchased in bulk for academic, corporate, or promotional use. eBook versions and licenses are also available for most titles. For more information, reference our Special Bulk Sales–eBook Licensing web page at www.apress.com/bulk-sales.

Any source code or other supplementary materials referenced by the author in this text is available to readers at www.apress.com. For detailed information about how to locate your book's source code, go to www.apress.com/source-code/.

Printed on acid-free paper

To all the defenders out there working unnoticed to keep us safe.

Contents at a Glance

Contents

About the Author

Raymond Pompon is currently the director of security at a global solutions provider in the financial services industry. With over 20 years of experience in Internet security, he has worked closely with federal investigators in cyber-crime investigations and apprehensions. He has been directly involved in several major intrusion cases, including the FBI undercover Flyhook operation and the Northwest Hospital botnet prosecution. For six years, Raymond was president and founder of the Seattle chapter of InfraGard, the FBI public-private partnership. He is a lecturer and on the board of advisors of three information assurance certificate programs at the University of Washington. Raymond has written many articles and white papers on advanced technology topics and is frequently asked to speak as a subject matter expert on Internet security issues. National journalists have solicited and quoted his thoughts and perspective on the topic of computer security. He is a certified information systems security professional as well as GIAC certified in the Law of Data Security & Investigations (GLEG).

About the Technical Reviewer

Mike Simon has an education in computer science and 25 years' experience designing and securing information systems. Mike is a well-known and highly respected member of the Northwest's information security community. Mike is faculty at the University of Washington Information School, a published author, an active collaborator in the PRISEM project and other regional initiatives, and a subject matter expert in the energy and finance sectors. He has also integrated with law enforcement through contacts with the FBI, the Department of Homeland Security, and InfraGard.

Acknowledgments

A huge thank you to my family for the boundless encouragement, love, and support. Thank you and I love you Rebecca, August, and Theo. Thank you to my mom and Jim, who nudged me to do this.

Dad, I wish you could read this. Maybe in some way you are. You taught me so much.

Much gratitude to all my teachers and fellow artists who inspired and taught me at the Richard Hugo House. Special thanks to you, Frances for opening up this geek's world.

To the rest of the Conjungi gang: Cory, Mark, Sara, and Julie. I learned so much from all of you and I miss the heck out of you.

Thank you to everyone who worked hard and fast to make this book a reality: Mike for showing me the way and going above and beyond to help get this book done. Dena, who set me straight on the audit details. Kyle for giving me pointers along the way. Jana for a rocking author photo. Rita, for keeping me and everyone on track. Susan for taking a chance on a new author. Light is the task where many share the toil.

Introduction

Far and away the best prize that life has to offer is the chance to work hard at work worth doing.

—Theodore Roosevelt

Growing up before the Internet invaded everything, my discovery of computers in my teen years was akin to discovering and exploring a new hidden alien world. That shiny TRS-80 in my high school library was a magical portal of unlimited possibilities. I'm happy to say that that magic still tickles my brain. As I grew in knowledge and skill, I delved deeper into technology's sorcerous mysteries: programming, dial-up communities, the Internet, hacking culture. It was here that I found IT security: the most engaging, most challenging, most thought-provoking aspect of computing. Security feels like a never-ending undersea duel between remote-controlled fleets of submarines during uncertain weather conditions.

Congratulations for choosing to work in IT security—doing combat engineering in the war zone of the Internet. It's exciting and exacting work, where a single lapse can mean a hole that an invisible intruder can creep into. Security can also be the kind of work that not everyone appreciates. Much like airport security, IT security gets in the way, slows us down, and creates a hassle. Many people see security as overhead that apparently contributes nothing to revenue or growing the customer base.

Security defines its best successes to be when nothing happens. After a long period of these kinds of successes, an organization ponders whether you are necessary or not. Then you have to deal with the bothersome chore of justifying what you've done to an auditor and the budget axe.

When things do go wrong, many quickly accuse the security team of negligence and ineptitude. Breaches often end up as headlines, embarrassing the whole organization. IT security teams can be trotted out by their own organization as the scapegoats. All of this humiliation is suffered while knowing that the bad guys have outspent, outlasted, and outwitted you.

It's not enough to discourage me, though. There is the thrill of the chase and arrest of the perpetrators. I've helped take down a tiny fraction of them, but that's ancillary to what matters. What IT security does is protect privacy, bolster confidence, and keep vital systems up. It feels good to make critical systems more durable and predictable—and maybe knowing that you've deprived some creep of one less victim. I am energized by designing new systems and making them resilient in the face of a horde of attackers. There's joy in digging deep and figuring out where the holes are, where the best place to bolster the defenses is, and then untangling all of this for the financial decision makers. It's more compelling than all the puzzles and video games in the world. IT security is an interesting and challenging field, which rewards dedication and open-mindedness.

An Audit Focus

This book is framed to walk you through building a security program for an organization about to be audited. Even if you don't think you're going to be audited, this is still a useful way to approach a security program. If you think you're not going to be audited, think again.

Even if you aren't being audited, it's useful to act as if you will. The threat of outside scrutiny focuses your attention and keeps you from getting sloppy. For some, the fear of an audit is greater than a fear of hackers. Audits force you to be thorough and organized in your work.

What Technological Knowledge Should You Pursue?

Where do you begin with all of this? IT security requires practitioners to have a strong working knowledge of the fundamental mechanisms of a wide area of technology. This includes experience with the implementation and management of those systems. IT operations such as help desk support, asset inventory, patching, and system configuration are all key components of an organization's defense. Since a majority of attacks come in via the Internet, a good understanding of Internet protocols and network technology is essential.

As you will be risk analyzing systems of software components and strapping controls onto them, IT security professionals should at least have a fundamental grasp of programming. A good measure of this is being able create something simple but useful in a basic scripting language like PERL, Bash, or PowerShell. Bonus points for doing something in Ruby/Python/Java.

IT security professionals also benefit from a basic knowledge of databases. Since most large IT systems are built upon a database of some sort, it's helpful to know a little SQL. You should at least be able to write queries and understand how tables and indices work. You don't need to become a DBA, but tinker with something like SQLite or MySQL.

As you can see, IT security professionals need to keep up with technology. Keeping up is part of the job. Since you're reading this book, it's likely that you already don't mind doing homework to improve your skillset. That's first lesson of IT security: never ever be complacent.

What Other Knowledge Should You Pursue?

One of the most interesting things about IT security is the requirement to study a diverse range of related disciplines. To be effective, IT security professionals need to branch out of technology. Within an organization, IT security works with many different departments at an operational level, including human resources, physical security, accounting, legal, business development, software development, and sales. This means helping these departments modify and redesign business processes to accommodate security and audit requirements. IT security professionals need to have knowledge of key organizational financial processes, such as budgeting, revenue flows (sales), disbursements, and the related business cycles. This book gets into how this happens.

Knowing the organization's sector and competitive space is also important, as you may be sharing and comparing information on common risks and regulations amongst your industry peers. Nearly every major organizational sector has peer groups dedicated to security that you should consider joining and subscribing to information feeds. Just plug ISAC (Information Sharing and Analysis Center) and your industry name into a search engine and see what you get.

Since many of the things that IT security does are projects, it's helpful to have project management skills. I've been managing projects for decades and I'm still not satisfied on how well I run a project. Many organizations get hacked because they've skipped a few simple but tedious details somewhere in the implementation or routine process.

IT security professionals should understand how corporate culture works and how it differs from organization to organization. This understanding is crucial in being a change agent and educator. It means being able to present orally and in writing. In addition, we should have a good working of the psychology of risk. This means understanding how people react to risk and how to frame risk so that they can make optimal decisions. You should also be aware of the common fallacies and traps people fall into when weighing risky decisions. We'll get into this a lot more in the book.

IT security professionals need to know something about the law. This includes obvious things like security and privacy regulations, including US federal and state laws, as well as international regulations, since the Internet is global. IT security professionals benefit from an understanding of contract law and liability, as well as the legal implications and requirements of commercial compliance standards and internal organizational policies. This is covered in more detail in the chapters of this book.

While IT security professionals should understand areas outside of technology, they should expect everyone else to be ignorant of security. So IT security professionals need to continually explain and justify IT security concepts for executives, project managers, human resource officers, legal counsel, physical security officers, and law enforcement.

How this Book Is Laid Out

This book follows a chronological progression of building a security program and getting ready for audit.

Part I: Getting a Handle on Things. A good way to develop a security program is to design with an audit in mind to focus attention and to ensure that all controls work as described. This section covers the audit focus, asset analysis, risk assessment, and scope design.

Part II: Wrangling the Organization. This section includes chapters on how to design, nurture, and incorporate an IT security program into a dynamic organization over time. You rarely have a chance to design a program when a new company is formed. Most companies are born without security and need it added later as they grow and experience more security incidents. A security professional is always growing and trimming their program to fit the needs of their organization. These chapters cover everything from high-level governance to how you work with the various teams.

Part III: Managing Risk with Controls. Once the risk and scope are fleshed out, controls can be applied to reduce the risk. These series of chapters cover the various types of controls and how you can best implement them. This is the biggest section, starting with control design and moving into the implementation details of technical and physical controls.

Part IV: Being Audited. This section covers the process of being audited. Its chapters describe how to hire an auditor and the mechanics of various types of formal audits. It also covers the healing power of internal audits and the auditing of your organization's critical partners and suppliers.

How the Book Is Laid Out

PART I

■ ■ ■

Getting a Handle on Things

CHAPTER 1

Why Audit?

A smooth sea never made a skilled sailor.

—Franklin D. Roosevelt

As the headlines fill with breach notifications and stolen identities, legislators and industry groups may add more security regulations to their lists that entail newer and tougher audits. If someone hasn't audited your organization yet, someone eventually will. As our dependency on IT systems grows, there will be more scrutiny. This means more rules, regulations, and contractual obligations regarding the security and resiliency of crucial IT systems. These new rules will come with audits to make sure that they are being followed. In one form or another, it is a safe bet to prepare for a new flood of compliance requirements and their accompanying audits.

You Will Be Audited

If your organization isn't being audited right now, it may just be just a matter of time. Many organizations have IT security requirements required by industry requirements and laws, but they don't realize it. If a business accepts credit/debit cards, holds employee records, or collects data on children, then the security program needs to conform to specific requirements. If a company is part of the supply chain for critical infrastructure industries—such as medical, financial, military, or public utility, then that company can be audited. Regulated IT activity can be as complex as processing health insurance claims or as simple as writing software that is used by banks. If a company is publicly traded or provides critical services for a public company, then its financial and IT systems can be subject to audit. Even law firms have been audited because of their vast collections of customer intellectual property.

Government and non-profit entities can fall under federal and state regulations that require an IT security audit. The Federal Information Security Management Act (FISMA) governs the security of federal agencies and requires an audit. For North American electrical utilities, there are demanding audits against the North American Electric Reliability Corporation (NERC) cybersecurity standards.

What Is an Audit?

An *audit* is a systematic examination by an independent expert on adherence to a well-defined standard. To be an audit, these three elements must be in place: the standard to measure against, neutrality of the examiner, and a systematic approach; otherwise, it's an assessment, which implies informality. The standard's governing body certifies the audit.

© Raymond Pompon 2016
R. Pompon, *IT Security Risk Control Management*, DOI 10.1007/978-1-4842-2140-2_1

Regulated Industries That Require Audits

Any company working in the financial sector is probably already familiar with the obligation of audits. This includes banks, insurance companies, accountants, securities firms, and even pawn and payday loan shops. If an organization handles financial information, they fall under the Gramm-Leach-Bliley Act (GLBA) and its Safeguards Rule for protecting the privacy of their customers. GLBA itself is vague about specific technical measures that need to be put in place, but instead focuses on a risk-based approach with controls chosen by the organization to reduce that risk. This is the risk-based approach that this book focuses on, because it is very flexible and efficient.

There are additional security guidelines for GLBA described by the Federal Financial Institution Examination Council (FFIEC), an interagency standards group of financial organizations. Even though the FFIEC is a non-regulatory entity, its guidelines are used as measures by auditors in the financial services sector. The FFIEC guidelines describe specific technological and procedural controls that should be in place. This is more akin to how other compliance frameworks and audits are structured. This list of controls is a guideline to verify risk treatment plans to make sure that you haven't missed anything. Both the general risk-based approach as well as the specific controls-based approach are useful for understanding how auditors evaluate IT security programs at regulated organizations.

Another large regulated sector is publicly traded companies that fall under the Sarbanes-Oxley Act of 2002 (SOX). Congress passed this law to prevent another Enron-like defrauding of investors. SOX has many requirements around transparency and conflict of interest, but there are special rules relevant to IT security as well. SOX requires companies to establish security controls around financial and messaging systems to protect their availability and integrity. E-mail is considered relevant to SOX because of its prominence in the Enron case. Because of the regulation involved, SOX requires an independent audit of these controls. SOX does not call out specific security technologies or tools, but is risk-based, like GLBA. Large banks are often publicly traded companies, so they find themselves under both GLBA and SOX audits.

The third-largest regulated sector is the medical health sector, covered primarily by the Health Information Technology for Economic and Clinical Health Act (HITECH) and the Health Insurance Portability and Accountability Act (HIPAA). These acts have strict security requirements for hospitals, health care clearinghouses, and health care providers (referred to as *covered entities*) to protect the privacy and integrity of patients' electronic personal health information (EPHI). Like GLBA and SOX, HIPAA is not specific about technology but does require that organizations perform a risk analysis and build appropriate risk management processes. Be aware that medical information (and the accompanying security/audit requirement) can spread far beyond hospitals and cover individuals and organizations that do any kind of data processing on health records, including health insurance, medical billing, or medical data analysis organizations. Most of these organizations must undergo a HIPAA security audit, either directly or indirectly.

Regulated Industries Without Explicit Audits

Speaking of health records, a smaller but important regulated sector is drug and medical device companies. If a medical treatment is going to get FDA approval, the IT systems involved in drug development, medical device manufacture, or testing require exacting security controls to guarantee the integrity of the medical records. This is covered by Title 21 of the Code of Federal Regulations (21 CFR Part 11) under Electronic Records. It has additional IT security requirements around electronic signatures, which is rare in other industries. There are no formal audit regimes for 21 CFR Part 11, but the FDA does review the controls and records as part of the approval process. Although there is no specific audit requirement, after-the-fact investigations after incidents are as rigorous as any audit.

Another regulated industry that does not require a formal audit covers companies that collect personal information on children under the age of 13. Congress passed the Children's Online Privacy Protection Act (COPPA) to protect children's privacy on commercial children's online services (web and mobile). In addition to rules around parental consent and disclosure, operators must have security measures in place to protect the confidentiality and integrity of the information they collect from children. Although COPPA doesn't require an audit yet, because of the considerable industry penalties involved, an internal audit is a good idea.

Companies that manufacture, store, or distribute hazardous or critical chemicals also have security requirements that include addressing IT security risks and physical threats under Chemical Facility Anti-Terrorism Standards (CFATS) regulation. Presidential Policy Directives consider a chemical facilities' critical infrastructure, and therefore companies need to ensure the security of any toxic, explosive, or vital chemical. No explicit regular audit of IT security systems is required yet.

Business Transactions Can Loop You into an Audit

Although the payment card industry is not a government-regulated industry, an enormous number of organizations, both private and public, accept credit or debit cards (payment cards) as a means of payment. The issuers of payment cards created a council, the Payment Card Industry Council, to develop a set of strict requirements, called the Payment Card Industry Data Security Standard (PCI DSS). The PCI DSS has over a hundred specific control requirements under the umbrella of twelve major control objectives. PCI DSS is not flexible and mandates specific risk treatments based on the common threats to the average payment card processor. Depending on the volume of transactions in the operation, PCI DSS can require an audit. This book covers the analysis and selection of controls that lead you to the required controls for PCI DSS.

If a business provides services on behalf of an organization in a regulated industry, then it can be subject to an indirect third-party audit based on those regulations. For example, companies that store or process payment cards on behalf of other companies are subject to PCI DSS requirements. Companies that supply software or services to financial firms can find their customers requiring them to be audited against GLBA requirements. Service providers that involve critical financial transactions of publicly traded companies need to adhere to SOX regulations. The federal government also tasks medical third parties with security requirements. Per HIPAA regulations, all business associates are contractually required to agree to have appropriate security controls in place and can be subject to audit. This requirement contractually flows downstream, so any suppliers of the third party that have contact with confidential medical data also fall under these requirements. The HITECH law now requires periodic HIPAA audits of both covered entities and their business associates.

Does your organization do any business in Massachusetts that involves collecting and storing customer or employee personal data? Massachusetts General Law Chapter 93H and the 201 CMR 17.00 statutes (a.k.a. Mass Data Protection Law) cover the protection of the personal data for any Massachusetts resident. The law spells out a list of security controls that must be in place. While not specifying an audit, it would be a good idea to check your program to ensure that it's compliant and functional. If something does go wrong, it always helps to demonstrate diligence and transparency by having a previous audit done.

Even if your customers don't have explicit regulatory requirements, they may still require that their suppliers with access to confidential data be secure. For example, law firms, consulting companies, and software contractors have found themselves under contractual security mandates from their clients because of the sensitive data they handle. It's becoming common for service contracts to include a "right to audit" clause with penalties for nonconformance.

■ **Sample Contract Clause Requiring Audit**   Vendor acknowledges that IT security is important to Customer. Vendor will follow IT security processes that meet or exceed industry practices of companies providing services similar to those detailed in this agreement. On an annual basis, Vendor will provide Customer with the most recently obtained third-party SSAE 16 SOC 2 Type 2 audit with a period of no less than nine months of the security of Vendor's service and its conformance with information security standards. With no less than one-week's advance written notice, Customer may conduct an onsite security audit of Vendor's systems containing Customer data.

A Lawsuit May Drag You into Something Worse Than an Audit

If an organization has e-mail or internal electronic communication, any kind of lawsuit can create *e-discovery* issues as plaintiffs seek out digital information related to their legal complaint. Under the Federal Rules of Civil Procedure (FRCP), companies must take measures to prevent tampering with subpoenaed data, referred to as *spoliation of evidence*. Judges can require proof of these measures if witnesses do not provide timely and complete data subpoena requests. If that information is not secure and available, this could trigger a prolonged and punitive investigation of an organization's IT messaging and storage systems. This kind of legal investigation can become far more invasive and adversarial than any audit. Findings of spoliation can lead to financial penalties and/or adverse findings in the case.

The worst kinds of lawsuits for IT security are the ones from customers accusing an organization of negligence in protecting their data. When things do go wrong, audits demonstrate your due diligence. Suppose a hack does happen: you can point to a thorough and timely audit as your organization's commitment to pre-empt problems. A self-regulating organization with an eye to testing and improving its security is in a much better position to defend itself legally and in public. In negligence cases, judges look favorably on a healthy security program backed up by an independent audit, and hacks appear more like bad luck than willful ignorance or IT penny-pinching.

Business-to-Business Audits

Depending on your industry, just the act of soliciting large and important customers can bring about an external review of your IT security program. Some industries, like finance and government, have security assessments built into their request for proposal (RFP) process. So you can easily find your own sales team leading customer prospects into the security team's office to answer questions. In those situations, it's always great to be able to pull out a recently completed audit report and hand it to them for review.

Sometimes the act of working with a new business partner or supplier entails an audit. For example, some credit reporting bureaus require security assessments of their customers to ensure that they are protecting the confidential information accessed through their service. It seems strange that a vendor would add security responsibilities on top of the payment that you're already making for their service, but that is what happens if the data is sensitive.

When companies are acquired, the purchasing entity sometimes conducts an audit of the IT systems as well. Many smaller companies do not have as robust and detailed a security program as their larger acquirer. This kind of audit can be one with dire consequences—especially if the staff of the acquired entity does not make the grade of the new parent company.

If an organization is seeking IT security insurance to assuage the damages that come from breaches and cyber-attacks, then they need to submit to some kind of security audit from the insurer. No insurance company wants to cover an organization for a loss without having some idea of their risk exposure.

Will/Should You Audit Your IT Security Controls?

Does your organization...

- Collect, store, or process financial transactions?

- Do business as a publicly traded company?

- Collect, store, or process payment cards?

- Collect, store, or process health or health insurance information?

- Collect, use, or disclose data on children under the age of 13 years?

- Develop, manufacture, or distribute FDA-approved drugs or medical devices?

- Manufacture, store, or distribute dangerous or important chemicals?

- Act as a service provider with access to customers' confidential data or to critical systems?

- Create and store electronic messages that could be subpoenaed as part of a criminal or civil investigation?

- Collect, store, or process personal information on citizens of Massachusetts?

Audit Misconceptions

Audits can be intimidating and there is a tendency for some people to be confused or misinterpret what an audit is about.

The Burden of Audit Is on You

In an audit, there is no presumption of innocence. An auditor will not ever assume that you are compliant. Instead, auditors assume that what they haven't tested yet is insecure. The burden is on your organization to prove to outsiders that you are compliant. This means that even if you think you're compliant, if you cannot produce the timely, accurate, and complete records as proof, then you may have problems. It is best to prepare ahead of time.

Aim Higher Than Compliance

It is a waste of resources to build an IT security program solely devoted to meeting a compliance requirement. It is true that some organizations just want to check the audit check box and move on. Many companies coast this way for years. By blindly implementing controls to meet compliance requirements, you are in danger of having an inefficient and ineffective security program. Compliance requirements are the result of negotiation and committee work, which means weak and delayed standards with incomplete coverage. New threats and technology always leapfrogs what regulation defines as necessary, especially if that regulation spells out specific controls or technologies. Building a security program just to meet compliance falls short of addressing the current risks your organization faces. Ultimately, that is the goal of a security program: reduce risk, not pass audit.

If you are going to the trouble of building an IT security program and have it pass audit, you should at least make sure that your security program is useful for your organization. Security controls are expensive—directly in the cost of technology and indirectly in the cost to people's time and convenience in running through them. Think of TSA airport security with all its backscatter imaging systems, guards, X-ray machines, metal detectors and long, long lines. If you're going to do all of that, why not make the controls actually effective and appropriate to your organization's business? Most audit requirements are designed for a typical organization with typical risks. Your organization isn't typical in at least the one aspect that makes it unique and valuable. The IT security program should consider this and not adopt a one-size-fits-all control regime.

Audits Are Useful

There is value in the auditor's concept of confirmation that security systems are in place and properly functioning. Many organizational IT departments quickly slap together onto an accumulation of disparate IT systems to keep up with demand. Over time, these organizations have bolted-on security controls, like firewalls and passwords, as needed at the last minute, without a plan or roadmap. Implementation guidance and boilerplate security policies are often cribbed from Internet searches. At some point, your organization will become utterly dependent on that IT system remaining functional and trustworthy. If someone with an outside perspective doesn't thoroughly examine it, why would anyone assume that an IT security program assembled in this manner is correct and complete?

There is a lot of value in that outside perspective. Just as the publisher of this book wouldn't let these words go to press without someone else reviewing them, you should feel the same about your IT security. It's too dangerous to assume that it's all working perfectly. This is what audits should be about: verifying what you think you've done.

Audits Make You Look Good

An audit with no significant findings is a worthy accomplishment. Your organization can issue a press release or send an announcement to all of your customers about these kinds of achievements. Sales departments are always looking for reasons to contact customers with good news. Besides reassuring customers that their data and transactions will remain undisclosed and untouched, audits demonstrate your ongoing commitment to privacy and security. By proactively seeking out and passing an audit, you show the world that your organization puts its money where its mouth is. You can work with marketing on delivering an ongoing campaign, extolling the trust and confidence that comes with industry audit certifications. Smart customers realize that passing an audit requires an organization to expend serious resources on IT systems. Audits may not always tell you if an organization is secure enough, but they will at least weed out the lazy and the ignorant. Like peacock feathers, a passed audit is a good indicator of health and strength.

The Audit as a Forcing Function

Audits are great motivators to build a security program. It is hard work to get a security program off the ground, much less in a semifunctional state to pass an audit. Left to their own devices, the IT department would rather focus on keeping the existing systems up and functional with a minimum amount of fuss. They are already busy patching, upgrading, adding capability, and helping users. Also, IT teams can be very protective of their systems. Changes, especially the large changes that the security programs sometimes require, can cause downtime or confuse the users. Their livelihood revolves around keeping things running. The last thing they have time to do is retool their systems because there is a *possibility* that a hacker *might* break in someday. However, an auditor is a real and present danger. Hackers are hiding somewhere out on the darknets and they may or may not bother to poke at your organization. The auditors are there in the office and in their faces, asking them hard questions. Even if they weren't moved by risk of breach or failure, the IT department and the users know that they will be held accountable for a failed audit.

To pass an audit, an entire organization needs to coordinate, pay attention, and put effort toward getting controls and processes in place. An audit mandated by the executive suite sets a tone and direction for the entire organization to build an IT security program as part of the organizational culture. Audits also provide a tangible milestone for leadership to measure the success of the IT security program. With the audit looming, it is also easier to get budget and resource approvals for necessary controls and changes.

One of the hard things about being in the security field is that you are the person who tells everyone else "No!" *No* to that new business idea. *No* to relaxing the stringing password policies. *No* to hiring that great developer with a long police record. *No* to the flashy new web site full of vulnerable code. *No, no, no*. With an audit in place, the security team can now point elsewhere for the blame. "Sorry, I'd like to do that but I'm afraid we'd have an audit finding." There is significant value in having a scapegoat for getting the unpleasant things done and denying the insecure requests.

Audit Types

The three types of audit standards covered in this book are Statements on Standards for Attestation Engagements 16 (SSAE 16), the Payment Card Industry Data Security Standard (PCI DSS), and the International Organization for Standardization/International Electrotechnical Commission standard, or ISO/IEC 27001:2013 (ISO 27001). With that certification comes a requirement of the auditor to be independent and follow a proscribed auditing methodology. For example, there are certified public accountants (CPAs) for SSAE 16 audits, qualified security assessors (QSAs) for PCI DSS audits, and certified ISO/IEC 27001 lead auditors. The critical difference between all audits is the formal standard used. It's worth briefly exploring how these different audit standards approach risk management.

ISO 27001

A striking thing about an ISO 27001 audit is its strong focus on the risk management process, with a weaker emphasis on using specific controls. The ISO 27001 audit requires the use of a classic management tool, the Deming Cycle (also known as the Deming Wheel, the PDSA Cycle, and the PDCA Cycle), which has four rolling phases: Plan (risk analysis), Do (risk mitigation), Check (internal audit), and Act (adjust controls). Organizations can select controls during the "Do" phase based on a pre-supplied list of best practice controls, but organizations can choose to skip controls in the list if they can provide sufficient justification for exclusion. Organizations are also encouraged under ISO standards to add new controls to ensure that they are adequately managing all risks. ISO 27001 audits also require organizations to identify and document a formal method of risk analysis.

ISO 27001 calls the IT security program the *information security management system* (ISMS). The ISMS must have certain standard features and roles, as defined in the standard. In general, ISO 27001 audits require more paperwork than any other audit. There is a strong emphasis on policy, procedures, and the creation of records related to the running of the ISMS.

The SSAE 16

The SSAE 16 actually has three types, called Service Organization Controls (SOC), and numbered 1 through 3. The SOC 1 audit is the most flexible in terms of control design. Yes, you still need to do a risk analysis, but what the auditor actually reviews are your control objectives and the controls supporting those objectives. The risk analysis focuses on protecting the systems involved in performing financial transactions and messaging. This audit satisfies SOX. The SOC 1 is issued by the American Institute of Certified Public Accountants (AICPA). The predecessor of the SSAE 16 SOC 1 was the Statement on Auditing Standards No. 70, or SAS 70. Some individuals still refer to the SSAE 16 SOC 1 as a "SAS 70" type audit, even though the standard has evolved.

The SOC 1 works with the audited party (you) writing control objectives (with some auditor's help) that mitigate the risks identified against financial transaction integrity. For example, a control objective would be written, "Controls will provide reasonable assurance that Electronic Access to Systems is appropriately restricted to authorized individuals." Then, you would select controls like passwords and firewalls to support this control objective. Unlike the ISO 27001, for a SOC 1, there are no pre-defined controls or objectives to pick from; you need to create your own based on the relevant systems and risks.

This changes when we move to SSAE 16 SOC 2. In a SOC 2, there are pre-defined control objectives and general control descriptions. As part of your audit scope, you can choose what SOC 2 control objectives you'd want to certify. The choices are Security, Confidentiality, Processing Integrity, Availability, and Privacy. Be aware that the Privacy objective is more business-process focused than security-focused and not covered in this book. For these control objectives, SOC 2 specifies controls through Trust Service Principles that must be in place to manage certain kinds of risk. This audit is a bit more specific with respect to certain kinds of controls, as opposed to the SOC 1. Overall, this is to make the audit more standardized (you either have this control in place or not) and easier for people to implement. It does come at the cost of the flexibility for the organization. The SSAE 16 SOC 3 audit is the same as a SOC 2, except the organization can make the audit certificate publicly available, whereas SOC 1 and SOC 2 audit reports are restricted to other auditors' review.

In an SSAE 16 audit, there are two explicit types, also numbered. A SSAE 16 Type 1 audit is a design audit, with a single visit to review the design of the controls and control objectives. Functionality and operational effectiveness are not measured. A SSAE 16 Type 2 audit is a performance audit that covers a three-to-twelve month period, with the auditor visiting several times during that period to examine how well controls actually work.

PCI DSS

The most restrictive type of audit in terms of control choice is PCI. Under PCI DSS, you must implement all the controls as described. Skip a control or implement it inadequately and you do not meet the standard. With ISO and SSAE 16, you can leave out some controls—as long as the failures don't jeopardize fulfilling the control objective and address risk adequately in the eyes of the auditor. The reason PCI DSS is far more restrictive is because it is centered on payment cards and payment card processing, which have well-known risks and well-understood IT systems. Therefore, PCI DSS can skip over some of the risk analysis and scoping exercise needed for other types of audits, and focus on the controls that the PCI council believes works the best to protect payment cards. Since systems processing payment cards are so widespread (think of all the e-commerce sites), there needs to be a cut-and-dried way to evaluate their security posture. Assessing against a list of controls goes a lot faster than having an auditor try to interpret a risk analysis and customized control objectives. It also requires less expertise on the part of the control implementer and the auditor.

Another difference between these audits is how frequently the auditor reviews the running controls. For PCI, the auditor performs a single comprehensive audit once per year. For ISO 27001, the auditor returns every six months to recheck the controls and the health of the IT security program. The ISO 27001 has some discretion in the frequency, based on stability of the environment and the strength of the controls.

Auditors Auditing

How do auditors perform an audit? There are several levels of investigation, depending on the importance and functionality of the control. The simplest form of evidence gathering is attestation: they ask you if something is true or not. Auditors can expand this into testimonials by asking many people in an organization and seeing if their answers line up. This actually works well. If an auditor asks three people about "the security policy around laptops in cars" and gets three different answers, then the so-called policy is not actually a company policy. For critical or technical controls, auditors will look for physical evidence. Audit teams gather this evidence by either direct inspection or by requesting copies of records and screenshots. Auditors usually do not ask for every single record, but use statistical sampling with confidence intervals to get a measure on things. In some cases, auditors may in fact look at every single record, especially if the majority of the samples are coming up negative. Auditors perform some of this work on-site, but can also work off-site as well. All formal audits mentioned here require at least one site visit to do physical inspection, with the exception of PCI DSS level 4, which allows self-reporting for low-volume payment card merchants.

What Is the Right Audit for You?

If don't already know which audit you should aim for, either you are lucky or you don't understand your organization's business. Most organizations have specific audits thrust upon them. If you don't know which to choose, it's worth noting that government regulators and large staid institutions prefer SSAE 16 audits. Watch out: they can be the most expensive, because only CPA firms can perform them. Some very large service providers literally do every audit that they can. To see this illustrated, just type "AWS Compliance" in your search engine and you'll see just how many there are. In the end, the best audit for your organization is the one that your customers and partners respect the most.

FURTHER READING

- **PCI Security Standards Council - information on the PCI DSS**
  https://www.pcisecuritystandards.org/pci_security/

- **ISO 27001**
  http://www.iso.org/iso/home/standards/management-standards/iso27001.htm

- **Information on the SSAE 16 SSAE 16**
  http://www.aicpa.org/Research/Standards/AuditAttest/Pages/SSAE.aspx

- **FTC security controls guide**
  https://www.ftc.gov/tips-advice/business-center/guidance/start-security-guide-business

■ ■ ■

CHAPTER 2

Assume Breach

When intelligence folks smell roses, they look for the funeral.

—MI5 Director-General Jonathan Evans, Address at the Lord Mayor's Annual Defence and
Security Lecture, London, UK, June 25, 2012

A security professional should expect and plan for things to go wrong, especially when hostile parties are constantly attempting to break their engineering constructs. This concept is as old as the history of warfare and defensive engineering.

The Lesson of Fort Pulaski

Near the coast of the state of Georgia sits the picturesque city of Savannah and the Savannah River. The Savannah River stretches out into the Atlantic Ocean through an estuary of brackish waters dotted with small islands. The size and depth of the river have made Savannah a major seaport since before America was a nation. After the War of 1812 and the British rampage through Washington, DC, the US government realized that its major ports needed protection from sea attacks. President Madison ordered the construction of a fort on Cockspur Island—a strategically perfect location in the southern channel of the Savannah River—to stop invading ships bound for the port. Ringed with marshes and oyster beds, Cockspur Island was only nine square miles but big enough to build a military stronghold.

The Invincible

In 1829, the US Army Corps of Engineers constructed Fort Pulaski, an impregnable fortress named after a hero of the American Revolution (see Figure 2-1). In addition to the natural defenses of the Savannah River territory, which included swamps filled with native alligators, the US Army added an impressive series of defenses. At the cost of more than 26 billion in today's dollars, they laid 25 million bricks to create walls that were seven feet thick—strong enough to repel any known bombardment. Inside, engineers braced the walls with thick ramparts to buffer artillery shells that made it through or over the walls. Outside, a moat that was seven feet deep and 32 feet wide surrounded the fort with only one entrance via a drawbridge. Beyond the moat lay a flat open plain. Any soldiers landing on the beaches of the island would have to race across hundreds of yards of open plain while under constant fire from 48 smoothbore cannons covering the entire circumference of the fort. Land assault would come with high casualties. The cannons' effective range stretched nearly a thousand yards, far enough to hit any ships passing up the river heading toward the city of Savannah.

Figure 2-1. *Fort Pulaski*

Figure 2-2 shows the range of the Fort Pulaski guns. The nearby shore was out of range in both directions, so only ships on the river could fire on the fort and be fired upon. But the ships would not have the protection of seven-feet-thick walls to protect them. The fort was impenetrable.

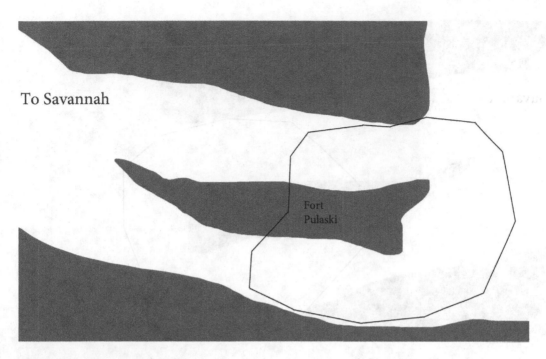

To Savannah

Fort
Pulaski

Figure 2-2. *Gun ranges of the fort*

Ownership Changes Hand

Things never go as you planned and foreigners never invaded the US coast. Instead, the state of Georgia seceded from the Union in February of 1861 and joined the Confederate States of America. The Confederate Army took over the port of Savannah and stationed 385 troops in Fort Pulaski. Now a key port town in the US Civil War, the US Army found themselves in the undesirable position of having to capture their own impregnable fort. By 1852, the Union Army had captured the nearby Tybee Island to use as a staging ground for assault. The Union sent several ships to test the defenses, but the scathing cannon fire quickly them turned back. The Union generals had two bad options: starve them out or besiege the island with a massive strike force and accept huge casualties.

New Exploit Technology Is Introduced

Maybe there was another option. The history of engineering is tied to the history of warfare, as the problems of war inspire new technologies. A former engineer, Brigadier General Quincy Gilmore had a crazy new idea. He knew there was new technology that the Union Army could use on Fort Pulaski. First tested only a few years earlier, no one had ever tried the newly developed rifled cannon in battle. Unlike the smoothbore cannon, the rifled cannon had a grooved barrel that forces the shell to spin through the air like a football. This spin acts like a gyroscope to stabilize the path of the shell, giving the cannon longer range and a straighter path (smoothbore, on the other hand, acts more like a fastpitch baseball with high pressures at the leading edge, forcing curved trajectories). General Gilmore placed his guns on the shores of Tybee Island, which were nearly 1,700 yards away from the walls of Fort Pulaski. He took his time setting up his artillery pieces in the marshy banks, safely out of range of the smoothbore guns of the fort. Figure 2-3 shows the gun ranges of Gilmore's shore cannons.

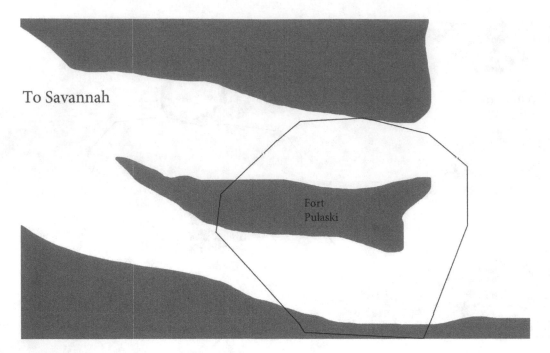

To Savannah

Fort
Pulaski

Figure 2-3. *Gun ranges of the Union rifled cannons on the shore*

After a final ignored plea to surrender the fort, Quincy opened fire on the morning of April 10, 1862. With only three rifled cannons, he fired shell after shell into one particular spot on the wall of the fort. After only 30 hours, shells punched a neat hole through the wall. Fearing that more shells would ignite the fort's powder magazine, the Confederate garrison surrendered and the Union Army took the fort. Not a single life was lost.

This was the first true test of the Fort Pulaski's defenses and it failed catastrophically. If you visit Fort Pulaski today, you can see the hole. The world was stunned by this historic military victory. Armies everywhere had to rethink their defenses because of the rifled cannon. As shocking as this event was in 1862, this was neither the first nor the last successful defeat of a so-called perfect defense. Even in contemporary times, we often hear murmurs of fear regarding a "digital Pearl Harbor," tying the worry about the weakness of current IT systems to our last major military disaster. What we may think of as invulnerable can easily become fatally weak in the face of technological advancement. In the IT profession, our advances come daily instead of over decades. It's a safe bet to assume that an attacker will eventually breach your network, with all its best defenses. This is further complicated by the intricacy of constantly shifting IT systems and the defenses of typical organizations.

The Complexity of IT Systems

We know that the Internet is far more complex than just HTTP servers and browsers, but to non-IT folks the Internet is only the Web. Based on that worldview, let's just look at only the Web. The mechanisms involved are so dizzyingly complex that the sum of all the components involved is beyond any single human's complete understanding.

The act of opening a single web page is an intricate collection of interwoven technologies, standards, and transactions. You type a site's name into your browser's URL bar, let's say **www.apress.com**, and press Enter. Your local machine needs to do a Domain Name Server (DNS) query to match www.apress.com to an IP address. To do this, it sends out a DNS query to whatever DNS server that was assigned to your machine. That server does not likely know the answer, so it must pass the query upstream to another DNS server. This goes upstream again to the ".com" DNS authoritative servers (wherever they are), which then pass it to the authoritative "apress.com" DNS server run by Apress, which then returns the IP addresses resolve to the "www." web server.

Networks on the Internet hand this IP address, server by server, to your client to use. DNS client and server software governs all of these interactions using standardized DNS calls and answers over specific ports and protocols between many different parties. The entire design of DNS is a highly distributed database run by everyone with a domain name on the Internet. Right now, that number is in the hundreds of millions. Anyone with their own DNS server is part of that system, which means that DNS is an agreed-upon naming and lookup system run by millions of participants; none of which you have influence or oversight on, but must all work together for the Internet to deliver a web page.

But wait, I was simplifying. I skipped an entire lower-layer set of transactions involving how Ethernet and IP addresses are tied together and routed locally and on the Internet. In this case, we are talking about two dozen or so top-tier global networks and ten thousand ISPs sending around two billion terabytes of information a day. All of this and we haven't even gotten started on opening a web page yet.

Now that the browser has an IP address, it can request a web page. The browser establishes a TCP session with the web server by issuing a request to connect, which travels over the web ports, protocols, and the local Ethernet LAN, through the local router, up to the local ISP, over the Internet, and down to the Apress web server. The web server completes the TCP handshake, with more back and forth over the Internet, to eventually establish a connection. Once linked up over TCP, the browser issues an HTTP GET request to the web server. The web server's response is the text HTML code of the web page. The browser interprets that page and starts to paint the screen. The page itself may contain hundreds, if not thousands, of other elements. The local browser interprets these elements, such as graphics and embedded web pieces. This in turn triggers more HTTP GETs, sometimes to different web servers and different domains.

This isn't even taking into account any active content like JavaScript or Flash, which run like mini-programs within the browser and trigger other kinds of Internet calls. Also, I'm not talking about a secure encrypted web page, because a discussion of HTTPS, certificates, and trust would take another chapter.

A Tangled Web of Code

All of the details of this are compounded by the complexity of the code itself. One piece of software in this everyday scenario does most of the heavy lifting: the browser. A single version of Firefox has around 13 million lines of code programmed by 3,600 different developers with over 266,000 specific changes in a single version alone. Let's not forget patching in new code changes, which happens about once every six weeks. So we have a single critical piece of the web that is so complex that the software is already beyond any single person's understanding. It's not the only piece of software involved, because we still need the operating system, the network stack, DNS servers, web servers, routers, and other networking software. All of these components need to cooperate with a gigantic set of standards. Each of these standards represents hundreds of hours of work by committee, detailed in inches of documentation that programmers must implement correctly in each of the respective software components. To the average user, this complexity is hidden by the interface and underlying infrastructure. Table 2-1 is a listing of some of the major standards involved in a web transaction. Each of these standards is dozens of pages of exacting technical detail.

Table 2-1. *Some of the Standards Involved in a Web Transaction*

Standard	Defined by
HTTP	RFC 7230
HTTPS	RFC 2660
TLS	RFC 2818
DNS	RFC 1032-1035 and many more
IP	RFC 791
UDP	RFC 768
TCP	RFC 793
CSMA/CD	RFC 2285
HTML	RFC 1866 and many more
ASCII	RFC 20
JPG	ISO/IEC 10918
PNG	RFC 2083
CSS	RFC 2318

Complexity and Vulnerability

Given the size and intricacy of a single IT system, how well do they all work in concert? Many organizations slap together IT infrastructure at the last minute to barely meet functional requirements. It is rare that you see quality or security requirements defined ahead of time. IT infrastructure grows organically as an organization expands, as systems are interconnected, upgraded, patched, modified, and jury-rigged to keep up with relentless business needs. What is left is a convoluted and bewildering infrastructure interacting with its environment in unpredictable and untestable ways. Software bugs, incompatibilities, misconfigurations, design oversights, misread standards, and obsolesce are prevalent within many IT infrastructures of notable size. These unplanned problems can create numerous opportunities for catastrophic sequences of failures that in turn give rise to gaps in security. Given the immense scale of typical IT systems, it is inevitable that pervasive security holes are the norm, not the rarity.

Researchers on both sides of the law are discovering new vulnerabilities every day. As I write this, the National Vulnerability Database is tracking nearly 75,000 known vulnerabilities in software. A single common browser plug-in had over 300 newly discovered vulnerabilities in 2015. A very popular network device manufacturer had nearly 75 new security holes in the same period. A widespread smartphone operating system had nearly 200 that year. The huge Heartbleed vulnerability of 2014 affected more than half of the Internet's web services. Nearly two years later, people are still patching and cleaning up systems from Heartbleed. These are all disclosed vulnerabilities, which are a subset of all the other vulnerabilities yet to be discovered. The large numbers are not surprising. The more a technology is used, in terms of number of users and time in production, the more valuable a target it becomes. The largest, most popular IT systems are always going to be the ones leading the vulnerability statistics. Unfortunately, there is a reason why these systems are popular targets. These are also the same systems that your organization will be inclined to use the most because they are the most useful, the most familiar, and often the cheapest. It is like the old saying on thermodynamics: You can't win, you can't break even, and you can't quit the game.

Technical Vulnerabilities

How are IT systems vulnerable to attack? To a computer, a number can be data or instructions. Most vulnerabilities occur when instructions are injected into data channels. Common attacks like buffer overflow,[1] SQL injection, ping of death, the Bash bug, and cross-site scripting are all examples of this. The system is expecting user-input data in a safe format, but an attacker takes advantage of a neglected verification and inserts new commands. Since computers are blind to the real world, attackers can easily fool them into executing new orders.

Subsystems that run their own instructions within the main system amplify the vulnerabilities present. Things like active web content (Java, Flash, and ActiveX) or operating system scripting languages (PowerShell, Bash, or batch files) can become new vectors for attack. Even systems with complex parsers like HTML or SQL can also have their own entire classes of vulnerabilities on top of the software application itself. The more flexible a system becomes, especially when it comes to accepting input carelessly, the more security vulnerabilities it has.

Security technology itself is not immune to these problems. Since complex systems require complex solutions, security controls can have vulnerabilities as well. Since these controls are often the primary gatekeeper to huge treasure troves of other systems, attackers often scrutinize them very carefully. Given the complexity of software and the inevitably of software bugs, I find it a warning sign when a manufacturer boasts of impossible-to-hack devices. Another error in judgement is to assume that by making one part of a system secure, the entire system becomes secure. Called the *fallacy of composition*, you see it when people expect a computer to be completely safe from attack merely because it has antivirus software or a firewall installed on it. Technology is complex and vulnerabilities are so numerous that you should always expect new attacks.

Attackers Are Motivated

A few years ago, I saw a job ad on a Reddit forum. It offered a "huge salary" with full health benefits, relocation bonuses, free lunches, and two free visits to security conferences a year. It was for a small startup in Saint Petersburg, Russia. They were looking for programmers with a strong C and assembly language background, good knowledge of Windows, and networking experience. The job title was "senior malware engineer." This wasn't the first solicitation I'd seen from underground cyber-criminals, but it was the most brazen.

Cyber-criminals can make a lot of money from breaking into systems. It's a safe bet to assume that they're better paid than you are. Because they are the profit center of their organizations, they have the complete support of their leadership. In fact, many hackers are entrepreneurs, working for themselves and totally self-motivated. These individuals do nothing but work all day (and night) finding new ways to break into systems. They are highly organized, with specialists in system penetration, planting malware, managing captured machines, laundering stolen data, and reselling captured systems. They have market places that rival modern e-commerce platforms and use business tools to track "sales" and projects.

Unlike defenders, these attackers are not constrained by rules. They cheat. They steal source code and look for holes. They trick users into running their software or entering passwords on fake sites. They comb social media and build detailed dossiers on the people in your organization. Then they combine that information and come up with devious attack schemes. It's easy to assume that there is an inexhaustible supply of vulnerabilities that attackers can tap into given enough time or motivation. The defenders are always playing catch up, always responding to attacks. In fact, cyber-criminals may have already broken into your network as you read this. This is the essence of principle of *assume breach*.

---

[1]https://users.ece.cmu.edu/~adrian/630-f04/readings/AlephOne97.txt

The Assume Breach Mindset

To not assume breach is naive. Could you assume perfect security, perfect trust, and perfect information over a long time? Just like Fort Pulaski, this thinking is dangerous. Arrogance is worse than ignorance. It is better to always be on guard, always be expecting an attack, than to be complacent and hope for the best. Security professionals must be continuously seeking to improve their defenses and looking for signs of breach. Just like the attackers, defenders should be thinking of new ways that their systems can be hacked.

This doesn't mean be pessimistic about the industry, though many people are. Over the years, I've heard many pundits say that we're losing the war against the hackers. The world hasn't ended yet. We're still using computers and the Internet and getting things done. We still get more value out of using computers and the Internet than we lose to attackers. I see that more systems than ever are now online and we are still protecting the majority of them. Victories or defeats are really about how you define the winning conditions. At some point, you have to let go and accept some losses. No security system is perfect and most of us are doing our very best to protect things. I know we'll be always outnumbered, always outgunned. It is a form asymmetric warfare, where there is a vast landscape of possible targets that you cannot possibly defend all the time. That's what makes it a challenge.

Living in Assume Breach World

What does it mean to accept the eventual failure of security? It is best captured in Norton's Law: All data, over time, approaches deleted, or public.[2]

We know that technology will fail. We know that people will fail. Failure can be defined as a system not conforming to your expectations. So change your expectations. Prepare for failure. Even if you can't fix the weak links, you can watch them, insure them, plan to replace/upgrade them, and prepare response scenarios for when they break down.

When you do your analysis, assume you won't know everything. Anything that you haven't thoroughly tested should be treated as insecure. Assume that there will be unknown systems on your networks, hidden critical data, data in the wrong places, unexpected connections, and excessive user privileges. Some of the systems most relevant to security will be inconspicuous or subtle. Follow the data flows, look for the systems holding value, and rethink what is critical. Plan for systems to change constantly and what the repercussions will look like. Build your controls with all of this in mind.

Assume breach is about people as well. Remember that there will always be people in positions of trust who can hurt you. Rigid security policies will be bypassed. Listen to the complaints, they will tell you something.

Assume breach is knowing that you should never fight alone. Find peers to trust and then share information with them. Share intelligence about what you see the bad guys doing. Share data on what worked for you in keeping them out. Build allies.

Lastly, no matter what you do and how much work you put in, there will be risks left over—residual risk. Organizations exist to get things done, to make money, to solve problems—not to avoid trouble. Your job is to assume that everything will go wrong and still help your organization get through it. That is assuming the breach.

---

[2]https://medium.com/message/hello-future-pastebin-readers-39d9b4eb935f

FURTHER READING

- **Better Than Free, by Kevin Kelly**
  http://kk.org/thetechnium/better-than-fre/

- **Heartbleed as Metaphor, by Dan Geer**
  https://www.lawfareblog.com/heartbleed-metaphor

- **Complex adaptive system**
  https://en.wikipedia.org/wiki/Complex_adaptive_system

- **Top 50 Products by Total Number of Distinct Vulnerabilities**
  https://www.cvedetails.com/top-50-products.php

- **U.S. code-cracking agency works as if compromised, by Jim Wolf**
  http://ca.reuters.com/article/technologyNews/idCATRE6BF6BZ20101216

CHAPTER 3

■ ■ ■

Risk Analysis: Assets and Impacts

The real trouble with this world of ours is not that it is an unreasonable world, nor even that it is a reasonable one. The commonest kind of trouble is that it is nearly reasonable, but not quite. Life is not an illogicality; yet it is a trap for logicians. It looks just a little more mathematical and regular than it is.

—Gilbert K. Chesterton

All your decisions regarding security and meeting compliance requirements should be driven by disk. The more accurate the picture of risk you ascertain, the more efficient and effective your security program will be. The next three chapters explore risk in the IT world.

Why Risk

Imagine the CFO of your company telling you that there's an extra $50,000 in the budget that you can spend on security. How would you spend it? After that, what would you say to the CFO when he asked you to explain your choices? Many of us are technologists and we love to buy new gadgets. But that may not always be what our organization needs. The well-organized security professional has a prioritized list of what she needs to do next. Where does that list come from? Risk analysis.

Risk is about avoiding unnecessary costs while maximizing revenue. Being hacked is expensive. So is installing a bunch of firewalls that don't do anything. Therefore, risk should drive security decisions. Before you spend any money, understand what risks you have, to which key assets, and how you plan to deal with them. Ideally, you align controls such that the most important controls are reducing the biggest risks. This also necessitates that you measure how much a control is reducing risk. The goal is that you work your way down, reducing risk after risk on the list, based on that priority. Risk analysis tells you where to focus your attention.

No, risk analysis won't always be perfect. However, careful and calibrated analysis is provably far superior to off-the-cuff guesses. Despite the apparent fuzziness of measuring risk, the components of risk can be quantified—at least enough to do comparative rankings of best to worst problems.

You should customize your risk analysis to your specific organization, at a specific point in time. Otherwise, there is a danger of missing major risks or overspending on insignificant risks. Risk analysis is dynamic. You need to update it on a regular basis to reflect the changing world. Valuable risk analysis is realistic, actionable, and reproducible.

© Raymond Pompon 2016
R. Pompon, *IT Security Risk Control Management*, DOI 10.1007/978-1-4842-2140-2_3

Risk Is Context Sensitive

Risk on its own is merely a number. A measure of risk is only meaningful when compared against another measure of risk. For some people, driving on a crowded freeway is too risky. For others, skydiving is just a fun way to spend a weekend. Saying something is "too risky" implies that the risk in question exceeds some other level of acceptable risk. Saying "it is safe" means it does not. Risk is a relative measure. What is acceptable to your organization?

Furthermore, that risk measure itself is only meaningful to a particular system and organization. Robert Courtney Jr. of IBM summarized this in his first law: "You cannot say anything interesting (i.e., significant) about the security of a system except in the context of a particular application and environment."[1]

Where is the context that we look at when examining risk? We can look right into our own organizations. In 2007, the Institute of Internal Auditors (IIA) released the *Guide to the Assessment of IT (GAIT) Principles*. The GAIT states: "Technology exists to further a business goal or objective. The failure of technology to perform as intended (i.e., technology risk) may result in or contribute to a business risk—the risk that business goals and objectives are not achieved effectively and efficiently." Furthermore, GAIT published principles pertaining to risk.

THE GAIT PRINCIPLES

Principle 1: The failure of technology is only a risk that needs to be assessed, managed, and audited if it represents a risk to the business.

Principle 2: Key controls should be identified as the result of a top-down assessment of business risks, risk tolerance, and the controls—including automated controls—required to manage or mitigate business risk.

The GAIT created these principles to guide auditors and the organizations they audit. It is a good compass in dealing with the confusing world of audits and compliance requirements. The GAIT principles are useful for dealing with IT risk as well any audit-related dilemmas.

Components of Risk

IT security professionals have a specific definition of risk: the event in which something bad happening to something we care about. Risk is composed of two subcomponents: likelihood (chance) and impact (something bad).

Saying, "If this machine gets hacked, all our data is owned" is a description of an impact, not risk. Risk analysis is also more informative than a list of disaster scenarios. Statements about "what could go wrong with" are impacts, which do not mean anything without an attached likelihood. The key to spotting these kinds of incomplete risk statements is to look for the word *could*. "The sun could go super nova!" Is that a risk that you need to consider?

Someone may complain, "We're getting tons of malware spam every day on our support e-mail box." This is statement about likelihood, not a fully formed risk statement. Without an impact (or a worthwhile measure of the chance of it leading to an impact), it is not a risk.

Watch out, it can get confusing, especially when non-security people say things like, "Our password lengths are too short and that's risky!" This is an incomplete risk statement. Insufficient password length is a statement about control deficiency that informs likelihood, which is a part of risk. Risk analysis tells you

---

[1]http://zvon.org/comp/r/ref-Security_Glossary.html#Terms~Courtney%27s_laws

more about actual threats to your organization than doing a gap analysis against which best practice controls you've implemented. Missing controls are vulnerabilities, which may or may not be relevant to risk. "Hackers are getting cleverer and better organized" is not a risk. It's an evaluation of a threat actor, which is also a subcomponent of likelihood. Likelihood is the combination of a threat and a vulnerability.

Statements like "the cloud is risky" convey no useful IT security information. Risk statements must include probabilities and calculated impacts to provide you with the data that you need to make trade-offs.

Calculating Likelihood

Sometimes when IT security professionals discuss likelihood, the response they receive is "It'll never happen." If this is from a C-level, often it is the end of the discussion. To avoid this from happening, you need to do your homework. Calculating the chance of something happening has two primary pieces: the likelihood of a *threat* acting against you and the likelihood of the threat leveraging a *vulnerability* in your systems. Here are some examples of threats:

- Malware

- Malicious insider

- Non-malicious insider

- Burglar/office thief

- Internet hacker

- Earthquake

- Pandemic

Within here, you can break down even further into things like prevalence of threat or capability of threat, as shown in Table 3-1.

Table 3-1. *Common IT Security Threats*

Threat	Capability	Prevalence
Malware	Untargeted, generic	Common
Malware	Targeted, customized	Rare
Malicious insider	Normal user, no rights	Common
Malicious insider	Sysadmin, full rights	Very rare
Non-malicious insider	Normal user has an accident	Common
Non-malicious insider	Sysadmin user has an accident	Rare
Burglar/office thief	Opportunistic	Common
Burglar/office thief	Targeted	Rare
Internet hacker	Script kiddie	Very common
Internet hacker	Cyber-criminal	Very rare
Earthquake	Richter 5.0 and under	Uncommon
Earthquake	Richter 5.1 and higher	Very rare
Pandemic	Debilitating	Uncommon
Pandemic	Fatal	Very rare

Remember that threats have to be able to act on something in order to cause problems. Threats and vulnerabilities are tied together so that certain types of threats only use certain types of vulnerabilities. Here are some examples of vulnerabilities associated with malware:

- Web sites

- Mail servers

- Web browsers

- Users, social engineering

Like threats, you can examine vulnerabilities in terms of attack surface, exploitable weaknesses, and resistance capability yielding the updated list in Table 3-2.

Table 3-2. *Examples of Vulnerability Factors*

Target	Attack Surface	Weakness	Resistance
Web sites	Many sites	Moderately patched	High resistance
Mail servers	Few sites	Well patched	High resistance
Web browsers	Large number of browsers	Poorly patched	Moderate resistance
Users	Social engineering	Large number of users clicking	Low to moderate resistance

Between these two factors, you can see how you could begin to get some idea on the magnitude of likelihood. You may have noticed that, in general, the threat vectors fall into two major types: natural disasters and human-caused attacks. You can assess these types of threats differently, with differing methodologies and models. These two types are covered in more detail in the next two chapters.

Calculating Impact

Going back to the GAIT principles, we know that risk flows from business objectives or the parts of the organization that make money, engage with customers, and/or do something useful. When in doubt, go back to the company's mission. Note that unless the organization is specifically a technology company, these business objectives are likely non-technical in nature. That doesn't mean that you won't quickly discover a lot of IT systems that directly support those objectives.

Ultimately, impacts relate to assets. Assets can be tangibles such as money, people, facilities, and IT systems. Assets can also cover intangibles like market reputation, intellectual property, contracts, or market advantage. Assets are anything your organization considers valuable and would feel pain losing.

When looking at impact on assets, you can break these down into breaches of confidentiality, integrity, and availability. Some assets have a different magnitude of impact to different types of breaches. For example, a breach of confidentiality against a database of payment cards would likely be considered a higher magnitude impact than a loss of availability to that same database. Having the system down is bad, but leaking all the confidential data on the Internet is worse.

Just as risk analysis entails doing an impact analysis, doing an impact analysis presupposes a complete and timely asset inventory. For risk analysis, asset inventory is one of the first steps. Your goal is to have a prioritized list of your most important assets.

IT Asset Inventory

Of all the types of assets, IT assets are often the most difficult to nail down. This is because it requires a lot of tedious grunt work to identify intangible things like software, data, and configurations. This means scanning with tools, interviewing people, reviewing documentation, and examining configurations. You take all of that, cross-reference the results, and repeat the scanning, interviewing, and reviewing. Why? Because IT systems are everywhere in an organization and the data is even more widespread. *Wired* magazine founder and visionary Kevin Kelly famously said, "Every bit of data ever produced on any computer is copied somewhere. The digital economy is thus run on a river of copies." Tracking down data in a dynamic organization, much less deciding on its value, is extremely challenging.

Chasing down data can begin by creating a detailed map of all the systems and data in your organization. Onto this map, you can draw out critical data flows and user action chains. Sometimes commercial tools can help identify critical data, like data leak prevention solutions or network scanners. Ultimately, you want to gather as much information as you can. What is on all of your file shares and who administers them? What are the most important servers on your network? The following are some ideas.

Key systems to include in an asset analysis:

- Domain controllers

- Mail servers

- Accounting servers

- HR servers

- Database servers

- Sales servers (customer and prospect lists)

- Internet-facing anything

- Point-of-Sale systems

- File shares

- Anything holding confidential data of any kind

It sometimes helps to do a little archaeology and dig up old network diagrams and documentation. Glean what you can from these documents and use it to generate questions when you interview key personnel both in IT and in business services. After all the work that you're doing to come up with your asset inventory, it's a good idea to document how you did it. Not only will this help you (or someone else) do it the next time (and you want to do this at least annually), but some audit standards require a documented asset inventory process. Later chapters describe how to document processes, but consider this a placeholder to write down how to do it.

Asset Value Assessment

Once you have an inventory of assets, you need to value it. Asset values change over time, so you should document and revisit this process at least annually. At this stage, you are looking at the value of assets to your organization, not necessarily the value of your assets to others. A file of customer credit cards has a different value to you than it does to a Latverian hacker. The valuation of your assets to malicious actors is covered in the discussion on adversarial risk analysis in Chapter 5.

You can categorize organizational data into different classes. This process, called *information classification*, usually breaks things down into several major categories. The most common types are *confidential* (secret), *internal-use only* (protected), and *public* (shared with the world).

You would likely classify the most valuable data objects as confidential, such as customer data, usernames/passwords, HR records, payment card numbers, product designs, sales plans, and financial records. Internal information normally includes things like source code, e-mail, or internal memos. Public information is the free stuff that you give away, like sales brochures, press releases, or product demo videos. Another thing to consider in valuing information is how old it is compared to its useful life. Obsolete data may not be as important as current data. Note that these are examples only.

Some organizations place different values on different things. Some government entities may classify much more information as public, as they may be bound by transparency rules. Firms doing research in highly competitive fields, like medical drug manufacture, may classify things much higher. You need to roll up your sleeves and customize asset analysis to your organization.

The following are examples of valuable assets:

- Intellectual property (source code, product designs, copyrighted material)

- Personal information (customer credit/debit cards, Social Security numbers, customer names, driver's license numbers, account numbers, passwords, medical information, health insurance information, vehicle registration information)

- Usernames/e-mail addresses and passwords stored together

- Message repositories (e-mail, chat logs)

- Customer-facing IT services that are revenue generating (e-commerce sites, streaming media, product catalogs)

- Customer-facing IT services that are support/non-revenue (web support forums, documentation, demo sites)

- Critical internal IT services (chats, help desks, accounting, payroll)

- Semi-critical internal IT services (web sites, e-mail, SharePoint)

However way you estimate the significance of your assets, you should ensure that upper management agrees with your valuation. Talking to your leadership is an important part of asset valuation. Lastly, the information classification scheme should be formalized in policy and communicated to all users; this covered in more detail in later chapters.

Assessing Impact

With a prioritized list of assets and critical business functions, you can work on the impact component of risk. IT systems can fail in many ways and you can categorize them all. A simpler way is to look at three major aspects: confidentiality, integrity, and availability. A breach of confidentiality means that information that should have remained secret has been exposed to unauthorized parties (e.g., hackers broke into the mail server, or malware just transmitted all the payment cards to a botnet). An integrity breach refers to an unauthorized and possibly undetected change (e.g., a disgruntled employee just broke into the HR system and gave herself a big raise). A breach of availability is the unplanned functionality loss of something important (e.g., our web server got denial-of-serviced, or our server room lost cooling and shut down). The National Institute of Standards (NIST) has codified this way of doing impact classification in their standard FIPS-PUB-199.

■ **Note**   NIST FIPS-199 Standards for Security Categorization is good for asset classification.

See http://csrc.nist.gov/publications/fips/fips199/FIPS-PUB-199-final.pdf.

Impacts against confidentiality, integrity, and availability are rated "low" for limited adverse effects, "moderate" for serious adverse effects, and "high" for severe or catastrophic adverse effects. It's simple, but it's a good place to start thinking about impact scenarios.

A common impact calculation is to estimate monetary damages from a breach of customer confidential records. Some analysts assign a dollar figure per record, such as *It will cost us $150 per credit card number that falls into cyber-criminals' hands*. However, there is some nuance in obtaining an accurate estimate of financial impact. At very low numbers of records, costs can be extremely low, but very high on a per-record basis. I have worked on some cases where the breached bank simply got on the phone and called the few dozen affected customers. There was no public disclosure and associated bad press. In very large breaches, affected parties can leverage economies of scale in dealing with millions of affected customers and lower their impact costs as well. Like many other things, it is worth the time and effort to research and brainstorm what the actual impact of losing customer records would be for your organization. A good place to start would be to come up with some plausible scenarios and run them by the legal or compliance department.

If your organization provide IT services with an associated service level agreement (SLA), then the impact estimation becomes much clearer. You can calculate losses due to downtime in hard numbers down to the second. If you don't know the SLAs in place, check the customer contractual language for paragraphs like the following.

SAMPLE SERVICE LEVEL AGREEMENT WITH PENALTIES

"Availability of services: Subject to the terms and conditions of this Agreement, Service Provider shall use its best efforts to provide the Services for twenty-four (24) hours a day, seven (7) days a week throughout the term of this Agreement with a minimum of 99.9% site availability in any given month. In the event that downtime falls below the 99.9% uptime threshold, for every additional hour of downtime, Customer shall be entitled to a pro rata reduction of 10% monthly credit of any payments due for that period."

Indirect Impacts

Beyond the direct impacts stemming from impairment of services to customers, successful attacks can go beyond monetary damages. There can be a loss of user productivity due to downtime, which you can convert back to dollars with some help from business leads. Impact can also include the slowing of response time and delay of service from IT as they clean up the security incident. There is also time lost in investigation and reporting to law enforcement, management, and regulation bodies. There is also reputation damage, something that can be controversial to quantify, but nonetheless a critical impact for some industries. Depending on the nature of the attack, there can also be a loss of competitive advantage. Some breaches were about the theft of industrial secrets, which has obvious competitive advantage impacts.

Some breaches involve public leakage attacks, as with WikiLeaks, Sony, or Ashley Madison, where malicious parties spill company secrets out into the Internet for the whole world to gawk over. Often such breaches result in interested parties like journalists and activists creating custom search tools to parse and scan through the leaked data to magnify the exposure of the breach. Even small organizations can experience ill effects from this kind of breach. Consider how your customers and executives would react if the contents of all their e-mail going back for years were made available to Internet search engines. In fact, some customers may find a vendor's e-mail system has compromised their own information. Think of what may be sitting in your lawyer's e-mail inbox.

Indirect impacts can also have a technical dimension that drives up IT resource and user overhead. These can include data corruption (requiring restoration from backup, assuming there is backup), impromptu software upgrades, loss of cryptographic keys or passwords (many breaches force everyone in the company to reset their passwords), increased regulatory scrutiny, investigative resources, and performance degradation (resource exhaustion from attacks, causing general slowness).

Compliance Impacts

Some of the worst kinds of impacts are regulatory. Compliance requirements like PCI and HIPAA have hefty monetary penalties associated with security breaches. One of the highest fines for security non-compliance comes from the North America Electric Reliability Corporation (NERC), which can issue fines against a utility company up to $1 million per day for security non-compliance. On top of direct fines, organizations victimized by breaches could also be subject to class-action lawsuits from victims for failing to protect data. In addition to that, the Federal Trade Commission (FTC) has the authority to sue for "unfair or deceptive business practices" because organizations "failed to adequately protect" customer data. Even if an organization successfully escapes a legal judgment, there could be still legal costs involved.

In the end, impact goes far beyond records lost. Impact calculations can be simple or complex, depending on your needs. The most important thing is to think things through and tie the results to reality.

Qualitative vs. Quantitative

When you put together your risk analysis, one of the big decisions to make is whether your analysis is qualitative or quantitative. Qualitative risk analysis does not use tangible values, but instead uses relative measures like high, medium, and low. This is how FIPS-199 is structured. Quantitative analysis uses numerical values, such as dollars, and can entail a bit of work.

Qualitative Analysis

Qualitative risk assessment is subjective, usually based on subject matter experts rating the various factors on a scale. You can represent this scale as anything measurable, from using words like "high/medium/low" to temperatures or colors, and even numerals. Note that I said numerals, not numbers. I do this to keep from making a cognitive error. A numeral is the name or symbol for the number. Think Roman numerals. You should not be performing mathematical operations with qualitative risk factors. The expression that "Risk = Likelihood × Impact" is not an actual mathematical formula, but a description of the relationship between likelihood and impact. One way to keep yourself honest is that if you're going to do mathematical operations, remember what you learned in middle school: keep track of your units. Just as you would never say "3 feet × 4 degrees = 12 feet-degrees," you shouldn't say "Likelihood 3 × Impact 4 = Risk 12."

Qualitative risk assessment gets a bad rap as being too vague or misleading. It's understandable when compared to quantitative analysis, where you say things like "There is a 20% chance in the next year of having six to ten malware incidents that cost the organization $900 apiece." It's not as clear when you say, "The risk of malware infection is medium-high." However, remember that humans make decisions based on this information, and ultimately our brains convert everything to a subjective score anyway. The confusion of a qualitative analysis is that two different people may look at the same data and one may say it's high and the other may say it's medium. The opposite mistake can also happen. Just because someone filled in hard numbers like "20%" and "$900" doesn't mean those numbers weren't guesstimates pulled out of a hat, making them just as subjective as saying "medium-low."

Clarifying Your Qualitative

So how do we avoid confusion? One good way is to define your qualitative labels and put them in two dimensions. Let's start with this simple but unclear risk list in Table 3-3.

Table 3-3. *Simple Risk List*

Risk	Rating
Malware on LAN	Not bad
CEO phished	Kinda bad
Insider	Bad
Stolen backup tape	Kinda bad
Stolen laptop	Not bad
Web site defaced	Kinda bad
E-mail hacked	Kinda bad
Colocation facility fire	Bad
Wi-Fi hacked	Kinda bad
Wire transfer fraud	Bad

You might guess that a risk is "kinda bad" if it fell into three different categories:

1. High impact and low likelihood
2. Low impact and high likelihood
3. Medium impact and medium likelihood

All three of these situations may be vastly different. High impact and low likelihood could describe a pandemic outbreak. Low impact and high likelihood could mean a flood of spam. Medium/medium could mean a malware infected laptop. In a single dimensional chart, all of these risks aggregate out to the same level. With respect to a decision process, it's confusing to differentiate between these different levels of risk. Remember, the goal of risk analysis is to clarify and reveal information for good judgement.

Heat Maps

I recommend presenting qualitative risk analysis as a heat map so that these two dimensions are visible. Figure 3-1 is a simple graphical way to show the two risk components. Here the one dimensional risk labels are spread out into a heat map. You still can see the worst risk in the upper-right quadrant, and the three "kinda bads" as a diagonal band across.

Somewhat Risky	Risky	Most Risky
A Little Risky	Somewhat Risky	Risky
Least Risky	A Little Risky	Somewhat Risky

Impact — High / Low axis, *Probability* — Low / High axis

Probability

Figure 3-1. *Risk heat map*

With this format, you can now place risks directly into the graph axes at their proper magnitudes. The darkening effect represents "badness" and is optional. Figure 3-2 shows the same risk list expanded with qualitative numerals instead of badness labels, which is easier to graph. You can see the difference in clarity.

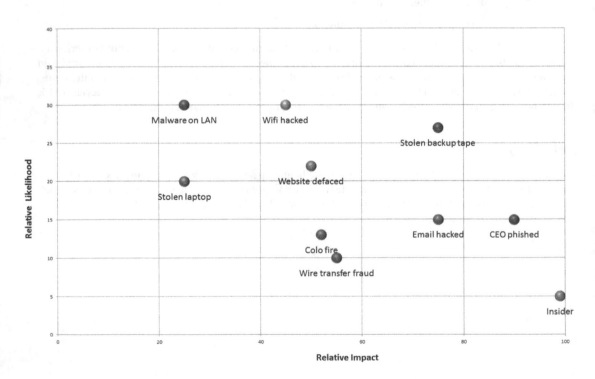

Figure 3-2. *Simple two-dimensional qualitative risk map*

Figure 3-2 shows multiple risks on a single qualitative table with proper labelling. You now have a tool that allows decision makers to rank and discuss risks in a relative manner. The goal here is to make decisions on which risks are treated with controls, avoided by stopping the activity, or accepted by taking on the risk. Even with no hard numbers, it is obvious in Figure 3-2 which items are considered more risky and why. This type of diagram can also serve as a discussion aid, so that decision makers can weigh in and say, "I feel the risk of malicious insider hacking is not that high an impact. Move it down." Now you have a valid and tangible starting point to discuss the factors involved in that particular risk.

Explaining Your Qualitative Ratings

Another way to reduce misunderstanding with qualitative models is to define your terms. You should do this at the outset as you are polling your subject matter experts and filling in the values. You can present this scale alongside the analysis so that it is clear to everyone involved what "moderate risk" actually means. Take a look at Table 3-3 and Table 3-4 for sample qualitative rating scales to include with your risk analysis. In Table 3-5, you can see that undetectable alterations to integrity are higher in impact than detectable ones. This is because if there are potential undetectable alterations, all the records are now untrustworthy.

Table 3-4. Example of Clarifying Likelihood

Rating	Meaning
Very Unlikely	Expected to occur less than once every 5 years
Remote	Expected to occur between 1 time per year and once every 5 years
Occasional	Expected to occur between 1 and 10 times per year
Frequent	Expected to occur more than 10 times per year

Table 3-5. Example of Clarifying Impact

Rating	Confidentiality Impact	Integrity Impact	Availability Impact
Minor	Under 10 records of confidential data exposed internally on an internal system but no proof of exploitation	Under 10 transaction records altered in a noticeable correctable manner	Several users offline for 1 to 5 business days. Customer-facing service offline up to an hour.
Major	Under 10 records of confidential data exposed internally to several unauthorized employees	More than 10 but less than a hundred records altered in noticeable correctable manner	Customer-facing service offline or data for more than an hour but less than a business day.
Critical	Under 10 records of confidential data exposed externally, more than 10 records disclosed internally	More than 100 records altered in noticeable correctable manner or records were altered in an undetectable manner	Customer-facing service offline or data for more than a business day.

Quantitative Analysis

Quantitative risk analysis uses real numbers and data in place of subjective measures. Remember in the end, it's likely that the security steering committee will make subjective judgements on how to manage these risks, but with a quantitative analysis, they have the best possible data in hand to make decisions. What does this look like? Let's take the previous description of threats and update it with real data, as shown in Table 3-6.

Table 3-6. *An Example of Analysis Using Quantitative Values*

Target	Attack Surface	Weakness	Resistance
Web sites	10 sites	Avg. 2 patches missing each	Firewalled
Mail servers	2 sites	No patches missing	firewalled
Web browsers	400 browsers	Avg. 14 patches missing each	host-based antivirus
Users	Social engineering	350 users	4% failed last phish pen-test training

As you can see, finding real data isn't that hard. If you've done a good asset analysis, many of these things should be at your fingertips. Your asset and impact analysis can also feed in real numbers in terms of monetary loss. You can find more data in industry source web sites and intelligence reports. The specifics of doing quantitative analysis in risk modeling are covered in more detail in the next two chapters.

External Sources for Quantitative Data

You can find more data in government and industry security reports. For example, California passed S.B. 1386, which requires any organization that suffered an exposure of more than 500 California resident's data must issue a notification to those persons. The organization also has to disclose that information to the state's Office of the Attorney General, which now publishes this information on its web site at `https://oag.ca.gov/ecrime/databreach/reporting`, which is very useful for working out likely risk scenarios.

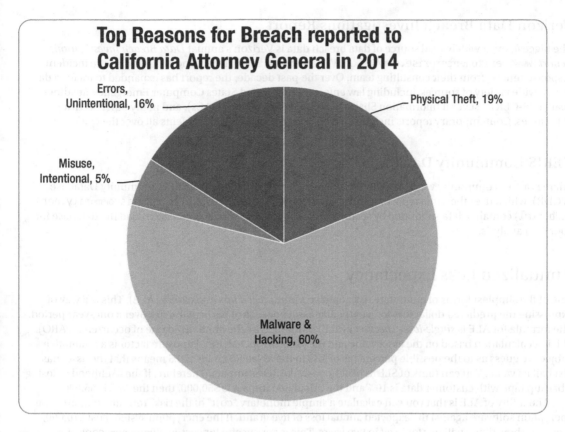

Top Reasons for Breach reported to California Attorney General in 2014

- Errors, Unintentional, 16%
- Physical Theft, 19%
- Misuse, Intentional, 5%
- Malware & Hacking, 60%

Figure 3-3. *Breach data from Ca. Ag for 2014*

This can give you a good idea on the likelihood of various risk scenarios. They also publish a lot more details on the breaches, including the actual notification letters sent out to victims.

Chronology of Data Breaches

Another free source of breach data is the Privacy Rights Clearinghouse (https://www.privacyrights.org/data-breach/new), a California nonprofit organization dedicated to educating people about privacy. They have a database going back to 2005 on reported data breaches found in news reports and media. Unlike California's Office of the Attorney General database, this database is a bit vaguer because of the limitation of public reports. However, there is high-level data on thousands of breach cases stretching back a decade to examine. Their data is also automatically broken down into useful categories and available for direct download into a spreadsheet or statistical tool. The confusing part is that they use different categories than the California Office of the Attorney General.

Verizon Data Breach Investigations Report

The biggest, most widely read source of data breach data is Verizon's annual *Data Breach Investigations Report* (www.verizonenterprise.com/DBIR/). Verizon began by analyzing and reporting on the incident response reports from their consulting team. Over the past decade, the report has expanded to include data from a wide variety of sources, including law enforcement, United States Computer Emergency Readiness Team (US-CERT), several Information Sharing and Analysis Centers (ISACs), and many other security companies. Contemporary reports include data on tens of thousands of incidents all over the world.

VERIS Community Database

There is also a community version of the Verizon breach report, called the VERIS Community Database (VCDB), which uses the same reporting and analysis structure. The VCDB (http://veriscommunity.net/vcdb.html) contains data submitted by security professionals like you. You can download the database for your own analysis.

Annualized Loss Expectancy

One of the simplest forms of quantitate risk analysis is *annualized loss expectancy* (ALE). This is a way of expressing the predicted dollar loss for a particular asset because of particular a risk over a one-year period. The formula for ALE is *single-loss expectancy* (SLE) multiplied by the annualized rate of occurrence (ARO). SLE is a calculation based on the asset value and the *exposure factor* (EF). Exposure factor is a qualitative subjective guess as to the possible percentage of loss to the asset. So an EF of 0.5 means that the asset has lost half its value. You can think of SLE as likelihood and ARO as impact. Therefore, if the likelihood of losing a backup tape with customer data is 10% and the calculated impact is $50,000, then the ALE is $5,000.

The utility of ALE is that you can calculate a simple monetary "cost" of the risk. You can compare tape encryption software against the expected annual loss of five grand. If the encryption system cost $10,000, then you show that it will pay for itself in two years. This is very useful for cost-justifying new control purchases. The hard part is coming up with plausible, defendable numbers for the SLE. As stated before, this is covered more in later chapters.

Formalizing Your Risk Process

All major compliance requirements require a foundational risk analysis based on an industry standard model. Without a model for guidance, a risk analysis can become distorted by individual biases and selective perception. This is especially true regarding cyber-risk, which is complicated and non-intuitive compared to physical risks. Here are some formal IT risk models to choose from:

- **ISO 27005:2011 Information Security Risk Management**
  http://www.iso.org/iso/catalogue_detail?csnumber=56742

- **PCI DSS Risk Assessment Guidelines**
  https://www.pcisecuritystandards.org/documents/
  PCI_DSS_Risk_Assmt_Guidelines_v1.pdf

- **NIST SP 800-30 (R1) Guide for Conducting Risk Assessments**
  http://nvlpubs.nist.gov/nistpubs/Legacy/SP/
  nistspecialpublication800-30r1.pdf

- **OCTAVE Cyber Risk and Resilience Management**
  http://www.cert.org/resilience/products-services/octave/

- **ENISA Cloud Computing Security Risk Assessment guide**
  https://www.enisa.europa.eu/activities/risk-management/files/
  deliverables/cloud-computing-risk-assessment/at_download/fullReport

Whatever risk modeling method that you choose (and more are introduced in the next two chapters), it is important that you document the risk assessment process. The process should be *systematic*, meaning that someone else can follow your process and come up with the same results. Many audit requirements, including PCI and ISO 27001, require that organizations have an annual formal risk assessment process that identifies threats and vulnerabilities, with documented results. You should redo risk assessments whenever there is major infrastructure change as well.

FURTHER READING

- **Doug Hubbard Decision Research (highly recommended!)**
  http://www.hubbardresearch.com/

- **Data Driven Security**
  http://datadrivensecurity.info/

- **Assessing Security and Privacy Controls in Federal Information Systems and Organizations: Building Effective Assessment Plans**
  http://dx.doi.org/10.6028/NIST.SP.800-53Ar4

CHAPTER 4

Risk Analysis: Natural Threats

Even with all our technology and the inventions that make modern life so much easier than it once was, it takes just one big natural disaster to wipe all that away and remind us that, here on Earth, we're still at the mercy of nature.

—Neil deGrasse Tyson

There are many ways to look at risk. One way is to divide risk into natural, accidental events and man-made intentional acts of aggression. Both types of risk are important, but there is some insight to be gained in looking at them differently. This chapter explores risk arising from natural and accidental threats.

Disaster Strikes

What is a disaster? What can go wrong when a random occurrence has far-ranging consequences? Consider this:

- A transformer in a nearby substation explodes and an entire nearby business park goes dark. The medical service company there has its own generators, so their server room stays up. However, the business park is on a hill and the local water pumps are offline. The landlord closes all the offices because none of the bathrooms are functioning and the local board of health is citing a sanitation hazard.

- A backhoe tears through an underground telecom conduit, breaking the primary T3 serving the nearby bank. Good news: the bank had a secondary Internet connection. Bad news: the second Internet connection ran through the same conduit as the primary. The bank is offline and the telecom company is digging furiously to expose the conduit to replace the broken lines. Then it starts raining. Hard. Now the hole is filling up with mud and water, slowing repair efforts.

- Heavy snowfall blankets the hills and streets of a major metropolitan city. Then temperatures drop, freezing the snow into slick ice. No wheeled vehicle in the city can drive faster than ten miles per hour. Roadways clog up with stalled cars. At a large software development company, hundreds of employees jump onto the remote access VPN and promptly overload it. Only 50 can work at a time out of an office of 200. Work now breaks down into shifts with many personnel forced to work off their cell phones and locally stored files until the snowplows can clear the roads.

© Raymond Pompon 2016
R. Pompon, *IT Security Risk Control Management*, DOI 10.1007/978-1-4842-2140-2_4

- A thousand-year storm (now more common in the age of climate change) hits and flooding takes out not only the data center but also an entire company's campus. It turns out that the campus was built in an ancient lakebed. Sewers are reversing and streets have become rivers. Even if they could work remotely, failing levees are forcing local employees to flee their homes.

- A 6.8-magnitude earthquake hits just south of a major city. At one company's data center, a large battery stack that was not properly bolted down pulls away from the wall by a few inches, breaking the main power coupling. The coupling is how all power flows into the server room. The emergency generator in the parking lot, despite being fully operational, is useless without a connection to the server room. Worse, outside feeds also come in over the same coupler. It's a specialized part and none are available locally. The company needs a new coupler flown in but the earthquake damaged the airport runway so nothing can land.

- A law firm is on the top floor of a prestigious downtown office building boasting an award-winning Venetian trattoria in the lobby. One evening, a fire breaks out in the kitchen of the restaurant. Fire fighters quickly douse the flames but they also close the building for days to inspect for damages. During that time, the power to the building is also turned off. The law firm servers go dark.

- In 2012, Hurricane Sandy damaged hundreds of thousands of homes and shut down power to dozens of data centers all over the New York metropolitan area. Data centers switched over to generators, but generators require fuel and the fuel trucks couldn't get through the flooded roads.

These are all natural disasters based on real events that significantly affected the organizations. Clearly, these kinds of risks are worth examining in more detail.

Risk Modeling

A risk model is nothing more than a taxonomy and a method of measurement that provides a picture of the likelihood and impact of potential damaging events. To be useful, a model needs to reflect reality as closely as possible. Therefore, you should choose the right risk model. One thing to consider is using different risk models for different kinds of risk.

You *could* use the same model for all of your risk calculations. Many knowledgeable risk analysts do, and come up great results. I want to illustrate a couple of different specialized models that I find useful. You may find the risk model that works best for your organization is entirely different. The most important thing is to think thoroughly about risk and build a practical methodology that is appropriate for your industry, threat landscape, and compliance requirements.

Let's consider the following list of risks:

- Earthquake

- Denial-of-service

- Fire

- Fraud

- Hazardous materials spill

- Industrial espionage

- Insider sabotage

- Intellectual property theft

- Landslide

- System failure

Examining this list, you may see two kinds of threats here. There is the threat of natural hazards and accidents, where bad things just happen. There is also the threat of adversarial risk, where bad people make bad things happen, either on purpose or through carelessness. So, this risk list can be split into two columns, as shown in Table 4-1.

Table 4-1. *Risks: Natural vs. Man-made*

Bad Things Just Happen	Bad People Make Bad Things Happen
Earthquake	Denial-of-service
Fire	Fraud
Landslide	Industrial espionage
Hazardous materials spill	Intellectual property theft
System failure	Insider sabotage

Given the distinctive difference in likelihood and impact between these two kinds of threats, it might be more accurate to model these threats differently. The likelihood of a random event that causes damage, such as a tornado or a technology failure, manifests much differently than intelligent adversaries (such as cyber-criminals or malicious insiders) who adapt their strategies to your defenses and choose when to attack. Likewise, the impact of natural disasters can sometimes be so vast and multifaceted that you might want to look at a more detailed impact model.

The next chapter is about adversarial threats, whereas the rest of this chapter is about natural/operational threats.

Modeling Natural Threats

In some ways, natural threats are easier to model than adversarial threats. Although there are still many unknowns, such as trying to predict earthquakes or weather, there is also a lot of scientific expertise and historical data to draw upon.

Like real estate, the three most important things about natural hazards are location, location, location. Location even factors in natural threats like pandemics, where large cities and regional travel hubs are at higher likelihood of outbreaks than sleepier locales. Location modeling is where your asset analysis comes in. To do any kind of natural risk analysis, you absolutely need to locate all the significant physical locations of your organization. With that, you can determine what infrastructure and hazards are present in each area. By *infrastructure,* I mean the following:

- Connected utilities (power, water, sewer)

- Communication providers serving that location and their entries into the building

- Nearest fire department

- Nearest major highway

- Nearest major airport

- Nearby waterways

- Nearby industrial activity

Based on this, you can gather information about what can go wrong. There are many resources available for getting this kind of data, most from governmental agencies. One warning: sometimes the data can require some work to decipher. For example, where I live, there is the Seattle Hazard Explorer, which is an interactive map that provides data on a dozen different possible natural hazards (see www.seattle.gov/emergency-management/hazards-and-plans/hazards).

It gives its results as a number range mapping of a "10% chance of exceeding in 50 years." Reading around the site, you learn that the number range refers to the force of the acceleration generated by an earthquake in terms of gravitational constant (G). So a number 50 would mean shaking to add power equal to half the strength of normal Earth gravity. As a reference, at numbers higher than 30 (or more than 1.3Gs), you can expect some building damage to occur. This gives you some idea of impact. The 10% refers to the probability of such quake in a 50-year period, thus you have likelihood. So with a little work figuring out the numbers, you have enough for a quantitative risk analysis for earthquakes in Seattle. Many of these sites require this kind of decrypting to get data for a risk model.

Here is a list of other good resources for researching natural hazards for North America.

- USGS Earthquakes maps
  http://earthquake.usgs.gov/earthquakes/

- USGS Natural Hazards map
  http://www.usgs.gov/natural_hazards/

- National Hurricane Center Storm Surge map for US Coast
  http://www.nhc.noaa.gov/surge/

- FEMA: Flood Hazard map
  https://www.fema.gov/national-flood-insurance-program-flood-hazard-mapping

- NOAA Severe Storm Labs
  http://www.nssl.noaa.gov/

- Power Outage Data Explorer
  http://insideenergy.org/2014/08/18/data-explore-15-years-of-power-outages/

As you assess natural hazards, you quickly realize that here is a huge range of possible threats. There are many things to calculate and consider. Here is a large list of possible natural threats for you to consider.

- Threat

- Earthquake

- Flood

- Blizzard / ice-storm

- Landslides/mudslides

- Building fire

- Forest fire

- Heat wave

- Hazardous material spill

- Gas leak

- Prolonged road closure

- Pandemic

- Blackout/electrical disruptions

- Solar flare

- Volcano

- Lightning

- Tsunami

- HVAC failure

- Aircraft accident

- Windstorm

- Communications failure

- Nuclear power mishap

- Civil disturbance

- Active shooter/domestic terrorism

You may notice that the last two bullet items are human-originated but still listed as natural hazards. In these kinds of threats, it's easier to model them as random events rather than intentional attacks against your organization. This could change if your organization is one that is attractive to highly motivated attackers, like a law enforcement agency which could appeal to political or nation-state attackers which then skews the normal random distribution of Internet threats. Use your best judgement.

Modeling Impact with Failure Mode Effects Analysis

Operational impacts involving technology can be tricky because of the intricate dependencies involved. Consider a situation like a power surge in a single colocation facility that causes a single rack to fail. This rack holds dozens of servers, including the main external DNS server for an entire company. Coincidentally, the secondary DNS in another facility is undergoing a maintenance event. Now the entire company's Internet presence is offline. Web, FTP, e-mail, and remote access are all down. Although this is an unusual chain of events, it still happens. Considering the severe impact of these kinds of problems, you might want to model these kinds of occurrences.

For operational risk analysis, consider looking at Failure Mode and Effects Analysis (FMEA). FMEA is based on a US military procedure. The model was formalized for general use and is currently published as International Standard IEC 60812. FMEA is a risk analysis methodology that focuses on the ways that components in a system fail and the downstream effects of those failures. Although it can be time-consuming, it is a very systematic and easy method for a team to use to get a complete picture of how complex systems fail. You will quickly see alternate design ideas, fail-over mechanisms, and monitoring requirements as you walk through an FMEA analysis.

The essence of FMEA is to

- Break down a complex system into its major functions.

- Analyze the functions.

- Determine the effects of the failure of each of the functions on the overall system.

Simple FMEA Example

Table 4-2 illustrates an example of how to break down an Internet banking system into functions.

Table 4-2. *System Example: Internet Banking System*

Subsystem	Functional Subsystems	Effect of Failure
Servers	Database server, app server, web server, DNS server	Immediate failure of entire system
Network Devices	Firewall, router, switch, cables	Immediate failure of entire system
Connectivity	ISP, local link, cables	Immediate failure of entire system
Facilities	Server rack, power, HVAC	Varies but assume near-term failure of entire system
Personnel	DBA, sysadmin, net engineer, programmer	Varies but assume failure of system within a few weeks

You can increase the availability of all the technological systems by adding redundant systems. However, adding more personnel and facilities is much more expensive. So let's dig deeper into these two functions. In Table 4-3, we can add another FMEA factor, the detection method for a failing function.

Table 4-3. *FMEA Example of Facilities*

Function	Effect of Failure	Explanation	Detection
Server rack	Immediate failure of entire system	Need rack to hold server	Beyond systems failing, none
Power	Immediate failure of entire system	Need electricity	Audible alarm in room on batteries
HVAC	Failure of system in 1–6 hours, plus possible equipment damage	Servers overheat	Thermometer alarm via SMS pager

In Table 4-4, we can add another layer of impact by looking at how personnel are affected by function failures.

Table 4-4. *Example of FMEA Breakdown of Personnel*

Function	Effect of failure	Explanation	Detection
Database admin	Failure of system within 30–60 days	Database logs fill up without admin to clear them	E-mailed alarms to admins
Sysadmin	Degraded performance, failure of system within 15–30 days	No maintenance by admins	User complaints
Net engineer	Degraded performance	No network fixes or optimization	User complaints
Programmer	Degraded performance	No bug fixes or features added	User complaints

As you can see, there are some problems with delayed failures caused by functions not being available. Coupled with poor detection capability, this could mean a serious problem emerging when you are least able to deal with it, like in the middle of the night. Anyone who works in IT will probably cringe when they read that the detection method is user complaints.

Breaking down a System

The first step is to break down a system into its primary functions. You can represent most systems, especially technological ones, as a hierarchy. In addition, large systems are built to serve a purpose. This is your beginning point: the primary mission of the system. From here, functional requirements will flow. Examine its structure as it fulfills its functions. You may want to look at how it performs those functions over time, considering environment changes on a scale of hours, days, weeks, and so forth. For example, an accounting system may have different functions and dependency cycles for month-end, quarterly profit reporting, and annual tax analysis. Remember to use your asset analysis and review those diagrams, documentation, data flows, and subject-matter expert interviews.

You should consciously decide and document what you consider to the boundaries of the system. This is useful for analysis and will come in handy in Chapter 6 when we discuss the concept of scope. What is a system? What should you include? What you should you leave out? For example, a typical corporate Windows workstation needs dynamic addressing, Active Directory, name services, clock synchronization, and a local area network. Maybe you can leave out authentication services, file sharing services, and Internet links. Maybe you should include Internet connectivity? It all depends on your business requirements.

When looking at larger systems, functions can be more than just components or technical services. You can look at things like facilities, personnel, ISPs, and other major systems. For example, here is a functional breakdown of a retail store's sales system:

- Point-of-Sale (POS) terminals

- Receipt printers

- Card readers

- Sales clerks

- Store network

- Store wiring closet

- Store server rack

- Store POS server

- Store network link to headquarters in another city

- Regional IT service technician (part-time)

This method is called the *top-down* approach and it is the most common way people approach an already existing system. You start big and work your way down into smaller and smaller pieces, stopping analysis when you feel that you understand enough. Another approach is *bottom-up*, where you start with components and build up to a complete system. This takes longer but is more complete.

Analyzing Functions

With the major functions defined, you can begin analyzing those functions for how they will fail. This means looking at dependencies, redundancies, inputs, and outputs. Like the overall system, you should begin with the goal of the function. How does the function fulfill its mission? What was the mindset of the designers of the function? These things can provide overlooked clues that can help you find shortcomings and possible flaws in the function.

You should also consider how this system feeds into other systems. In the workstation example, that system could be considered part of the "marketing subnet." Are there any implications and feedback loops because of that relationship? Perhaps the marketing department does monthly video broadcasts; so now you realize that each workstation should also have speakers or headphones as critical functions.

Things to look at when analyzing a function:

- Command inputs (the range of possible changes that can be made)

- Breadth of command inputs (How many external parties can issue commands to the function?)

- Data flows (size, speed, and path)

- Internal feedback mechanisms (Can the function monitor its own status? How does it react?)

- External feedback mechanism (Can the function receive warnings from the outside? How does it react?)

- Does the function provide feedback to outside systems? How and how often?

- What does the function require from outside systems to function? What happens when it doesn't get it?

- How does the function handle load? What does it do when overloaded? Idle?

- Does the function adjust its own parameters? How?

- How long can the function run without rest/maintenance? External adjustment?

Determining Failure Effects

Modeling failures within complex systems full of interacting components is a challenge. Large systems can be non-linear, where a minor change in a single subsystem can resonate with large consequences. Systems also have a history, as they have evolved and been adapted from earlier, simpler systems. Over time, their purpose may have changed. Sometimes that legacy of changes is reflected in the components in the system. For systems already in place, it is important to perform analysis on systems, as they exist, not based on the original specifications or idealization of plans yet to be implemented.

When brainstorming failure modes, you should consider exactly what that failure would look like. Be sure to take into account the scale (how bad) and the duration (how long). For some kinds of systems, scale and duration could be limited or prolonged depending on how the system reacts and recovers from problems. In some cases, disruption is momentary and evades detection. I have seen more than a few cases where a server quietly crashes, reboots, and comes back up all between the cycles of a five-minute uptime check of the monitors. Users, however, did notice because all of their transactions failed and data was lost. Improving function failure detection is an important part of failure effects analysis.

Drawing a system can also help illustrate which failures modes can be the most catastrophic to a system. Figure 4-1 is a simple diagram of an Internet banking web farm.

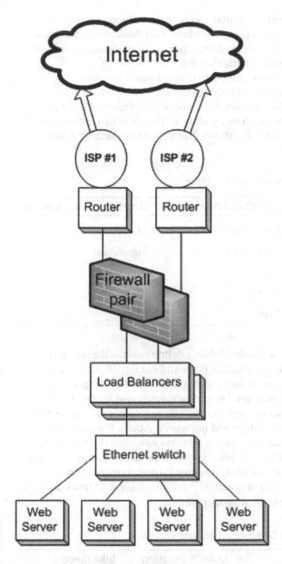

Figure 4-1. Internet banking system

Can you spot the single point of failure in the example? Hint: it's probably the cheapest piece of equipment in the entire stack. Drawing a system on a whiteboard during a group brainstorming session can be very effective; not only for spotting failure points, but also in creating general understanding on how the system *actually* functions.

Business Impact Analysis

If you are responsible for the organization's business continuity plan, then this type of analysis is useful for the Business Impact Analysis (BIA) section of the business continuity plan. Business continuity is a requirement of ISO 27001, PCI DSS, and SSAE 16 SOC 2 and 3. Sometimes this role falls on IT security and sometimes the role falls on a dedicated business continuity team. In any case, it's essential to understand the process.

BIA identifies the functions that are necessary to the organization and what the effects of an interruption would be. Through BIA, you create disaster impact scenarios based on those mission-critical services to help determine what resources you might need to get business operations going again. This all fits very nicely into the risk analysis methods discussed so far in this chapter.

A way to enhance this analysis, especially for disaster scenarios, is to break down duration of unavailability or degradation of function. For the following examples, I have divided the period of unavailability into three times: one day, three days, and five or more days. These times allow a response plan to address specific kinds of interruptions, but also can work with an escalating crisis. You can use whatever periods you think are appropriate for your organization. Table 4-5 shows one way of categorizing different downtime periods for a typical office.

Table 4-5. *Example of Impacts to Normal Business Operations for the Office*

Function	Duration: 1 day down	Duration: 3 days down	Duration: 5+ days down
Water & Sewer	Minor	Significant	Major
HVAC	Minor	Significant	Significant
Electricity	Significant	Major	Major
Elevator	Minor	Minor	Minor
Connectivity (Phone & Net)	Significant	Major	Major

One thing you may notice from the example in Table 4-5 is that I didn't define specific threats; just functional interruptions. I used FMEA is to treat offices services as functions and combined threats into a basic assumption of an interruption of service, regardless of reason, with a defined area of impact. You can use this shortcut with the FMEA model so that you do not need to look at every possible threat. This automatically rolls up the threats of fires, cable cuts, blackouts, pipe breaks, and severe storms into a single threat vector. For example, you could focus on an electrical outage and not worry about if it was caused by a backhoe accident, windstorm, regional blackout, or an earthquake. All you focus on is the loss of the function and effects. You can also use FMEA and ignore all the various types of threats and group common likelihoods together. For the BIA, you can also break down into likely durations; so in your scenario planning, you can just focus on a function interruption event of specified duration. Table 4-6 shows more examples of rolling natural threats and likely durations into an analysis table.

Table 4-6. *An Example of Threat Mapping with FMEA to Generalized Failure Threats*

Threat	Effects on Services	Outage Duration	Likelihood
Earthquake	Regional, all services	5+ days	1-Rare
Large earthquake	Widespread, all services	5+ days	0- Very Rare
Flood	Regional, all services	2–5 days	3-Unlikely
Blizzard/ice storm	Regional, transport	2–5 days	5-Possible
Storm	Regional, power & com & transport	2–5 days	5-Possible
Building fire	Facility, all services	5+ days	3-Unlikely
Civil disturbance	Facility, transport	2–5 days	1-Rare
Hazardous spill	Facility, all services	2–5 days	1-Rare
Pandemic	Regional, personnel	5+ days	3-Unlikely

(continued)

Table 4-6. (*continued*)

Threat	Effects on Services	Outage Duration	Likelihood
Bomb threat	Facility, all services	1 day	3-Unlikely
Blackout	Regional, power	2–5 days	Possible
Volcano	Regional, all	5+ days	1-Rare
Lightning	Facility, power & comm.	2–5 days	1-Rare
HVAC failure	Facility, equipment	2–5 days	5-Possible
Aircraft accident	Facility, all services	5+ days	1-Rare
Communications loss	Regional, comm.	1 day	5-Possible
Nuclear mishaps	Regional, all	5+ days	1-Rare
Sabotage/terrorism	Facility, all services	5+ days	3-Unlikely

Here's how you can use this mapping—along with combinations of outages—to get a simpler breakdown of the various impacts to business operations that a disaster would create. In this example, I model a service company with two customer-facing services: customer support calls and consulting. Of the two, the call center is the most important because it facilities immediate customer communication. If a customer calls and the lines are down, the company reputation sinks. Consulting services can be delayed but call answering cannot. In this example, most of the offices are in Nevada, except the sales offices, which are in Chicago. These are the facilities:

- Main office: Las Vegas, NV
- Sales office: Chicago, IL
- Call center: Reno, NV
- Call center: Las Vegas, NV

In Table 4-7, I break down the first cut of the outage scenarios for this example.

Table 4-7. *Sample Scenario Overview*

Scenario	Example	Likelihood	Impacts Critical service: Customer call center	Other Impacts
Scenario 1: All services in the state of Nevada heavily damaged	Major earthquake	Very rare	Major: Complete outage	Major: Corporate outage, sales office becomes primary contact
Scenario 2: Service outages in the Vegas area	Storms, flooding	Possible	Minor: Reno call center takes all calls; capacity reduced	Minor: Corporate outages; sales office becomes primary contact
Scenario 3: Personnel in the Vegas area are disabled	Pandemic	Rare	Minor: Reno call center takes all calls; capacity reduced	Minor: Corporate outages; sales office becomes primary contact
Scenario 4: Main office is unavailable	Building fire	Possible	No direct impacts	Minor: Corporate outages; sales office becomes primary contact

(*continued*)

Table 4-7. (*continued*)

Scenario	Example	Likelihood	Impacts Critical service: Customer call center	Other Impacts
Scenario 6: Reno call center is unavailable	Building fire	Possible	Minor: Vegas call center takes all calls, capacity reduced	No additional impacts
Scenario 7: Vegas call center is unavailable	Building fire	Possible	Minor: Reno call center takes all calls, capacity reduced	No additional impacts
Scenario 8: Chicago consulting office is unavailable	Building fire	Possible	No direct impacts	Minor: Corporate takes over sales calls as needed

As you can see in this example, things seem to be pretty well in hand except for a statewide disaster scenario. In this case, the risk has been identified and leadership can choose to mitigate that risk or accept it.

Documenting Assumptions

Whenever you work on these kinds of analyses, there will be assumptions. You need to identify them as you go along. Do not let them be invisibly baked into the resulting analysis. The results can be misleading if the assumption turns out to be false or misunderstood. The easiest way to avoid this is to solicit multiple perspectives in the analysis. Once you have identified the assumptions, they to need to be documented along with the analysis. You should also have leadership review and approve these assumptions when you present your analysis. They may have different assumptions that could change your results. Here are some sample assumptions to go along with the earlier examples:

- Unless otherwise noted in the analysis, all staff can telecommute to perform their job functions with at least 75% efficiency.

- Services hosted outside of the state remain available and functional. They are considered "always available" during an emergency due to the low probability that both services are unavailable at the same time. External hosted services include chat (cloud-based), accounting (outsourced), HR payroll (outsourced).

- IT personnel suffer no more than 25% incapacitation in an interruption event.

FURTHER READING

- **Microsoft's IT Infrastructure Threat Modeling Guide**
  https://technet.microsoft.com/enus/library/dd941826.aspx

- **IEC 60812 Ed. 2.0 b:2006 Procedure for failure mode and effects analysis (FMEA)**
  https://webstore.iec.ch/publication/3571

CHAPTER 5

■ ■ ■

Risk Analysis: Adversarial Risk

Cybersecurity is perhaps the most challenging intellectual profession on the planet both because of the rate of change and because your failure is the intentional work product of sentient opponents.

—Dan Geer, CISO In-Q-Tel

Intentional attacks against IT systems from motivated malicious attackers are the heart of the challenge in IT security. Malicious attackers work around your controls, actively hide from detection, and zero in on highly valuable systems and data. This chapter explores how you can analyze and predict adversarial attacks.

A Hospital under Attack

In the fall of 2004, twenty-year old Christopher Maxwell of Vacaville, California, came up with a great moneymaking scheme. Already a skilled programmer, he wrote a devious little network worm. The malware used two Microsoft Windows vulnerabilities—LSASS and RPC/DCOM—to break into a Windows computer and install his remote control tools. The program would silently scan for other machines to attack and be joined to his fleet of already infected machines (called a *botnet*). Once an infected machine was up and running, it would stealthily surf to a few web sites that Maxwell ran, and then click the banner ads. Since Maxwell was getting paid per-click from these ads, all those thousands of captured machines would create the illusion of popularity for his site. It was a grand idea; however, not a very original one. This was what cyber-criminals were doing at that time. Maxwell figured most Internet advertising was a shell game anyway, so who cared? Besides, since the victim machine would only be out a few computing cycles and tiny bit of bandwidth, what was the real harm? He made nearly a hundred grand this way. Easy money.

In early January of 2005, at a large medical facility in Seattle, the entire network suddenly seized up in the middle of the morning. Something was burning through Northwest Hospital's computing systems, jamming all network traffic with scanning sweeps looking for new targets. Diagnostic and lab services couldn't update patient records. The intensive care unit's terminals went dead. Even the automatic operating-room doors locked down. Anything on the network was either shut down or turned into a shrieking beacon of network noise. IT staff disconnected a machine, cleaned out the malware, and got it functional. As soon as they put it back on the wire, it became reinfected. Northwest Hospital was in tough spot. It seems that Maxwell's worm had a bug; the malware was probing too quickly for fresh victims and saturating the network.

Because of the magnitude of the damage, Northwest Hospital called the FBI for help. The FBI cyber-crime unit put their best people on the case. Within a year, Christopher Maxwell was wearing handcuffs. During his interrogation, Maxwell was horrified to learn that his worm had crashed a hospital's network. He never intended to commit a crime of that magnitude. The judge sentenced him to 37 months in prison.

© Raymond Pompon 2016

R. Pompon, *IT Security Risk Control Management*, DOI 10.1007/978-1-4842-2140-2_5

Adversarial Risk

When most people talk about hacking and computer security, scenarios like Northwest Hospital are what they have in mind. Some "hacker" unleashes a computer worm that wreaks all kind of damage, both on the network and in the real world. These are some of the kinds of incidents that security professionals need to understand and prevent. We can understand them better by modeling the attacker and the attack.

Building a risk model for a human-based attack against technology is challenging. Adversarial tactics change frequently based on rapid shifts in technology, new monetization schemes, and innovative new attack methods. Consider how much the state of IT risk changed on April 7, 2014, when Heartbleed was announced. Suddenly network devices, including network security devices that were once considered secure were now perceived at a much higher state of risk due to a change in the likelihood of compromise. Risk levels changed rapidly for many government agencies on June 5, 2013, when Edward Snowden leaked the National Security Agency's (NSA) operational secrets. In both cases, the census of perceived risk models around the security of encryption and insider access were changed forever. You are more likely to update your adversarial risk model with more frequency than your natural and operational risk models.

Overview of Attacker Types

To model adversarial risk, you need to look at how an adversary would attack your systems, keeping in mind their goals, capabilities, and methods. To make things easier, let's break adversaries into four basic types:

- *Cyber-criminals*: Crooks who hack that are external to your organization. They are out for monetary gain.

- *Insiders*: Disgruntled, reckless, or crooked users within your organization. They have varying motivations.

- *Hacktivists*: Political hackers who often seek to expose wrongdoing by exposing protected data.

- *Cyber-militants*: Professional experts in hacking doing espionage or sabotage on behalf of their country or cause.

Cyber-Criminals

There is a vast ecosystem of parasites in the cyber-criminal world. You have young entrepreneurs like Maxwell, sweeping the Internet indiscriminately looking for opportunistic victims. In recent years, these opportunistic criminals have organized and professionalized, resulting in more specializations and more sophisticated scams. Just like old-fashioned criminals, the cyber-crooks have organized into gangs with global reach. Within that group, there are also the "jewel thieves" of the Internet: highly skilled cyber-criminals who target high-value targets and often make off with millions of dollars in stolen data.

Insiders

The concept of malicious insiders covers a wide gamut. The most famous are the disillusioned system administrators who see themselves as the hero in their own story, like Edward Snowden or Chelsea Manning. Sometimes insiders are agents of an outside criminal conspiracy, abusing their position of trust to enable a crime. Sometimes they are opportunists who steal what is in front of them. Some are angry and seek revenge against a perceived wrong. Another class of insider is the careless or reckless individual. People with poor judgement who do dangerous things like download pornography, or pirate movies at work, which can result in expensive lawsuits. They are also people who accidentally release private data on the Internet through carelessness or ignorance. Whatever the case, the impact of their acts is often extreme because of their direct access to systems and valued assets.

Hacktivist

Political hackers run the spectrum, from vicious pranksters like Anonymous to the cyber-activists who feel they are hacking to promote the social agenda of their collective group. In most of these cases, the political hacker attacks by releasing loads of private material on the Internet. Sometimes insiders are politically motivated, as stated earlier. One case worth knowing about is Aaron Swartz, a brilliant engineer who had a history of liberating records that he thought should be public goods from closed systems. He did this with the Pacer court documents, the Library of Congress bibliographic dataset, and JSTOR. JSTOR is a repository of academic journal articles, which Swartz downloaded onto a laptop hidden in a closet at MIT. He was arrested and charged as a cyber-criminal. He faced a possible 35-year prison term. Contrast that with the 37 months given to Maxwell, who crippled a hospital for his own financial gain. Unfortunately, Swartz committed suicide under the weight of the prosecution. It was a tragedy for all involved, as his technical and intellectual contributions helped shape the Internet. The point being that hacktivist motivations can be hard to discern in advance and they are not like ordinary cyber-criminals.

Cyber-Militants

Beyond hacktivism, these are well-trained, well-funded security experts used by nation states, corporations, or large non-government organizations (like ISIS). They may infiltrate networks to spy or cripple critical infrastructure. Sometimes they hack to spread disinformation or propaganda. Some are hired mercenaries being well paid by a variety of masters. They are mostly known by their capability and their actions, which are in a different class than an ordinary hacktivist or cyber-criminal.

Understanding Attacker Capability

Like IT professionals, there are many levels of attacker capability. From the script kiddie, who is only as good as the tools he barely understands, to the seasoned professional who codes her own exploits and rootkits. You need to assess how likely an attacker can smash through your defenses and how likely a particular type of attacker would come after your organization. There many factors that go into this, but let's look at four big ones: technical capability, trickery capability, timing, and techniques.

Technical Capability

Since we're talking about IT security, the attacker's IT skills and tools are a major factor. At the lowest end, we have the aforementioned script kiddie. They aren't necessarily young kids, but simply technical novices. Their capability begins and ends at the user interface for the tool they are using. They don't necessarily understand what is going on under the hood, but they do know just enough to be dangerous.

Technical capability also refers to an attacker's ability to evade or break through IT security controls. An unskilled attacker could be stymied by antivirus software, while a skilled attacker may know how rewrite and pack their malware such that it is undetectable.

The Bare-Minimum Threat

Many security professionals use a measure of the minimum threat level that IT security systems must withstand. Security thought leader Alex Hutton referred to this as the Mendoza Line for Security[1], taking a reference from baseball. The Mendoza line in baseball refers to Mario Mendoza, who has the minimum batting average acceptable in major league play. For Alex, the Mendoza Line for Security is the capability of the point-and-click penetration testing system, like the Metasploit Framework. If a tool like Metasploit can penetrate your Internet perimeter, then any script kiddie that comes along will crack you wide open. It's the bare-minimum threat capability.

Advanced Threats

At the highest end of the spectrum are the seasoned professionals. There are indeed hackers out there who understand technology and attack techniques so well that they can find flaws in nearly any system, given enough time. During the investigation of Operation Flyhook[2], one of the lead forensic experts remarked that the Russian suspects were some of the best Windows integrators he'd ever seen. It is a telling quote about the capability of some hackers. Many of them have an understanding of a software system on par with or exceeding the original designers of that system. In addition, attackers view that system with a hostile eye, looking for any weakness to exploit. Given the complexity of most systems, you can see how they can chisel their way in.

Attack the Available Power-ups

Advanced attackers often create their own tools for finding or exploiting vulnerabilities. Some of them give or sell these tools to others, providing a pathway for the lesser skilled to follow. Exploit timelines usually goes from discovery, to a proof-of-concept tool (usually a script), to a point-and-click tool, to finally, a fully capable module as part of a penetration tool. Whereas an advanced attack requires time and skill, once a tool is available, it falls to the Mendoza Line for Security. This is how a nearly impossible hack yesterday can become a commonplace attack tomorrow.

Trickery Capability

In addition to their technical capability, attackers cheat. They build complicated deceptions and weave a chain of lies to ensnare victims. Some attackers go through great lengths to impersonate your company and staff, constructing very genuine-looking e-mails or web sites. Some generically masquerade themselves as authority figures, like the FBI or the IRS, and blast out waves of phony e-mail notifications soliciting credit cards or login credentials.

A few are particularly devious and target an industry or organization with a *watering hole attack*. This is where an attacker researches their target organization to find out which web sites their users visit frequently, like a popular industry blog or an affiliate site. The attacker breaches that affiliate system, which usually has weaker security than the target organization. On the site, the attacker plants web-borne malware or a phishing capture page, in hopes that their target visits it and becomes infected. A popular technique is to put up an enticing video that requires users to install a plug-in that is booby-trapped with malware.

Social engineering is a con game facilitated by technology. The following are some of the facets of a con that are useful in understanding social engineering:

- *Ring of familiarity*: The attacker uses social proof (presents business card, carries a clipboard, has an official logo on a web site) to establish authority.

- *Urgency*: The attacker uses time pressure ("Act now or pay a fine!") to distract the victim into not thinking clearly.

- *Incentive*: The attacker offers something for you to win or lose: "Pay this fine or be charged interest!" or "Claim your annual bonus!"

- *Story*: Some of the best cons involve stories that engage the victim's interest in some way.

To reemphasize the power of trickery, nearly all large breaches involve some kind of social engineering. Some hackers say they achieve 100% success with phishing campaigns against sizeable organizations.

---

[1]http://riskmanagementinsight.com/riskanalysis/?p=294
[2]https://en.wikipedia.org/wiki/United_States_v._Ivanov

Time

The amount of time an attacker spends attacking you is another deciding factor as to whether you suffer an impact or not. Usually this factor is directly related to the technical skills and motivation of the attacker. A script kiddie is doing the network equivalent of walking down a street of cars looking for unlocked doors. As soon as he spots one, he'll pop the door and snatch whatever he can carry off in a hurry. The window of risk is short. Some attackers set off massive Internet-wide scans for vulnerabilities and then return a day or so later to the identified vulnerable machines.

A more sophisticated attacker spends days or weeks researching her target, probing and testing until just the right opportunity arrives. Once in, she may spend more weeks and months sneaking around the network until she finds her final target. The StuxNet malware attack against Iranian centrifuges involved waiting months for a worm to reach its target. The more-organized hacking groups perform time-consuming and project-intensive attacks; for example, mass phishing campaigns use management tools to assist in keeping track of victims and their status.

Techniques

There are many permutations of how an attacker can combine their technical ability, deception, and available time. Many of the techniques are available only to attackers with the right amount of time or technical ability.

Proximity of Attacker

One aspect of attack technique is the *contact method of attack*. Most attackers attempt only network attacks, coming in only over the Internet. Some attackers come sideways over the Internet but via third parties or business partner connections, having broken in there first. Other attackers may come from the neighborhood, jumping on wireless connections to get into the network from the inside (infamous hacker Alberto Gonzales broke into TJX retailers from its wireless connections using a laptop in the store's parking lots). Dumpster-diving attackers rifle through an organization's trash, hoping to find some useful secrets. One attack technique is to leave USB drives loaded with malware laying around nearby so that unsuspecting users will pick them up and use them inside.

Some attackers physically come into your organization, either by burglary or by social engineering. Once inside your building, they can plant malware, connect key-logging devices, hide spy cams, install their own wireless taps onto your network, or just walk out with hard drives or backup tapes.

Cornucopia of Techniques

Table 5-1 lists a bunch of attack techniques with their respective attributes. Regarding the time and skill needed, a well-funded attacker can easily purchase the necessary expertise to supplement their own lack of time or skills. Also, you should be aware that these characteristics can quickly vary as new tools are made available.

Table 5-1. *Attack Techniques*

Technique	Time Needed	Skill Needed
Able to create malware that evades antivirus	Not much, tools available	Low; tools available.
Able to evade standard intrusion detection tools	Some time needed to test tools	Some skill needed.
Uses chained exploits in attack	Some time to ensure exploits all work correctly on target's environment	Moderate skill; some tools available.
Finds new vulnerabilities (zero-day) and develops attack	Weeks/months to find exploit	High skills needed. These skills can be specialized in web apps, operating systems, or a particular type of application/platform.
Uses wireless man-in-the-middle attacks	Minutes, assuming Wi-Fi clients available to attack	Not much; tools available.
Perform brute force password guessing attack	Hours/weeks/years, depending on strength of authentication	Low skills needed.
Able to perform decryption attacks on broken algorithms	Minutes to days, depending on algorithm and traffic captured	Low.
Able to perform decryption attacks on unbroken algorithms	Minutes to years, depending on algorithm and traffic captured	Highly specialized skills needed.
Use of social engineering in conjunction with attack	Minutes to days, depending on research needed in attack	Medium skills needed.
Use of physical penetration in conjunction with attack	Minutes to days, depending on research needed in attack	Medium skills needed.
Intelligence gathering pre-attack	Hours to weeks, depending on depth of research desired	Low/medium skills needed; some tools available
Use of watering hole web sites to lure victims	Days or weeks to find and penetrate watering hole	Medium to high skills needed.
Use covert or side-channels to facilitate hidden communication with compromised hosts	Hours or days depending on root kit	Low, tools available

Understanding Attacker Incentives

Beyond technical capability, the other major attacker attribute is their motivation. There is definitely some truth to compensating for skills with sheer determination. Depending on the incentive, some attackers can be very dangerous threats. Based on that, you should consider what things your organization has or does that could motivate an attack. You can get an idea about this from reviewing your asset analysis. Let's break that down a bit.

Monetary Incentives

When looking at monetary incentives, sometimes the value is straightforward. If your organization is storing payment cards or involved in banking, then you are a big juicy target for attackers. If you are doing e-commerce for any kind of good that criminals can easily resell on the black market, like electronics or media, then you are a valuable target. The incongruity of this situation is that your data may be worth more to criminals than to the organization itself. For example, for those working in the financial services industry, you can run systems holding personal financial details that are worth hundreds of millions of dollars to identity thieves. However, customers may only be paying a tiny fraction of that to process that same data. This can lead to strange situations, where attackers may have better financial support in stealing the data than you are given to protect it. Always consider the value of your assets to adversaries. To quote the CISO of the University of Washington, Kirk Bailey, "Data is a cash crop."

Account data is also easily monetized. Things like bank logins and PayPal accounts are obvious valuables worth stealing, but data thieves also harvest many other types of accounts. The accounts can be used to ring up fraudulent charges to fake sellers, launch spam at other victims, or do click-fraud. Table 5-2 lists a sample of commonly stolen accounts.

Table 5-2. Commonly Stolen Accounts

Uber	eBay	Netflix
Mobile phone	Xbox	Google Voice
Facebook	E-mail	Spotify
Minecraft	Amazon	Twitter
World of Warcraft	FedEx/UPS	iTunes

Some of these accounts may only be worth a few cents on the black market, but with the power of automation comes high-volume turnover. A good piece of malware can infect about one million computers worldwide. Small amounts of money can easily add up to a big payoff, all with very little work needed. It's safe to assume that if an account has a password, then it's worth stealing by someone.

Monetization Schemes

Beyond stealing data, there are many other ways that attackers can monetize a hacked computer. Like a good hunter, no scrap of the animal goes to waste. Let's look at the Northwest Hospital case again. The secondary monetization scheme that Maxwell used was pay-per-install fraud. Many independent software manufacturers provide free applications with embedded pop-up advertising. They also pay marketing companies to entice people to download and install this software to increase their popularity. These software companies pay marketing companies from the revenue of the software's pop-up ads. Criminals like Maxwell use their malware to directly install adware onto a victim's computer, thus generating quick revenue without having to do any marketing. You still see this scheme in use in some mobile malware. The important lesson is that fraudsters find ways to subvert legitimate business models all the time. To see where the trends in hacking are going, you need to follow the monetization schemes. Here are some of the more popular ones over the years:

- *Click jack/ad fraud*: Use your machine to click banner ads

- *Pay-per-install*: Install ad-supported software on your machine

- *Crypto ransom:* Pay us to decrypt your data that we locked up

- *Fake AV fraud:* Trick you into paying for antivirus software you don't need.

- *Spam relay:* Use your machine to relay spam.

- *ID theft:* Use stolen credentials for impersonation fraud.

- *Carding:* Use stolen payment cards.

- *Bitcoin mining*: Use your machine to mine (calculate) bitcoins.

- *Botnet for denial-of-service:* Use your machine (and thousands of others) to bombard someone else's site with network traffic for ransom.

- *Malware delivery*: Use your server to host malware to infect other machines.

- *Phishing platform*: Use your server to host fake phishing site to trick others.

- *Fake ad/SEO injection:* Inject banner ads or content onto your site to deliver or help deliver malware.

- *C&C server*: Use your server as a command and control server for other hacked machines (botnet).

- *File repository*: Use your server to store/sell/serve illegal materials (child porn, pirated media).

- *Stealing and using/reselling organizational secrets*: Such as pricing guidelines, proprietary models, contracts, internal security or audit reports, regulatory findings, information on acquisitions/mergers/divestures.

It's worth mentioning that the audits covered by this book are addressing specific types of monetary-incentivized IT risks. The risks that an SSAE 16 SOC 1 covers are unreliable or misleading financial reporting because of fraud, misuse, corruption, and loss of financial transaction records. PCI DSS primarily addresses the risk of confidentiality breaches of payment card numbers for use in fraud, with some lesser emphasis on protecting integrity and availability.

Political Incentives

Politically motivated hacking can come from amateurs and professionals alike. Amateurs are also sometimes enticed with patriotism based on nationalism and sense of duty. Sometimes amateur gray-hat hackers rise up and decide to act, like the Anonymous group. Professional political attackers are often very dangerous, as they are usually well-funded and well-trained cyber-warriors.

Political hacking can take the form of espionage with covert attacks into messaging systems and financial records to build dossiers on enemies and affiliates like spies, whistle-blowers, unfriendly journalists, and double agents. They can also be looking to gather intelligence for future attacks or steal military secrets. Their attacks can disrupt marketing systems to slow recruitment or to inject their own propaganda. Sometimes political attacks are direct, with attempts to disrupt weapon and industrial systems causing infrastructure damage and financial loss. Sometimes political attacking means implanting malware that lies in wait to disrupt a system when a trigger is depressed. Many political attacks take the form of denial-of-service flooding attacks as a protest against a particular cause.

Targets for political/nation-state espionage and sabotage:

- Media and journalists

- Universities

- Health organizations

- Military agencies and related industries (aerospace)
- Police departments
- Energy utilities and companies
- Critical infrastructure (water, sewer, communication)
- Financial institutions
- Large industrial companies

Personal Incentives

Some motivations for hacking appear completely irrational. Instead of asking why someone would do that, consider that people may have different priorities. Some people throw up their hands and don't try to understand these motivations. As John Maynard Keynes said, "The market can remain irrational longer than you can remain solvent." So don't discount personal incentives that appear to provide no apparent benefit to the attacker. Let's look at the detail on motivations seen in these kinds of attacks. Be aware that attackers may have a blend of these reasons.

Counting Coup

Some hackers hack for the sheer joy of hacking. They are breaking in "because it's there." Others may be trying to win prestige and fame for being the first to pull off an impossible hack. The organization that boasts of the "unhackable" system is daring a certain community of attackers to come after them. The results of this kind of hacking usually results in humiliation for the hacked system, as web sites are defaced and secrets are leaked. *Counting coup* refers to how Plains Indians used to win prestige for bravery by merely touching an enemy in battle, but not injuring them. Some hackers do this with systems.

Ideology

This is like political hacking, but often with a vaguer cause—and often with an even vaguer objective. Their focus is to throw a spotlight on wrongdoing. They see themselves as whistleblowers righting an injustice. Ideological hackers often work alone. Snowden and Manning are good examples of ideological insiders.

Duress

Some insiders are pressured into committing cyber-crimes. Some are doing it to support an addiction. These kinds of attacks are hard to spot because the attacker often doesn't appear to have a motive. I have seen cases where sysadmins end up hacking their own systems in order to cover up mistakes that they made. Fear of being fired actually led them to doing something that really did get them fired. Often there is something going on in their personal lives that are compelling them into action.

Ego

The classic disgruntled sysadmin is a known threat to many security professionals. These kinds of insiders are the most dangerous because they have deep technical knowledge as well as an intimate knowledge of the environment that they're compromising. They can feel affronted from being passed over for promotion or from simply having their ideas ignored. They can seek revenge in a variety of ways, from simple destruction to complex blackmail or leakage attacks. Some egotistical attackers feel that they are above the rules because of their superior technical knowledge, and they act accordingly.

Deviant Motivations

Perhaps the most inexplicable are the socially deviant motivated attackers. There have been more than a few cases where one user (usually a man) is hacking the network to stalk or harass another user (usually a woman). There are also attackers breaking into laptop cameras to facilitate their voyeuristic needs. Some of the worst cases are when seemingly normal users are discovered to have large caches of child pornography on their work computers. Despite the awkwardness and distastefulness of these kinds of incidents, they should be considered in a risk assessment.

Common Attack Techniques

Another way to model attacks is to look at the attack techniques. A few attack methods are useful to understand when determining the risk to your organization.

Kill Chain

One of the common attack models for this is the "kill chain" analysis. Originally developed for analyzing military physical attacks (a.k.a. actual warfare), Lockheed Martin adapted the model for IT security. The *kill chain* refers to each of the stages an attacker must succeed in doing in order to achieve security impact. The idea is that if a defender can break any link in that chain, they can block the attack.

There are seven links in the kill chain model:

- *Reconnaissance*: The attacker scans the network for vulnerabilities and/or researches the organization for weaknesses.

- *Weaponization*: The attacker develops an exploit or attack technique based on the reconnaissance.

- *Delivery*: The attacker delivers the exploit and breaches the organization's defenses.

- *Exploitation*: The attacker succeeds in capturing a machine or machines within the organization.

- *Install*: The attacker installs a rootkit that allows him to retain control of the captured machines over time.

- *Command and control*: The attacker uses that remote control to act upon the network as if she were a normal user.

- *Actions on objective*: The attacker now goes after his final objective.

The final stage, action on objective, is sometimes called a *pivot*. It can involve restarting the kill chain internally as the attacker goes after the final objective. For example, the first attack gives the attacker access to a sysadmin's workstation. Now the attacker will move laterally through the network to find the database server holding all the payment card numbers and break into that.

■ **Note** Check out the Lockheed Martin white paper "Intelligence-Driven Computer Network Defense Informed by Analysis of Adversary Campaigns and Intrusion Kill Chains." (http://www.lockheedmartin.com/content/dam/lockheed/data/corporate/documents/LM-White-Paper-Intel-Driven-Defense.pdf).

Stealing Authentication

One useful technique for attackers is to impersonate users. With a user's authentication credentials, they can appear to be legitimate and generate no suspicious hacking traffic that can set off intrusion detection systems. Any audit logs of actions appear as that user. As far as the system is concerned, nothing is amiss. Some organizations do have user-behavior anomaly detectors, but they are still rare and hard to tune. What exactly do I mean by *stealing authentication*? There are several ways this happens:

- *Guessing*: Some users choose poor passwords and have usernames that are easily guessed. Some organizations don't bother to change their default accounts. So guessing or brute-forcing (trying all combinations) a bunch of passwords can occasionally be successful. Organizational names can be harvested off social media sites or guessed based on naming conventions, and turned into usernames easily.

- *Phishing or social engineering*: Simply trick a user into giving you their username and password. They can create a fake e-mail and a fake web page, use a browser pop-up window with a login box, or simply call up the user and pretend to be the help desk. If the attacker is physically onsite, maybe the user has their password on a note under their keyboard.

- *Sniffing*: If a system doesn't encrypt its passwords when being transmitted, an attacker with access to the local wire (or wireless) can use a network sniffer to copy the passwords.

- *Man-in-the-middle*: This is a little more sophisticated attack that also requires the attacker to have access to the network that the victim is using. In this case, the attacker inserts himself into the authentication transaction. When the server asks for the password, the attacker blocks the call and creates his own call to the user asking for the password. The user answers, the attacker copies and relays it back to the server. This trick not only works for passwords, but also for other forms of authentication, like tokens and biometrics. In this case, the attacker sends back an error message to the victim and uses the stolen credential to get in.

- *Local theft*: Most systems make you log in once and then don't keep reprompting you for authentication every time you do something. What is happening is that once you've authenticated to a server, your machine is given some kind of ticket for a duration of time. This ticket is stored in the memory of your computer and is used in place of authentication every time that you need to perform an action with the remote system. In Windows, this is called a Kerberos ticket. On the web, it is a session cookie. An attacker can use malware or direct hacking to simply copy this ticket out of memory.

Modeling for this kind of attack means that you should assume an attacker is going to steal a user's authentication. Based on that, how would an attacker make use of it on your system? What would that look like and what kind of damage could they do? This can drive decisions down the road for controls to help detect and contain this technique.

Exfiltration

Once an attacker is in your network, what are they going to do? If they intend to steal data, they need to find that data and copy it back out. This is called *exfiltration*. It is not always an easy problem for an attacker to solve, as sometimes they need to copy large amounts of data. Some organizations have data leak prevention that looks for large data transfers of a certain type. So attackers need to find a way to disguise or conceal the data. A common technique is to send the data out via encrypted web traffic to a web server under the attacker's control. Some attackers compress, encrypt, and then send the data out in small chunks hidden inside normal traffic, like DNS or Ping. Different organizations have different channels available (or unavailable) for exfiltration, which can squeeze an attacker's options. This should be considered in risk modeling an attack as well.

Building the Adversarial Risk Model

Now that we have examined a wide range of adversarial models, let's build a risk model and populate it with data.

A good risk model that is formal but still practical that incorporates many of the elements I've been presenting is *factor analysis of information risk* (FAIR). It's also an open standard and widely available. It supports both quantitative and qualitative analysis and is relatively easy to use. FAIR's likelihood component, which it calls *loss event frequency*. Loss event frequency consists of *threat event frequency* and vulnerability. Threat event frequency consists of two factors: contact and action. *Contact* refers to how likely the threat will come in contact with an asset. *Action* refers to the likelihood the threat will attack the asset, once it comes into contact. The vulnerability factor consists of control strength and threat capability. Impact is defined in FAIR as *probable loss magnitude*.

FAIR also breaks down impact into more detail subfactors. For the purposes of this example, let's collapse those factors into a single measure. I also use the same terminology I referred to earlier for this model for simplicity's sake. FAIR also uses frequency in its risk modeling. *Frequency* refers to the count of observable events, which is great when doing quantitative analysis with past data driving your calculations. For this example, I am going to stick with likelihood since we're still doing qualitative analysis and it refers to the future probability of an event.

Remember, your risk model needs to fit your organization and in some cases, your organization's way of expressing things. Although some audits prefer to stick to the book definition of a formal risk model, you can still modify things as needed. You just need to be clear and consistent in how you do your risk assessment. Remember, the process should be repeatable by someone else.

■ **Note**   More information about factor analysis of information risk (FAIR) is at the FAIR Institute (www.fairinstitute.org).

Qualitative Example

Tables 5-3, 5-4, and 5-5 walk through an example of some risks for a typical organization.

Table 5-3. *Sample Qualitative Risk Table: Part 1, Vulnerability*

Risk Scenario	Control Resistance	Threat Capability	Likelihood of Vulnerability
Malware infection on a desktop PC	*Moderate*: AV resists 75% of all attacks	*Strong*: Lots of new malware out there	*Moderate*: Subfactors moderate and strong
Insider steals source code	*Weak*: No controls for insiders	*Moderate*: All internal users have read access; only two sysadmins with full access	*Moderate*: Subfactors strong and moderate
Office intruder steals a laptop with data	*Moderate*: Door entrance is partially staffed	*Moderate*: It doesn't take much beyond daring to steal a laptop	*Moderate*
Denial-of-service attack against web site	*Weak*: No controls beyond basic firewall	*Strong*: A distributed DoS attack would overwhelm us	*Moderate High*

Table 5-4. *Sample Qualitative Risk Table: Part 2, Threat*

Risk Scenario	Contact Likelihood	Attack Likelihood	Likelihood of Threat
Malware infection on a desktop PC	*High*: Malware is always coming in	*Very high*: Lots of web-based and e-mail malware	*High*: Both subfactors high
Insider steals source code	*High*: Internal users in constant contact with source	*Very low*: Low chance of insiders; small user base	*Unlikely*: Very low chance despite high contact
Office intruder steals a laptop with data	*Moderate*: Some crooks working downtown	*High*: If a crook gets in, there are lot of nice laptops to steal	*Likely*: Subfactors moderate and high
Denial-of-service attack against web site	*Low*: We mostly fly under the radar	*Low*: Our site is pretty boring and static	*Unlikely*: Both subfactors low

Table 5-5. *Sample Qualitative Risk Table: Part 3, Risk*

Risk Scenario	Likelihood of Vulnerability	Likelihood of Threat	Likelihood	Impact
Malware infection on a desktop PC	*Moderate*: Subfactors weak and strong	*High*: Both subfactors high	*Likely*	*Significant*: could slow productivity for days
Insider steals source code from CVS	*Moderate*: Subfactors weak and strong	*Unlikely*: Very low chance despite high contact	*Moderately unlikely*	*Highly significant*: Our source code is key to our business
Office intruder steals a laptop with data	*Moderate*	*Likely*: Subfactors moderate and high	*Moderately likely*	*Significant*: Laptops cost $ and could have data on them
Denial-of-service attack against web site	*Moderate High*	*Unlikely*: Both subfactors low	*Moderately unlikely*	*Insignificant*: We don't care if our web site is offline for a bit

Quantitative Example

With some work, you can convert these qualitative measures to quantitative calculations of frequency based on real-world data. Some of the data can come from your asset analysis, some from vulnerability scanning, and some from industry reports. Tables 5-6, 5-7, and 5-8 look at the malware threat, but narrow the threat contact vector for simplicity. We're just going to look at browser-borne infection via web drive-by.

Table 5-6. *Sample Quantitative Risk Table: Part 1, Vulnerability*

Risk	Control Resistance	Threat Capability	Likelihood of Vulnerability
Malware infection on a desktop PC via web	Our antivirus has been rated 85% effective	75% of company browsers fully patched and hardened	40% likelihood from (1-0.85)+(1-0.75)

Table 5-7. *Sample Quantitative Risk Table: Part 2, Threat*

Risk	Contact Frequency	Attack Frequency	Frequency of Threat
Malware infection on a desktop PC via web	500 users surfing approx. 40 sites per day	1 in 1000 web sites have malware per industry reports	20 web malware hits per day

Table 5-8. *Sample Quantitative Risk Table: Part 3, Risk*

Risk	Frequency of Vulnerability	Likelihood of Threat	Likelihood	Impact
Malware infection on a desktop PC via web	20 hits per day	40%	Almost 1% per day, or 4% per week; probable infection every 5 months	$600 in IT cleanup costs, lost productivity

In this example, I made up numbers roughly based on industry data; however, much of that data—and more—is out there. Here are some external resources for data:

- **Microsoft Security Intelligence Report**
  https://www.microsoft.com/security/sir/default.aspx

- **Akamai State of the Internet: Security report**
  https://www.akamai.com/us/en/our-thinking/state-of-the-internet-report/

- **Cisco Security report**
  http://www.cisco.com/c/en/us/products/security/annual_security_report.html

- **Symantec Security Threat Report**
  http://www.symantec.com/security_response/publications/threatreport.jsp

- **Mandiant Intelligence Center Report**
  http://intelreport.mandiant.com

- **Virus Bulletin Effectiveness Results**
  https://www.virusbtn.com/vb100/latest_comparative/index

- **AlienVault Open Threat Exchange**
  https://www.alienvault.com/open-threat-exchange

- **Health and Human Services Breaches Affecting 500 or More Individuals**
  https://ocrportal.hhs.gov/ocr/breach/breach_report.jsf

These are just simple examples but should mostly show you that it isn't that hard to do a decent risk analysis. There are entire books, classes, certifications, and user organizations focused on calculating and presenting IT risk results. At some point in your IT security journey, it might be helpful to check them out.

FURTHER READING

- **CERT Insider Threat Center**
  http://www.cert.org/insider-threat/cert-insider-threat-center.cfm

- **Northwest Hospital, Successes and failures apprehending malware authors**
  http://www.planetheidi.com/Pompon-VB2010.pdf

- **Society of Information Risk Analysts**
  https://www.societyinforisk.org/

- **FDIC Cyber Challenge: Exercise**
  https://www.fdic.gov/regulations/resources/director/technical/cyber/purpose.html

PART II

Wrangling the Organization

CHAPTER 6

Scope

Just boil the ocean.

—Will Rogers, American humorist,

A proposed solution to the threat of submarines (1917)

Scope, simply, is what you care about protecting based on what your compliance and risk analysis uncovers. The assets, processes, and personnel in the scope are where you focus your controls to reduce risk. Since it isn't always feasible to defend all your assets from all the threats, scope answers the question about what must be protected. The following are some examples of scoped assets:

- Cardholder data, financial transaction data, protected health information

- IT systems storing, processing, or transmitting data under scope

- Software running on those IT systems

- Infrastructure supporting those IT systems

- Facilities housing those IT systems

- Personnel managing and operating those facilities and systems

- Processes and procedures describing operations related to those facilities, systems, and personnel

Developing Scope

It is important that the scope developed accurately reflect the logical, physical, operational, and human factors of an organization. Furthermore, a scope with respect to audit has a time-dimensional component as well, referring to when things fall under scope. A good definition of the process comes from PCI DSS: "The process of identifying all system components, people, and processes to be included in a PCI DSS assessment to accurately determine the scope of assessment."[1]

There are many factors that drive scope analysis within an organization. Certain industries, as discussed in Chapter 1, have specific compliance requirements they must obey that may mandate specific scope definitions. For example, a merchant accepting payment cards is required to have a PCI DSS scope. Sometimes scope encompasses an entire organization and sometimes it covers only a single business unit.

---

[1]PCI DSS v3.2 Template for Report on Compliance," Section 3, Description of Scope of Work and Approach Taken, https://www.pcisecuritystandards.org/documents/PCI-DSS-v3_2-ROC-Reporting-Template.pdf

If your scope is not well defined and controlled, auditors can redefine the boundaries. You may have built a security program based on the assumption of a particular scope. If you missed something, an auditor could determine that your scope is incomplete— and that there are other things in scope that haven't been protected. Worse, because of this oversight, you could be missing vital controls and oversight over those overlooked areas. For example, you limited your scope to a single set of servers that process and store payment cards, forgetting about the tape backup system that has copies of all the stored cardholder data. What if you didn't set up proper access control or encryption on that backup system? Not only would you have an audit problem, but the cardholder data is at risk of exposure as well. A correctly defined scope can save you time and money because you can focus your efforts on the right things. An incomplete scope can turn an audit into a struggle if things that you didn't expect to be audited suddenly did.

Scope is critical to the design of the IT security program because it shows where the work needs to happen. Scope also features prominently in most published audit reports. It is possible and sometimes desirable to have multiple scopes for different audits in the same organization. They can even overlap, as shown in Figure 6-1.

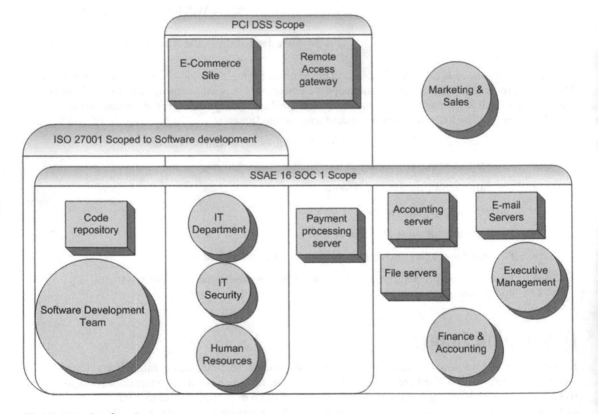

Figure 6-1. *Overlapping scopes*

The ultimate scope design depends heavily on the focus, boundaries, risks, and the compliance requirements of the organization. This necessitates a closer look at compliance requirements.

Compliance Requirement Gathering

If you don't know the legal and regulatory compliance requirements that you are subject to, then it is very hard to define a scope. If you remember from the first chapter, there are a large number of possible requirements regarding IT security. I will not rehash them here, but instead focus on the three types of audits that this book covers.

The SSAE 16 SOC 1 covers the Sarbanes-Oxley legal requirements for publicly held companies. PCI DSS covers the payment card contractual requirements for organizations issuing, accepting, processing, or storing payment cards. Many compliance requirements can be satisfied with an SSAE 16 SOC 2/3 or an ISO 27001 scoped to the chosen services.

The products, services, locations, and processes in the scope can also be determined by customer requirements and contractual terms. For example, a Software-as-a-Service (SaaS) company may be required to follow PCI DSS because one of its customers is using the hosted software to store cardholder data. The SAAS company did not set out to be PCI DSS compliant when it built its service offering, but a customer's chosen usage model has brought their systems under scope.

Zero in on PII

After you've looked at your organizational, compliance, and customer obligations, then the next big thing to look at for scope is *personally identifiable information* (PII). This is the private information that can be traced back to an individual. In many jurisdictions, PII usually originates with a full name plus some other confidential identifier. It can also include things like usernames and passwords. There are varying definitions of what is considered as private information, depending on standard, regulation, or law. In general, a single piece of information that distinguishes one individual from another can be considered an identifier. In some contexts, even things like telephone numbers, e-mail addresses, and facial photographs can qualify as confidential data that must be protected. When thinking about what to put in scope or not, consider how someone would feel if his or her information was published on your web site for all to see and index. If it would make a reasonable person angry and possibly litigious, you should consider putting that data into scope. The following are some examples to help figure this out.

Identifying information

- Full name

- Date of birth

- Social Security number

- Passport number

- US state ID or driver's license number

Personal information that when combined with identifying information can be considered PII

- Date of birth

- Personal identification numbers (PIN)

- Name of spouse or family members

- Vehicle registrations

- Bank account numbers

- Payment card data

- Spousal information
- Children's information
- Military records
- Religious preference
- Gender
- Race/ethnicity
- Image of signature
- Mother's maiden name
- Medical insurance number
- Information that relates to an individual's past, present, or future physical or mental health or condition, the provision of health care to the individual, or the past, present, or future payment for the provision of health care to the individual, and that identifies the individual or for which there is a reasonable basis to believe can be used to identify the individual.[2] Any information an individual gives to related to a financial product or service, or related to a transaction involving financial products or services. Biometric data such as fingerprints, photographs, or voice recordings.

Things that might be considered in some jurisdictions as personal even though they are routinely shared openly or are available from public sources

- Home telephone number
- IP address
- Home mailing address
- E-mail address
- Marital status
- Employment history
- Property ownership records
- Place of birth
- Educational history
- Maiden name
- Names of banks used

Things that would not be considered personal information

- Work address
- Work telephone number

---

[2]HIPAA Privacy Rule definition of protected health information.

PCI DSS scoping

The PCI DSS audit scope if focused primarily on payment card data and the systems and processes in place to protect it. This is pretty much everything associated with a payment card, both visible and invisible, which is referred to as the *cardholder data environment* (CDE). Per PCI DSS, the data in scope encompasses *cardholder data* (CHD) and *sensitive authentication data* (SAD). Cardholder data includes the *primary account number* (PAN), which is the payment card number. Cardholder data can also include the PAN along with the cardholder name, expiration date, and/or service code.

Sensitive authentication data is defined by the PCI DSS as the "security-related information (including but not limited to card validation codes/values, full track data (from the magnetic stripe or equivalent on a chip), PINs, and PIN blocks) used to authenticate cardholders and/or authorize payment card transactions."

In addition, PCI DSS requires you to protect the data scanned off the magnetic stripe. The tiny three- or four-digit code on the back of a card is used for authentication. Like a password, it must be kept so secure that it can never be saved in long-term storage (okay in memory, but never to disk).

Although not part of PCI DSS (since we are talking about payment cards), you should also be aware the printing the last four digits of the card number along with the card expiration date on a receipt is a violation of Fair and Accurate Credit Transaction Act (FACTA).[3]

SSAE SOC 1 Scoping

Remember that the overarching goal is to curb fraud, misuse, and loss of financial transactions. Specifically, the SOC 1 report is intended to be an "evaluation of their internal controls over financial reporting for purposes of comply with laws and regulations such as the Sarbanes-Oxley Act and the user entities' auditors as they plan and perform audits of the user entities' financial statements."[4] This is why SSAE 16 SOC 1 audits are scoped for financial systems and the services that support them. Primarily, this scope covers products and services used by customers, and includes key systems, processes, and operations that affect those scoped products and services. Any messaging or workflow systems related to financials can also fall within scope, such as the system used for customer orders or the system used for purchase orders. Scope also includes any IT services pertaining to these applications, such as change control, backup, and software development. Any system that holds or processes significant financial reporting elements can cause a misstatement in financial reporting and is considered a *material weakness*.

Supporting Non-IT Departments

All of these types of audits pull the IT department into scope, but don't forget the other departments. Departments that support key processes and controls may also be in scope. For example, since human resources is typically responsible for hiring and background checks, their processes need to be in scope. Call centers can easily fall into a PCI DSS scope if they are involved in taking, recording (both digitally and on audio), or looking up customer payment card numbers.

Double Check

One thing about making decisions on scope is that you should never proceed alone. Your legal department can also help. You may need to explain how the technology works and draw some diagrams, but working with legal can give you a better picture. Scope is also something that you should run by management and system owners before you finalize it. There may be specific business requirements that management will want to move in to (or move out of) scope that you didn't know about.

---

[3]https://en.wikipedia.org/wiki/Fair_and_Accurate_Credit_Transactions_Act#Truncation_of_credit_ and_debit_card_numbers
[4]http://www.aicpa.org/InterestAreas/FRC/AssuranceAdvisoryServices/Pages/AICPASOC1Report.aspx

Writing Scope Statements

The scope definition must be absolute and exact, as audits are built upon the scope statement. Since organizations can have complex and intertwined processes, the boundaries of the scope need to define exactly where the audit should stop, with the assumption that controls are in place to enforce boundaries. SSAE 16 and ISO 27001 auditors review the scope statement in meticulous detail. There should be no ambiguity in interpretation that could lead to audit or control gaps. Scope statements must be easily understood for ISO 27001, SSAE 16 audits, and PCI DSS Report on Compliance (PCI DSS ROC), since they are featured on the front page of the reports. The statement should include the business process or organizational units as well as the locations involved. Here are a few examples:

- The information security management system for the protection of client information held in the file server systems operated by the Wichita office (ISO 27001)

- The information security management system that supports and protects the confidential information related to the clients of Dewey Fleecem & Howe Attorneys at Law, stored at its domestic and international offices and business continuity sites (ISO 27001)

- The global services for customer service centers located in Honolulu, Hong Kong, New York, Sao Paolo, Paris, and Mumbai (SSAE 16)

- The hosted systems supporting the MYZER Financial System (SSAE 16) at all locations of Puget Regional Bank (SSAE 16)

- The City of Gotham Department of Accounting Services and Computer Services' IT environment (SSAE 16)

Control Inventory

The things that reduce risk to assets are controls. In an IT security program, controls are built to support *control objectives*, which are goals supporting the objectives. We'll get more into control objectives later in the book. Right now, you need to know that controls are important in protecting scoped assets. It's very helpful to understand the controls that you have already as you define scope.

There are a few ways to look at controls. There are administrative controls, which describe processes and policies; technical controls for IT systems; and physical controls. Another way to look at controls is their function: preventative controls try to stop a risk from occurring, detective controls alert when risk events occur, and corrective controls repair the impacts from risk events. You can map these all together, as shown in Table 6-1.

Table 6-1. *Examples of Controls*

Control Type	Administrative	Technical	Physical
Preventative	Acceptable usage policy, change control policy, security awareness training	Antivirus software, firewalls, passwords	Door locks, security guards, fences
Detective	Access rights review, unauthorized change reviews, audit log reviews	Intrusion detection systems, uptime monitoring, data leak detection	Burglar alarms, surveillance cameras, temperature monitors
Corrective	Business continuity plan, incident response plan, NDA lawsuits	Back up tapes, failover ISP connections, laptop tracking software	Fire suppression, generators, exploding dye packs

Control Effectiveness and Efficiency

Once you are satisfied that a control is operating consistently, another consideration is how efficient the control is. Efficiency is not a requirement for most audits, but it is a powerful concept for your security program. But what is good? A useful way to look at this is to examine control effectiveness and efficiency. Control effectiveness refers to both a control's coverage (the amount of scoped assets that it covers) and its strength or stopping power. Some auditors think in terms of strong vs. weak controls. Usually, preventive controls are considered stronger than detective and corrective controls. Control efficiency is really control effectiveness divided by cost—or simply, the bang per buck.

How do you measure control effectiveness? For technical controls, vulnerability testing and penetration testing can give you a good idea of what works and what isn't working so well. Many of the resources in the last chapter can also provide hard data on control effectiveness. Here are a few organizations that publish analysis reports on the effectiveness of many technical controls and security tools.

- Virus Bulletin (`https://www.virusbtn.com`)

- West Coast Labs (`http://www.westcoastlabs.com`)

- ICSA Labs (`https://www.icsalabs.com`)

Your controls analysis is also important once you establish governance (explained in the next chapter) and you need to bolster or change controls to achieve your control objectives. You should document the results of your controls analysis, because it is an audit requirement for ISO 27001, as well as a good idea.

Scoping Adjacent Systems

Once you've defined on your scope, some systems and processes are clearly under scope while others may be harder to decide upon. For example, say you're scoping a payment card–processing environment. Obviously, the servers and databases doing the actual card processing are in scope. However, is the storage area network providing the disk space for them in scope? Yes. Are the system administrator workstations? Yes, if they have direct access to the cardholder data environment. Is the corporate file server in scope? It could, if it is also on the same network as the storage area network in the CDE. Adjacent systems can fall into scope if they have unbounded access to systems in scope. An indirect path to the scoped systems is just as important as a direct path. The key is how you manage access to the scoped systems. If the pathway to scoped systems is access controlled, perhaps by a fingerprint-scanning gateway, then the scope can end at that gateway. Figure 6-2 is a diagram that illustrates this concept.

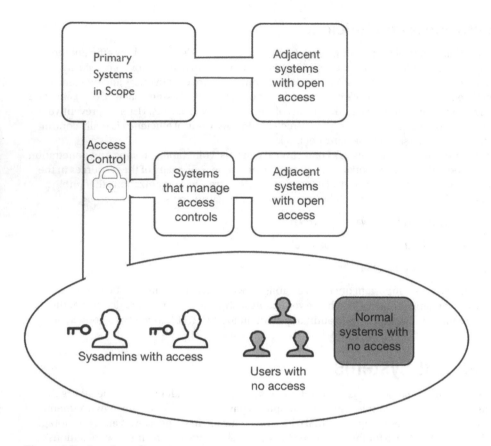

Figure 6-2. *Scoping adjacent systems*

Trace a line from a system; if it can touch the systems in scope unimpeded or with a key to the lock, then it's in scope. If it's not (shaded systems), then it's out of scope. Notice how the system controlling the access and its supporting infrastructure are also in scope. This is a nuance that eludes some people, so remember that. If an unauthorized person can affect the access control system, then they could get access to the rest of the scoped environment. This is why access control systems must be controlled as well.

Scope Barriers

Once you define a scope, you need to build a barrier around it and manage access. If you can't erect a strong barrier, then detailed monitoring and logging can be used as compensating controls. If everything within the scope is so important that it needs to be protected, this implies that everything outside the scope is less important and not as well protected. Any unauthorized access or changes that happen outside scope should not be allowed to contaminate the scoped assets. This can get tricky when you look at how porous the scope barrier might need to be. Personnel, data, and requests for service could all pass back and forth through a scope boundary as needed. Controls need to be placed on all of these flows.

Technical Barriers

As we are dealing with IT systems, let's look closely at the technical controls that you can use as choke points in a scope boundary.

Network Barriers

The most common scope boundary tools are network security devices. The ideal is *air gap* separation, where there is no connectivity at all between scoped systems and the other systems. Often this is infeasible. The most useful device here is a firewall, though this can get expensive when you need to segregate large numbers of systems with a lot of data flow. Virtual LANs (VLANs) that run off managed switches are a useful compromise. However, remember the scoping rules around access control infrastructure; the switches themselves fall under scope.

Logical Access Barriers

Authentication systems should be segregated across scope barriers. It can be very challenging to properly secure the same Active Directory (AD) tree for both scoped and non-scoped users. Remember that infrastructure supporting access control into scoped areas is also under scope. You will find it easier to have separate domains or AD branches for each trust zone. It's best for you to use strong authentication into scoped zones, such as two-factor authentication.

Application Barriers

Logical access within applications is highly variable in terms of form and function. Nevertheless, the general rule is that administrative access to scoped applications must be controlled. This can mean either restricting administrative access to scoped or trained individuals, and/or only allow administrative access from controlled subnets. You need to control the ability to modify data or logs within an application as well. For scoped applications, even normal user application access should be subject to reasonable access controls, such as username and password. Automated data integration and feeds from sources outside of scope also need to be controlled; not only for authentication but also for the quality of the data. It's helpful if applications push their data feed out from secured scoped zones, rather than requiring that untrusted clients pull data.

Combined Technical Barriers

Figure 6-3 is a simple diagram pulling all the technical controls into a single scope perimeter. You may notice that there are many firewalls in this diagram. They need not be physical appliances, but could be virtual firewalls or subinterfaces. The administrative access is done through *jump workstations* in their own segregated zone. Administrators authenticate to the jump machine and then move through into the scoped secure zone.

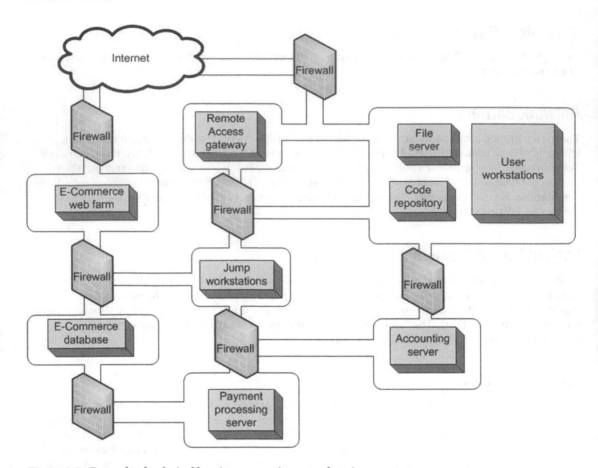

Figure 6-3. *Example of technical barriers supporting scoped environments*

Physical Barriers

There should be physical controls to separate scoped equipment as well. Sometimes the scoped hardware is already secured in a dedicated collocation facility. Otherwise, locking the server room door and controlling access to the keys can be done. In the case of shared server rooms, locking cages and racks can be used. Buildings on lower floors with windows are also a consideration. Don't forget supporting infrastructure, so cabling and power should also have some physical controls protecting them.

Process Barriers

Just like everything else, you should control business processes as they cross the scope barrier. In Figure 6-3, you can see how two common processes are supported. One is change control, where administrators can use the jump workstations to pull code changes from code repository and then push them to the e-commerce servers. I cover more of this change control process in Chapter 13. The second is how payment data can be pushed from an e-commerce database to the payment database, with a final push to the accounting server. In general, you should be pushing or reaching out from the scoped environment, as opposed to having unscoped (and less trusted) machines pulling or reaching in.

Third-Party Process Dependencies

The most difficult processes to manage with scoped systems are processes involving third parties. In some cases, third parties can even be different divisions of the same organization that are not directly under the control of the group being audited. A common third party is the collocation company used to house the scoped equipment. In all of these cases, the requirement is to segregate them as much as possible by using the previously mentioned controls. Additional processes for managing risk with third parties are discussed in Chapter 23.

Scoping Hints

Although we have introduced some controls here, later chapters get into more detail on their implementation and uses. One thing to remember with scopes (and all security) is that you do your best and refine later. Over time, as successive audits and business cycles are run, you may want to change scopes and move scope barriers. That is natural and a good way to evolve your IT security program. This is covered more in Chapter 7, which focuses on governance.

Start Small and Expand

If possible, start as small as possible. It's not always feasible or easier, but you can reduce scope by centralizing assets and departments. Look for redundancies and dispersed systems and see if you can consolidate them. It may also be possible to scope to one facet, location, or division of the business, and then build upon that after things are working. To do this, you may need to merge and split departments and personnel, which can be messy and complicated. However, some organizations realize some efficiency gains by restructuring to support dedicated departmental functions.

But Not Too Small

A scope that is too small can be more trouble than it's worth, especially if you're dividing an organization with firewalls and segregated processes. Sometimes it's just easier to put an entire company in scope, wrap the barriers around the external perimeter, and go from there.

Simplification

You can reduce a scope by eliminating superfluous access. It sounds simple, but it can be difficult to take something away from someone that they're used to having. For example, I have seen some organizations where the entire development team had full root access to all the servers. This put that entire team, and all their systems, in scope for audit. Removing that access immediately simplifies everything, if you can convince the development team they can still get their job done. If someone's job doesn't require them to have access, they should not have it. Even if they only require occasional access, perhaps some new process can replace the always-on access.

Sometimes after analysis, you may find some processes or systems that are too expensive to keep in scope. These could be systems with a wide surface area and are spread around everywhere. These could be fragile or immature functions that are difficult or expensive to secure and contain. These could be things that are distant and out of your direct control, yet you are still dependent on. There could also be things that are new or subject to rapid change, so they're hard to pin down. The question to ask is whether you eliminate these processes all together. I have seen cases where companies ceased or modified a line of business when confronted with the high cost of securing them. Another way to eliminate a process is to outsource it, pushing the security and compliance requirements to someone else.

FURTHER READING

- **Guide to Protecting the Confidentiality of Personally Identifiable Information (PII) 800-122**
  http://www.nist.gov/customcf/get_pdf.cfm?pub_id=904990

- **Open PCI Scoping Toolkit**
  https://www.isaca.org/Groups/Professional-English/pci-compliance/
  GroupDocuments/OpenPCIScopingToolkit.pdf

CHAPTER 7

■■■

Governance

Amateurs talk about tactics, but professionals study logistics.

—General Robert H. Barrow,
USMC (Commandant of the Marine Corps) noted in 1980

How do you win in a game where the landscape is constantly changing and your opponents look for new ways to trip you up? Like Fort Pulaski, the defenses of yesterday become useless against today's threats. What good is planning if everything you're using can be made obsolete overnight?

Let's step back and talk about the concept of tactics versus strategy. Some people use the terms interchangeably, but there is a distinct difference. Strategy refers to long-term plans towards a set of goals. Tactics are the short-term things you do to achieve those goals. Since it's in the quote by General Barrow, I'll define logistics as well. Logistics is how we coordinate resources to support the tactics in accordance with the strategy Say your mission is to capture a castle. Your strategy is this: we plan to invade the castle indirectly using subterfuge. However, your tactics are this: we are going to pretend to lay siege to the castle but we'll also send a disguised messenger in with a fake letter from the enemy king giving the garrison permission to surrender. The logistics would involve forging the letter and disguising the messenger. By the way, this really happened in 1271 to a Crusaders castle.[1] It's another great story to add to your war chest of security anecdotes.

Therefore, in IT security, our tactics are how we deal with risks: implementing controls like firewalls, antivirus software, password schemes, and encryption. Tactics will change as the risks and technologies change. Your strategy is how you analyze and assess risks, set scopes, and define goals. *Strategy* defines how your organization decides which risks should be eliminated and which you should just live with. Logistics flows from that strategy to supply resources to perform the tactical work. *IT security governance* concerns defining your strategy and logistics. Strategy and logistics shouldn't need to change as much as tactics. Tactics will always be changing, as the threats and landscape changes.

For IT security, management is at least as important as technology. Technology is powerful but must be properly selected and used in order to be instrumental in stopping attackers. Governance is about ensuring that adequate and proportional security measures are acquired and managed by the organization. Governance defines who does what and when, so that security is properly addressed. Most importantly, governance creates and promotes the security goals, as there is no universal thing as *secure*. What is acceptable as secure has to be defined based on an organization's threshold of acceptable risk. Lastly, governance is means that the organization authorizes and commits to the IT security program from the highest levels of management.

Some organizations will outsource their tactical tasks, but strategy is your own. You can bring consultants and advisors to help you build a strategy, but just as the risk is yours, so should be the plan in dealing with it. Luckily, there are great road maps on how to organically grow a governance process that fits your organization's needs.

---

[1]https://en.wikipedia.org/wiki/Fall_of_Krak_des_Chevaliers

© Raymond Pompon 2016
R. Pompon, *IT Security Risk Control Management*, DOI 10.1007/978-1-4842-2140-2_7

Governance Frameworks

There are many ways to do IT security governance. Some may fit your organization more naturally than others may. Here are some of the major governance frameworks:

- **National Institute of Standards Cybersecurity Framework**
  http://www.nist.gov/cyberframework/

- **Control Objectives for Information and Related Technology (COBIT)**
  http://www.isaca.org/COBIT/pages/default.aspx

- **Health Information Trust Alliance (HITRUST)**
  https://hitrustalliance.net/hitrust-csf/

- **ITIL ISO 27001**
  http://www.iso.org/iso/home/standards/management-standards/iso27001.htm

Choose your governance system with care. Once a system like this is in place, they are hard to replace. This is especially true if you're in the middle of an audit period. Over time, systems can grow and force you to do things the way the system wants, not necessarily the way you want.

The ISMS

We talked about the focus of different audits in earlier chapters, like how the SSAE 16 SOC 1 is focused on financial records and the PCI DSS is focused on payment cards. ISO 27001's focus is on IT security governance, which they call the Information Security Management System or ISMS. Since ISO 27001 has a pretty good model for security governance, this chapter will follow its path in building a governance system.

The ISMS Governance Strategy

Briefly, governance is the work of a cross-functional team that manages the IT security program for an organization in a continuous process of analysis and actions. Governance according to the ISMS approach uses the *Deming Cycle* of continuous improvement, also known as Plan-Do-Check-Act (PDCA). The following is the action plan for getting an ISMS off the ground:

1. Establish the ISMS.

   a. Set up an ISMS security steering committee.

   b. Draft a charter defining the steering committee's roles and responsibilities.

   c. Obtain executive management's approval of the charter and the security steering committee.

2. *Plan*. The steering committee commissions an analysis of assets and compliance requirements. It publishes security goals and scope based on these.

3. *Do*. The steering committee and related stakeholders commissions an analysis of risk and controls. It reviews these in light of the security goals, decides upon risk treatment options, and assigns work to be done based on them.

4. *Check*. The steering committee commissions an analysis of control effectiveness and appropriateness within the organization against the previously published goals and scope.

5. *Act*. The steering committee adjusts the risk treatment plans accordingly to ensure that goals are being met. The steering committee then returns to step 2 and begins the Plan phase again to continue refinement and improvement of the security program.

Let's break each of these down now.

Establish the ISMS

The ISMS is a key part of your strategy for the management of risk in your organization. Before you get started on the Plan-Do-Check-Act part of the ISMS, you need to set it up. This involves forming the steering committee, assigning key roles, drafting your charter, and getting organizational buy-off on the endeavor.

The ISMS Steering Committee

When doing IT security, you never want to go it alone. Security is hard, but things get much easier with a whole team pulling together. A strong team is a multi-disciplinary team. Having team members with different skills and different perspectives of how the organization runs will make identifying risks and treating them much easier.

IT Security

Who should be on the ISMS steering committee? You need some obvious members, like the chief security officer (CSO). The CSO will lead the committee and be responsible for setting the agenda and running the meetings. Please note that the CSO is a role that I am using for convenience not necessarily a title. The CSO's job title could be security manager, information security officer, IT security lead, or even network security potentate. The title isn't as important as the role, which belongs to the most senior individual in the organization responsible for managing the IT security program.

Other Security Departments

You should also include any other security departments, such as the leads representing the other domains of security outside of IT. For example, you should include someone from either physical security or facilities. If there is a head of business continuity or disaster response, they should be included as well. In smaller offices, business continuity and physical security duties usually fall onto the office manager, who would be an excellent addition to the ISMS committee. Some organizations have a separate department (and requirement) for data privacy, so they should be involved as well.

Leadership

An absolute requirement would be representation from the executive leadership of the organization. Ideally, the higher ranking the better. If you can get someone who represents the organization's board or the CEO, that would be best. Sometimes you can't get so lucky, so the CIO or VP of IT may be the best you can get. Whoever this is, their role is to put executive authority behind the committee decisions and to supply the necessary resources (budget and people's time) to getting things done. Without explicit and concrete executive support, an ISMS will stall before even getting off the ground. Until that happens, all of your efforts will be an academic exercise with little or no real impact to the organization. At the very least, the committee's work should roll up to the CEO for formal acceptance of risk. The CEO's job is to ensure the safety of the organization, even if he or she can't or don't have time to participate in the day-to-day work committee.

Audit

As part of the Plan-Do-Check-Act, you should have a representative from the Check phase of the cycle. This means an internal auditor on the committee, or at least an occasional report to the committee from the external auditors. They provide an independent assessment of the progress towards the ISMS goals. As members of the committee, not only could they provide direct feedback on control shortcomings, but they can also provide insight into the design of security program metrics to measure and track effectiveness. Note that if you are doing an ISO 27001 audit, you are required to have an internal audit role within your organization. Chapter 22 is entirely focused on internal audit.

Specialized Departmental Roles

Other appropriate organizational experts should be part of the ISMS committee. You'd want to have someone from the legal team to weigh in on proposed policies as well as to navigate the complex shoals of liability that can arise from IT risk. The legal team can also act as an authority on compliance regulations and contractual issues involving IT. Since IT risk translates to financial risk (as well as financial expenditures), a representative from finance is a strong addition. With so many security policies involving how staff perform their job, a member from the human resources department is another key role. HR becomes especially important when security policy violations involve employee disciplinary measures, as well as IT security initiatives that touch employee privacy.

IT

Since we are talking about IT security, you will want at least one person from the IT department on the committee. Some organizations are large or tech-oriented enough that there may be several different groups of IT personnel. So maybe you'd want one person each from software development, IT operations, the help desk, and projects. Or perhaps you don't want to load up your committee with techies, so you could have one person who could represent all of those teams, such as the IT director. It all depends on your organization and its culture.

Major Departmental Heads

The ISMS committee should have representative from a cross-section of business within the organization. These are the department heads who represent the important business processes and user communities that are affected and protected by the ISMS. In larger organizations, these department heads are likely already meeting for other reasons. In that case, you could use that forum as an opportunity to get their feedback and opinion on risk matters. These department heads act as system owners, weighing in on decisions and analyses tied to the daily business of the organization. Without them on the committee, you risk doing things in a vacuum and failing to engage user's support. As my old boss used to say, without input from the business, your security program will be like throwing sod down on cement and expecting it to grow.

ISMS Committee Guests

In addition to the standing membership, the ISMS committee could benefit from occasional guest members or speakers. These members can come both inside and outside the organization.

Inside the organization, you can include other department heads not formally in the ISMS committee. Perhaps these departments don't even have a strong IT presence within the organization, but could still provide some new insights or warnings. This could include marketing, sales, customer service, manufacturing, academics, research, transportation, or even the cafeteria. You could also look at asking one of your standing department heads to bring in a representative from one of their underlying sub-departments. For example, facilities could bring someone from janitorial to talk about what goes on after dark. The IT help desk could bring in a support phone tech to talk about how they do password resets over the phone. The idea is to keep the ISMS fresh with new ideas and leave no stone unturned when it comes to possible internal risk.

External expertise is also valuable to the ISMS committee. If an ISMS is just starting out and all the participants are new the process, then having a security consultant on the committee would be extremely beneficial. If there is outside counsel with expertise in areas of the law beyond your in-house knowledge, this person would be a good drop-in member. Subject matter experts could guest lecture on occasional topics as well. This could include key vendors, technical consultants, regulators, and even cyber-cops. I have seen several federal cyber-police agencies willing to go onsite to organizations and provide advice on the protection of critical infrastructure. Do you remember the security organizations that I discussed back in Chapter 1? They are a good source for these kinds of speakers.

Also remember that the ISMS committee is as organic as your security program itself. The membership will ebb and flow, as your organizational and security needs change. It is not a fixed committee but one you can add and change members on over time.

Duties of the ISMS Committee

The duties of the ISMS committee are to work together to do the following:

- Provide the authority and leadership for IT security for the organization. To lead and to lead by example with respect to security.

- Incorporate IT risk into overall organizational risk plan that may include other forms of risk beyond IT.

- Decide on what is acceptable and unacceptable risk for the organization based on regulations, compliance requirements, contractual agreements, and organizational needs.

- Ensure for planning and budgeting to provide sufficient resources to control unacceptable risk in the organization.

- Ensure that there are adequate policies and procedures created, maintained, and enforced to control unacceptable risk in the organization.

- Provide reports to senior leadership on the health of the ISMS, including audit status.

- Agree on new and proposed changes to high-level security policy for the organization.

- Approve security policy exceptions and perform formal risk acceptance when needed.

- Sponsor and oversee security control projects and ensure that adequate resources are available to complete them.

- Review security incidents and security policy violations.

- Take an active role in major security breaches and breach notifications.

- Review security and audit scope changes including assessing new and changing third-party relationships.

- Assist in the recruiting, hiring, and the succession of the CSO.

- To stay abreast of major security, compliance, business, and asset changes within the organization to facilitate optimal decision-making.

Key Roles

Now that you have the membership of the ISMS committee established, what are everyone's roles?

CSO

As we discussed earlier, the CSO is the top security person leading the ISMS committee. This means setting and running the agenda for the meeting, as well as keeping the discussions on topic. As the most knowledgeable expert in IT security in the group, she should also act as teacher and explainer for the rest. The CSO should make sure that the committee reviews critical policy and control project proposals at the appropriate time. Since the CSO is running the ISMS as part of her day-to-day job, she is likely the main point of contact for all ISMS committee business and communication. The CSO also directs the various assessments, including the risk, asset, and compliance analyses. The CSO has the functional responsibility for security, she is charge of directing the IT and security administrators to implement and maintain the controls. The role of CSO is so important that this role should be part of the CSO's job description. The CSO's authority is derived from a formal delegation of authority from the head of the organization. This can be direct or indirect via a chain of command, but the ultimately the CSO has been officially tasked with security by the leader of the organization. This authority can be documented in a memo, in the ISMS charter (endorsed by leadership), in their job description, or all of the above.

Asset Owner

The asset owner is the one responsible for the security of their assets. They empower and delegate the task to the CSO to find and reduce risks to their assets and associated business processes. The asset owner provides support and resources for the CSO to do her job. The asset owners are also the ones who help determine the information classification of the data within their systems. If they appear to be making ill-informed or irresponsible choices, the CSO (and perhaps the legal department) needs to educate them on the possible consequences of their decisions.

The ultimate asset owner on the ISMS committee is the leadership role or C-level executive. That role is the asset owner of the entire organization and would have final say on support and resources allocations for the CSO, which is probably no different from their role outside of the ISMS committee. By default, this person is also ultimately responsible for ensuring that risk is kept to minimum acceptable levels and nothing goes horribly wrong. Again, this is probably not different from their role outside the committee. Be aware that there will be struggles with asset owners and security requirements. Asset owners may occasionally resist security control work and operations due to their own priorities. For example, they may not want their systems down for an urgent zero-day patch if they are facing their own deadlines. The ISMS committee forum is one place that these requirements can be resolved. For ideas on how to manage these obstacles, see Chapters 8, 9, and 10.

Asset Custodian

The Custodians are the people who manage and take care of the assets for the owners. Generally, this means the IT operational personnel. Their role is to implement, operate, and maintain the various defined controls that manage risk to the assets. They are responsible for maintaining the control operational records, which auditors may need to review. They must also report any deficiencies or deviations to defined risks, assets, and controls to the CSO so they can be dealt with. Custodians also work ensuring information is maintained according to data classification policies set down by the ISMS committee. Upcoming chapters go into the specifics of how controls can be implemented and maintained.

Asset User

Asset users can refer to anyone in the organization, whether or not they are a member of the ISMS committee. The asset users are anyone who uses the IT assets defined in the scope of the ISMS. They are responsible for exercising due care to protect the assets by following the ISMS defined policies and operational procedures. Upcoming chapters define how asset users are educated on and managed with ISMS rules of conduct.

Auditor

The auditor role is the tester of the ISMS. Their job is to monitor the ISMS and report on deviations and shortcomings of the process. Because they are in a watchdog role, they must be independent and not in the chain of command of any of the ISMS custodians or the CSO. This role is not the same as penetration testers or vulnerability assessors, which are usually hired by the CSO to test for vulnerabilities from outside the organization. Auditors are given full authority to see everything going on within the organization at any time. The trade-off is that auditors are not allowed to implement or maintain controls. They are testers only. This function is described in more detail in Chapters 21 and 22.

Roles and Responsibilities Diagram

The RACI diagram is a helpful tool for managing roles and responsibility. It is a responsibility assignment matrix named after the four commonly assigned duties: Responsible, Accountable, Consulted, and Informed. They are described as follows:

- *Responsible*: The person(s) assigned to work on this task

- *Accountable*: The person(s) in trouble if the task isn't done correctly

- *Consulted*: The person(s) contributing information to this task

- *Informed*: The person(s) who need to be updated about the task

Figure 7-1 shows a RACI diagram for the ISMS for the Plan-Do-Check-Act process.

	Senior leadership	ISMS Steering committee	Asset owners	CSO, Custodians (IT)	Auditors (Internal, External)
Plan the ISMS	Accountable	Responsible	Consulted	Consulted	Informed
Do the work of the ISMS	Accountable	Responsible	Consulted	Responsible	Informed
Check the ISMS	Accountable	Informed	Informed	Informed	Responsible
Act on the results of the ISMS	Accountable	Responsible	Consulted	Consulted	Informed

Figure 7-1. *RACI diagram for the ISMS for the Plan-Do-Check-Act process*

ISMS Charter

Now that you've hammered out an ISMS committee, you need a document defining your ISMS. The ISMS charter formalizes the ISMS and lays out the scope, roles, goals, frameworks, and operational details of the steering committee. It can even specify the risk assessment methods and acceptance criteria.

Sample ISMS Charter

Information Security Management System Charter for Puget Regional Bank
The purpose of the Information Security Management System (ISMS) is to:

- *To ensure confidentiality, integrity and availability of sensitive information of Puget Regional Bank, its customers, and business partners*

- *To ensure management and employee accountability for information resources including assets and information entrusted to them*

- *To ensure compliance with legal and regulatory requirements*

- *To eliminate or minimize risk to Puget Regional Bank's IT resources*

- *To reinforce Puget Regional Bank's core ethical values*

Sponsorship: *The Chief Technology Officer (CTO)*
Scope: *Puget Regional Banks's scoped assets*
The ISMS Committee: *An ISMS committee will be formed to define and lead the ISMS. The ISMS committee will be responsible for:*

- *Setting goals for security projects and program*

- *Defining organizational policy regarding IT security based on those goals*

- *Communicate with leadership and the organization regarding the security goals*

- *Strive to achieve those goals by defining control objectives for risk treatment*

- *Measure the effectiveness and performance of the controls and control objectives*

The committee will annually review membership and recommend changes after considering the needs for continuity and expertise as well as the need to encourage change and opportunities to participate. The Office of the CTO will provide administrative support.
The current ISMS membership includes:

- *IT Security Officer (ISO) - Chair*

- *Director of IT Services - Co-chair, CTO proxy*

- *Puget Regional Bank Lead counsel*

- *Lead Internal Auditor*

- *Director of Continuity of Operations*

- *Director of Bank security*

- *Director of Customer Services*

- *Director of Remote Customer Services*

- *Director of Credit Services*
- *Director of Mortgage*
- *Director of Collections*
- *Director of Human Resources*

Meetings: *The 3rd Tuesday of the first month of the annual quarter. The committee can have emergency meetings if any member calls one*

Decision-making: *Decisions by consensus of the ISMS committee with disputes taken to the CTO for resolution*

Attendance: *Regular attendance by ISMS Committee members is mandatory. ISMS Committee members can designate proxies to attend in their stead if unavailable.*

ISMS Committee members can invite additional attendees as appropriate

Communication: *In addition to this charter, membership list, schedules, and other docs will be posted on the ISMS Intranet web site. During the next meeting, the meeting minutes from the previous meeting will be approved and posted on the ISMS Intranet.*

ISMS Strategy: *To achieve its stated purpose:*

- *The Puget Regional Bank ISMS program will employ a risk-based approach to analyze, and compare threats to and vulnerabilities in, information resources with respect to their criticality and value to Puget Regional Bank.*

  - *The ISMS program will also determine compliance with country, community, federal, state, and other regulatory information resource requirements. The results of the risk assessment will be used to determine appropriate, cost-effective safeguards and countermeasures.*

- *All assessment findings and recommendations, as well as the safeguards, procedures and controls implemented, will be documented and reported to the Puget Regional Bank Chief Technology Officer.*

- *The Internal Audit department will maintain an ongoing assessment program to test and evaluate the effectiveness of preventative, detective, and corrective information security controls to ensure their continued effectiveness against evolving risks and threats.*

- *The Puget Regional Bank ISMS will be managed by security policies.*

- *The IT Security Department will work with various departments as necessary to develop and maintain comprehensive security standards and procedures designed to implement this security strategy and security policies.*

- *The ISMS Committee will accept requests from any business unit, group, or department to add or make modifications to security policies or controls.*

  - *The ISMS Committee will address requests at their discretion based upon an analysis of the request.*

- *Puget Regional Bank's IT Security Policy will be available to all Puget Regional Bank personnel via an Intranet-based application, or other appropriate medium.*

  - *Puget Regional Bank personnel will be informed when policies or control standards are created or changed.*

  - *A communication plan will be developed for security policies, standards, and procedures.*

Obtain Executive Sponsorship

The final piece of establishing the ISMS is to get executive management approval of the charter and the security steering committee. As you can see in the sample ISMS charter, the executive sponsor for Puget Regional Bank is the chief technology officer, which in this example is a bank senior vice president. You will want your sponsor to be as highly placed as possible in the organization. You will find it also helpful if that sponsor appreciates the gravity of an IT security program and can provide guidance to its operation.

Plan: Implement and Operate a Security Program

Now that the ISMS is established and the committee is up and running, the committee can get to work. The first step is to plan how you are going to deal with the risks.

Now the committee needs to make sure that it has an accurate and timely analysis of assets and compliance requirements. If the committee doesn't have them, then the ISMS committee needs to kick off a project to have them done. It's likely that your organization has already done something along the lines of asset analysis, as most normal IT departments have some kind of inventory. The ISMS committee can brainstorm an initial compliance analysis be in a short session or two. What you don't want to do is sit around for months waiting for analyses to be completed before taking action. A little work yields decent and usable results right away. The committee can spin-off projects to get better data later. The plan will never be perfect anyway, so why wait?

Decide upon and Publish the Goals

The committee can now take the ISMS charter's goals and make them a little more specific, which will form the basis of your security policy and organizational communication. This also illuminates the scope, as you are getting specific about requirements.

Based on the Puget Regional Bank ISMS charter example, this could be a published goal:

> *Puget Regional Bank will strive to adhere to the Sarbanes-Oxley and Gramm-Leach-Bliley Acts by protecting the confidentiality, integrity, and availability of its financial systems and customer data. Security, privacy, accuracy, and uptime are the goals of Puget Regional Bank and its IT systems.*

The use of saying *will strive* indicates that you will put serious effort into achieving these goals, but you are not necessarily guaranteeing that you will succeed perfectly for all time. You should always assume breach, but still try your best to avoid it. This is different from when you write internal policy statements, which use clear directives regarding mandatory duties such as "should, will, must, shall."

Please note that this goal includes two different overlapping compliance requirements, which is common in complex environments. We could have just as easily added PCI DSS to that list as well, since there are probably payment card numbers involved in some financial transactions.

This goal can be the preamble when you publish your security policy and do your security awareness campaign. It's important to communicate this goal to everyone. You are going to ask every user and IT to do some kind of work on security. Explain to them why this matters.

Define Control Objectives

With goals, you can begin to draft control objectives, which are the specifics with respect to assets and requirements. The organization builds controls to achieve those control objectives. Consider the following Puget Regional Bank sample assets in Table 7-1.

Table 7-1. *Assets and Control Objective Requirements*

Assets	Requirement
Databases with customer data records	Confidentiality, integrity, availability
Customer-facing web site	Integrity, availability

The following are some potential control objectives based on these two assets and requirement combinations:

- Controls provide reasonable assurance that physical and logical access to Puget Regional Bank databases and data records are restricted to authorized persons.

- Controls provide a reasonable assurance that all changes to the Puget Regional customer web site are approved and performed by authorized personnel.

- Controls provide reasonable assurance that Puget Regional Bank critical systems and infrastructure are available and fully functional as scheduled.

For an SSAE 16 SOC 1, these kinds of control objectives are a critical part of the audit. The SOC 1 is both the most flexible and most challenging in this aspect. You have the privilege and the burden of writing your own control objectives. For other audits, the compliance framework dictates a specific control objective. This is the first objective for SSAE 16 SOC 2 and SOC 3 under security:

Security commitments and requirements are addressed during the system development lifecycle including design, acquisition, implementation, configuration, testing, modification, and maintenance of system components.

Under the PCI DSS, this is the first of 12 control objectives (called a *requirement* in the standard): "Install and maintain a firewall configuration to protect cardholder data."

Underneath that control objective (or requirement), the PCI DSS specifies a dozen or so specific controls that need to be in place to support it.

In ISO 27001:2013, there are 14 *control groups* that are analogous to control objectives. With the ISO 27001, you need to create a document called a Statement of Applicability based on these control groups. We'll get into that soon.

Assignment of Role and Responsibility

One thing to keep in mind when working on control objectives is to think about how you are going to achieve them. This means formally assigning the control objectives to someone to work on and then requiring a continuous monitoring process. It's common for the ISMS committee to assign the majority of IT Security control objectives to the CSO. This is a big reason why you have the formal CSO role. Left to themselves, most people neglect risks that aren't directly their problem. They're probably already busy doing something else. Formal assignment of roles helps minimize that.

Do: Risk Treatment

Now that you have a defined goal and scope, you can map your risks and controls to them. Like before, if you haven't done a risk assessment or a controls analysis, you absolutely need to do them now. Again, if you don't have time, then brainstorm a qualitative assessment for now, while commissioning a more detailed one that you can use in the near future. You'll be repeating this planning step at least once a year, so you can expect things to change anyway. Now you can pull all of these things together and build a risk table as shown in Table 7-2.

Table 7-2. *Sample Risks and Controls Table*

Asset	Require	Risk	Controls
Databases with customer data records	Confidentiality, integrity, availability	Malware infection	Antivirus software, firewalls, limited access
		Application attack	None
		Insider theft or sabotage	Limited access, background checks
		Physical theft or damage	Locked server room door, fire suppression
		Accidental data leak	Limited access
Corporate web site	Integrity, availability	Defacement	Firewall
	Integrity, availability	Denial-of-service attack	Firewall, redundant ISP

Given this, the ISMS committee can determine if these controls are sufficient to lower these risks to an acceptable level. This calculation can be done out-of-band by the Security Officer and then presented to the ISMS committee for review and approval. Only the most tech- and security-savvy ISMS committee is going to sit through the process of analyzing controls and risks for each scoped asset. However, the committee does have to buy-off on the analysis, since they recommend and sponsor control projects to close those gaps. Table 7-3 demonstrates how this can look.

Table 7-3. *Risk and Control Analysis of Effectiveness*

Asset	Require	Risk	Controls	Effectiveness
Databases with customer data records	Confidentiality, integrity, availability	Malware infection	Antivirus software, firewalls, limited access	Acceptable
		Application attack	None	Deficient (no controls applied)
		Insider theft or sabotage	Limited access, background checks	Insufficient risk coverage
		Physical theft or damage	Locked server room door, fire-suppression	Insufficient risk coverage
		Accidental data leak	Limited access	Insufficient risk coverage
Corporate web site	Integrity, availability	Defacement	Firewall	Insufficient risk coverage
Corporate web site	Integrity, availability	Denial-of-service attack	Firewall, redundant ISP	Acceptable

As you can see, the ISMS committee has found that a number of risks are not being sufficiently addressed. The next big question to address is what to do about them?

Risk Treatment

After you've looked at your risks and current controls, the ISMS committee will likely discover controls that are managing risks insufficiently. They basically have four choices at this point:

- Ignore the risk, pretend that you never saw it, and hope that it will go away
- Accept the risk and hope that it never happens
- Eliminate the risky activity
- Reduce the risk through controls

Since ignoring the risk is a great way to end up in an extremely embarrassing and expensive litigious situation, most ISMS committees don't go there. *Negligence* is when you fail to do what is reasonable to prevent something bad from happening to others. Organizations are sued and fined for negligence.[2] Ignoring risks is negligent. I'm pointing this out because some organizations can ignore risks and get in trouble. This usually happens by accident because they are so disorganized or their security programs are so ineffective. You won't be like that, though.

That leaves choosing between accepting the risk, eliminating the risk, and risk reduction. Nevertheless, before we get into these choices in detail, you need to be aware that people can be irrational when dealing with risk. An apocryphal study found that people spend more for flight insurance coverage for "death by terrorism" than they would for a more inclusive policy that covers death for any reason. People can get stunned by scary headlines about large breaches and make judgments on small sets of data, especially large impacts are concerned. There is a tendency for people to overly focus on the magnitude of an impact and ignore the probability. Some unscrupulous vendors even use this technique in their sales and marketing material. In the security industry, this is called Fear Uncertainty and Doubt (FUD) marketing. It's not a rational or efficient way to make risk decisions. Remember that if you spend your money dealing with a few unlikely but high impact risks, you may not have enough to deal with the numerous common threats. This can lead to a death by a thousand cuts.

Risk Acceptance

An ISMS committee may want to accept certain kinds of risk. Risk acceptance is the deliberate and carefully considered formal act of declaring that an organization will deal with the consequences of a risk impact. This is not ignorance, where you pretend the problem doesn't exist. This is a conscious choice, documented in writing, that the risk is acceptable. This is usually done for risks that where the impact or likelihood is small. It can also be done for risks where the cost of managing that risk is higher than the impact.

For example, a company may say that it is accepting the risk of a super-typhoon wiping out its Hong Kong sales office; the impact is potentially high, but the likelihood is somewhat low. There are already controls for normal typhoons and the sales functions aren't critical to company operations, so for now the risk is accepted.

When doing risk acceptance, the ISMS committee must be very explicit about documenting what they are accepting and why. The criteria for accepting risk should also be formalized, so that auditors and other interested third parties can review the decisions. To an outsider, risk acceptance can look like negligence to customers, auditors, or regulators. If something goes wrong on a risk you've accepted, then you really better be ready to deal with the consequences. Be very sure about your impact calculation. Lawsuits and failed audits are not pleasant experiences.

---

[2]https://www.ftc.gov/news-events/blogs/business-blog/2015/12/wyndhams-settlement-ftc-what-it-means-businesses-consumers

The ISMS committee should track and review accepted risks at least annually. Risks can change for a number of factors, both internally and externally, and the ISMS committee should revisit and re-decide on the risk acceptance.

Lastly, once a small risk is accepted, there is a tendency for people to think that a precedent is set and all similar small risks should be automatically be accepted. Remember risk is cumulative, like drops of water in a bucket. The more little risky things you accept, the more risk you take on as a whole. A lot of little risks are as bad as one big risk. Don't fall into the trap of saying "We allowed this thing, so we might as well allow more like it." It all adds up. If you're doing quantitative risk analysis, you can calculate this cumulative risk.

Risk Elimination

There have been times when an organization did a risk analysis on a particular process and decided to drop that process entirely. The risk could simply be too high and the cost of reducing that risk just not worth it. Maybe the process is not that critical to the organization. In some cases, the organization may find a way to redesign or reorganize the process so the risky functions are no longer performed. Perhaps the process could be folded into another function, and the risk moved that way.

This kind of work can involve research, experimentation, thorough analysis, and imagination. Moreover, sometimes the resulting product does not reduce the risk in any significant way. Systems interact, both internally within the organization, and externally with the outside world. Risks almost never live in isolation and solutions can sometimes produce newer and bigger problems. In any case, risk elimination means that this particular risky process and its assets are shut down and with them, the associated risk. From an IT security perspective, this is the optimal solution. Unfortunately, the organization may have different priorities.

Risk Reduction with Controls

This is the most common choice that people make when confronted with risk. It's likely that your organization is already trying to reduce perceived risks with controls. It's become automatic to install firewalls, passwords, and antivirus for IT systems. It's a suboptimal solution because the risk is rarely reduced to zero, but it's the generally accepted solution and is often good enough. Let's revisit the sample table of risks for Puget Regional Bank. In the analysis, several risks were not reduced enough by controls:

- Application attacks against the database and customer records

- Insider theft or sabotage against the database and customer records

- Physical theft or damage of the database and customer records

- Accidental data leaks of the database and customer records

- Defacements of the corporate web site

The ISMS committee can now propose new control projects for these risks. At this point, the ISMS committee does not have to select a particular control. It merely needs to decide that someone owns the project of reducing this risk through controls. The committee usually assigns these controls projects to the CSO to oversee, with the various departments doing the work. This is probably a good time for another RACI diagram. In Table 7-4, I present a different format of RACI diagram, breaking things down by risk.

Table 7-4. RACI Diagram of Top Risks

Risk	Responsible	Accountable	Consulted	Informed
Application attacks	Developers	CSO	Database owners	ISMS committee
Insider theft	IT	CSO	HR	ISMS committee
Physical theft	Facility security	CSO	IT (owns the server room)	ISMS committee
Accidental leaks	IT	CSO	Users	ISMS committee
Defacements	IT	CSO	Marketing (who owns the web site)	ISMS committee

Often a risk can be reduced by using many different types of controls. It may take some work to determine which control works best in your organization. For example, with the Application attack, risk against the database could be reduced by hardening the software with the programming work done by the developers (as shown in the preceding example). Alternatively, perhaps IT could install an application-aware filtering firewall or proxy in front of the database to stop attacks before they get there. For the physical theft risk of the databases, facilities could add better door locks or IT could implement database encryption. An ISMS sub-committee may have to do a bit of work to find a solution that is acceptably efficient and effective. Control design is covered more in Chapter 12.

Risk Transfer

There is actually a fifth option, which is a hybrid of risk elimination and risk reduction: risk transfer. For a risk transfer, you transfer either the impact or risky activity itself out of your organization. Many companies choose to outsource their payment card operations for this reason. They haven't fully eliminated the risk, because their customers will still be angry if hackers steal their credit cards. However, the outsourcing company can be contractually bound to pay for the damages if this happens. The trick is estimating the impact so that the party taking on the risk transfer can properly compensate you. You also can try to transfer to a third party that could lower the likelihood of the risk occurring as well. A third party payment card hosting company will likely have better controls in place than in this area and (hopefully) be fully PCI DSS compliant. So you can hope that not only is the impact transferred, but the likelihood has been reduced by superior controls.

Another way to transfer risk is to simply buy cyber-insurance against the risk. There were already many insurance options for disaster related IT risks. Now many hacking or data breach risk premiums are available. Be warned however, insurance companies may interpret a covered loss much differently than you might. You should make sure that your policy really covers what you think it does before you consider a risk transferred. In addition, many insurance underwriters perform an audit much like we are describing in this book of your organization's IT security program to calculate the cost of your premiums. Depending on the risks and the state of your organization, you may not save much money.

Documenting Risk Treatment

Once all of this done, the ISMS committee should document their proposed risk treatments. For each risk listed, the ISMS committee needs to commission a plan. Revisiting our risk list from Puget Regional Bank, let's make a new table. Here in Table 7-5, we see the ISMS committee has decided to transfer the risk of physical theft by moving the servers to a co-location facility. They have also decided to accept the risk of insiders as the nature of the system makes controlling that risk prohibitively expensive.

Table 7-5. Sample Risk Treatment Table

Risk	Asset	Treatment	Description
Application attacks	Database and customer data	Controlled	Developers recode app to reduce vulnerabilities
Insider theft	Database and customer data	Accepted	Cost and complexity of controls too high (see attached report), IT reduces access to only core team, access logging provides audit trail, ISMS committee revisits this risk in three months
Physical theft	Database and customer data	Transferred	IT has a project (see attached plan) to move servers to Glenda ISP secure colocation facility
Accidental leaks	Database and customer data	Controlled	IT installs a data leak prevention tool to scan for customer data in e-mail
Defacements	Customer-facing web site	Controlled	IT performs regular vulnerability scans and patching

Statement of Applicability

As we noted earlier, the formal ISO 27001 standard requires a document called a *Statement of Applicability* (SoA). This looks a lot like Table 7-6, except it focuses on controls instead of assets, so make control reference the first column. The SoA is a why-we're-doing-this strategy (and in some cases, it's a why-we're-not-doing-this) document with the respect to controls. You create it by going through a list of best practice controls and map risks and requirements to them. Table 7-6 is an example based on Table 7-5.

Table 7-6. Sample Statement of Applicability

Control	Risk	Compliance	Effectiveness	Justification/Description
Security requirement analysis and specifications	Application attacks against database and customer data	SOX, GLBA	Deficient	Developers will recode app to reduce vulnerabilities
Administrator and operator logs	Insider theft of database and customer data	GLBA	Insufficient	Cost and complexity of additional controls too high (see attached report), IT will reduce access to only core team, access logging will provide audit trail, ISMS committee revisits this risk in three months
Equipment protection	Physical theft of database and customer data	GLBA	Insufficient	IT has a project (attach summary of a plan) to move servers to GlendaNet's secure colocation facility
Electronic Messaging	Accidental leaks of database and customer data	GLBA	Insufficient	IT will install a data leak prevention tool to scan for customer data in e-mail

The ISO 27001 standard strongly encourages you to use the ISO 27002 list of security techniques as your best practice controls list, but it's not an absolute requirement. ISO 27001 does require you to explain, formally, why you aren't using a particular control in their best practice list. For example, say you intend to use the PCI DSS as your list of controls in your ISO 27001 (killing two birds with one stone), you need to either include the controls in ISO 27002 that are missing from the PCI DSS or write a few paragraphs for each missing control justifying why you're not using it. The most commonly acceptable reason is that the controls would apply to a non-existent or unscoped process. No auditor is going to be satisfied with you saying you're not doing a control because it's too expensive or too difficult to implement. That starts to smell like negligence.

Check: Monitor and Review Security Program

This being the world where you should assume breach, it's unlikely that a control will reduce a risk to zero. Therefore, once the controls are implemented and running, they should be monitored for effectiveness and appropriateness. These are two different measures. Effectiveness measures how well a control is functioning within the organization. Appropriateness is measuring how much that control actually reduces risk. Often people make the mistake of only measuring effectiveness, but not looking at what the outcome of the risk reduction effort. For example, "In the past three months, we have reduced our malware infection rate by 20% (appropriateness). Our antivirus control is now active on all servers, based on the Q2 internal audit (effectiveness)."

The committee can compare these measures against the actual cost of a control to determine if the control should be replaced or the risk treatment changed. This is explored in much more depth in Chapter 22 on internal audit.

Act: Maintain and Improve Security Program

The last step in the cycle is for the committee to adjust the ISMS based on the information found during the Check phase. The goal is continuous improvement of the security program—improving not just the effectiveness and appropriateness of the controls, but also reducing the cost of controls. Anything can be adjusted not just controls but scope and goals. This is covered in more detail in Chapter 24.

FURTHER READING

- **The Deming Wheel**
  https://www.deming.org/theman/theories/pdsacycle

- **FDIC Technical Assistance Video Program: Cybersecurity**
  https://www.fdic.gov/regulations/resources/director/virtual/governance.html

- **Responsibility assignment matrix**
  https://en.wikipedia.org/wiki/Responsibility_assignment_matrix

---

CHAPTER 8

■ ■ ■

Talking to the Suits

A ship in harbor is safe, but that is not what ships are built for.

—John A. Shedd

Many years ago, the CTO asked me to a give a five-minute presentation to the rest of executive leadership regarding the recent risk analysis my team had completed. It was a huge project for the security team, spanning months of work examining every possible IT risk to the company we could imagine. The final report was nearly 50 pages long, filled with quantitative details on multiple sources of threats and multifaceted impact calculations. This was my first appearance before the entire executive team in a single room. Since I had only five minutes, I condensed our results into a handful of slides covering the top three risks. I arrived early and set up my laptop and the projector. As the execs strode into the boardroom, the CEO noticed my title page, "The Top Risks to the Company." He asked as he sat down, "Oh, you're going to talk about our competition?"

I was stunned. No, my presentation covered things like earthquakes, stolen laptops, and malware. More importantly, he was right. I was the tail wagging the dog. IT security risk is important, but it might not represent any of the *top risks* to the company. We were a growing startup just starting to gain traction in the marketplace. Losing enough key sales could mean a downward slide for the entire venture. It was an epiphany for me. Security is there to serve the business, not the other way around.

Ultimately, I did come to understand that security was important for the organization, but only because it was important to customers. Having strong protections in place to guarantee privacy and availability were good, being able to demonstrate to the outside world was better. After that, I framed all my messaging that way. This meant in addition to building a strong security program, I would pursue audits and certifications for the sales and marketing team to show off. When I talked to management, I emphasized the effect a breach would have on corporate reputation. I would talk up how a security project could provide new secure customer services and raise reliability. I studied our competitors' security efforts and made sure that we matched or exceeded them. Once I knew what mattered to the organization and aligned my work accordingly, I had no trouble getting budget or support for my security program.

When Security Appears to be Anti-Business

IT security and audit sometimes have the reputation for being anti-business. It isn't hard for me to rattle off a list of common complaints.

- Security puts us behind the curve. You block new technology all the time with the reason "because it isn't safe."

- Security always says "No!" They kill so many good ideas. Now we don't even tell them what we're doing anymore.

© Raymond Pompon 2016
R. Pompon, *IT Security Risk Control Management*, DOI 10.1007/978-1-4842-2140-2_8

- Security is sore loser. When their objections are overridden, they say things like, "You're going to do that insecure thing even after we told you how dangerous it is? You'll be sorry..."

- Security yells at us when we're the victims. I was just surfing the Web trying to find something and my browser got hacked. Now I don't have my laptop and I'm being told I was a careless newbie.

- Security is always pushing obsolete and convoluted solutions down our throat, like making us create and remember weird passwords or making us patch all the time. My computer spends more time patching than doing useful work.

The worst is when security is seen as the Department of No. It's easy to see how a lot of that happens. Business units are often told to find new ways to make customers happy with no restrictions on IT risk or compliance requirements. If security doesn't find out until after something is already rolling along with a lot of organizational momentum, then the security requirements appears as the obstacle. The security team is seen to rush in and try to put the brakes on before something terrible happens. Sometimes it seems like management, by accident or design, has set up an adversarial relationship. It's a tough burden to be the person telling people they can't do something. But isn't security the final word on what happens or doesn't happen?

Who Really Decides?

The ISMS steering committee represents the leadership of the organization. If the committee was formed properly, there is either executive management in the committee, or they have the authority of management. There may also be times when members of the committee would present results and decisions to the entire leadership of the organization, such as the board of directors or CEO. The entire point of the steering committee is to make sure IT security properly supports and empowers the organization's business. IT security's role in all of this is to present and explain IT security issues so that leadership can decide what to do about them.

Security explains what needs to be done, laying out the costs, the reasons, and the timing. Leadership, through the committee or alone, decides on a course of action. Sometimes that action could be too risky for the security representative. In that case, the security officer needs make the matter clear with no misunderstanding. Ending that misunderstanding is a critical part of the security job. Once matters are understood, if management still decides otherwise, then that's what the organization wants. Like it or lump it, that's the way it is.

Likewise, security solutions must fit the culture of the organization. IT is there to fulfill their needs and run business processes, which means taking on risky behavior. To succeed, sometimes organizations have to push beyond the safe boundaries and do risky things.

Since every organization is different, how does the security team find this understanding and make use of it?

Understanding the Organization

The obligation is on the security team to understand the organization, not the other way around. If by luck, the organization is willing to learn and understand IT security, then the security team must do its patient best to explain things to them as many times and as many ways as they are willing to endure. The security team should not speak in terms of IT security, remembering that even words like "risk" may have a different meaning. In finance, risk can be seen as attractive because high risk often entails high reward. You must translate things into the language of the organization. How do you do that? By finding out what is important and exploring how security affects organizational goals. You begin by asking.

How to Ask

Before learning what to ask, it's important that you understand *how* to ask. Many IT security professionals used to be IT professionals, and very few IT professionals are famous for their charm and charisma. Speaking to machines all day will do that to you. So let's go over a few basics on asking questions.

The first rule is obvious but is still worth stating: when you ask a question, be sure to listen to the answer. While they are speaking (even if you didn't ask a question), take notes, preferably on paper. Do not type answers into a device. It's distracting, slow, noisy, and people may think you're reading your e-mail. Write notes on paper or pay close attention and remember. Listen to their entire answer before you speak again. Speaking of speaking again, if they're describing a problem, it's not helpful to try to *top* their problem with a bigger problem of your own. This is an investigation, not a complaint competition. After they describe their problem, you may either ask a question related to what they've just said or confirm that this is everything. If they are done, summarize what they've just told you in your own words. Not only is this good for understanding of the issue, but it builds rapport with the other person. Note that this technique is useful beyond asking questions of executive leadership. It is useful for a broad range of communication with humans and humanoid life forms. It's worth practicing, even if you think you've mastered it. You can also work on ascertaining how confident or satisfied they are in the answer they are providing.

Who Do You Ask

When learning about an organization and its processes, anyone is fair game. You definitely should ask your boss and your peers. When you're doing your risk, asset, and compliance analyses, you'll have a great excuse to talk to every major department head. The same goes if you're working on a business continuity plan. Whatever your organization does, that is whatever customers it serves, you should definitely talk to as many of the people directly involved in that process chain. Sometimes this is easy if an organization is a for-profit business, you just follow the money. For academic institutions, you should talk to the teachers and librarians. If you're completely bereft of ideas, hit up HR and get an organizational chart to review for ideas. Not everyone will have all the answers (although the senior leadership might come close), but a thorough process of investigation will get you most of the answers. Keep in mind the "I" in IT. Data flow also provides insight here. Wherever the "I" moves around, and whoever touches it, may have something interesting to tell you.

What to Ask

Now, what do you need to know? Here's a list of things that you can ask straight out or try to figure out based on descriptions of the business.

- What is the business model?
  - How do we get revenue to operate? How does it happen? When does it come in?
  - How do we lose money?
  - How important is agility or the ability for the organization to change processes quickly?
  - How important is organizational stability? Do we rely on having cash reserves or credit? Do we live hand to mouth from sales?

- What is the organization's secret sauce?
    - What are the things we do that no one else can do?
    - Does it involve intellectual property?
    - Does it involve particular expertise?
    - Does it involve unique processes?
    - Do we have special government mandates to do things that other organizations can't?
    - Does our organization or business model depend on consumer trust?
- What information do people need to do their job?
    - Which processes need what information and when?
    - How do they get it?
    - What happens if they don't get it?
    - What happens if it's inaccurate?
    - What happens if it's seen by a third party?
- What are the biggest challenges facing the organization as a whole?
    - Growth? Survival? New markets? Changing regulations? Competition? Shrinking customer base? Shrinking budget from legislature?
- Who does the organization serve?
    - Who are the current customers?
    - Who are the biggest customers and what do they want?
    - What do the majority of the smaller customers want?
    - Who are the customers that aren't worth having as customers?
    - What customers do they want to go after?
- Where is the organization going?
    - What do we all hope happens? How does the organization define success? What could stop us from getting there?
    - What are the biggest problems right now?
    - Are we planning on growing? If so how? New locations? Bigger sizes? Acquisitions and mergers?
- What are the major internal systems or processes?
    - How do we handle sales and revenue?
    - How do we purchase goods and services?
    - How do we circulate information internally?

- What physical locations do we have presence? Don't forget unmanned storage facilities and data centers.

- How do we communicate with customers and outside entities?

- How do we onboard and terminate employees? Contractors? Interns?

- Who are our key partners and suppliers? What do they do for us? How do we work with them? How do we bring them on? How do we remove them?

- What do we do with legacy information and systems? Is there an asset life cycle?

- What IT equipment do we own? Rent/lease? Outsource? Do users BYOD (bring your own device)?

- What are the major IT projects planned for the next few cycles? What problem are they trying to solve?

What to Do with This

Once you've gathered this information, the question to ask yourself is how can security help with these things? What should you be spending your time on? Sometimes what is important is completely non-intuitive to a techie. For example, in some companies, the sales department's priorities are higher than the operation's priorities.

How does the security team become an active participant in driving new technology and innovation for the business and IT-side of the house? As organizations grope into the dark future, IT security can shed some light about potential obstacles. In this way, IT security can allow the organization to move faster and avoid pitfalls.

Answering Questions

The other side of asking questions is answering them. When you present risks, you can expect there will be questions. You also need to expend resources to implement security controls, so you need some combination of money or time (which is also money, per the ancient maxim). If you've ever experienced asking executive management for money, you know how difficult it can be. As my favorite superhero, *Too Much Coffee Man*,[1] says: "In the land of toast, the butter is spread very thin." So how do you justify your request?

Do the Research

If you're proposing to do something that is going to cost serious money, you had better have your facts straight. By facts, I mean evidence as hard as you can get it. Quantitative analysis beats qualitative because actual numbers and dollars are what executives are used to dealing with. Nothing sounds more wishy-washy than *something bad might happen*, or worse, saying that you need a hundred grand because *the risk is yellow-orange instead of green*.

---

[1]http://www.tmcm.com/tmcm/

If you're implementing a control, have a good idea about how much risk reduction you're getting and why. Lay out the costs of the control, including the initial costs and ongoing cost. Include hard costs (what you're going to pay in dollars) and soft costs (how it impacts staff and process). Show them the calculations and the data sources that you used. Present alternatives so that they can see what they're trading off against. Compare this to peers in the industry. Explain the value of your defense in clear terms they can understand.

- *Bad*: We need a new Razorwall firewall because, otherwise, we'll get hacked and all our data will get *pwned*. IT is doing a lousy job locking those boxes down, so we need more technology to make up for it.

- *Good*: We currently have a high risk of Internet penetration across all of our customer-facing web sites. We've tried patching, but IT just can't keep up with the new vulnerabilities. We want to put in a smarter firewall that will automatically block most of these attacks before they reach the web site. It'll cost us $27,000 to install and another $5,000 a year to maintain. It's the cheapest alternative we've found. We already have people in IT who are familiar with this technology, so installation and maintenance is a slam-dunk.

- *Better*: Our last penetration test showed 16 critical vulnerabilities on our corporate and marketing web sites. Based on this information and industry averages, there is a 50% chance in the next six months that our sites will be broken into and defaced. Worse, hackers could use our sites to host malware, which means we could be infecting our customers who visit our site. IT needs nearly three weeks to schedule, test, and completely patch the web site each cycle while new vulnerabilities appear at a rate of four per month. We have several ideas on how to take care of this. IT is looking into speeding up their patch cycle, but they said they need more personnel. The IT director is planning to submit a proposal to you on that. I am recommending a better firewall for the web site to buy us more time to complete patching. It will also protect us against other threats as well as support new web site services as we roll them out. I have a detailed project plan and budget for the firewall, but the initial cost will be $27,000 in the first year and $5,000 per year after that. Another alternative would be to have someone else host our web site. I have some numbers on that if you're interested.

Don't Wander Outside Your Area of Expertise

When confronted with questions you can't answer, don't try to make stuff up. If you're basing your answer on hearsay (something someone else told you), then say so. We all can't be experts in everything. Even security is a wide and deep field with many disciplines and details. If you don't know or aren't sure, tell them so and that you'll get back to them with a definitive answer. And then get back to them. There is nothing wrong with "I don't know but I'll find out." As the saying goes, better to remain silent and be thought a fool, than to speak and to remove all doubt. This is especially true with the world of finance. I have seen security project proposals rejected because of incorrect return on investment (ROI) financial models.

How to Talk Their Talk

It's hard enough to do the job of keeping hackers out and auditors pleased. Don't add communication problems to your list. You should communicate on their terms, not yours. Speak in language that they understand, not with a lot of technical jargon. If you're going to use jargon, use jargon that's part of the culture of the organization.

When speaking to executives, match the medium of their preferred mode of communication. Since leadership primarily communicates with their voices, face to face, then that's likely how you should communicate. If you send a long e-mail full of technical details, it's unlikely that it will be read in a timely manner, if at all. I've found the best way to communicate is to talk in person in a brief meeting and then follow up with summarizing notes.

You should always try to communicate in a business-positive manner. This means getting away from saying, "No, you can't do that! We'll get hacked!" and moving toward, "Here's a better way to do that," or "If we do it this way, we can go faster and take on more risk in this area, which could give us a competitive advantage." Here's an example:

- *Bad*: "Marketing's new web site uses 56 bit SSL. That crypto is broken and isn't PCI compliant. We need to halt that project right away and get it fixed."

- *Good*: "It's come to my attention that Marketing's new project, the gift shop web site, is using weak and obsolete encryption. This could be a problem if anyone expects their communication to remain secret. I believe that there is an option for customers to enter payment card numbers on the site, so we could be facing PCI DSS audit sanctions. I'd like to work with IT and Marketing to upgrade the encryption. This may slow down the project, but this fix should be pretty easy to install."

- *Better*: "For any customer-facing web site that asks for payment card numbers, we always use newer encryption systems. Our customer's expect us to do a quality job securing their data and it reduces our legal exposure. Furthermore, upgrading encryption doesn't cost us any hard dollars, it's just a configuration option. Now, I believe there are a few new web projects that aren't meeting this standard. I'd like to work with Marketing and IT to resolve this..."

In the final example, I focused on setting a high standard of quality for customers. Only then did I move on to the potential deviation, immediately weaving in a solution. I would expect the response to this to be a nod and a wave to move on. I also didn't propose halting the project, since this kind of thing is usually fixable a matter of hours, once you get the right people involved. If I get push back, then I'd explain how I have the backing from leadership to get this done right away.

When going into a meeting with leadership, have a printed agenda to hand them. Bonus points if you included the agenda in the meeting invitation. I like to hand them a paper agenda so they can make notes on it while I'm speaking. In addition, it's a nice indicator that I'm organized and not wasting their time. Time is one of the most precious things to executive leadership.

Neutron Stars

A neutron star is a tiny hyper-dense star with immense gravity that affects things millions of miles away. When I convey information upstream, I like to use neutron stars: tightly packed chunks of information with strong ties to important things like customers (money), business objectives (money), or potential expenses (money). I also like to include vivid scenarios and examples that are concrete and have direct consequences. If need to, I'll cite facts or even pull in outside experts to help support my case.

Explaining Risk

When explaining risk, either to a single executive or to an entire board, it is a good idea to use a multimediated approach. This means presenting orally, in writing, and visually. This doesn't mean have a bunch of PowerPoint slides with your speech typed up as bullets that you read. This is where your risk models can come in handy, as many of them translate into interesting and informative visuals. For example, Figure 8-1 is a slide explaining a phishing/drive-by web attack.

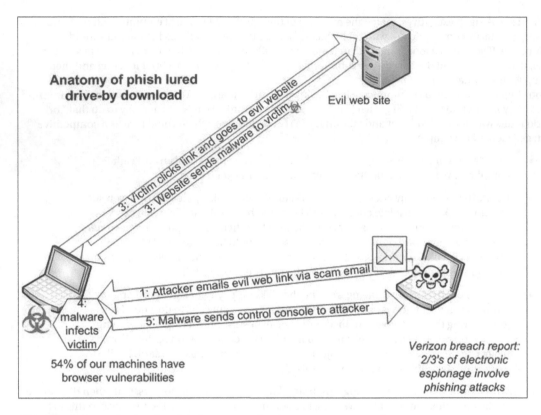

Figure 8-1. Example visual explaining an attack

Whenever you can, use visuals, analogies, and stories to explain risk. Avoid walls of boring text. Keep things concrete and tie them to dollars as much as you can. You don't need to do all this work for every single risk that you ever explain. It is a useful thing to do for top risks or explaining a particular nasty new attack that you need resources to remediate.

If you're talking to any executives with a background in finance or financial audit, you can also talk about risk in terms of *assurance*. Assurance is a measure of how sure you are something is what it says it is. You may have noticed that the control objective examples given in the scoping chapter used the expression *reasonable assurance*. Assurance is the good thing that risk erodes but controls reinforce. Therefore, you can talk about risk thresholds in terms of falling below reasonable assurance.

It's a good idea when presenting a problem to offer solutions. Follow the negative with a positive. This new risk is below our tolerable threshold, but here's what we can do mitigate it to an acceptable level. Be upbeat and positive. You can solve most of these problems if you think and work hard enough.

Finally, you have to realize that to an executive, some risks are worth taking. Success in business is about taking risk. Sometimes that risk may seem unwarranted, but it's not your decision. As long as everyone understands what risk they're accepting, you have to do your best to accept it and minimize the potential damage.

Proposing a Course of Action

By pulling all of this together, you can build an entire presentation on a course of action to deal with risk issues. Perhaps it is the launch of the new ISMS or maybe it's a response to failing audit. Whatever it is, you need to sell to executive management a plan and a budget for security. How do you use all of these techniques cohesively?

First, lay out the narrative of your presentation. When I say *narrative*, I am being deliberate. Present as if you're telling a story. There are many ways to go about this. One is to begin with the current aspiration. You paint the vision of where you want things to be and how everything is going to be fantastic in this new, beautiful, secure world where all of your customers and regulators love you. New ventures and business processes can be spun up free of worry from hackers and auditors. Life is good. We just have a few obstacles that we need to get over, which are …. Then you lay out your plan and budget, citing milestones and what they'll bring to the organization at each step of the way.

If you have the time, it's a good idea to brief the key audience members (including your boss) ahead of the meeting. The goal of this to uncover potential objections and put participants at ease. Consider how the project lead for the mobile banking project would feel if you gave this presentation cold about how the software is full of security vulnerabilities. You don't want him to feel ambushed, which could put him on the defensive and close his mind to your suggestions. A briefing ahead of time (sometimes called a "pre-wire") can open the door to compromise and collaboration.

Sample Presentation on a Mobile Banking Project

I start with a slide like the one shown in Figure 8-2, which discusses the project and reminds everyone about the timeline and what's at stake. At this point, everyone can also review the virtues of the project and the benefits that the organization will receive from pursuing it. This starts the presentation on a positive note and shows that you are all on the same side. It's likely that everyone else is aware of this information, but I'm just setting the tone.

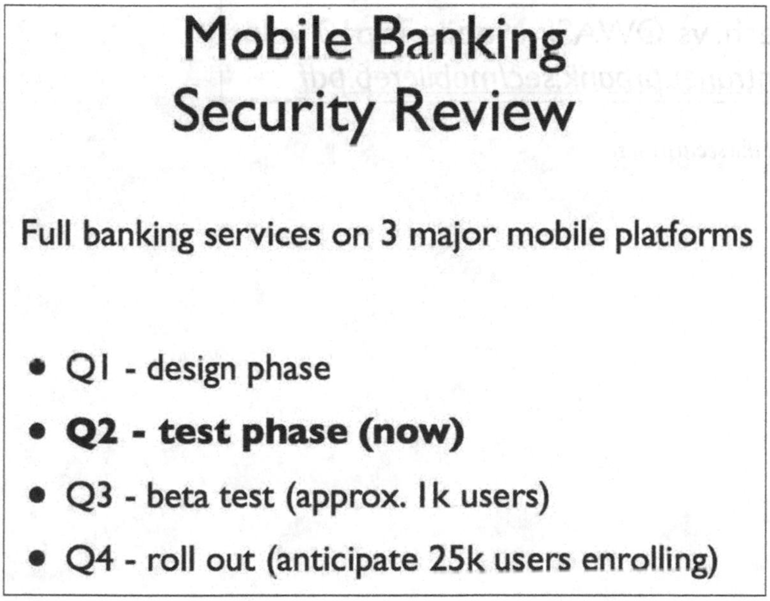

> # Mobile Banking
> # Security Review
>
> Full banking services on 3 major mobile platforms
>
> - Q1 - design phase
> - **Q2 - test phase (now)**
> - Q3 - beta test (approx. 1k users)
> - Q4 - roll out (anticipate 25k users enrolling)

Figure 8-2. *First slide: Why are we here?*

Now that the introductions are over, let's get right to the problem, as shown in Figure 8-3. The slide doesn't waste executive's time or try to hide the bad news. I include details here because I don't want to appear flippant or hysterical about risk. These are the facts: our company's mobile security product has some serious security problems. (When presenting, I may not chose to read aloud all (or any) of the particular details on the slide.) The slide includes a link to the actual report because this information may make someone in the room look bad. For example, in this case, the code has security vulnerabilities in it. If the VP of Development was in the room, I want to be able to give him a chance to check the results himself. Also, I want others to be able to get to the gory details if they want it.

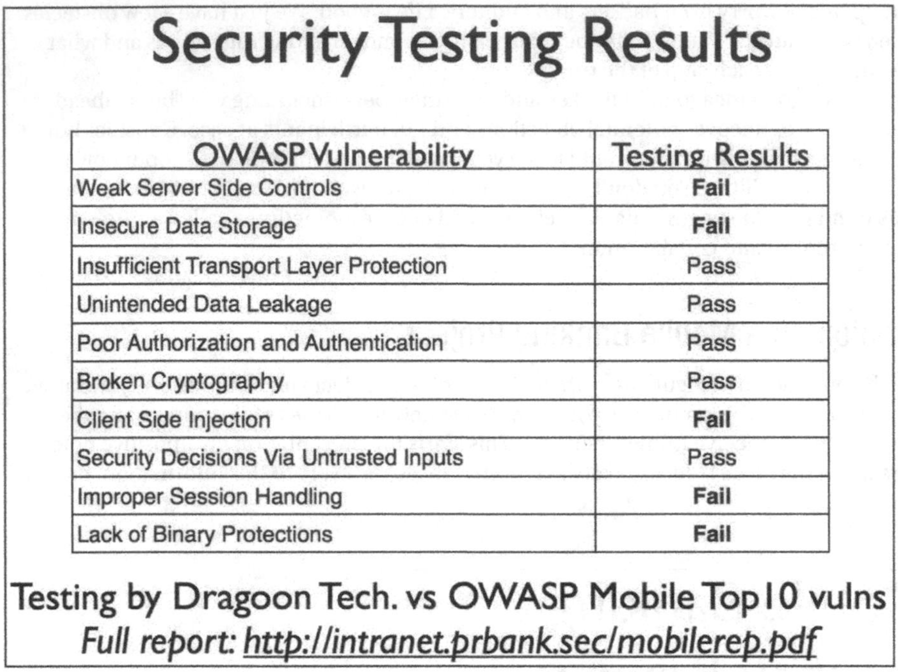

Security Testing Results

OWASP Vulnerability	Testing Results
Weak Server Side Controls	**Fail**
Insecure Data Storage	**Fail**
Insufficient Transport Layer Protection	Pass
Unintended Data Leakage	Pass
Poor Authorization and Authentication	Pass
Broken Cryptography	Pass
Client Side Injection	**Fail**
Security Decisions Via Untrusted Inputs	Pass
Improper Session Handling	**Fail**
Lack of Binary Protections	**Fail**

Testing by Dragoon Tech. vs OWASP Mobile Top10 vulns
Full report: *http://intranet.prbank.sec/mobilerep.pdf*

Figure 8-3. Showing the details of the security test

In the next slide, shown in Figure 8-4, I analyze the report. The company paid a lot of money to have the security analysis done. I'm going to show that the report was used strategically. This slide shows the conclusion of the report: our mobile project developers aren't capable of producing secure code. Notice how I frame this as a quality issue, not a security issue. This ties the problem back to customer satisfaction, not just the security geeks crying, "Hacker!" I also drop the big bomb, if it hasn't already dawned on everyone in the room: we are about to release a product into beta test that has huge security problems. And the methods used to expose these problems are associated with one of the most common frameworks for assessing web security risk, not some obscure super-hacker tool. This means that if we publish as-is, every script kiddie with an Internet link will know about these problems as well. If we stop to fix them, however, the whole project will be delayed. No one in that room is going to want to delay the project. No doubt, sales and marketing has already promised the delivery of a mobile product by this date. We're in a tight spot.

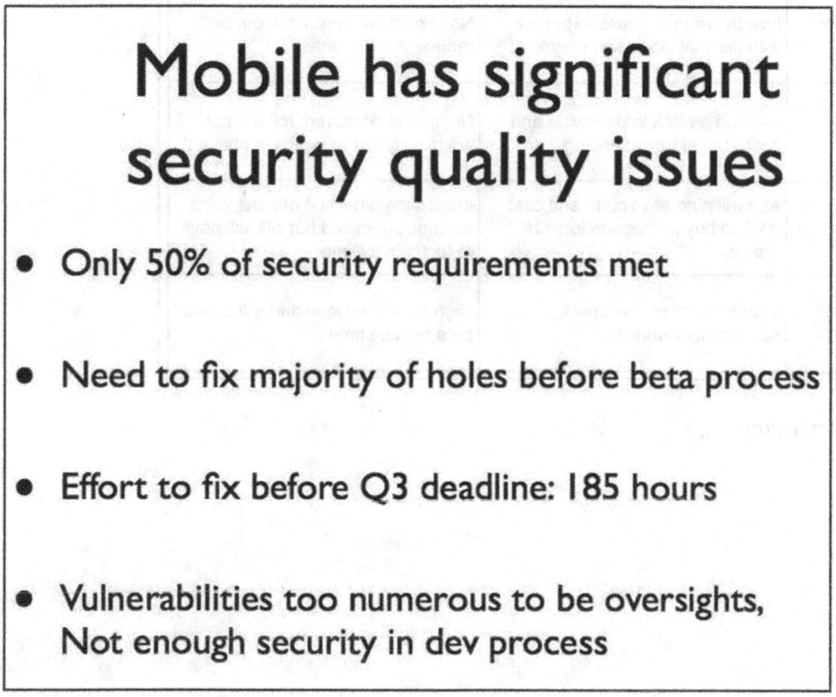

Mobile has significant security quality issues

- Only 50% of security requirements met

- Need to fix majority of holes before beta process

- Effort to fix before Q3 deadline: 185 hours

- Vulnerabilities too numerous to be oversights, Not enough security in dev process

---

Figure 8-4. Analyzing the analysis

Now that I've dropped the bad news, I'd better have a good story on how to get the company out of this jam. In Figure 8-5, I lay out some short-term and long-term fixes, summarizing the effort and effect.

Proposed Solutions

Solution	Effort	Effect
Sec Architecture review in design phase of products	Low by using in-house expertise with minimal slowdown to project	No impact on current roll-out but reduce vulns in phase 2
OWASP Mobile training for dev team	Will add a week to dev cycle and cost $1k per dev attending	No impact on current roll-out but will greatly reduce vulns in phase 2
Security code review software	App will auto-scan code and cost $35k to buy & integrate into QA process	Immediate detection of most vulns as code submitted but will still have to factor in fix time
Dragoon consulting assist in closing bugs to meet Q3 deadline	$32k for contract security development work	High for this release and will make beta release time

Figure 8-5. Introducing the solutions

In Figure 8-6, I jump to the first big decision: pay some money to meet the deadline, or push out an insecure and weak product. Short and sweet. Obviously, I want the problem fixed, but it's not my call, and I do not have $32K in my own budget to fix things. This is a critical risk acceptance question.

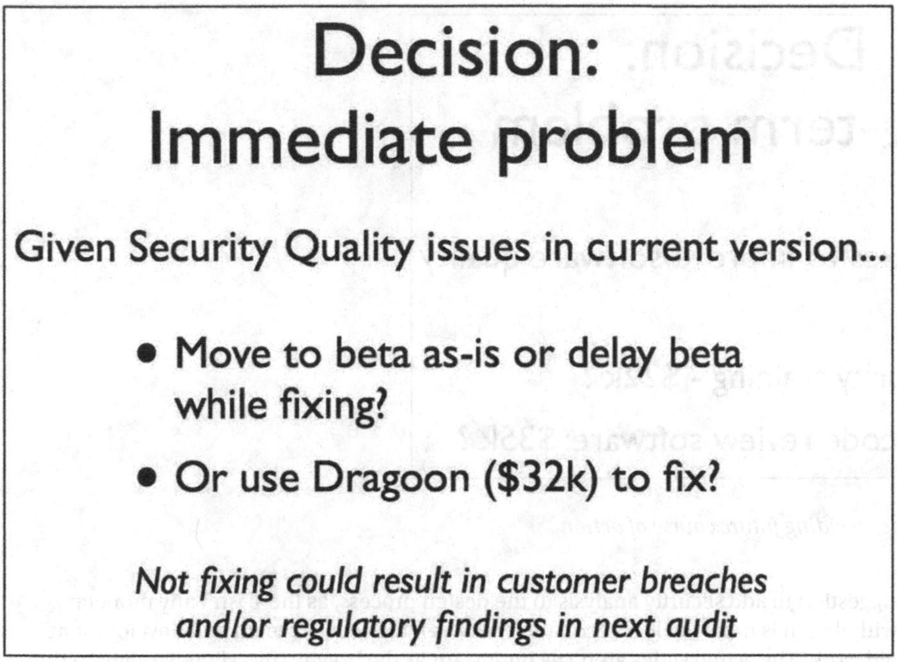

Decision: Immediate problem

Given Security Quality issues in current version...

- Move to beta as-is or delay beta while fixing?

- Or use Dragoon ($32k) to fix?

Not fixing could result in customer breaches and/or regulatory findings in next audit

Figure 8-6. *Penultimate slide: solving the immediate crisis*

Never let a good crisis go to waste. In Figure 8-7, I'll also make sure that this never happens again by improving software quality with both training and security feedback in the development process. Both are two new controls to raise the security strength of all the development work.

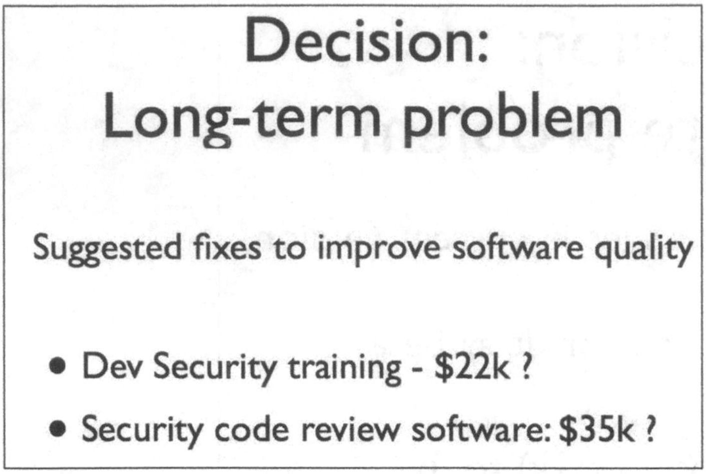

Decision:
Long-term problem

Suggested fixes to improve software quality

- Dev Security training - $22k ?
- Security code review software: $35k ?

Figure 8-7. *Final slide, deciding future course of action*

I've left out the suggestion to add security analysis to the design process, as there isn't any monetary spending associated with that. It is more likely a negotiation between the security team and development team on how this would work. The actual slides aren't as important as the brevity (five slides straight to the point) and the consideration of the audience's perspective.

FURTHER READING

- **Admiral Grace Hopper explains technological limitations to management**
  https://www.youtube.com/watch?v=JEpsKnWZrJ8

- **Explaining Risk to Non-Experts: A Communications Challenge, by Peter Sandman**
  http://www.psandman.com/articles/nonexpt.htm

- **The Secrets of Consulting: A Guide to Giving and Getting Advice Successfully, by Gerald Weinberg**
  http://www.geraldmweinberg.com/Site/Consulting_Secrets.html

- **Manager Tools: How to be Persuasive in a Presentation**
  https://www.manager-tools.com/2007/11/how-to-be-persuasive-in-a-presentation

■ ■ ■

CHAPTER 9

Talking to the Techs

It will be hard work. It's always hard work, and hard work from everybody within the team—technical director, mechanics, drivers, engineers—everyone in the team.

—David Leslie, racing driver

There are times when the hardest thing a security professional can do is work with the IT department. It's strange since many security professionals have come from an IT background. Speaking for myself, I moved into security from network engineering after a large firewall project. Of course, IT professionals work on security tasks their whole career, from cleaning up malware to managing user accounts and passwords. The IT team is on the front line of security every day. If your organization is hacked, they're going to be just as busy as you are, if not busier. When the auditor delivers a failing report, it's going to reflect on IT's efforts. Even worse, high-powered hacking groups and spy agencies single out IT personnel as high-value targets. They know sysadmins have the best access privileges in the company. If they can take over their accounts, the whole network is their buffet table.

So why do IT and security not get along sometimes? One of the biggest reasons is that IT's entire job revolves around making sure things don't break and their workload is manageable and building out whatever new thing that the business requested. Sometimes new security controls or processes impact one of these things. Sometimes that alteration is drastic, like when introducing change control or formalized user account management for the first time. This can really burden the IT team with unplanned (and often in their mind, unnecessary) work that could set them back significantly on their other projects. Security controls can also introduce new failure points or roadblocks in IT systems.

There are also sometimes clashes of technical expertise. Many people in IT have specialties and may understand the technical nuances of threats, vulnerabilities, impacts, and controls better than the security team. Therefore, there can easily be disagreements on risk assessment and treatment decisions. As there are no universal standards for what is acceptable security yet, members of the IT team may favor a different approach than the ISMS committee or IT security team. Many IT experts have favorite solutions or vendors, which they may feel are superior to the chosen solution.

You need to overcome these barriers because IT is critical to a successful security program. They will make or break the implementation of the technical controls. They are the eyes, ears, and hands of the IT security group. In the end, both groups are part of the security team and serve the business together.

IT Security vs. IT

So far, I've been speaking as if IT security is in a different department than the IT. That may not always be the case in every organization. However, you should be aware the job focus is different. I am distinguishing between the security team and the IT around the implementation and management of technical security controls. The CSO leads the security team, as well as being responsible for assessing and managing risks. The IT team has direct hands on the technology, managing the day-to-day business of keeping the systems and controls running properly.

In the big picture, their goals are the same: keep the tech up and support the business. However, some security requirements may run counter to availability and operations goals of general IT. First, it's a question of responsibility and leadership. Security is not a technology *add-on* that you apply or install into existing IT systems. Many IT people are tech-heads, which is why they're so good at their jobs. They may think they've fixed all the security problems by implementing controls. As we've seen so far, security is a lot more than just implementing controls. Security begins with goals, risks, and decisions, not some device or software package. It is about deep analysis of risk and requirements. Sometimes the solutions aren't technological. Sometimes the technology itself is the risk. Understanding technology does not mean someone understands security.

Second, there is a divergence of goals. The security team's highest priority is managing risk to the level acceptable to management. The IT team's priorities are satisfying user demands, implementing projects, and dealing with outages. In general, the IT department's mission revolves around granting access to information and resources, not restricting access. All things being equal, IT prioritizes availability and integrity over confidentiality. While security cares more about confidentiality than the other two. When push comes to shove, I've seen IT departments opt to let something be insecure to maintain uptime and keep users happy, despite the elevated risk. There are also cases where security has to reverse a decision that IT has made like this. The security team and ISMS committee own decisions around risk, not the IT department.

A key part of the security team's job is managing the risk of insiders. Some of the most damaging types of insiders are in the IT department. I've even seen cases where a malicious insider was leading the IT department. As the most knowledgeable and powerful tech users in the organization, there are times when an IT staff member can develop a sense of entitlement around technology. These individuals are more prone to feeling that rules are for the users, not them. By accident or on purpose, this can lead to security vulnerabilities or insider malfeasance. This is why you should separate the security group from IT, and give security the mandate to review the IT team's work. Sometimes security people can go bad or be careless too. So give IT full system privileges and give read-only access to the security team. Security is more of an oversight and management role, while IT does the actual work.

There can be some overlap, but in general, Table 9-1 breaks it down.

Table 9-1. *Security Tasks vs. IT tasks*

Security Tasks	IT Tasks
Approves and reviews firewall rules.	Implements and runs firewalls.
Review and responds to IDS alerts.	Implements and runs IDS system.
Runs vulnerability scans.	Fixes found vulnerabilities.
Monitors encryption settings.	Manages VPNs and storage encryption tools.
Writes and reviews security policies and standards.	Provides input and follows polices and standards. Writes procedures.
Reviews admin logs on privileged systems.	Works on privileged systems.

Techie Traps

I've mentioned the problems and misunderstandings that security and IT can run into, but not at a detailed level. Let's look at some specific problems and how to deal with them.

The Infinitely Long IT Work Queue

IT is busy. So busy they don't have time for your security project. They won't say no. In fact, they will probably cheerily accept the work—and then dump your project into a to-do list hundreds of tasks deep. Why should a security project be treated any different from all the other *critical* business requests that are pouring into the IT queue every day? Okay, before we start complaining, let's back up and look at how IT works.

The IT department is probably understaffed (just you ask them if you aren't sure) and they have a full plate of things to do. It may seem like all they need to do is read a few pages of documentation, run a few commands, and the work is done. If you've ever worked in IT or even with a computer, you know that is rarely the case. The simple freedom to choose which projects to work on might be a difficult goal for them to achieve. IT staff often start their day putting out fires and dealing with angry users. This is on top of whatever routine maintenance they have to do and the projects they already had scheduled. This doesn't include the typical IT system, which is a big haystack of legacy architecture, often poorly implemented and full of bugs. Since IT serves the entire organization, they are often also handed new high priority tasks on a daily basis (or even several times per day). Security tasks must compete with other business divisions for prioritization in the queue.

Some folks perceive IT as having time for *just one more thing*. Well, if they do, it means something else isn't getting something done. Sometimes the things that aren't being done can directly affect security like ensuring antivirus clients are working or removing accounts for terminated users. Throwing new security work into the IT work queue can be like squeezing a balloon. Reduce risk with one control could mean increasing risk on others by taking away attention to critical work or creating new unforeseen systems interactions.

To manage this, you need to work with the IT leadership to ensure that security risks are being addressed by priority. Be realistic about what you can ask IT to complete in a timely manner. You may need to prioritize and help them chose what can be actually finished. This is why you've done an extensive risk analysis and know what's important.

Poor IT Hygiene

Related to this problem is the IT team that has neglected or hasn't had time to clean up after themselves. Here are some examples of security hygiene that is overlooked in the bustle of everyday business:

- Expired HTTPS certificates still in use

- Terminated local user accounts still enabled

- Open but unused firewall ports

- Out-of-date access control lists

- Partially implemented projects leaving critical files around

- Overly permissive access permissions ("we did that just to get things working until we get a chance to come back and fix them... someday")

- Critical system configurations not backed up

- Audit logging not set up properly

- Out-of-date antivirus signatures or clients

- Missing patches on local systems (Usually, the OS is patched, but the browser? Critical apps? Utilities? Java? Acrobat? Flash?)

- Obsolete encryption algorithms still enabled

- Important passwords not rotated in a timely manner

- Missing or out-of-date documentation on critical systems (impacting business continuity)

- Old data or configuration files remaining uselessly in directories

- Retired hardware and media not scrubbed for disposal

- Entire desktops or servers gone off the radar for patching and updates

- Out-of-service operating systems still in active usage

All of these kinds of things need to be kept up to maintain the same expected level of risk control. This means the security team needs to schedule a regular audit for these things and assign cleanup tasks to IT. There's been more than one occasion of a serious breach happening because IT thought a machine was patched with current antivirus when it wasn't.

The Black Hole

Another similar problem related to IT workloads is "the one firewall engineer" or the one security-savvy developer. All the security projects and maintenance tasks get bottlenecked because there is one person in IT who can do it. No one else in the department has the skills (or the willingness) to do that particular complicated job.

There are several strategies to deal with this. First, if that security work is not a recognized part of that person's job, it should be. Often by explicitly assigning that task to that individual, they can be freed up from other tasks and concentrate on opening up the bottleneck. You can also have them document and train other staff to perform these tasks, so that the workload can be spread out. Sometimes this means slowing down the pace of work so that they can document and train, and thus everyone can move faster later.

Perpetual Design

Like many other IT projects, security projects can become stuck in a perpetual design phase. IT may have opinions and insights into security matters. There could be long hours of discussion and analysis, only followed by the realization that more discussion needs to be done. Sometimes you're cursed with the opposite, with no workable ideas or feasible solutions. Maybe there are problems or ideas, but no one is willing to bring them up for fear of being assigned new work. The whole design process can get difficult when both IT and security are bringing different perspective to the table. A Socratic method with multiple perspectives is desirable as inputs, but not at the expense of a stalled project. Security's role is to hear them and let them know that they've been heard, and then ensure them that the design work is completed.

There are several different approaches to help fix this. The first is to make use of the segregation between security and IT. The security team and the ISMS committee should decide upon the type of control and define the requirements for the control. IT can choose the specific technology and vendor, as long as it meets the requirements. When teams are stuck on designs, then this is a good time to bring in outside help. A consultant or value-added reseller may be useful. If there is still discord, it is helpful to remind the design team that they are all working to improve customer service and reduce risk to the company.

Sometimes design paralysis is caused by mistaken goal that the design needs to be free of flaws before going into operations. No design is going to be perfect. In fact, very few designs remain the same once implementation begins. The whole point of PDCA is continuous improvement. You unlikely to get something exactly right the first time. Try something, measure it, and make changes. Gradual improvement in the face of the real world will move you closer to perfection much faster than trying to think of every possible scenario before beginning.

Dragging Projects

Once a project is underway, it could stall or be perpetually delayed. Sometimes the causes are clear, like lack of funding or the necessary skill sets. Other times, it's not as clear. Like any other IT project of consequence, you need to establish clear milestones and deliverables to track the project's progression. The ISMS committee needs to clearly assign project responsibility. There should be no doubt which individual is responsible for making sure the project is completed per the requirements. Never assign a project to a department or a team, instead assign it to the manager of that team. That manager can delegate the work within the team. If necessary, you can create a RACI diagram to show who is responsible for what parts of the project.

Sometimes projects can be delayed because there are disagreements to the solution. This can include individuals who did not voice complaints or had their concerns ignored, and work silently behind the scenes to delay things. This isn't usually outright sabotage, but simply the de-prioritization of key project tasks but always with a plausible excuse. The security team needs to engage complaints head-on from the beginning. Even if they don't agree with what people say, they do need to make sure that everyone has been heard and knows that they've been heard. Remember the listening skills laid out in the last chapter. It is also helpful to get explicit buy-in from department heads before assigning projects. This means asking them if someone on their team can complete the project and getting their assent. If things really get ugly, you can always blame the auditors for forcing the organization to do this.

Other Tools

You can use few other tools when working with IT. Don't forget simple things like appealing to their professionalism. Everyone is on the same team and things need to be secure. It seems obvious but sometimes reminding people of that can get them on-board.

Another tool to getting their buy-in to a new process is the *IKEA effect*. This cognitive phenomenon describes how people place a higher value on products that they assemble themselves. Instead of forcing a new control or policy onto the IT department, make the team part of the process. Have them submit the first draft, or allow them to critique the procedure that you're proposing. As I mentioned before, let IT choose the specific solution, with their favored vendor. As long as the end product is the same, who cares how it gets there? Make them a part of the security process in whatever way you can. Give them advanced warning when you think something big is coming, like a big patch or a major audit finding.

Remember that IT is a department with their own needs and wants. When rolling out something new, consider what's in it for them. Can this new security process help them serve their users better? Can it improve efficiency for them? Can it save them money? Can they use it to push off unwanted work? Can they use this project as a learning opportunity or a chance for advancement?

Speaking of learning opportunities, a useful thing for the security department to do is to enlist *security champions* throughout the organization. Like everyone else, the security team is probably understaffed and can't be everywhere at once. Security champions are your technical leaders in other departments. Both IT and the development departments are excellent places to cultivate and support champions. Once you get permission from their boss (or ask them to nominate a champion), you give these folks extra training and tools. You can invite them to ISMS committee meetings as observers. They become the departmental experts in a particular control or security process. Good controls to find champions for include change control, system hardening, vulnerability scanning, secure development, and e-mail malware filtering.

Don't Over-Argue

When all else fails, you may find yourself in an intractable disagreement with someone. If so, don't prolong it such that you make a permanent enemy of them or anyone else. Your task is to state your case as clearly as you can and leave it at that. You rarely can change someone's mind by repeating your argument over and over again in exhausting detail. You probably have a better chance of swaying any bystanders with maintaining the high ground by not losing your cool and becoming annoying. Once you've made yourself clear, agree to disagree and seek another strategy to move forward. Maybe you need to appeal to authority or the ISMS committee. Maybe you need to concede and make up for it some other way. However, don't remain in a pointless argument. No one wants to sit around and watch two techies go at it for hours or multiple meetings.

Working with Other Security Pros

Sometimes collaborating with other IT security professionals can be a challenge. There are a wide variety of security specializations and backgrounds. Remember that there a lot of different standards and best practices in the security field. Not all of them line up with each other in the details of philosophy or execution. In addition, auditors are security professionals as well, and you may occasionally disagree with some of their conclusions. If you're a security professional reading this, you may already disagree with me.

In addition to the techniques that I've mentioned so far, as well as your good listening skills, the next best thing to do is to understand what different security professionals do and how they got there. There are many paths to management and mitigation of risk. Disagreement among security professionals is often about which path is better, even though the goal is the same.

IT Security Roles

There are many different kinds of jobs and roles within IT security. For simplicity's sake, I'm going to break them down into three functions: builder, tester, and responder.

Builder

This book is mostly for builders. Builders design, implement, operate, and maintain security systems and technical controls. Many of these security professionals have come from traditional IT careers. The role is about building IT systems and processes that can withstand attack. Sometimes the focus is small, on a single type of technology, and sometimes it covers an entire organization. Whatever it is, it's all about defense. The following are the kinds of job titles that security builders have:

- Chief Security Officer
- Director of Security
- Security architect
- Network security engineer
- Security software developer
- Security systems administrator
- Information assurance analyst
- Technical director
- Security analyst

Tester

Testers get to break things. It's sometimes considered the most fun job in security. They act like hackers and find the holes before the bad guys do. They use all kinds of tools and techniques, sometimes getting very hands-on in trying to subvert the technology. Auditors also test things, although they are more upfront as they review procedures and documentation. The goal again is defense, but this role is more about making sure things were built to last. These are some of the job titles:

- System, network, and/or web penetration tester
- Application penetration tester
- Source code auditor
- Vulnerability researcher
- Exploit developer
- Ethical or white hat hacker
- Security research engineer
- Security auditor

Responder

When all else fails, you call in the responders. These are the folks who clean up the mess or tell you what when wrong and who's to blame. They can wade into the aftermath while maintaining a cool head. Some of them are involved in legal work, gathering evidence and building a case. Others focus solely on the cleanup efforts. These are the job titles:

- IT forensics expert
- Security operations center analyst
- Forensic analyst
- Incident responder
- Malware analyst
- Computer crime investigator
- Prosecutor specializing in information security crime
- Intrusion analyst
- Disaster recovery analyst
- Business continuity manager

Hiring for Security

You may want to expand your security team by hiring or bringing in contractors or consultants. Given the variety of skills and experiences associated with security roles, the following are some questions that you can use when examining candidates.

How Do They Do Risk Analysis?

Given how this is a bedrock skill for what we need to do, you should definitely ask the candidate to describe how they have performed risk analysis in the past. You could even ask them to walk through an analysis with you by giving them a hypothetical problem. See what they focus on and what methods they use. Do they use quantitative or qualitative analysis? Do they know the difference? How do they gather evidence? Do they focus solely on technology or best practices? Do they dismiss new and possible unproven technologies out of hand? Do they mention or understand the legal implications of risk? How about compliance and audit issues? Do they have pet risks that they fear? Can they prioritize risk? Are they focused (or even aware) of potential business drivers behind the risk? Do they use a published risk model? Or do they do it ad hoc?

How Good Are They with Compliance?

Does the candidate understand the compliance requirements that you have? Have they acted as an assessor or auditor on them? Have they implemented to pass audit? Do they understand what passes a control and what fails? Do they understand scoping and scope barriers? Can they audit a third party for that compliance regime? How do they keep up with changes to the audit requirements over the years? A competent individual in a compliance requirement understands the intent behind each control objective. An expert knows how to subvert the rule.

What Controls Are They Familiar With?

Which controls has the candidate worked with in the past? Yes, you'll hear a lot about specific vendors and technologies, but has the candidate integrated them into a running organization? Maintained them? Audited them? Replaced them? Beyond technical controls, what about working on processes and policies? What about physical controls? Are they overly focused on one kind of control and weak in the others? Do they understand that they have this weakness? Do they understand the applicability and efficacy of control types? For example, what risks does transmission encryption mitigate? What risks does it not mitigate?

How Do They Meet the Challenge?

How does the candidate keep up with security? It's a constantly changing field. Do they read, attend conferences, meet with peers, or do online training? See if they push themselves, not just to maintain but also to learn new things. Do they pursue new certifications and skills? Do they have a mentor? Do they mentor others? I'm a big fan of individuals with a "constant learning" attitude. Not having this outlook can be an indicator of burnout.

FURTHER READING

- **Phoenix Project**
  http://itrevolution.com/books/phoenix-project-devops-book/

- **How do I get someone to change without upsetting anyone? You can't.**
  http://fishbowl.pastiche.org/2004/03/21/charles_rules_of_argument/

- **Sysadmin advice**
  http://everythingsysadmin.com/

- **Yak Shaving**
  http://projects.csail.mit.edu/gsb/old-archive/gsb-archive/gsb2000-02-11.html

CHAPTER 10

■ ■ ■

Talking to the Users

There is nothing more difficult to take in hand, more perilous to conduct, or more uncertain in its success, than to take the lead in the introduction of a new order of things.

—Niccolò Machiavelli, *The Prince*

Despite their great importance to the organization, users are best known to security people for just one thing: trouble. Users download malware along with their questionably funny cat videos. Users hate to patch their software. Users click links in e-mail. Users choose passwords based on the name of their dog. Users click through security warnings so they can get their job done. Users resist new security programs. Users break security, along with many other things.

When trying to take over a system, you want to exercise control at the element with the greatest variety of behavioral responses. In most organizations, this element isn't the technology but the users. Both the defenders and the attackers know this. Attackers take advantage of this by tricking and subverting the users. Security professionals are faced with attempting to build controls for the unwilling and the unaware. It's a Sisyphean struggle.

Users are not passive objects that do what you command. How the system functions can affect their daily workflow significantly. Users need to get their jobs done just like everyone else. In addition to all the problems they have with their job, they don't want to struggle with the security system as well. Consider the very real example of my spouse who is a research scientist involved in human subject testing. In order to access some of her research systems, she has to use three different username/password combinations as well as a token. Think about how often a non-techie, who is in a hurry to get work done, has to remember which authentication codes to use at which gateway, without locking themselves out. It's no wonder the users hate security.

Specific Challenges for the Users

My intent in this chapter is to show that the problem—and more importantly, the solution—lies not with the users but with the security team. Here are some specific hurdles that users encounter when dealing with security systems.

© Raymond Pompon 2016
R. Pompon, *IT Security Risk Control Management*, DOI 10.1007/978-1-4842-2140-2_10

Complexity

The use of security systems, as designed by IT security professionals, can easily overwhelm the average person. Consider the common security maxim of using at least eight-character passwords with a combination of uppercase and lowercase letters, and rotated every three months. Oh, and you should always use a different password for each system you use. And never write them down. The very fact that "password managers" software exists tells you how daunting this task can be. Yet we subject the users to this every day. But hey, picking on passwords is just low-hanging fruit. There are other unreasonable things that we expect users to do, such as the following:

- *Transferring confidential information securely over the Internet.* Can they e-mail it? No, not unless it's encrypted. How can they tell if it's encrypted properly? In many cases, the user can't know because some mail encryption happens within the infrastructure. Can they upload it? It depends where and how. Can they use a file-drop service? No, not unless we say that it's safe.

- *Knowing what is confidential and what isn't.* Remember the long descriptions of PII from the chapter on scope? Now imagine a user having to keep track of that. I hope that everything that is confidential is correctly marked confidential.

- *Keeping software patched.* It's one thing to approve the system patches and let them run. It's another when secondary apps like browsers and browser plug-ins need patching. Browsers are complex; patching may also break useful functionality. On top of that, there are evil web sites that spoof patch update messages to trick users into getting infected with malware.

- *Understanding what software is supposed to be running on their computer and when a program should be considered suspicious.* Even better, being able to tell if their computer is running slow because there's a system problem vs. when it's infected.

- *Being able to tell if an e-mail or web site (complete with the company logo) is real or a phish.* Meanwhile, attackers are actively working on new and better ways to impersonate and trick people.

- *Being aware of when encryption, antivirus, firewalls, and backups are working properly.* All of these services work invisibly to the user. Most of the time the services work fine, except when they don't. But users assume that they are always being protected.

Different Paradigm, Different Goals

Users come from a different world than IT and security. They have a different perspective based solely on how the technology presents itself to them and their daily workflow. You should never expect users to understand how systems work or the limitations of infrastructure.

The user's perspective may not necessarily include working to keep data private and free from corruption. They are likely to assume that security is *someone else's problem* (probably yours) and they are just there to do their job. Some users forget security advice and work around the controls if they need to get something done. There is a behavioral concept called *diffusion of responsibility* that describes the tendency of people not take helpful action when alone. Normal people have an implicit assumption that they are not responsible to do anything not explicitly assigned to them, so they just move on. Writer Douglas Adams nailed this concept brilliantly in his *Hitchhiker's Guide to the Galaxy*, by harnessing this power for a sci-fi camouflage screen called Somebody Else's Problem.[1]

---

[1]http://hitchhikers.wikia.com/wiki/Somebody_Else's_Problem_field

Since users have different motivations, users tend not to notice security or risk requirements. If a user does notice security controls, they often feel like they're impeding their useful work. This is where the sentiment that security gets in the way of business comes from. They have limited time and resources to deal with what they are tasked with finishing. Pop-up security warnings and authentication prompts can be distractions at best, roadblocks at worse. Users quickly learn to see the controls designed to protect them as obstacles that need to be worked around. This tends to happen in systems with rigid, unworkable, or vague rules imposed by security without context. Unfortunately, some security administrations see this rule-beating behavior as rebellion. They respond by trying to overpower the resistance with even stronger enforcement and tighter rules, which only creates more resentment. Often the problem is that the user's goals and security goals are inconsistent and work against each other.

Culture Clashes

When the security team redesigns a business process, they run the risk of damaging the value of that process. This risk is more likely when the change is made without careful and through analysis of the goals and legacy of that process. There is a concept called Chesterton's fence,[2] which warns that if you don't understand the purpose of a fence, don't pull it down; a bull could run you over. The next step beyond that is the cobra effect,[3] which refers to a poorly conceived change that makes things worse. This does not mean you should never alter or remove a process. It means you should be careful and make sure that the new process still achieves that same goal as before. Usually this simply means working with the users and taking the time to observe the process in action.

Tools for Helping Users

Given the gulf between our expectations of the users and the reality, we need some tools to bridge the gap.

Empathy

Empathy builds trust, and trust is your lubricant for working with users. The goal of empathy is not to *feel bad* for the other person. The goal is to *understand* the other person. It's about understanding and finding a connection. Remember your listening skills: don't interrupt, let them talk, and summarize back what they've told you. At this point, it's not about solving the problem or making the pain go away. It's about acknowledging what they're telling you.

Don't blame the victim. When someone gets phished, malware infected, or has a laptop stolen, the first reaction from some security people is to berate the user for being careless or stupid. People don't set out to be tricked or robbed. Think about you'd feel if it happened to you. So don't judge right off the bat. You can always educate later.

It's easier to empathize if we can experience the behavior itself. When trying out new security processes, take away your elevated system access and special tools (like password managers and non-company standard browsers). You can also try timing yourself and see how long it takes. If it's a new authentication system, try locking yourself out. What does the messaging look like? How does the reset process function?

One last trick to understanding through the user experience of a process is to document it, step-by-step, for a complete newbie. Every user action should become a bullet point in your how-to list. You'll find that a number of familiar things that were invisible to you now jump out as difficult or confusing. Sometimes even the sheer length of the process, once written down, can seem daunting for an unfamiliar user. All this information can feed back into your final design.

---

[2]http://www.chesterton.org/taking-a-fence-down/
[3]https://en.wikipedia.org/wiki/Cobra_effect

Let the Work Flow Smoothly

Redesigned processes can gain an additional leverage by following the natural flow of existing systems or task sequences. Take advantage of the existing plumbing and make the secure way be the most natural way to do things. The progression of decisions and arrangement of tasks can have a huge effect on how a system operates. Other times, you can redesign an entire process from scratch if the old system was based on paper-driven workflow. This is where you can take advantage of automation and have forms auto-filled, enforce task sequences, and monitor for bottlenecks in the flow. Another technique is to push decisions and power to the edges of the system, to give users more control over the process. Here's an example that embodies these ideas:

Old manual process

1. Manager e-mails a note to IT for new user access.

2. IT receives request and forwards to HR for approval.

3. HR checks records and send back approval to IT.

4. IT responds back to manager with note saying approved and ETA for change.

5. IT creates new user account and temporary password.

6. IT e-mails manager with new account name and asks them to schedule new user training.

7. Manager contacts new user to tell them to call IT for training.

8. New user contacts IT, schedules training, and receives temporary password.

9. Auditors reconcile paper trail of e-mails with existing user database.

All right, this looks like a process based on an old memo paper process. It's thorough but slow and cumbersome. Maybe we can automate this with a simple workflow.

New automated process

1. Manager enters request for new user in user management system (UMS). UMS automatically notifies HR for approval.

2. HR approves in UMS and IT is automatically notified.

3. IT creates account and temporary password, and enters into the UMS that it is done.

4. UMS notifies manager to schedule training.

5. Manager contacts new user to tell them to call IT for training.

6. New user contacts IT, schedules training, and receives temporary password.

7. Auditors receive a report from UMS to reconcile with existing user database.

Perhaps we can use automation to create the account as well and shave off more back-and-forth work. We'll make sure that the system is keeping detailed records and sending notifications to keep the auditors happy.

Improved automated process

1. Manager enters request for new user in user management system (UMS). UMS automatically notifies HR for approval.

2. HR approves in UMS and account is automatically created with temporary password. Notification is sent back to manager to schedule training. UMS also notifies IT about a new user and training that needs to be done.

3. Manager contacts the new user to tell them to call IT for training.

4. New user contacts IT, schedules training, and receives temporary password from UMS.

5. Auditors receive a report from UMS to reconcile with existing user database.

Sometimes the best control for a risk is inconspicuous. When faced with a task, consider looking at a policy control instead of a technical control. Maybe it's really expensive and error-prone to do automated security source code scanning on every developer submission. A new policy that requires another developer to sign-off on a peer code review for each submission is cheaper and can be more useful. Or maybe not. Why not test out both and see which works better? Vendors are often willing to offer proof-of-concept tests of their tools. See if they can beat a manual system.

Work with the Users

If you can't walk in the user's shoes, then walk alongside them: do user acceptance testing. . User acceptance testing has additional benefits beyond security and is often a key part of the software development process. Sometimes this process can be formal and done in a lab environment with recording equipment. Other times, you can do it more informally. It is important to ensure that all aspects of the working system are explored in testing. You can get a lot of good feedback from handing your instructions to some key users and asking them to walk through it while you observe. Not only does this give you good feedback on what's understandable and what's clunky, but it also fosters better user relations. When users can give you direct feedback, it makes them feel more comfortable about being included in the design process.

As with many things in security, one of the key characteristics of a good system is simplicity. Simple things are easy for users to understand and easy for auditors to review. Simple things have clarity, where security decisions and warnings are relevant and apparent. Security warning banners are one area where things can become cluttered and confusing. Banners are powerful tools if used judiciously. Banners work best when crossing key barriers, like moving onto a scoped system or logging in from the Internet. A warning banner on every single system login results in users blindly clicking through them without reading. Worse, it trains users to click through banners in general, so when they change or something important is added, they do not see it.

Users need to be given the clear and relevant information they need to make security decisions. Perhaps the most interesting example of this has been the evolution of insecure HTTPS certificate warning alerts over the years for web browsers. The early messages were full of useful information, but confused users:

```
Data you send to this site cannot be viewed or altered by others. However, there is a
problem with the security certificate. The name on the certificate is invalid or does not
match the name of the site. Do you want to proceed?
```

Over time, things were simplified and included some direct advice:

```
There is a problem with this certificate - it is not trusted. We recommend you close this
page and do not continue.
```

Now the message is dead simple:

```
Your connection is not secure - [Go back] or [Advanced]
```

Any extra information, as well as the option to continue, is underneath the Advanced button that should (legitimately) deter inexperienced users from moving forward.

One thing you can do with user adoption is to provide resources. This can include short training videos (use a screen recorder) that aren't mandatory but simply available. An intranet-posted frequently asked question (FAQ) list is a useful thing as well. You should always include a note that provides a way for the users to ask for help or send feedback. It is critical to make it possible for users to get help without feeling stupid for asking, or risking being belittled. When they do provide feedback, if it is sarcastic or angry, don't take it personally. Even with the best of design work, some processes are just going to be difficult and slow. Just let them vent and do what you can to make things easier.

The alternative to a counter-intuitive, ineffective process is to remove the control. This sounds like heresy but it is occasionally worth considering. You can shift your resources from enforcement and training to another control somewhere else, that compensates for the risk. Perhaps a combination of detective and corrective controls is a better use of energy. Maybe it's worth revisiting if the risk could be accepted or the assets moved out of scope.

Get Users on Your Side

One of the most powerful things you can do in security is to align the user's goals with security. Sometimes management is willing to help with this by leading by example or providing incentives. Things like free coffee cards and periodic security awards given to users who exemplify good security behavior are useful. They do cost money and may not work for some users. There are other powerful techniques that can help enlist people to fight the good fight, as described next.

Explain Why You're Doing This

It may seem obvious, but actually demonstrating the risks and dangers of hacking can sink in the importance of what we're doing. Make the examples tangible and personal, showing exactly how an attacker would phish the user and how their stolen credentials would be used. Explain to them exactly how antivirus software works and its limitations. Show them how cyber-crooks buy and sell private information on darknets. Go into detail about how auditors will be reviewing their actions and what a finding write-up will look like. In many cases, the success of an audit may directly affect sales and user's employment status, so you can mention this as well. You may scare people a little. That too can help make the lesson stick.

Explain the intention and vision of controls, so that people understand what things you are trying to prevent. There is also a tendency for users to do things if a control allows them. Explaining the intention of a control can help keep them on the right path if a control doesn't work as intended. For example, explaining why the credit card numbers are scrambled with encryption will signal to users that if they see credit card being stored unencrypted, something is wrong. You can also explain how the control and risk fit into the overall business objective, so they can tie the security activity back to their own work and livelihood.

Nothing like a Good Analogy

Engaging the users to help you with technical security matters is difficult. If they could be made to understand in some manner, things would be easier. Analogies are a powerful tool for explaining things.

A good example is confidential data leakage, which I covered in the chapter on assume breach. Confidential data can be copied everywhere invisibly throughout an organization. As you read in the chapter in scope, whatever system is holding confidential information immediately falls into scope. There are also issues of confidential data left behind on old media, which needs to be properly deleted. How do we convey this non-intuitive concept to users?

Well, you can use the analogy of fecal matter. Tell users that confidential data is like dog flop. It stinks, it smears, and no one wants it outside of a sealed container. Anything that it gets on needs to be scrubbed thoroughly. If it's on your shoe (or your laptop), you can unwittingly spread it around the carpets and floors. You don't want a nugget of it rolling around with all of your mail. Even the tiniest speck of it will contaminate whatever it's adhered to. If you even think you smell it, you want to find it quickly and contain it. You don't want to be near it. You sure as heck do not ever want to touch it. If you spot it, you need to call the special people (security or IT) to come clean it up quickly. Do you see how you can build the imagery to make confidential data so repulsive that users will want it as far away from them as possible? That's the power of analogy.

Contextual Shift

Another way to harness the user's own mindset is to do a contextual shift. Change or clarify their perspective on security and their obligations to the organization. For example, a standard security policy statement may say:

All employees will endeavor to protect the confidentiality, integrity, and availability all critical information and stored customer data.

Yawn. Sure, whatever. The users will get right on that. How about flipping that statement around and making it clear as to what they're actually doing?

- Our customers decide who sees their data

- Our customers decide who gets to modify their data

- Our customers have access to their data when they want it

Although this says the same thing, we've now underscored the duty of data custodianship for the entire organization. This isn't just a policy statement, it's a mission statement. It's an expectation, which is easier to meet than a performance objective. It's a reminder to IT and all the data handlers of their responsibilities. We are all working to serve our customers by protecting their data.

Security Awareness Training

Now let's pull this all together for some user awareness training. First, user awareness training is a powerful tool for security, but not necessarily as a means to prevent users from being tricked by hackers. Security awareness training is your first, best chance to get in front of all of your users and explain everything we've talked about so far. It's your chance to break the ice and get them onboard with the security program. Soon they will be dealing with controls and security procedures, so here's your opportunity to show you care about them and really sell them on the program. Use analogies, explain why, and put things in context. Lead them through the dangerous waters of the Internet and show them how to be safe.

Security awareness training is about affecting user decisions. However, there are only so much a user can remember and only many decisions that you can significantly affect. So choose your battles carefully. What are the few key decisions you want users to make? Think about what's useful and feasible. Take into account their mindset, incentives, average daily attention span, and technical ability. Here are three things I think that I can reasonable expect most non-technical users to grasp and internalize:

- The threats are real and security can't be everywhere, so it's everyone's job to protect the organization. We will all work together on this.

- If you see something suspicious or out of place, call security and we can help.

- When we ask you do something, there's a good reason why.

Whenever you can, make the training relevant and personal with real examples from the organization. Use threats and impacts that tie directly back to what the organization operates. As a bonus at the end of the training, it's a good idea to provide them with some home-based security advice. Not only does this maintain their security mindset when they're off the job but it makes them feel like they've gotten a little gift from you. This is also why I don't mind giving users home security advice when asked, as long as it's succinct.

Lastly, some regulatory environments mandate security awareness training, so take attendance. If you're not doing training live in a classroom, then consider using a security awareness quiz. Not only does this create an audit trail for later, but it also encourages participants to pay attention. Just don't go overboard on the quiz questions. I've used quizzes of less than a dozen questions and if they don't get enough answers correct they can retake it as many times as they want. I figure if they didn't learn it during the training, they're learning during the quiz questioning.

FURTHER READING

- **Security vs. Design: Standing at Odds?**
  http://uxmag.com/articles/security-vs-design-standing-at-odds

- **Humans in the Loop: Human-Computer Interaction and Security**
  http://www.cs.dartmouth.edu/~sws/pubs/humans.pdf

- **Bounded Rationality**
  https://en.wikipedia.org/wiki/Bounded_rationality

- **Usable Security**
  http://usablesecurity.com/

PART III

Managing Risk with Controls

CHAPTER 11

■ ■ ■

Policy

A common disease that afflicts management and government administration the world over is the impression that "Our problems are different." They are different, to be sure, but the principles that will help to improve quality of product and of service are universal in nature.

—W. Edwards Deming, *Out of the Crisis*

Security policy is the bedrock for controls and processes. An effective security policy serves the users, business processes, and technology of the organization. The policy should be universally understood and relevant for the current risks. This chapter explains security policies and how they should be developed and used.

What Is Policy?

How many times have you heard someone tell you: We can't do that, it's against policy. For some, it seems like policy is the blunt instrument used to prevent people from doing anything useful. True story: one organization had a policy that required a thirty-minute training session to use the bathroom. The *potty policy* was in place because the bathroom was on a different floor from the work area and it required traversing a secured area. Policy required that everyone entering the secure area behave in a certain manner. There were also special keys needed to access that area, which required additional key handling training. Essentially, it took eight different steps and a sign-off from the security department to relieve oneself. The ironic thing is that you can both see how this is necessary (access to a secured, scoped area) and absurd. That can be the nature of policy.

So what should policy contain? Policy is what guides people's behavior at a high level within the organization. With an IT security program, the security policy flows directly from the ISMS charter and its defined goals. There should be one security policy for the entire organization that covers the organization's stand on IT risk. There can be other policies, as well as other security documents, that support this top policy. Usually the top security policy is a simple, universal, and aspirational statement noting that the organization has risks and that everyone will work together to reduce those risks to an acceptable level. Most security policies are all the same; only the names differ.

What does the security policy do for an organization? It's how management communicates to the people of the organization about what it wants them to do regarding security. The security policy is the highest law of the land with respect to IT security. Legally, it demonstrates the organization's commitment to the security program, which can be useful in both audits and lawsuits.

An organization should try to avoid creating a security document for every possible risk and control in the world (though some may try to). The security policy provides the purpose and target for the security program, so that even if there isn't a specific policy regarding a situation, at least the intention is present to guide people's behavior.

© Raymond Pompon 2016
R. Pompon, *IT Security Risk Control Management*, DOI 10.1007/978-1-4842-2140-2_11

What Isn't Policy

People unfamiliar with this kind of documentation conflate policies with procedures and standards. These documents have different names with differing purposes and audiences. At the highest level is the organizational security policy. Below that, additional policies are used to describe the high-level goals for various functions. Under those, you have standards to describe the acceptable level to which the policy must be implemented. Appearing last are the procedures that detail how the work should be done. Figure 11-1 illustrates this relationship.

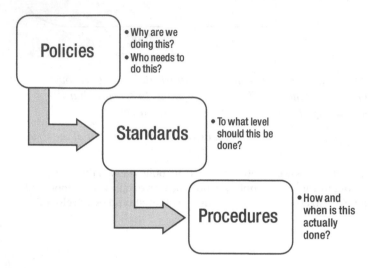

Figure 11-1. *Policy, standards, procedures*

Therefore, you could have a policy stating encryption should be used for confidential data transmissions and storage. Then an encryption standard describes the acceptable encryption methods, like AES[1] and key length. Then you can have procedures on how to set up encryption on various devices.

Another type of documentation is records, which are the proof that you did things according to policy, standard, and procedure. They can include machine-generated logs as well as meeting minutes, decision summaries, memos, schedules, and ticketing system notes. These are created as people do the day-to-day work. Records are what the auditors are going to need to see in order to validate you are doing what you're supposed to be doing.

Chapter 13 is entirely on documenting procedures and standards. In addition, in each of the chapters on controls, there is more information on the kinds of policies, standards, and procedures needed for type of control examined in the chapter. This chapter is going to focus primarily on overarching organizational security policy.

Writing Policy

How do you go about writing the security policy? Before I get into specifics, you should consider few things.

---

[1]http://www.nist.org/nist_plugins/content/content.php?content.39

Policy and the Law

Policy and the law are intertwined. Policies are written partly to ensure the organization is conforming to the legal or regulatory requirements of the organization's industry. Security policy is no different. In your case, you are looking to conform to IT security laws, regulations, and contractual agreements. This means the written policy itself has deep legal implications. Poorly written policy can mean there are gaps or errors in your compliance coverage. Published official organizational policy that your staff cannot understand or do not follow can have severe legal blowback.

An incomplete or unimplemented policy at best is a non-policy. At worst, a policy that staff disobey or ignore can be considered a deceptive business practice. There have already been many significant legal judgments against organizations who have promised customers certain IT security protections that failed to live up to them. Here is just one example from the FTC case files:

> *Review your privacy policy and double-check that what you promise—expressly or by implication—comports with your day-to-day practices. Like any other claim, what you say about how you handle information has to be truthful and backed up with solid proof. The FTC's lawsuit alleges that Myspace's policy made assurances the company didn't honor.[2]*

On top of the legal problems, your auditors will verify with your users whether policy is being followed. Be cautious about what you require in your policy. Include only the statements with should/shalls/wills/musts/mays that you know that users will obey. Having a policy that requires users to do things that they won't or can't do can only lead to problems.

Keep It Simple

Since your users need to read and understand the policy, you should make your policy as brief and readable to non-technical people as possible. Policy should be simple, not simplistic. It does need to encompass all of your high-level security and compliance requirements. That said, it is still feasible to do most security policies within a single page of text. Remember, this is the top-level security policy. The lower-level policies, standards, and procedures can be longer and do not need to be distributed to the entire organization.

Policies Don't Have to Be Perfect

There is the temptation to make every policy perfect, to cover every possible situation, and to address every complaint. Don't spend weeks or months in committee trying to hammer out the Magna Carta. Remember that policy is simple and broad. Take a reasonable shot at it and include a policy amendment process. As you find things that don't work in your policy, update and republish it. You don't want to change your policy every couple of weeks; once or twice a year is reasonable. If you need to, you can also include policy exceptions for certain departments or processes, depending on your scope and compliance requirements. Perhaps the security policy only covers the employees and contractors that need to follow a certain set of guidelines. For example, there may be a universal but weak security policy for all users and a more stringent policy for the IT department (who have elevated privileges and thus stronger rules).

---

[2]https://www.ftc.gov/news-events/blogs/business-blog/2012/05/
why-ftcs-myspace-case-matters-your-business-part-3

Key Policy: Security Policy

The organizational security policy is the most important policy that you create with respect to your IT security program. It is the foundation for all of your other policies and a primary requirement for nearly every audit on the planet. Note that this policy is called the Written Information Security Program (WISP) if you are a Massachusetts-based company and you need to comply with 201 CMR 17.00.[3]

What should be in your policy? Start with your ISMS charter. Some organizations use the same document for both, but it's best to keep the policy simple since all users are going to read it. However, you can derive a lot from your ISMS charter, including the scope, purpose, and overview. Remember, you don't need a lot of detail because the policy is a broad set of goals that everyone will be working toward.

Components of the Policy

There are some important pieces that you should have in your policy. These can be called out with section headers or they can simply be separate paragraphs. You can do whatever is most understandable for your organization. The critical pieces are explained in the following sections.

Scope

Scope describes who should follow this policy. If you aren't having the policy cover the entire organization, then you can specify the groups of users and divisions. Scope should define the data and the IT systems that are covered by this policy.

Policy Goal

The policy goal is your high-level generic statement that says something to this effect: *Security is good while leaking and losing data is bad, therefore we will have an IT security program to try to prevent the bad things from happening.* Look back to your ISMS charter for ideas. This section usually looks the same across the board for all policies: *We're going to protect the Confidentiality, Integrity, and Availability of our systems. We're going to follow all applicable rules related to the data we have in our possession.*

Governance

Tell your users who owns this policy and who is responsible for implementing policy. This is where you designate a coordinator, like the CSO, and give them power to run the security program. The coordinator should have a direct chain of authority for security from the highest level of the organization. You should also lay out the fact that you'll have ongoing maintenance of the policy, such as an annual review and updates. The governance section can also state that additional documents will be coming to flesh out this policy.

Risk Management

You should have a statement that identifies risk to the organization's objectives and establishes controls based on those risks. If you want, you can spell out the control objectives here, but use brief, plain English. You can also mention that you'll hold vendors and third parties to a certain standard and assess the risk of using them. Lastly, you can mention that your organization is aware that bad things will happen (assume breach) but you have processes in place to deal with it.

---

[3]http://www.mass.gov/ocabr/docs/idtheft/201cmr1700reg.pdf

Expectations for User Behavior

The final critical section is your message to the users on what you need them to do. First, you need them to read and abide by this policy and any other policies that may come their way. Users should report policy violations. If a user is unsure about policy, they should ask questions rather than making assumptions. You can keep this section high-level, as you'll have more detailed user behavioral expectations in the acceptable usage policy.

Sample Security Policy

So how does this look? Here's a sample.

Goal

The Executive Management of ORGANIZATION is committed to protect all company information assets, from all threats, and to provide all needed resources to implement an Information Security Management System. For this purpose, an Information Security Policy for all ORGANIZATION information assets has been authorized. This policy's purpose to enable core ORGANIZATION functions by protecting the confidentiality, integrity, and availability of ORGANIZATION's data from unauthorized access, unauthorized modification, and unplanned outages.

Authority

The Chief Technology Officer (CTO) is the senior executive in charge of the ORGANIZATION's IT assets. The CTO assigns and entrust the implementation of this security policy to the Security Officer.

Scope and Limitations

This policy applies to

- *All IT systems owned, managed, leased, or provided by ORGANIZATION;*

- *All employees, contractors, and users of ORGANIZATION IT resources;*

- *All data considered confidential which includes but is not limited to proprietary information, sensitive personal information, and intellectual property owned by ORGANIZATION or its customers or business partners*

Security Policy Objectives

ORGANIZATION will

- *Maintain, approve, publish, and require acceptance of security policies, standards, and procedures that express the ORGANIZATION strategy for protecting IT systems and data.*

- *Maintain appropriate security governance functions to establish, oversee, and evaluate the implementation of ORGANIZATION security controls.*

- *Identify, nominate ownership, publish, and require acceptance of acceptable usage rules for system assets and data.*

- *Ensure that all users understand their responsibilities, are aware of relevant security risks, and are held responsible for their actions.*

- *Protect ORGANIZATION physical facilities, equipment, and digital media from unauthorized physical access, damage, or loss.*

- *Protect ORGANIZATION IT networks and the supporting infrastructure from unauthorized access, corruption, or interruption.*

- *Maintain and communicate IT operational roles and processes for controlling risk with technical processes including encryption, change control, configuration management, vulnerability management, and prevention of malicious software.*

- *Control logical access to data and IT based on business requirements and roles.*

- *Review critical systems and logs for signs of unauthorized access and damage.*

- *Maintain, train, and follow secure application development and maintenance processes to minimize unauthorized access, modification, or downtime to developed or supported applications.*

- *Maintain and communicate incident management processes to ensure quick reporting, tracking, remediation, and analysis of security incidents.*

- *Review and track risks with third parties and business partners to ensure ORGANIZATION security objectives are met.*

- *Review and update security controls and processes to maintain compliance with legal, regulatory, and contractual requirements.*

- *Maintain, communicate, and test business continuity processes to mitigate unplanned interruptions and outages of critical system processes and networks.*

Policy Governance

This policy is subject to change and annual review by the ISMS committee appointed and approved by the by Chief Technology Officer. Changes to policy will be communicated to all users in a timely manner. All users are expected to behave in accordance with this policy. Violations or questions about the policy should be brought to the Security Officer.

Approved by Chief Technology Officer
Dinah Might

Key Policy: Acceptable Usage Policy

The second key policy related to security is the acceptable usage policy (AUP) or data handling policy. Where the main security policy sets the tone for the entire organization's security program, the AUP governs the user's specific behavior. This policy is pivotal in guiding all user interactions with the organization's IT equipment and data. Because this policy involves user behavior and can have severe sanctions for non-compliance, it should be written with the cooperation of the human resources and legal departments. You want to ensure that all of your users formally agree to this policy before allowing access to IT systems. The following discusses the major pieces of an AUP.

Goal

You should state the goal in this section. It's not anything new: you want users to behave responsibly in order to protect the organization's data and IT systems. It's fine to repeat the goal from the main security policy and/or ISMS charter. The users have probably already heard it, but repeat it anyway. Repetition strengthens memory.

Scope

It's likely this section is also repeated from the main policy. You could have a different usage policy for system administrators because of their elevated privileges. In that case, the scope could be slightly different and only cover the IT team. You could just as easily have a single scope that covers everyone's behavior. Use whatever makes sense for your organization. Remember that nothing is set in stone. You could start with a single policy and then later decide to split the policy for admins or developers as the need arises.

Privacy Disclaimers

This is an important section and may vary by local jurisdiction. The essence of this is to warn the users that when they use organizational resources, they will be monitored and recorded. If users store things on organizational systems, then it can be searched. This is a privacy disclaimer saying that users have less privacy than they do on their own personal equipment. Some jurisdictions, such as the European Union, allow users to label folders or files as "personal" and they are treated as more private than organizational stores. Be sure to check with your HR department and legal counsel when writing this section.

The privacy disclaimer is absolutely essential if you need to do any forensics or incident investigations involving users. It is also required if you are going to do content filtering to block pornography or objectionable web sites, as well as any kind of e-mail filtering. All the users' web traffic activity needs to be scanned for that particular control to work. It's also needed for audit logging of administrator actions on scoped systems, which is a major audit requirement for many compliance systems.

Lastly, the privacy disclaimer can even call out a warning that if the organization comes across evidence of criminal violations on organizational records, law enforcement will be called and records will be turned over to them. In the United States, if you find evidence of child pornography on a machine, you must report the violation. You also may need to turn over internal records if there is a legal investigation involving any of your users. It's a good idea to spell this out to users in advance. If nothing else, it might deter them from doing something they shouldn't.

Handling the Data

Do you recall how data gets everywhere in an organization and Kevin Kelly's description of the Internet as a copy machine? It's important that you define confidential data to your users in terms that they understand. Give examples of organizational intellectual property and clarify who owns it (not the user). If users could potentially encounter a customer's confidential data, explain what it looks like. Be sure to point out that they are custodians of their customers' data, which these customers have entrusted to them for safekeeping. Explain how important it is that they not copy and send confidential data around carelessly.

Handling the Machines

Now that you've talked about handling data, you should talk to them about handling the hardware. This includes how they web surf, how they e-mail, and software usage. This is also a good opportunity to remind them again that users should have no expectation of privacy: if you use our equipment, we will watch you. Users can use organizational equipment for occasional personal tasks but there should be appropriate usage. Now that you've said that, you need so spell out what is inappropriate.

Define Misuse

Many things may seem obvious to a security professional that still should be explained. This includes the things user's shouldn't do, like surf pornography or download malware. Obviously, you don't want people to do these things but you also want to warn them that you may discipline them if they do. Right out of the gate, users should not be pirating copyrighted materials using organizational equipment. They shouldn't be surfing pornography or sending sexually harassing messages. No threats or spam, which includes sending mass e-mails about their favorite political cause or charity.

Another minefield of acceptable usage is bring your own device (BYOD). You need to explain the rules for which types of personal hardware are allowed to touch the organization's systems or data, if any at all. If users can bring their own hardware to work, like smartphones, what are the expectations? Can you enforce security controls on their devices, such as mandatory locking PINs? Can you do a remote wipe on the device if it has organizational data on it? This can get so complicated that you may want to have a separate BYOD policy that you require users to agree to before allowing the connection.

Another aspect of BYOD is BYOS, or bring your own software. You do not want users installing their own software, possibly full of malware and vulnerabilities. You can have a policy that all software on organizational computers must be approved by IT or security.

Social Media

It's a dangerous line between allowing free speech and restricting what people can say about the organization on social media. You don't want to stir up anger by telling people what they can or cannot say on their personal social media accounts. At the same time, you don't want an employee tweeting out racist comments using their company smartphone.[4]

You need to make it clear that only certain departments or individuals are empowered to speak on behalf of the company. You also need to assert control over what users post from their organization-supplied equipment, such as nothing obscene or racist. You can remind users not to share confidential information about the organization.

Security Responsibilities

Finally, you need to spell out the responsibilities for the security that every user has. The first one is easy: it's the user's responsibility to be familiar with the security policies and to abide by the procedures and standards. Drilling down into that, users should use and maintain the security controls that they are given; no turning off their antivirus software to speed up their machine's performance. You never want users tinkering with security or IT systems outside their authority. Explain that only the security department has authority to hack or audit internal systems. Along with that, tell them no sharing of passwords or authentication tokens.

You want users to report security problems, policy violations, and incidents immediately. By the way, when users report problems, thank them. It's not always the most obvious thing to do (remember the "someone else's problem" problem), so you need to encourage that behavior. Reminding that it's their duty in the acceptable usage policy is a good idea.

Sanctions

After all that explanation, you need to put some teeth in the policy. Tell the users that if they violate policy, there will be consequences. You don't have to spell them out here, but you need to mention that something bad could happen. More on sanctions is covered in Chapter 15, which focuses on people controls.

---

[4]http://www.nytimes.com/2015/02/15/magazine/how-one-stupid-tweet-ruined-justine-saccos-life.html

Sample Acceptable Usage Policy

Use of IT Resources

Overview

Users of ORGANIZATION's IT resources need to observe these rules in order to protect the confidentiality, integrity, and availability of ORGANIZATION's systems and data.

Scope

This policy sets forth the rules regarding employee usage of ORGANIZATION's electronic media and services (computers, e-mail, telephones, voice-mail, fax machines, external electronic bulletin boards, on-line services, and the Internet).

This policy applies to all ORGANIZATION users, which includes employees, contactors, consultants, and temporary employees at ORGANIZATION.

This policy applies to all equipment that is owned, leased, or rented by ORGANIZATION.

Policy: Protect confidential data

Users should take all necessary steps to prevent unauthorized access to this ORGANIZATION and Personal confidential data. Examples of ORGANIZATION confidential information include but are not limited to company private, corporate strategies, competitor sensitive, trade secrets, and intellectual property specifications. Examples of Personal confidential information includes Social Security numbers, financial account numbers, addresses, and full names.

All users must protect confidential information of ORGANIZATION and personal confidential stored by the ORGANIZATION by obeying the following rules:

- *Confidential data must never be sent in e-mail or messaging in an unencrypted form. If an e-mail is received containing confidential information, the sender and the Security Department must be informed.*

- *Confidential data must never be stored on laptops, workstations, or computing devices in an unencrypted form.*

- *Confidential data must never be stored on cloud computing services, such as Dropbox, iCloud, Google Drive, and similar services without formal approval from the IT or Security department.*

- *Confidential data must never be stored on portable media in an unencrypted form. Portable media includes USB sticks, hard drives, data tapes, or floppy disks.*

- *Approved acceptable encryption tools for storing confidential data is available from the ORGANIZATION IT department. Only the specific encryption tools from the IT department are approved for confidential data. Users should not install their own encryption tools.*

Limit Personal Use

Occasional personal usage of ORGANIZATION's IT systems for personal purposes is understandable and acceptable. However, users may not use ORGANIZATION IT systems in any way that would be considered obscene, indecent, hateful, malicious, racist, defamatory, fraudulent, libelous, treasonous, or promoting the use of violence to others.

Users should not use ORGANIZATION IT systems for non-job-related solicitations, such as other commercial ventures or personal/political/religious causes.

All users must conduct themselves in a professional manner when corresponding with customers or colleagues.

Users must not connect personal computing devices to the ORGANIZATION networks without permission of the Security Department. Personal devices can be connected to the guest Wi-Fi network.

No Expectation of Privacy

ORGANIZATION reserves the right, without warning or permission, to review any employee's data files, e-mail messages and usage records to the extent necessary to ensure that IT systems are being used in compliance with the law and ORGANIZATION's policies.

ORGANIZATION will not guarantee that any electronic communications will remain private or confidential. For security and maintenance reasons, authorized individuals can and will monitor systems and network traffic at any time without notification.

ORGANIZATION reserves the right to access and disclose any messages sent over its networks and to monitor electronic activity without regard to content.

Copyright Infringement

Approved software includes all software provided to employees by ORGANIZATION IT department. Only software supplied or authorized in writing by the IT department will be considered approved.

Individuals may not take ORGANIZATION software home for personal use. Software audits will be conducted on a regular basis. Discovery of any unauthorized software will constitute a violation of this policy.

The use of ORGANIZATION systems to distribute, store, or collect non-business copyrighted media files, such as music or movies, is prohibited.

Social Media

Only the ORGANIZATION marketing department and executive management is authorized to speak in public on behalf of the ORGANIZATION. Employees are expected to use their best judgment when making personal comments on social media about the ORGANIZATION and distinguish their opinions as their own and not the ORGANIZATION. ORGANIZATION's trademarks, logos and any other intellectual property may not be used in connection with any social media activity. Social media usage by employees when using ORGANIZATION property and systems is also subject to the terms and restrictions set forth in this Policy. Employees assume all risk associated with social networking and blogging.

Authorized Security Controls

If you suspect an ORGANIZATION IT system of being compromised or subject to unauthorized access, please contact the Security department immediately.

Users are assigned specific system ownership responsibilities and usage privileges associated with their specific job roles. Wherever feasible, ORGANIZATION has implemented technical security controls to limit access to authorized users. However, ORGANIZATION realizes that preventative technology has limitations. Users shall not to exceed or attempt to exceed their access privileges beyond their assigned scope of access.

Removing or disabling antivirus or security software without explicit written permission from IT is a violation of this policy.

Users must not perform or give permission to perform any security testing of ORGANIZATION without written permission from the Security Officer or Executive Management.

Consequences of Violations

If you need clarification of any aspect of this policy, contact the Security department.

Failure to comply with this policy may lead to discipline up to and including termination and all available legal remedies.

Policy Changes

This policy will be reviewed on an annual basis and may change regulations or requirements. Users will be notified of the changes and be required to acknowledge their acceptance.

Policy Rollout

The security policy and the acceptable usage policy are absolutely the right things to roll out as part of the security awareness training. After you explain the threats and attacks against the organization, you can then present these policies as your organization's response. The Internet is scary, so this is why we all need to do these things. This is an also great opportunity to answer questions and clarify points about the policies. If you have to, you can roll these out electronically via video presentation or canned e-mail or video. It's not as effective, but it's better than nothing.

The best time to roll out all of this is when an employee first comes on board. If you can, have the HR department deliver the policies as part of their new-employee orientation. They're already reading and signing a bunch of documents, so why not add this one? You should roll out policies once a year afterward and every time there is a change in policy.

One thing you need to do is formally capture each user's acceptance of the policies. They can sign it at the bottom of the policy (put in a signature block) or agree electronically on some kind of policy management system (there are a lot available). Not only do you need this proof if you have to deal with a policy violation, but it's essential for audit. You should also do this as part of every policy rollout, so annually or upon policy change. Your goal should be 100% compliance with policy acceptance. It's not easy, but it's not impossible either. Like everything else in this program, it mostly takes hard work.

FURTHER READING

- **Attorney Benjamin Wright on Policy**
  http://hack-igations.blogspot.com/2016/01/infosec-policy.html https://computersafety.wordpress.com/2008/10/28/internet-pornography-in-the-workplace/

- **SANS policy templates**
  https://www.sans.org/security-resources/policies/

CHAPTER 12

■■■

Control Design

Security is like dentistry. You go to the dentist twice a year for reviews and advanced questions, but you don't go to the dentist to brush your teeth. The security team should function like the dentist: regular checkups and expert issues.

—Robert Garigue,
IT Security thought leader, former CISO of Bell Canada & Bank of Montreal

Controls are what you use to reduce risk. Controls can reduce likelihood or impact, and if you're lucky, they can reduce both. The selection and arrangement of controls is an important step in the IT security program. This chapter explains how to design controls.

A Control Not Used Is a Control Wasted

During the financial crisis of 2008, it was a terrible time to sell a house, but a great time to buy one. My wife and I had just fallen in love with a gorgeous brick Tudor with amazing hardwood floors and a huge finished basement. It was the house of our dreams and super cheap because the sellers were mired in tax court and bankruptcy. The IRS was on the verge of seizing the property, but if we purchased immediately, we could get it. Unfortunately, my credit union wouldn't underwrite a loan to a property buried in this risky mess. We ended up at a large bank capable of handling the more sophisticated risk. Our loan officer was set up in a small office in a strip mall; his bank recently shotgun-married to a large national bank due to failing assets. He sat at his desk, grumbling and tsk-ing as his hands slapped against the keys of a bulky black laptop with the new bank's logo stenciled across the case. "I'm sorry. This new system just won't let me enter your loan information!"

He shook his head, turned around, and reached into his desk drawer. With a smile, he pulled out a second laptop. This one was brand-new and still adorned in advertising stickers from the store. He stacked the new laptop right on top of the other one. It fired it up with a chirp and he began keying in my personal financial details. I raised an eyebrow and opened my mouth, but he silenced me with an upheld hand.

"Oh, the laptop the new bank gave me is so locked down, I can't do anything. Don't worry, with this one, I can get your loan done and approved in a few minutes." I clenched fists under the table. As a security professional, I was horrified that my financial information was being input into this potentially virus-riddled piece of plastic from a CompUSA fire sale. But we wanted this house and this loan was our only shot at getting it. I ground my molars together and gave him a tight-lipped smile as he completed my application.

Here I faced the adage that I had always been warned about: If the controls are too unwieldy, the users will work around them, usually in a more insecure manner than you can imagine. No doubt the gigantic bank was totally unaware that this was going on, especially in that first year of the too-big-to-fail-driven hasty mergers and turnovers.

We are faced with compromises like this from time to time. However, as security professionals, we can do better at control design so people don't have to take risks just to get things done.

What Is a Control?

We've already talked about controls as the tools that you use to reduce risk. Now we're going to dive deeper into how controls should be selected and used in conjunction to support control objectives. Most technical professionals are already familiar with controls. In fact, control installation and maintenance make up a lot of the day-to-day work of IT security. Because of this overhead, the best controls are fire and forget. Unfortunately, few of them are. But since they are such a heavy burden, it's worth talking about designing them so that they're easier to live with. Consider this a metachapter on controls before we get into the specific controls in upcoming chapters.

What Is a Good Control?

A good control has many facets, but the primary function is to adequately reduce a known risk. Your goal is to design controls that meet your compliance requirements as well as a *reasonable standard of care*. What does this mean? In 1932, there was a landmark legal case involving tugboats towing barges. An unexpected storm hit the boats, and the barges broke free and sank. There were lawsuits, and in the end, the tug operators were found to be negligent for failing to equip their boats with radios (a new technology at the time). The tug operators claimed that radios were so new that no other tug operations in the region were using them. They were still found negligent by Judge Learned Hand, who stated, "There are precautions so imperative that even their universal disregard will not excuse their omission."[1]

This concept is relevant to your choices and designs of controls in protecting your organization. You should consider your compliance requirements, especially the ones calling out specific controls, as the *minimum* standard of care in your design. Furthermore, remember the Mendoza Line for Security: your network must be able to at least resist the attacks of commonly available point-and-click hacking tools. These kinds of basic security controls are what you need to use so you don't look negligent.

Proportionate to Risk

Control strength should be matched to risk. The obvious best thing to do is build your strongest set of controls for your largest risks. Breaking this down a bit further, when the risk's impact is high and the likelihood is high, then most of your control work goes into mitigating that risk.

What about when the impact is low, but the likelihood is high? These are the predictable, everyday risks, like spam, non-directed malware, or equipment failure. They're the background radiation of the Internet: you know they're going to happen and cause a minor problem. They should be managed like chronic problems, with basic preventative controls. Since they are so common, it's likely that through sheer multitude of occurrence, a few events are going to get through your controls. In these cases, you should also have a few responsive controls to build resilience to the potential impacts.

Risks where the impact is high, but the likelihood is low are interesting risks to manage. Think of rare occurrences that can be devastating, like malicious insiders or building fires. Often preventive controls for these kinds of risks are expensive or cumbersome. The risk stance should be one of precautionary vigilance, with detective controls set up to look for leading indicators of this risk coming to culmination. This could be as simple as audit logging on insider action with oversight by the security department. You may not prevent the risk from occurring, but you could catch it early enough in the act to mitigate severe damage. Restorative controls can also be set in place to help reduce the impact in the rare event something occurs. Fortunately, many of the restorative controls can be used to resolve many kinds of impacts, not just the ones associated with these risks; for example, failover facilities in case of building fires.

---

[1]https://scholar.google.com/scholar_case?case=8197801632769400398&q=60+F.2d+737&hl=en&as_sdt=2002

In some cases, risk cannot be feasibly controlled. Consider Courtney's second law,[2] which states: "Never spend more money eliminating a security exposure than tolerating it will cost you." Courtney's law also has two corollaries: "Perfect security has infinite cost," and "There is no such thing as zero risk."

Standardized and Measured

Good controls are standardized across the organization, with a centralized management hub. This doesn't mean that you have a single console at headquarters that controls all of your firewalls (although you can if you want). It speaks more to having standards and procedures for controls so that they are implemented in a repeatable and measurable manner.

Good controls are designed so that their functions can be verified and measured. Remember the old management adage: *If it moves, then graph it.* All controls should have some kind of reporting mechanism, regardless of whether they are technical controls. The easiest-to-monitor controls are designed to send feedback about their functionality directly and quickly. If the control can't do the reporting, then a verification procedure should be built into the control operation. For example, consider a detective control of video camera recording the entrances and exits into a secure area. Some camera system can e-mail alerts when they detect motion in their area. If your system does not have this kind of feedback on functionality, then you could add a periodic (weekly, monthly?) verification procedure to review video logs to ensure that the system is working. The effectiveness of controls, especially after being deployed in your environment, is examined in detail in Chapter 22.

Documented

Related to standardization and measurement, is control documentation. Auditors will not consider a control secure if the design is not clearly expressed. This documentation would definitely include the policies, standards, and procedures associated with the control. It also can include flow charts, network diagrams, and narratives that spell out how the control functions and what it should accomplish. For SSAE 16 audits, these control descriptions are a mandatory part of the audit report, going into section 3 of the report. All controls should be documented in some way, not only for auditors, but also for your own organizational usage. Having documentation around controls is valuable for internal management and operational training.

Control Lists

For specific control ideas, you should definitely be looking at the compliance control lists within ISO27002:2013 and PCI DSS. If you are going to be audited against these standards, you will need to implement every control that applies. In the case of PCI DSS, every control in the standard does apply. In addition to the large myriad of technical controls for sale by IT security vendors, there are also other control lists available by standards bodies and organizations. Here are some:

- **NIST SP 800-171**
  http://nvlpubs.nist.gov/nistpubs/SpecialPublications/NIST.SP.800-171.pdf

- **Cloud Security Alliance Cloud Controls Matrix**
  https://cloudsecurityalliance.org/group/cloud-controls-matrix/

- **CIS Critical Security Controls**
  https://www.cisecurity.org/critical-controls/

- **Australian Signals Directorate Top Mitigations**
  http://www.asd.gov.au/infosec/top-mitigations/mitigations-2014-table.htm

---

[2]http://tools.ietf.org/html/rfc4949#page-81

Controls in Combination

You've already read about preventative, detective, and corrective controls, as well as administrative, physical, and technical controls. That's nine different ways (in combination) that a control can be applied to a risk. You've also already read the first two the GAIT principles, but there are more. Take a look at the third.

GAIT PRINCIPLE 3

Business risks are mitigated by a combination of manual and automated key controls. To assess the system of internal control to manage or mitigate business risks, key automated controls need to be assessed.

Notice how it says *combination* of controls can mitigate risks. Sometimes you can't find a perfect control that completely manages your risk. However, using multiple controls, of all nine permutations, you can reduce risk to acceptable levels. In a combination of several controls being applied, there are hundreds of possibilities. You can also use overlapping controls to manage the same risk, if one control fails then the others hopefully can mitigate the risk. For example, if a firewall filters 80% of in-bound malicious executables, your user awareness training is 30% effective, and the workstation antivirus blocks 80% of the infections. Do the math on the effectiveness of these three different controls.[3] Together these controls remove all but 3% of the infection attempts. Add a robust patching routine on browsers taking out another 80% and you're doing better than 99%. This is called *defense in depth* and it's a good way to layer your controls on critical risks.

Key Controls

If a control's failure to eliminate a risk results in a failure of a critical business process, then that is a *key control*. In the audit world, if a control failure leads to not achieving a control objective, then that is also a key control. Key controls are a primary risk prevention tool, standing between your organization and a breach or failed audit. For this reason, key controls are usually preventative controls.

Since key controls are so critical, they should be as reliable and robust as possible. Since complexity can lead to unexpected behavior, simple controls are better. Also, key controls should be backed up by other controls in case they fail. This is also a form of defense in depth. For example, you have a control objective that no unqualified or dishonest personnel will be given access to IT systems managing financial transactions. Your key control could be pre-employment screening for previous criminal convictions as well as reference checks of stated credentials. Nevertheless, you can add a supporting control to ensure that this key control functions properly, such as a quarterly reconciliation of IT system users to HR records to ensure that no accounts were added without HR's approval.

Compensating Controls

What happens when a compliance requirement mandates a specific control but you cannot implement that control? It could be for feasibility reasons, such as a critical legacy system that may not be able to accommodate a particular control. Some old mainframes are still in use to store and process payment cards

---

[3]Probability math: $(1 - 0.80) \times (1 - 0.30) \times (1 - 0.80) = 0.028 = 3\%$

but do not have mechanisms for strong authentication or encryption. Sometimes compliance-mandated controls can't be implemented because of immense cost. For example, an organization may have built an entire network infrastructure using firewalls and switch appliances that only use a single user, forcing the entire IT team to share a single generic login and password.

This can be a serious problem for organizations facing PCI DSS, which has very strict requirements about implementing their control regime. Enter *compensating controls*, which are additional controls added to take the place of the required control. You should be aware that PCI DSS has the following criterion, which must be met for accepting compensating controls:

- The controls must meet the same goal as the originally stated requirement ("intent and rigor").

- The control design must be at least as effective as the original control.

- The compensating controls must be *new* additions. You cannot re-use existing PCI DSS controls from the same asset-risk pair as compensating controls.

- The controls must over-compensate for the additional risk of going off required controls.

The compensating controls must work better than the original control. Often this works out to be either multiple additional controls or time-consuming administrative controls. This can mean that compensating controls can be more expensive and difficult to manage than original control requirement. In general, compensating controls work best as a temporary stopgap until the real control can be put in place. You will also need to explicitly document the reasons and mechanisms of these compensating controls and be prepared to defend them to auditors. Within the last few pages of the PCI DSS standard, there is a compensating controls worksheet that must be filled out.

Auditors review compensating controls with a lot of suspicion and ambivalence. You can expect your compensating controls to receive a lot of scrutiny. Even then, they may not be acceptable.

Control Functions and Failures

As you know from the concept of *assume breach*, the way that security systems fail is an important condition to consider during the design process. Many novice IT security practitioners become overly reliant on controls, especially technical controls. Consider commonplace technical security controls like firewalls and antivirus. In the beginning, these were considered optional controls that offloaded operational security work, such as hardening and patching. Now not only are these tools ubiquitous but also they are considered so essential that the idea of not using them is considered negligence. Like them or not, many IT systems are dependent on perfectly functioning technical controls.

Control Failure Modes

When analyzing a control's failure state, consider what happens to its security functionality. Does a control fail open or closed? When it fails or becomes overloaded, does the control shut down the entire function it's protecting or does it open up and allow all traffic to pass unimpeded? A control that fails open is useful if your primary concern is availability, but at the cost of access control. A control that fails closed will protect the assets behind it, even if it means shutting down the entire channel. Some hackers will flood traffic at network security devices that fail open, knowing that they can slip their attacks through once the shields are down. Other hackers may purposely overload network security devices for a denial-of-service of attack. You should make sure that your control's failure mode matches your requirements.

Control Flexibility

Look at a control's flexibility. In some ways, this is useful because the control can handle many different types of situations without a lot of pre-configuration. On the other hand, flexibility usually entails complexity. Complex systems are more prone to unexpected failures.

Control Functionality

Consider how the control works. Some controls work by what Marcus Ranum refers to as *enumerating badness*. This means the control has a long blacklist of known attacks that it will pattern match and filter against. This is fast and cheap to implement, which is useful for high-speed controls or for reducing complexity. However, there currently no complete list of every possible attack in the universe. All that attackers need to do is come up with one new attack that the isn't on the blacklist, and they can sneak through. Some controls use lists of all acceptable behavior (white lists) and then filter out everything else. They are powerful security controls, as well as fast and cheap. However, they do require a lot of maintenance, because every time a new acceptable behavior is needed, it must be programmed into the control.

Lastly, some controls use anomaly detection to try to learn what is normal and acceptable, and then reject things that do not conform. These systems are also often complex (because they are flexible) and not always accurate (what is normal?).

For your controls, especially your key controls, you should look into all of these aspects. Based on the control functionality and its failure modes, you can decide if your design should include additional controls or high-availability options for technical controls.

Control Cost

Very few controls are fire and forget. Controls require care and feeding in the form of monitoring, patching, licensing, and adjusting. This is true whether a control is administrative, technical, or physical. Even policies have to be written, rolled out, explained, reviewed, and updated. This raises the question: What is the total cost of a particular control? What specific costs should you consider in costing a control? There are hard dollar costs like the following:

- Purchase and licensing

- Ongoing support and maintenance

- Installation and testing (if hiring outsiders to do the work)

And there are soft costs, which can include the following:

- Installation and testing (if using staff to do the work)

- Disruption to work for users

- Monitoring of functionality

- User and administrator training

- Documentation of configuration and functionality (at least for audit)

One way to look at control costing is to break out the cost per protected node per risk. For example, a firewall costing $10,000 may seem like a bargain, but not if it's only protecting a small office of five users from network attacks only. There have been times where I've looked at my budget in this way. Let's say that I have $100,000 to protect 500 users. That means I can expect to spend $200 per user, which needs to cover all of my risks and compliance requirements.

Some tools are licensed by the user, while others may require some thinking to break out. There have been times where a vendor has presented a security solution to me and I responded, "I am not paying $1,000 per host just for intrusion detection." Having an idea of what your controls cost can help you make trade-offs in design.

Reducing the Cost of Controls

Since controls can get expensive, here are some ideas on how lower the costs.

Best Practices Can Be Expensive

What are *best practices* for security? There are lots of lists claiming to contain best practices, but for who and when? Remember that security and technology are constantly evolving. Any best practice list that cites specific controls and risks is likely to be obsolete soon after publication. I like to think of best practices as someone telling me, "This worked in our organization once upon a time, so it should work for you." In other words, they're precomputed risk/control trade-offs from somewhere else. Usually, they don't include any accompanying data to back up their claim as to why they are a best practice. I'm sure that many of these controls are useful and may be relevant for your organization; however, considering that the average control framework of best practices has at least 80 specific controls, blind implementations can get expensive. If you are basing your security on a best practice list, make sure that you analyze each control to see how much risk reduction you're actually getting for your money.

Legacy Systems

Securing old, but vital, legacy systems can get very expensive. Especially if you have to factor in software development to add security controls that don't exist on the system. Even if you can get controls working on a legacy system, there may be higher-than-normal operational and support overhead to maintain. If it's hard to put controls on the system, can you wrap the system in controls? Segment your legacy systems with firewalls, VLANs, and subnets. Then offer proxy or filtered access into the systems with lots of strong authentication and logging. In some ways, you can treat that legacy subsystem as its own scoped environment with its own policies and processes specific to access and operation.

Over Focus on Technical Controls

Technical controls are sometimes the most expensive controls of all. Not only in the cost of the technology and licensing, but also requiring skilled IT personnel to install, manage, and maintain them. A lot of technical controls can be replaced by solid processes and low-level IT work. Timely and continuous patching of software can be better than a sophisticated intrusion prevention system. An up-to-date accurate inventory and version management system can be as powerful as a vulnerability scanner. Change control policies and procedures can be very useful tools in hardening and managing deployed systems. Developer training can reduce security holes in software before they ever have to sit behind firewalls. Periodic log review and user access audits can control insider risks as well as many expensive management solutions. In the banking world, mandatory vacations for key personnel can help detect fraudulent internal activity.

Infrequently Used Key Controls

Key control failures can be expensive in terms of potential breaches and in audit findings. However, you may use some key controls only occasionally; for example, a quarterly reconcile of users to HR records, an annual software inventory, or a quarterly Internet vulnerability scan. If these controls are important, then it may be worth it to spend a little now to save more in the long run. If possible, spread out or increase the frequency of the key controls. This way, problems are caught earlier and a control failure isn't as catastrophic. I've seen annual user-rights reviews where it was discovered that entire departments had full local admin privileges for the past ten months. Think about how much damage that could have caused. Doing the reviews quarterly, or even monthly, might actually be less effort, since the workload is reduced. When designing controls, there are a lot of ways for you to get creative—not only with the controls themselves, but also in combination with other controls. Maybe you can retain the annual review but add a scripted alarm to send an e-mail whenever a user is added to the admin group. There are many simple and cheap ways to bolster key controls. Even if you don't know the answer, you can talk to your experts in the IT department.

FURTHER READING

- **Security Engineering**
  http://www.cl.cam.ac.uk/~rja14/book.html

- **Controls and GAIT**
  http://itrevolution.com/audit-101-for-devops-resource-guide-for-the-
  phoenix-project-part-3-correctly-scoping-it-using-gait-and-gait-r/

CHAPTER 13

■ ■ ■

Administrative Controls

Don't write with a pen. Ink tends to give the impression the words shouldn't be changed.

—Richard Hugo, *The Triggering Town*

There is a tendency to lean for security practitioners to heavily on technical and physical controls. Machines do the same thing every time, forever and ever. Humans are more variable in their execution of tasks. However, we aren't at the point where machines run themselves (I for one welcome our new robot overlords). Administrative controls are how you manage all this technology and associated controls in accordance with your stated security goals. We've talked about Courtney's laws before. Now here's one more.

■ **Courtney's third law states** There are no technical solutions to management problems, but there are management solutions to technical problems.[1]

There are many ways to interpret this (including having management fire all the tech staff and outsource them!) but let's look at how we use documented processes to manage technology. This definitely includes how we manage technical controls, but administrative controls are also very powerful in managing normal IT operations.

Control Maturity

As a consultant, I listened to many clients tell me they had good processes, but they just didn't ever write them down. They were sure everyone did the right things, but no one documented anything. When we began to check on what was actually going on, we discovered that there was a lot of divergence among what each person thought he was supposed to be doing. Worse, we often encountered complicated but critical tasks performed by a single person that were completely mysterious to upper management. When that person went on vacation or got ill, those tasks stopped. For some organizations, things were done differently, based on the time of the day and the amount of time that people had available. This may all be fine for some business and technical processes, but it's precarious for security controls that you depend on. It's also a deficiency finding during an audit.

---

[1]http://zvon.org/comp/r/ref-Security_Glossary.html#Terms~Courtney%27s_laws.

Many organizations have a verbal work culture. They prefer face-to-face meetings and conference calls to e-mail and chat. They value getting together and hashing things out to investigate and decide on critical matters. There's nothing wrong with this, but there should be some written processes for some things. For one, conveying information verbally is excellent for establishing a personal and deep connection with people. It's also time-consuming and inconsistent. Some verbal processes simply do not scale. Once you get beyond a dozen people in a single discussion, meetings can last for hours. Many organizations now are globally dispersed, so setting up a conference call for status check-ins can get tricky when you have more than three time zones. Lastly, verbal processes do not leave behind permanent records that can be reviewed and analyzed later. If you missed any of these big meetings and no one took minutes (converted verbal to written), then you are short out of luck. Also, no records means no metrics.

Capability Maturity Model

One of the ways that organizational processes are assessed is with the Capability Maturity Model (CMM). The CMM was developed to evaluate and rate military contractors on how well they might perform on software projects. The CMM helps determine things like how repeatable a process is, whether a process can be taken over by another individual, and how a process can be measured. To do this, the five-step scale shown in Figure 13-1 was developed.

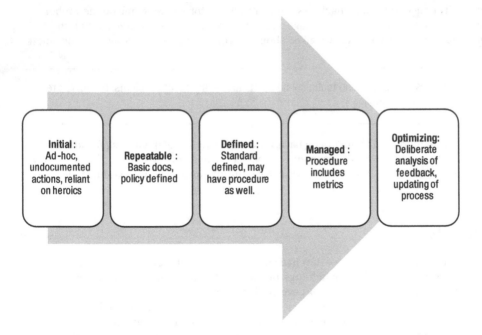

Figure 13-1. *Capability Maturity Model*

The CMM is so handy and powerful that some auditors (including myself) have used it for rapid assessment of an organization's security processes. Consider the security of an organization with no published security policy—where users are added and removed haphazardly. Patching takes place when someone *gets around to it* rather than on a schedule. Think about how hard it would be improve processes if there is no consensus on how they are performed. It may sound like I'm beating a dead equine here, but one of the biggest challenges I've had in moving organizations to a secure and audited state was convincing them to document their processes (and follow those documents).

The Power of Good Admin Controls

Some people say that using documented processes and following checklists slows them down and they get less work done. In reality, having defined methods for performing complex tasks build accuracy and speed. There are less errors (and less redoing) and better understanding of the process. With documented processes, work can be handed off to newcomers with less-handholding and training. Finally, documented processes are easier to automate because the algorithm has already been laid out.

Keep Them Updated

To be useful, administrative processes need to be reliable or they are worse than useless, they are misleading. An unsuspecting admin using an outdated process document could easily cause major system failures or create new security vulnerabilities. Documents need to be kept current to match the relevant tasks and environments. You should not carve administrative processes in stone; they should be fluid and always be checked and updated as needed. The first step in making sure this happens is assigning ownership to a process. The owner does not need be the one updating the process either, only to ensure that an update is performed. For example, ownership of the move/add/change user process could be given to manager of the helpdesk. She could then assign the updating of the procedure as needed. Managers need to ensure that their staff is given the responsibility and the time to update documents. An old management trick is to assign updating the process to a new hire that is paired with a veteran to assist them. As the newcomer learns the process, they also can work to update the document. Many technical document management systems can be set up to e-mail reminders to the owner periodically to review and update procedures.

Some organizations use internal wiki sites to store all their administrative policies. Since wikis are designed to support living, evolving documentation for a large number of people, they work well for this kind of thing. All changes are visible as well as who performed them and when. Policies can be set up to hotlink standards and procedures. Explanatory documents and external sites can also be linked as needed.

Differences in Documents

You read about the different kinds of administrative controls back in Chapter 11, on policy, so let's dive deeper. There is a top security policy document for the organization, which defines the high-level goals. In Figure 13-2, you can see how you can have more policies for specific control objectives with specific audiences in mind.

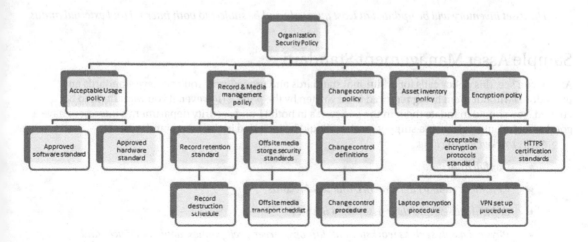

Figure 13-2. Example of policy relationships

This is not *the perfect list*. As things mature and go obsolete, you need to add and drop policies around different control objectives. In addition, you may choose to break down these control objectives into different groups or combine them in other ways. The coverage and upkeep is what is important, not the individual documents.

From these policies, you can build up the standards to describe how technology should be used to support the policy. The standard can lay out minimum baselines for settings, acceptable technologies, and responsibility matrices.

Below the standards are the procedures, which are the *run books* to tell people step-by-step how to perform tasks. Procedures can be detailed with screenshots and specific commands or they can be checklists for implementation. Many organizations develop standardized templates for procedures, with version numbers, to help people keep things straight. There are plenty of examples of policies, standards, and procedures for the specific control objectives. Let's jump right into some of those critical IT operational policies the support security right now.

Critical Admin Control: Asset Management

You may remember how important inventory is from the chapters on risk analysis (Chapters 3, 4, and 5). You'll want a policy covering this and making sure responsibility is assigned to get it done. Next is a sample policy describing what should be included.

Sample Asset Management Policy

ORGANIZATION will identify, track, and record all IT and IT-related assets. The IT Operations Department will be responsible for maintaining standards and procedures related to IT assets. These standards will include:

- *IT assets and IT-related tracked*

- *Asset details tracked*

- *Baseline workstation and server configuration standards*

- *Approved software applications*

- *Asset inventory procedure*

The asset inventory will be updated at least quarterly and be subject to both internal and external audits.

Sample Asset Management Standard

As you can see, this policy calls for additional standards and procedures. You can have standards and procedures without them being required to be written by the policy. However, if you want them to be created, you should mandate them in the policy. It's in both IT and security department's interest to have a good asset inventory. Here is a snippet of what should be included in the asset standards.

Assets tracked will include:

- *Confidential data*

- *Contracts, support agreements, and legal records*

- *Software assets and their associated licenses*

- *Physical assets such as workstations, laptops, servers, cell phones, network devices and security equipment*

- *Portable digital media such as floppy disks, tapes, external drives, Bernoulli boxes, and USB sticks*

- *Local and offsite virtual guest imaged, saved machine images, and the virtualization servers*

- *Internal and third-party tokens, cryptographic keys, certificates, and passwords for accessing offsite data resources*

Asset details tracked:

- *Hardware: Brand, make/model, MAC address, Serial #, Location, Owner*

- *Tokens & Certificates: Code key, Affiliation, Owner, Expiration date*

This policy will be reviewed on an annual basis and may change regulations or requirements.

Critical Admin Control: Change Control

When introduced into environments for the first time, some organizations see Change control as a major pain in the posterior. I've heard the complaints: "Oh, the paper work! And getting approval before IT does anything? Do you realize how much that will slow things down? This is just like auditors, making us jump through hoops just to do our job!" In fact, there is proven business value in change control.

Change control is a foundational control for SSAE 16 SOC 1 but is also a requirement in PCI DSS and ISO 27001. Change control is a powerful control for ensuring that systems are maintained in a known, tested state. Since updates, patches, and new configurations are performed in standard, predictable ways, IT operations are efficient and stable. The IT Process Institute found that 80% of unplanned outages were because of poorly planned changes.[2]

Change control means there is a documented process that governs all modifications to scoped systems. Access to those systems is minimized and monitored. Tools should record all changes for later review by system owners and auditors. In general, change control forces IT to pay attention to what they're doing. Figure 13-3 describes a typical flow for change control.

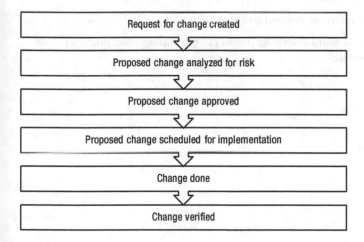

Figure 13-3. *Change Control Process flow*

[2]http://www.itpi.org/the-visible-ops-handbook-review.html.

Sample Change Control Policy

The purpose of the Change Control Policy is to ensure that our organization's IT department can deliver quality updates to our internal customers. Good change control accommodates change through proven processes, ensuring clear requirements and reliable results. Change control is done to reduce the risk of unauthorized changes, unplanned outages, failed changes, emergency changes, and operational delays. Policy requirements:

- *Requests for changes to critical IT systems will be coordinated in a timely, transparent, and efficient manner*

- *There is a Change Control Board comprised of representatives from IT support, IT applications, IT operations, and the departments being served*

- *Changes can be proposed to the change control board by anyone within the organization through the IT support help desk*

- *Change requests must include reason, systems affected, back out plan, location of code for change*

- *Whenever possible, proposed changes will be tested and the test results submitted along with the change request*

- *Changes to Production Hosted systems must be approved by the Change Control Board*

- *The Change Control Board will meet weekly, or sooner as needed, to review and approve proposed changes*

- *Proposed changes are assessed for potential impact to eliminate unnecessary or disruptive changes are minimized*

- *Changes will be carried out solely by the IT operations team - Changes must be verified to be complete and correct by the change requester*

- *Unauthorized changes will be considered a security policy violation and individuals will be held accountable for violations*

- *These Change processes will be subject to internal and external audits.*

The Operations group will maintain a standard describing proper change management processes. This standard will include the following components:

- *Roles and responsibilities*

- *Requests*

- *Change planning and testing*

- *Evaluation: approval/rejection*

- *Maintenance windows*

- *Verification*

- *Rollback*

- *Documentation*

- *Emergency changes*

This policy will be reviewed on an annual basis and may change regulations or requirements.

Change Control Standards

There should be standards around change control that support the policy by defining key items within change control. These standards should include:

- What constitutes a change?
  - Application changes?
  - Hardware changes?
  - Operating system changes?
  - Network changes?
  - Facility changes?
- How are changes classified?
  - How is risk of change effects determined?
    - Experience with change?
    - Impact to neighboring systems?
    - Scope of change?
    - Time to complete change?
    - Systems involved in change?
    - Quality Assurance review of change?
  - What are emergency changes and how can the normal process be bypassed for an outage but documented and explained
  - What are low-risk pre-authorized changes that do not need approval?
- What is an acceptable back out plan?
- What are the acceptable change windows?

Change Control Tracking

Part of the change control process is detecting if anyone bypassed it. There should be additional controls in place supporting the change control process that monitor for unauthorized changes. A number of technical controls can be used to keep track of changes, including file integrity monitoring or cloud configuration logging.

Because of the utility of change control, it's a good idea to track metrics around the process to demonstrate how effective the system is for improving IT and security operations. Here are some useful metrics to consider:

- The number of changes that meet requirements (successful change)
- System uptime
- The number of unauthorized changes
- The number of emergency changes
- The average time to perform change

- Outages caused by changes

- The accuracy of change time estimates

Critical Admin Control: Application Security

Application security is big and important—so much so that entire books and security certifications exist on the topic. Application security is critical, and I don't want to omit it, but I don't have the space to do it justice either. So you should just be aware that I'm skimming the surface of this major area of security.

Application security refers to writing and acquiring software applications that meet a security standard. It involves security in designing the software, how the software is coded, how the code is protected, and how secure the code is in different risk environments. Next is a sample high-level security policy on application security that should give you an idea of the expectations. The standards and procedures related to application security can get deep, but are worth looking into if you do internal development of applications that process or store confidential data.

Sample Application Security Policy

The ORGANIZATION will maintain and follow secure application development and maintenance processes to minimize unauthorized access, modification, or downtime to ORGANIZATION applications.

To support this objective:

- *The Security Department and the Software Development department will develop, publish and use secure coding standards based on industry best secure development practices*

- *Software Developers will have adequate secure application education & training*

- *Software Developers will use a Threat model and will be educated on common attacks, such as the Open Web Application Security Project (OWASP) Top Ten Vulnerabilities, to inform their threat model.*

- *There will be adequate separation of privileges between development, QA, and production environments.*

- *Development and Test data will not contain confidential information or personally identifiable information.*

- *Source code will be protected from exposure, tampering, and loss.*

- *As part of software release, the Software Developers will ensure that test data and accounts are not present.*

- *On an ongoing basis, the Security department will facilitate third-party security tests of in-house developed applications*

- *Software Vulnerabilities will be tracked, risk rated, and remediated.*

- *The Security department will conduct periodic reviews to test compliance against this policy.*

This policy will be reviewed on an annual basis and may change regulations or requirements.

Application Security Standards

Many application standards can flow from the preceding sample policy. One that comes to mind is a standard around vulnerability assessment, which might work well as a RACI diagram, as follows.

Function	Responsible	Accountable	Consulted	Informed
Vulnerability assessment	Security	Development	QA	App owner
Vulnerability scoring	Security	Development	QA	App owner
Remediation	Development	App owner	QA	Security
Verification of remediation	Security	Development	QA	App owner

A second important standard would be the guideline for developers to follow, which could look like the following sample.

Sample Secure Software Design Standards

- *Sessions and authentication data will be protected from impersonation, unauthorized modification, and session hijacking*

- *Web applications will facilitate client-side security through the use of browser directives*

- *User error screens will not reveal confidential or detailed system configuration information*

- *Application authentication mechanisms will be robust and resist brute-force guessing attacks*

- *Applications will validate input and output data*

- *Administrative or configuration data will not be visible to unauthorized users*

Software Acquisition

Just as important as developing software that is secure to a tolerable level of risk, is acquiring software that meets that standard. The acceptable usage policy guides users in making sure they only use approved, known safe software. Likewise, the IT department should work with the security team when on-boarding major software applications, especially if those applications interact with scoped systems or data.

To make this job easier, there should be a software acquisition policy that requires the security department to analyze and approve new IT systems. There can also be an accompanying standard that provides criteria for measuring the security and acceptability of new applications. This standard could include things such as the following:

- Applications must support existing organizational control objectives and policies. For example, authentication systems much support organizational password standards, logging systems must support organizational logging standard

- Software must be third-party tested for security vulnerabilities with no significant vulnerabilities present

- Internet-facing web application systems must be tested against the current OWASP top ten vulnerabilities with no significant vulnerabilities present

161

- Software should be capable of producing human-readable configuration information for audit and configuration review

- Manufacturer must disclose all maintenance and administrative access modes including any "developer backdoors" or automated callbacks outside of the organization

- Applications performing security functions must have up-to-date product assurance certification of advertised functionality from well-known independent evaluator such as Underwriter Labs (UL), Federal Information Processing Standards (FIPS), ICSA CyberTrust, or National Information Assurance Partnership (NIAP)/Common Criteria.

Critical Manual Control: Record and Media Management

Your organization's records are a critical asset, so you should have policies and procedures in place to protect them. Some policies distinguish between paper and electronic records, while others combine into a single policy.

Critical records almost certainly include e-mail and internal messaging systems, as these are the kinds of records that are relevant in litigations and criminal investigations. When it comes to lawsuits, it's always better to be able to produce the relevant, and only the relevant, records when requested by the court. Organizations that are unable to provide records in lawsuits are often viewed by judges with suspicion. Organizations can risk legal penalties and negative inferences in the case for not being able to find critical records. This means that the security and IT departments should work with legal counsel to develop a realistic record retention schedule. Business norm in the United States is a retention period of seven years. The IT department should make sure that they have adequate capacity and technology to be able to store and find records.

Speaking of lawsuits, quite a few breach negligence cases stem with an organization losing or improperly disposing of things like laptops and backup tapes. Media, such as drives and tapes that contain confidential information needs to be properly tracked, secured, and when the time comes, thoroughly destroyed.

Sample Record and Media Management Policy

ORGANIZATION recognizes that record management is important. To meet that goal, ORGANIZATION will have standards and procedures in place to inhibit the intentional or negligent withholding, alteration, or destruction of internal records. Records and media containing confidential and personal private information will be protected against unauthorized exposure. To meet these goals, the ORGANIZATION will do the following:

- *Critical records will be identified and documented in a standard and communicated to all relevant persons within the organization*

- *Location and responsibility for records and media will be tracked*

- *Record retention standards that are feasible and appropriate to the organization will be defined and approved by legal*

- *Records will be protected from physical and electronic threats with controls*

- *Records will be stored in a manner that they can be retrieved quickly when requested. A procedure for record retrieval will be written and updated.*

- *Data archival and destruction timelines will be tracked and records scheduled for destruction when due.*

- *Media and records will be securely erased or destroyed in such a manner as to make inadvertent recovery impossible and intentional recovery impractical. Standards will be developed to describe the secure erasure and destruction processes.*

- *Procedures will be written for records and media being transported off premises*

This policy will be reviewed on an annual basis and may change regulations or requirements.

FURTHER READING

- **Checklist Manifesto: Using documented procedures**
  http://atulgawande.com/book/the-checklist-manifesto/

- **Visible Ops for Security: Change control and more**
  http://www.itpi.org/visible-ops-security-review.html

- **Build Security In Maturity Model: Application security**
  https://www.bsimm.com

- **American Bar Association: Records management & documentation**
  http://www.americanbar.org/newsletter/publications/law_trends_news_
  practice_area_e_newsletter_home/documentspoilation.html

CHAPTER 14

■ ■ ■

Vulnerability Management

Another flaw in the human character is that everyone wants to build and nobody wants to do maintenance.

—Kurt Vonnegut, *Hocus Pocus*

Most of the time, you shouldn't work too hard at being exceptional. You're better off first making sure that you avoid doing anything too stupid. If you are hacked because of some unpatched hole that's been sitting around for months, you will look stupid. Where did that hole come from? We know that no matter how secure we make our systems, new vulnerabilities will be found. Your challenge is to find and fix the holes before the attackers exploit them. The process you use is called vulnerability management. It is a process that combines both technical and administrative controls, calling upon many different aspects of security and coordinating work between different departments.

Vulnerability management is featured prominently in PCI DSS requirements, although you find it in most other audit requirements as well. Vulnerability management can be a real grind, but it's an important and powerful process. Enough to warrant a whole chapter devoted to it.

The activities associated with vulnerability management can be broken down into four general categories: hardening, scanning, prioritizing, and patching, as shown in Figure 14-1.

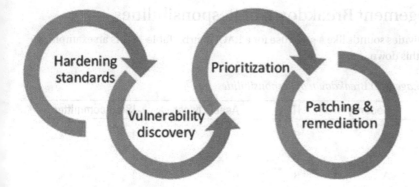

Figure 14-1. Vulnerability management activities

In some audit and control regimes, these are wholly defined separate controls, but for this chapter, we are combining them into a single practice.

Organizing Vulnerability Management

Let's begin with the policy to define what we want vulnerability management to be within the organization.

Sample Vulnerability Management Policy

To reduce exploitable security vulnerabilities in systems for ORGANIZATION in a timely manner, there will be:

- *Hardening standards for all asset classes as a requirement before they go live*

- *Monitoring of vendor vulnerability notifications for critical applications*

- *Monthly internal vulnerability scanning of local area networks of critical systems*

- *Quarterly external vulnerability scanning of entire organization's Internet perimeter*

- *Annual penetration testing of entire organization's Internet perimeter*

- *Application security testing for critical custom applications for every major release*

- *Vulnerability scoring and prioritization of all discovered vulnerabilities*

- *Patching and remediation of all high and medium scored vulnerabilities on critical assets within 30 days of discovery*

Responsibility for these activities will be assigned and tracked by the ISMS committee. Quarterly vulnerability reports and vulnerability management schedules will be reviewed by the ISMS committee to monitor the ongoing state of risk within the organization.

Systems covered by this policy must be tested to meet these standards before being released onto operation. This includes physical and virtual machines, both locally and offsite in public hosting or cloud providers.

This policy will be reviewed on an annual basis and may change regulations or requirements.

Vulnerability Management Breakdown of Responsibilities

Assigning all of these work activities sounds like a good use for a RACI matrix. Table 14-1 is an example of how you might want to break this down.

Table 14-1. *Vulnerability Management Breakdown of Responsibilities*

Activity	Security	IT	Asset Owner	ISMS committee
Hardening standards	A	R	C	I
Vulnerability notification	A	R	C	I
Internal scanning	A	R	C	I
External scanning	R,A	C	C	I
Penetration testing	R, A	C	C	I
Application security testing	R, A	C	C	I
Scoring and prioritization	R, A	C	C	I
Patching and remediation	A	R	C	I

Hardening Standards

Before you begin managing vulnerabilities, you need to know what is considered *secure* for your organization. Like everything else, it is informed by risk and business needs and described with administrative controls. These standards are the *you must be this tall to ride* checkpoint for any device or service going live in your organization. Next is an example of a base standard for hardening. You'll see that it calls out for more standards beneath it to describe the specifics. These standards form the bedrock for scanning baselines, risk analyses, implementation work, and technology acquisition decisions. This is a good example of the clarity and utility that strong administrative controls can bring.

Sample Hardening and Vulnerability Management Standard

The IT department and the Security department will maintain this approved standard for performing vulnerability management. This standard will address identifying, remediating, and documenting technical vulnerabilities for the following types of assets:

- *Security devices*

- *Internet-facing servers and network devices*

- *Corporate servers and network devices*

- *Accounting systems and network devices*

- *Desktop computers and laptops*

- *Virtual or public-cloud servers and services*

The IT department will be responsible for maintaining a configuration management and device-hardening standard for ORGANIZATION servers. This hardening standard will include descriptions of

- *Baseline firmware configuration*

- *Baseline operating system configuration*

- *Baseline software packages installed*

- *Baseline software packages configuration*

- *Hypervisor configuration*

- *Public cloud access, host, and network configurations*

- *Approved resource monitoring and management tools*

- *Administrative access requirements*

- *Approved network services*

- *Documentation requirements*

These standards will be updated no less frequently than annually. The IT department and the security department will also update these standards based on new technology, organizational changes, and risk changes.

This policy will be reviewed on an annual basis and may change regulations or requirements.

How to Fill in the Hardening Standards?

Some IT departments look to the security team to lead in defining the standards. While it is important that they have buy-in to what is in the standard, it is reasonable to give them a starting place. Many software, hardware, and Internet service manufacturers include secure configuration guides with their products. In general, you should be hesitant in working with technology vendors who do not offer such guidelines. Some of your compliance requirements may specify specific standards to meet for scoped devices. In addition, there are several independent sources of hardening standards. Here is a short list of some to consider:

- **Center for Internet Security (CIS) Host Benchmarks**
  https://benchmarks.cisecurity.org/downloads/multiform/

- **National Security Agency (NSA) Secure Configuration Guides**
  https://www.nsa.gov/ia/mitigation_guidance/security_
  configuration_guides/operating_systems.shtml

- **National Checklist Program Repository**
  https://web.nvd.nist.gov/view/ncp/repository?authority=
  Center+for+Internet+Security+%28CIS%29&startIndex=0

- **Department of Defense Information Assurance Support Environment Security Requirement Guides**
  http://iase.disa.mil/stigs/srgs/Pages/index.aspx

- **Microsoft Server Hardening**
  https://technet.microsoft.com/en-us/library/cc526440.aspx

- **Apple Security Guide**
  https://www.apple.com/support/security/guides/

- **Amazon Web Services Security Best Practices**
  https://aws.amazon.com/whitepapers/aws-security-best-practices/

- **Microsoft Azure Security Practices**
  https://azure.microsoft.com/en-us/documentation/articles/best-
  practices-network-security/

You will find literally hundreds of pages of ideas here. Over time, you will probably add items to your lists as new risks and compliance issues are uncovered. Stepping away from the specifics, here are some general things you should consider including in your hardening standard:

- Remove or rename default pre-installed accounts

- Change default passwords and shared secrets

- Protect and log administrative interfaces

- Prevent unknown code from running

- Disable unnecessary services

- Disable poorly encrypted services

- Disable poorly authenticated services

Lastly, if you have systems that don't require Internet connections, then don't connect them to the Internet. It seems the default expectation for every device and application is that it be granted full Internet connectivity. If it isn't necessary for the service the device is providing, disable Internet access. You should question and reconsider any vendor that argues with you on this point, especially when it comes to mandatory Internet-connected maintenance links back to the vendor's network. Some devices may not even allow you to disable their Internet connectivity. For these systems, you can look into either giving them a fake or non-existent default gateway. That'll usually prevent them from connecting to the Internet. If systems are disconnected from the Internet, there should still be mechanisms in place to have them patched in a timely manner. This can be as simple as temporarily connecting them for patching or using portable media to deliver updates.

Vulnerability Discovery

Now that you have standards, how do you know they're being met? The prudent answer is you should assume they aren't and check for yourself regularly. This means a schedule and assigned responsibility to do the checking. The standards and procedures for this can include the following:

- Vulnerability discovery frequency scans

- Type of discovery scan

- Who is authorized and is responsible to scan

- Who receives the results

- How results are protected (as they contain confidential information about your organization's weaknesses)

As you can see, vulnerability management can be a grind. It is necessary to do it this way to be thorough and prevent a potential surprise attack against systems you assumed were impregnable.

Vulnerability Notification

There are many technical tools that you can use for vulnerability discovery, but they're not required. You could do vulnerability discovery manually with an accurate, detailed inventory and an updated list of published vulnerabilities. However, with the average of several of machines to every employee, this gets hard to manage very quickly. It still is a prudent to subscribe to e-mail notification or Really Simple Syndication (RSS) lists of vulnerabilities from your major vendors. Responsibility for reading these notifications and responding to them needs to be assigned as well. For example, a security analyst could be on a "Microsoft Patch Tuesday" e-mail notification list and be responsible for alerting IT about upcoming urgent problems. In addition to software manufacturers, there are many independent sources of vulnerability notifications. If you are member of an ISAC or a security organization, you can get alerts on industry vulnerabilities there. Here are some other good resources:

- **National Vulnerability Database**
  https://nvd.nist.gov

- **US-CERT**
  https://www.us-cert.gov/ncas/alerts

Discovery Scanning

As discussed back in the chapter that introduced assume breach, one of the key problems in information security is knowing what you have and where it is. How can you have a complete picture of your vulnerabilities are if you can't identify all of your assets? In addition, how do you know if your published standards are being followed? Therefore, the primary step in vulnerability management is doing discovery scanning. This involves using technical utilities to sweep your systems to identify computers, appliances, services, software, and data.

One of the most basic of these tools is network port scanner software, which runs on one or more hosts and sweeps the network looking for services running. Network scanners can also do fingerprint-based pattern matching to identify known software packages. This is done with a series of probes to a list of addresses and automated analysis of the responses.

Scanning can be done internally, on your private local area networks, and externally on the Internet perimeter. External network scanning needs to be done from an Internet host outside of your organization's perimeter. External scanning can give you a "hacker's eye view" of how your Internet-services appear to attackers. You may be surprised as to what is visible and what is not visible from this perspective, which makes this kind of scanning always worth doing.

One of the most popular port scanners is Nmap, an open-source network scanner that's been around for almost two decades. Nmap runs on wide variety of operating systems and is available at `https://nmap.org/`. This is how you can use Nmap to get an inventory and footprint of a network:

```
$ sudo nmap 192.168.0.1-16

Starting Nmap 6.01 ( http://nmap.org ) at 2016-03-13 14:07 PDT
Nmap scan report for 192.168.0.1
Host is up (0.0063s latency).
PORT STATE SERVICE
80/tcp open http
1900/tcp open upnp

Nmap scan report for 192.168.0.10
Host is up (0.0025s latency).
PORT STATE SERVICE
22/tcp open ssh

Nmap scan report for 192.168.0.14
Host is up (0.00011s latency).
PORT STATE SERVICE
3689/tcp open rendezvous
```

There are also many other free and commercial tools out there that can do automated asset and configuration discovery. There are some tools directly available from vendors that can do configuration scanning and analysis of their products and services. For example, many network device manufacturers have device configuration scanners and many large cloud-hosting services provide inventory tools.

The key is to do regular discovery scanning so you have an as accurate and freshest picture as you can. This entails having a recorded inventory and standard to compare the scans against. Changes in your vulnerability and inventory are worth tracking as well. If a system has a history of vulnerabilities, perhaps a new design is needed instead of frequent patching. Scanning frequency is important as well. I have seen some organizations do daily scanning and analysis of their rapidly changing environment. You have to be careful, though, as some network scanners can create a significant load on the network. Having an accurate scope of the scanning can help reduce noise and time in a scan as well. You should only scan the things that you need to scan, instead of trying to saturate the network with probes. The following are things to look out for when discovery scanning:

- Unmanaged hosts—such as equipment that's fallen off IT management's radar—that could be missing patches and critical controls, such as antivirus.

- Out-of-office laptops and mobile devices that occasionally return from the field full of vulnerabilities and malware.

- Non-standard equipment—such as Wi-Fi hotspots—that people have sneaked in from home and plugged into the corporate network.

- Virtualized guests that can suddenly appear on your network or within your cloud environment. With virtualization, it's easy to spin up boxes and forget about them.

- New devices that you didn't know were network aware until someone plugged them in, like the proverbial Internet refrigerator.

- Spying devices planted on your network by the bad people. You definitely want to try to find these.

Vulnerability Scanning

The next step after discovery scanning is to do vulnerability scanning. Many discovery scanners have vulnerability scanning functions as well. Like network port scanners, vulnerability scanners can actively send network probes at a server and attempt to decipher the responses. The scanner functions in two ways. One way is to determine the exact version of software being run and then match that software to published vulnerability lists. The second way is to do a harmless attempt at a hacking attack and see if it succeeded. This method is slightly dangerous but far more effective in determining if there is a potential problem. At http://sectools.org/tag/vuln-scanners/, you can see a large, but not necessarily complete, list of vulnerability scanners. There are also vulnerability scanners that specialize in just scanning common types of services, such as database scanners or web scanners. This is how the free, open source, web scanner Nikto (https://cirt.net/Nikto2) looks in action:

```
$nikto-2.1.5>perl nikto.pl -host 192.168.0.5
- Nikto v2.1.5
---------------------------------------------------------------------------
+ Target IP:          192.168.0.5
+ Target Hostname:    scandog.chaloobi
+ Target Port:        80
+ Start Time:         2016-08-15 15:40:17 (GMT-7)
---------------------------------------------------------------------------
+ Server: Apache/2.2.29 (Unix)
+ Server leaks inodes via ETags, header found with file /, inode: 78545071, size: 633,
mtime: 0x526692b64c840
+ The anti-clickjacking X-Frame-Options header is not present.
+ Allowed HTTP Methods: POST, OPTIONS, GET, HEAD, TRACE
+ OSVDB-877: HTTP TRACE method is active, suggesting the host is vulnerable to XST
+ 6545 items checked: 992 error(s) and 4 item(s) reported on remote host
+ End Time:           2016-08-15 15:41:26 (GMT-7) (69 seconds)
---------------------------------------------------------------------------
+ 1 host(s) tested
```

Some vulnerability scanners can work passively, by examining captured network traffic, otherwise known as sniffed traffic. The scanner looks at the network requests and responses and tries determining what software versions are in use. Another passive type of vulnerability scanner is an agent-based one, which is a small piece of software running on every host on the network. This type of scanner can be very accurate since it has direct access to the local software and configuration, at the expense of having something running on every box in your organization. Some passive agents also watch the local network traffic to help identify unagented machines that haven't been inventoried yet.

Vulnerability scanning of your network is a requirement of many audit regimes. PCI DSS requires at least quarterly vulnerability scans both internally and externally. In general, scanning frequency should be based on how frequently your environment changes and how often new vulnerabilities in popular software are discovered. Quarterly is just an industry average. Some organizations do monthly, weekly, or even daily scanning.

Some organizations choose to have outside security vendors do their vulnerability scanning, especially the external scanning. This is useful because of the expense and expertise required to do a thorough and accurate vulnerability scan. Some of the best commercial vulnerability scanners are not cheap and need a trained operator to interpret the results. The PCI DSS and many regulatory regimes require that a qualified vulnerability assessor perform the external vulnerability scans. This is not just because of the expertise needed but it also provides an independent third-party opinion of the vulnerabilities found.

Penetration Testing

Going beyond vulnerability scanning is penetration testing. Like the vulnerability scanner that can try a harmless version of a hacking attack to test for a vulnerability, penetration testing takes this a step further. A penetration test is an active attempt to break into your network. Some people conflate vulnerability scanning and penetration testing, but they are not the same thing. For one thing, penetration tests are usually an order of magnitude more expensive than a vulnerability scan. Penetration tests can also include techniques not normally found in a vulnerability test, including password-guessing attacks, social engineering phishing tests, wireless scanning, and even physical break-in attempts. It's one thing to point a software-scanning tool at your web server and another to have a security tester try to burgle your premises.

Good penetration testers combine techniques, such as rooting through your trash (dumpster diving) to determine potential targets, applying physical penetration to plant network bugging devices, and using custom-built hacking tools. A fun example of how this works is the short-lived TV series *Tiger Team*, which is available online just a search engine query away.

An annual penetration test by a qualified third-party firm is a PCI DSS requirement. These are different from quarterly penetration test, although often the same assessor can perform both. Regarding qualification, the PCI DSS requires organizations to use vendors certified in PCI DSS scanning. These vendors are called *approved scanning vendors* (ASV) and are listed on the PCI DSS site at https://www.pcisecuritystandards.org/assessors_and_solutions/approved_scanning_vendors.

Dynamic Application Testing

Another form of security testing more specific to in-house developed software is application security testing. There are many types of application security testing. Some firms specialize in testing specific types of platforms, such as web applications or mobile apps. Another way to do vulnerability testing is to offer *bug bounties* and to crowdsource the testing of your software. Bug bounties involve offering prizes (usually cash) to whoever submits a valid vulnerability (and keeps it quiet). Some businesses specialize in organizing and running your bug bounty program for you.

If you do sell or provide software services for an in-house developed application, you should define and publish a process describing how you will receive and deal with vulnerabilities discovered outside of your organization. This is a major topic that is more in-line to secure application development, but it is worth mentioning that it is something you should investigate. A good starting point on building this process is at https://blog.bugcrowd.com/security-vulnerability-submission/.

Prioritization and Risk Scoring

Now that you've been doing all this vulnerability scanning, you need to have a process in place to deal with this influx of data. If you've never done vulnerability scanning before, you'll quickly discover the tsunamis of data a single scan produces. Furthermore, most scanning tools and vendors will include a priority score along with their results. Usually these are based on the Common Vulnerability Scoring Standard (CVSS) that rates vulnerabilities from the lowest 1 to the highest 10. The CVSS uses factors like exploitability, complexity, and necessary authentication to service the scope. Its calculation method is explained more at https://www.first.org/cvss.

Problems arise having a third party use CVSS because often they don't understand your environment and the potential interactions vulnerabilities can cause. I have seen harmless vulnerabilities scored as 10, and have had penetration testers break in using two vulnerabilities scored as a 3. Furthermore, research has shown that CVSS is not a good reflection of real world likelihood and impact of attack.

The conclusion to draw from this is that regardless of what the scanner or vendor reports, you need to do your own analysis and prioritization of the vulnerabilities discovered. Obviously, anything not meeting your published standards needs to be addressed. For PCI DSS covered entities, you are also required to patch any vulnerability scored higher than a CVSS level 4. Even then, you may still have a long list of items to fix. What should come first?

Higher Priority

The first things you should look at are the vulnerabilities that are easily exploitable over the Internet. If there is an existing hacking tool that a script kiddie can just push a button and execute from a Wi-Fi café that takes down your site, then you need to fix it immediately. Many scanning tools and third-party assessors will provide this type of exploitability information in their vulnerability report. If they don't, reconsider your scanning vendor. You can also check some known lists, like the Exploit database at https://www.exploit-db.com/. You'll find that these same vulnerabilities also fall into the category of *things you need to fix so you don't look stupid* and/or negligent. If the whole Internet is in a panic about the new Ahab Hole in BigWhale Servers, then it's prudent to get on that quickly.

On the inside network, the highest priority items are going to be the common services that touch the outside world in some way. Right now, this translates into Internet browsers and their associated scripting languages. A medium-rated vulnerability that is running on 95% of your user's browsers that surf the Internet all day long is a bigger priority than a highly rated vulnerability on a seldom-used service that never talks outside the local network.

Lastly, you should use organizational factors like the impact calculations you've done during your risk analysis to prioritize vulnerability remediation work. This is where what you've determined may diverge from what an outside-scored vulnerability tells you. You know which things need to be available 24/7 and may hold confidential data, as well as which things you don't care as much if they are breached. An outside party's scoring vulnerabilities may not. The CVSS calculation actually has variables for this including collateral damage, prevalence of vulnerability and the impacts. You can use these to refine your scores. The calculator at https://www.first.org/cvss/calculator/3.0 is helpful for doing this.

Lower Priority

Things that are deep in your network, protected by multiple layers of controls with little or no connection to the outside world can probably be prioritized lower. For example, consider a web server, an application server, and a database server, each separated by a proxy firewall. The web server touches the Internet, so it would have high priority. You could deprioritize a firewalled database with no direct outside access.

You should also be aware that low priority vulnerabilities often do not remain low priority forever. The cycle of innovation in the hacking world moves quickly. A vulnerability could be scored low because it requires a complicated manual attack and the service only runs on local area networks. The following week, a new worm could be released that includes an automated exploit of that vulnerability and the worm is designed to run on inside networks.

More Food for Thought

Beyond re-scoring and prioritizing vulnerabilities, the security team should also be doing analysis on the nature of the problems discovered. What caused these vulnerabilities to appear? Is there a breakdown in automatic patching routines? Are systems not being built according hardening standards? Should new controls or processes be put in place?

Patching

With the deluge of vulnerabilities and the rapid proliferation of attack tools, patching should not be a painful, one-off exercise for any organization. Regular patching of every system should be a procedure and performed regularly. This includes the capability to patch the fragile, can't-ever-go-down systems that people rely on. It's a safe bet that a new high-priority vulnerability will be found and the IT department will have to scramble to patch. Work out and test the plan now before you have to do it under fire.

A deadline for patching based on priority should be documented and communicated. A common standard is thirty days maximum for high priority vulnerabilities, although you might want to be able to go faster. When something scary is running around, you may have a window of days if not hours to get things locked down.

Having spent a large portion of my career in and around IT operations, I appreciate just how much work is involved in patching. It definitely is the hardest part of the grind of vulnerability management. This is where having clear prioritized vulnerabilities and a well-functioning change control system in place can help your organization patch fast.

Some vulnerabilities can be a real beast to fix and you may find that they can't be fixed within your defined schedule. This is where you need to document your best efforts and work them like small projects. You never want to throw your hands up and just forget patching because *we're replacing that system next year anyway*. This is how you end up looking like a monkey when your organization is hacked. If nothing else, write up a plan, have the ISMS committee buy off on the risk acceptance, and set deadlines to have the vulnerability remediated.

Scan Again

An often-overlooked aspect of patching is *patch verification*. An essential part of the remediation process is to rerun the vulnerability tests to ensure that the patch actually closed the hole. Only then can a vulnerability be considered closed.

FURTHER READING

- **Pen-test standard**
  http://www.pentest-standard.org/index.php/Main_Page

- **NIST Special Publication 800-40 Rev. 3, Guide to Enterprise Patch Management Technologies**
  http://nvlpubs.nist.gov/nistpubs/SpecialPublications/NIST.SP.800-40r3.pdf

---

CHAPTER 15

■ ■ ■

People Controls

Men and women range themselves into three classes or orders of intelligence; you can tell the lowest class by their habit of always talking about persons; the next by the fact that their habit is always to converse about things; the highest by their preference for the discussion of ideas.

—Henry Thomas Buckle

There's a lot in this book so far about working with people. As the element with the greatest variability in your security program, people can make or break your efforts to manage risk. This chapter focuses on controls explicitly for dealing with people. In most sizable organizations, there is a human resources department (or person) dedicated to overseeing personnel operations. They have an instrumental role in building and managing the security program.

Policy for the People

Here is a sample security policy covering Human Resource security that outlines their responsibilities:

Sample Human Resource Security Policy

ORGANIZATION will ensure that all users including employees, contractors, and third parties understand their responsibilities, are qualified for their assigned roles, are aware of relevant security issues, and are held responsible for their actions. The Human Resources (HR) department will be responsible for the following security processes:

Employee on boarding and off boarding

The HR department will be responsible for overseeing the hiring and separation processes for contractors and employees initiating/terminating their work with ORGANIZATION. The HR department will track the processes for distribution/collection of company equipment and work with IT to ensure the prompt provision/removal of access rights. The ORGANIZATION assigns the primary responsibility for the provision/removal of access rights to the IT department. The IT and Security department will work together to ensure that only authorized personnel have privileges on the ORGANIZATION systems.

© Raymond Pompon 2016
R. Pompon, *IT Security Risk Control Management*, DOI 10.1007/978-1-4842-2140-2_15

Background Screening

Because some ORGANIZATION employees and contractors will have direct access to sensitive information, prospective ORGANIZATION employees and contractors must be background screened before being they are granted access to sensitive systems or data. The HR department will own and maintain a documented process for performing background checks on potential employees and contractors. The Security department will work with the HR department to develop a standard describing the acceptable background check criteria that users must meet in order to be granted access to sensitive information. The Security department will work with HR to develop a standard and schedule for re-checking background checks on an ongoing basis.

Agreements

As ORGANIZATION has many terms and conditions of employment, HR, the Security department, and management will share the responsibility for ensuring ongoing training and compliance with the security policy, the code of ethics, non-disclosure agreement, acceptable usage policy, and the proprietary information and inventions agreement.

Training

The HR and Security departments will be responsible for making sure all employees receive annual security awareness training as well as any needed security skills training. Some security-specific responsibilities may require additional skills and knowledge, HR and management will work to provide training resources as needed. The HR department will track and retain records of employee training, skills, experience, and qualifications as pertains to security matters.

Disciplinary Process

ORGANIZATION considers misuse of its IT systems or violation of security policy as grounds for disciplinary action up to and including immediate termination. The HR and the security departments will work together to ensure proper follow-up actions are taken in the event of a violation.

Employee Role Changes

An important part of user management is ensuring proper and authorized user account additions, closures, and changes. The HR department plays a pivotal role in keeping IT and security teams informed about employee changes, which can include on-boarding (hiring), off-boarding (termination), or role changes. It's never fun to have a new employee start work and find that IT has no idea the person is starting that day. Then IT has to scramble to set up their account and get their equipment, which can lead to mistakes like giving the user too much access. IT needs to have adequate warning when new users are needed.

It is also helpful to have either a separate process or defined extra steps for account work involving system administrators and individuals with elevated access. You may want to include additional approvals, additional checks, and faster turn-around time on terminations for these types of accounts.

In the other direction, user account deactivations are even more important. Having an active user account open and available after an employee leaves the organization is big problem. First, it's a security vulnerability to allow a former employee to have unauthorized access when you have no control over their actions. Second, it's a threat to the employee, as they could be blamed for actions taken with their still active account. Third, it's a glaring audit finding and in some regulatory regimes, a fine.

For security and sanity's sake, all user accounts should be created and removed as part of a documented request and approval process. The goal is to be able to produce the entire chain of events when an auditor randomly picks out a user and says, "This guy here, it shows his account was created on August 15th, 2016. Show me HR paperwork authorizing his account creation and what level access he should have." If you don't have this, you will have a problem. Let's hope that the problem is just an audit finding, and not a rogue user that someone created. The real question to fear from an auditor is this: "I see that Melinda quit on February 15th, yet she still has an active account on these systems. Can you explain that?" Usually the explanation is that someone flubbed up and you feel the need to crawl under a rock. To prevent these kinds of things from happening, it's a good idea to have someone (like security) do periodic (at least quarterly) account reviews to ensure that every user can be tied back to an authorized person in the organization.

To unpack all of this, you should have procedures that include the following:

- Standard user addition, termination, and modification

- Administrative user addition, termination, and modification

- Quarterly account reviews

In addition to these, you should consider attaching some *service level agreements* (SLA) to ensure timely notifications and set expectations. Even if your organization doesn't use internal SLAs, you can include time expectations as part of the procedure or standard in the preamble. Some things to define service level agreements on are:

- IT needs notification at least X days for new accounts in order to set up a system and account

- Termination notifications should be given at least X business days before the employee's last day of service to ensure that the account is set to expire upon their leaving.

- In the event of urgent terminations, IT and Security should be notified immediately so that appropriate measures can be taken.

That last item refers to a touchy but important area of user management: urgent terminations. This could be the unexpected firing of an employee or a round of layoffs. These are the painful separations where IT and Security need as much warning as possible. I realize that in the real world, this can mean a matter of hours or even minutes, and sometimes needs to be contained to only a few individuals. In any case, urgent terminations must be coordinated between HR and Security. These are the events where leaving an account open a few minutes after an angry person has left the building can lead to incidents with large impacts.

Background Screening

One of the most controversial security controls is background-check screening. Unfortunately, it's also one of the more common controls in place. Some say pre-employment screening is necessary in order to properly investigate and weed out potential malefactors before being given access to sensitive information. This is why you see full complete checks of criminal and credit history required for all financial and medical organizations. Others say that overly broad background checks are invasive and discriminatory. Just in my own part of the world, two laws were been recently passed restricting pre-employment credit checks[1] and criminal background checks[2] in the Pacific Northwest. Both measures do have provisions for background checks where it is deemed "job related." Considering the various compliance and security requirements of the sensitive systems, it looks like background checks are still going to be big part of security controls.

---

[1]http://www.oregon.gov/boli/TA/pages/t_faq_credit_history_july_2010.aspx.
[2]http://www.seattle.gov/council/meet-the-council/bruce-harrell/job-assistance-legislation.

Since there is such a concern, there are many things that you can do to make sure that employee privacy is protected. First, make sure that you check extensively with the HR and legal when you embark on a background check program. The rules can vary quite a bit by venue.

Second, your checks should be proportionate and risk-based, not based on as how much information on a person you could vacuum up. Not every user may need the same depth of background check. Just remember if a user is moving from a lower level to a higher level of access, they should have additional background checks as needed.

Third, get the person's consent. HR and legal will insist on this, but it still bears repeating. Usually background check requirements are noted in the job description and a consent form provided as part of the job offer process. In fact, some job offers should be worded so that they are contingent on the prospective employee agreeing to and passing the background check. You should also give the applicant a chance to disclose if they have any known violations or incidents that could come up in the background check. It says a lot about person's character if they're willing to reveal this about themselves instead of hoping that it won't be uncovered in a records search.

Last, keep the background check private. At the very least, you need the person's full name, home address, date of birth, and Social Security number. This data is by definition personally identifiable information, which should be protected. Only HR needs to see this and the details of the background report. Preferably, you can even limit this in HR to a specific individual or role performing the check. Even auditors and the security department should be barred from accessing the details of a person's background check. In nearly every circumstance, security and auditors only need to verify that a check was performed, and the background-check cover page should be sufficient for that. If that's not possible, an HR representative can simply black out the details on a photocopy to sanitize the audit record. You shouldn't need to store background check details for more than two years, but you can hold onto the sanitized audit proof they were done.

When to Check

Nearly every security and compliance requirements list mandates a background check before a user is given access to confidential resources. The ideal time is upon hire before they are provisioned an account and office key. I have seen cases where employees were hired with pending background checks. In these cases, the security team blocked the issuance of login credentials until HR provided assurance that the check was done. It's always awkward for a new employee to be on site but not have access to any computers, but it was the right thing to do. Organizations with more secure needs also repeat their background checks on all personnel every few years, just to make a new unknown criminal violation hasn't occurred. Some organizations even have procedures in place to do covert background checks on users if someone reports them acting suspicious.

If a person has ended their relationship with the organization and then is returning (quit and then rehired), they should be considered starting from scratch as far as background checks have concerned. Some organizations give the candidate a few months of leeway, but the more prudent organizations re-do the check regardless of how much time has elapsed. This can also apply for contractors being transitioned to full time employee status. Background checks are relatively cheap to perform and another check can occasionally uncover interesting new facts. In other words, it's a control that provides a meaningful risk reduction for its relative cost.

Who to Check

Everyone who has access to confidential information and systems (which are defined in your policy and scope) should be subject to background screening. This means physical and logical access to systems, so you would include janitorial staff and maintenance workers. Fortunately, most modern building management companies who cater to businesses can attest to doing this on all their staff. When I say anyone who has access, I mean anyone who can touch the systems without supervision or in the normal course of their work. Occasional vendor support personnel who need to work on your hardware can be escorted physically or electronically with screen-sharing software. If a vendor or contractor requires unmanaged access, they need to be checked or have their company formally attest to a background check. A note on these attestations: they should be in writing or in the contract and they should include information on what the individuals are background-screened against.

Any user given higher access should be checked as well. If you don't do full background checks on normal users but then promote one to a database administrator of the payment card system, then you need to apply the full check at that point. This too is a common oversight, so be careful.

What to Check

Before we get into specifics of what should go into a background check, let's revisit the purpose: to measure the risk of a user acting maliciously. The information you discover as part of a background screening provides information about a person's past actions, which in turn inform you about their character and motivations. If any information is returned, it will likely point toward a person being untrustworthy. It's mostly about disqualifying someone, not qualifying them. A completely clean background check is by no means a guarantee that someone will be honest and reliable.

One of the simplest and most useful indicators about a person's character is to call and talk to their former employers and references. Make sure that you confirm the position title, the period of employment, and the job duties they performed. Establishing a good rapport with the reference can yield a lot of helpful information about the candidate. Since the majority of your candidates are unlikely to have criminal records, this technique will yield a lot of information you would not get otherwise. Remember to keep records of your conversation for both the auditors and in the event that there are any hiring-discrimination lawsuits.

Another easy verification is to check their educational and professional certification credentials. It's surprising how often this isn't checked; it's also very revealing about the truth behind some inflated claims. These are both verifications that can be done without tripping over any privacy or legal restrictions.

When looking at background checking candidates from outside the United States, it is common to do a passport verification (which encapsulates some home country checks) as well as residential address verification for the past five to seven years. If the person has lived in several international locations over the past years (not uncommon for tech contractors), then each of the national jurisdictions should be checked.

The more serious background checks involve criminal, terrorist, and sex offender records. These are best done by a qualified agency that can run them and give you a report. Be sure to be thorough and include global, federal, and state criminal records. HR probably already wants to do a legal working status check, which includes citizenship or immigration status. Lastly, you can do a civil litigation records check to see if this individual is party has a history of being sued. Court records checks should go at least seven years back.

Background screening that includes credit checks are controversial to the point of being legally restricted in some states and countries. The good news is that a standard credit check does not affect the candidate's credit score or ability to get credit. It isn't the same type of credit check that is done during a loan application process. The goal here is to look for candidates who might be predisposed to theft because of large or serial debts. This could be indications of potential addictions or gambling problems that could put the person in a compromising position. Things like credit history, bankruptcies, tax problems, liens, and civil court judgements could end up these kinds of reports. These kinds of checks are usually asked for in any organization or position involving the direct access to financial data or transactions. The unfortunate problem is that many trustworthy individuals in modern America do have some blemishes on their financial record. It's been my personal experience that these are usually because of previous large medical bills.

Where permitted by law, drug testing can be done as part of a pre-employment screen. Many organizations and jurisdictions do not condone drug testing, so be careful with this requirement. Some consulting companies often find themselves being pushed to have these done for staff doing work for military or financial organizations. This can become problematic given the privacy attitudes of some highly skilled IT engineers. Some may even reject the idea on principle. Lastly, in some state jurisdictions, adult use of some recreational drugs is perfectly legal, while remaining unacceptable at the federal level. This can create jurisdictional dilemmas.

What to Do When There's a Problem

Most of the time, background-check screens come back clean. The only discrepancies you may encounter usually come up during the reference or previous employment checks (which is why I encourage doing them). However, if you have an issue, how do you proceed? The first question to consider is if they predisclosed the issue. If not, then there is a big question mark regarding the candidate's honesty. Someone, usually HR, can ask the candidate about the problem and hear their story. See if there are mitigating circumstances or if the information received was incorrect. If they claim that the information in the report is inaccurate, then the candidate needs to work directly with the agency to correct it.

If what turned up was correct and unambiguous, then the organization faces a decision. Some things are going to clear showstoppers, such as the following:

- Dishonesty, such as any falsified information on any of their provided information.

- All fraud, including (but not limited to) payment card/check fraud, embezzlement, fraudulent trading, forgery, counterfeiting, money laundering

- Any computer crime

- Economic/corporate/business/industrial espionage, which can turn up as a civil lawsuit as well as criminal

- Bribery, corruption, extortion

- Theft, burglary, possession of stolen property

- Felonies, terrorism, drug trafficking, crimes against persons

- Producing, supplying, importing, or trafficking controlled drugs/substances

If a candidate doesn't have any of these problems, there is a possibility for appeal and review. Remember what is uncovered during this check should be used as part of a risk analysis. Given the information and their explanation, HR, the hiring manager, and someone from the security department can discuss the risk. You don't need a large committee for this; a single person from each represented department is sufficient. When looking at the issue, you can consider the age, the magnitude, and the relevance of the incident to the proposed position. Decisions should be documented and kept private within the HR department.

Employment Agreements

It's likely the organization has many terms and conditions of employment, not just counting the ones imposed by the security department. It's common for the HR department to ensure that all the relevant policies and agreements are presented and explained to the candidate. HR usually is also responsible for making sure the person signs off on these documents and has copies available. The following are the major agreements and policies that you want the candidate to agree to:

- Legal non-disclosure agreement (usually drafted by the legal department)

- Proprietary information and inventions agreement (usually drafted by legal to protect ownership of intellectual property developed while employed)

- Security policy (the high-level organization-wide policy)

- Acceptable Usage Agreement

These are the common minimum documents. Some organizations also throw in a code of ethics, sexual harassment/anti-discrimination policies, and even the employee handbook for the candidate to review and sign.

Rather than present people with mountains of paper and track ink signatures, some organizations use electronic distribution systems to push out these documents and capture approval. Some electronic signature systems require employees already have internal network access, which means they're already online before agreeing to follow policy. In those cases, someone needs to be assigned to be responsible for ensuring that they are all approved in a timely manner. If they are not, then that person's access credentials should be revoked and their supervisor notified.

Security Training

The content and goals of security awareness training were covered in Chapter 10. The actual rollout of the training can be done in a variety of ways. Some organization's schedule annual in-person classes that all employees are required to attend. Some organizations do this via online live or pre-recorded broadcast. Some even create or contract out computer-mediated training sessions. Responsibility for providing the training can be split with the HR department, who can be responsible for scheduling and delivering the training. The security group should always be responsible for the content. As everything else discussed here, security training should be a mandatory requirement for a user gaining access to sensitive systems. Other methods of security awareness are available as well. This can include the following:

- Security awareness quizzes

- Security brown-bag meetings or training videos on other security topics

- E-mailed or intranet-published newsletters and security warnings

- Office posters and banners with security tips

- Reminder cards left on people's desks for bad/good security behavior ("Please lock your workstation when you leave.")

- Periodic incentive awards for good security behavior (cookies at the security brown bag session)

These kinds of things should be seen as complements to the main security training, not replacements.

In addition to basic security awareness training, the HR department should ensure that individuals with security responsibilities are qualified and properly trained for their roles. Since security threats and technology change frequently, this can mean continuing education for staff. Staff members who hold professional certifications are already required to maintain educational credits to keep their certifications. The organization can work to support this by subsidizing some or all of their training and certification costs. New controls and tools should also entail technical training for the operators and implementers. This doesn't mean that you have to send the entire network-engineering department off to weeks of firewall training, but sending one or two is prudent, especially if a new system is being brought online. Records of all this training should be kept and tracked.

Sanctions for Policy Violations

When individuals violate security policy, there needs to be consequences. The obvious consequence is termination, which may be warranted in some cases. However, in some situations and venues, this may not be possible. This is an area where you can get creative. The goal should not to be punitive, but instead to ensure that this never happens again. If you do terminate someone, then consider making public the reason for the termination for deterrence effect.

If the violation was accidental, then the consequences can be as simple as a reminder or additional security awareness training. In the past, I have sent repeat offenders to "security traffic school" for additional and more detailed security training. The behavior could have been accidental or a one-off, or it could be a chronic problem. Be sure to calibrate the sanction response based on that.

When addressing violations, it is best to be clear and open in your discussions with the offender, and focus on the tangible observed behavior. For example, you can say something like, "I have been informed that you have violated X policy." Then you state the policy before continuing with, "This may have been an accident or your intentions were good, however this does violate our policy. We need to make sure that this will not happen again." You should explain the reason for the policy and the consequences that can occur if it is ignored (the least of which is an audit finding all the way up to a security incident).

Sometimes people raise objections, such as the fact that other people are violating this same policy. Here you should redirect them back to the violation being discussed with statements like, "That may be true and we will deal with that but we are talking about your policy violation right now. Can you confirm that this will not happen again?" The organization should always keep a record of the incident so you can see if this is a chronic problem or a pattern of behavior.

In situations where termination is not possible due to union or legal constraints, then revoking or reducing access privileges can reduce the threat significantly. It also sends a strong message regarding the unacceptable behavior.

In cases where security policy violations also overlap with criminal violations, the organization should strongly consider turning the matter over to law enforcement authorities. The following are some of the situations in which law enforcement should be contacted:

- Child pornography

- Threats of violence

- Stalking or harassment

- Hacking or espionage of others outside of the organization

Depending on the stance of the acceptable usage policy, the organization could also be in a position to turn over digital evidence to the authorities without a warrant. In these cases, the security department should oversee the secure collection of the evidence and protect it from tampering. We'll cover this in depth in Chapter 20, which focuses on response controls.

Managing the Insider Threat

During the risk analysis, we looked closely at the large threat of malicious insiders. Because of this risk, access for trusted users must be controlled. A wide variety of controls and tools can be brought to bear. However, like all risks, insider risk can never be reduced to zero. As long as you allow humans in the loop, you have to trust them to do their jobs correctly at some level. Let's break down these controls.

Monitoring

Strong oversight is a both a good detective control as well as a preventive control as a deterrent factor. You should have video surveillance monitoring in place in all your key secure areas. Recording all entries and exits from the server room can help spot suspicious after-hours behavior. Monitoring on administrative access and actions is absolutely necessary on systems holding confidential data. There are a number of logging tools built into most operating systems that record administrative actions. In addition to the built-in tools, many commercial products and add-ons are available to enhance the recording, analysis, and reporting on those actions. The monitoring records should be held in a tamper-proof system that is separated from the usual administrative systems. This can mean parallel systems that are managed solely by security with either no or read-only access by the IT department. You do not want people removing the records of their own misdeeds. Logging is discussed more in Chapter 20.

Least Privilege

A simple way to reduce the risk of insider abuse is to reduce the number of people who have access. It sounds trivial but I have seen some organizations where half the company has full administrative rights because of poor architecture. Out of the population of all users, the percentage of system administrators should be a single digit. If more than 10% of your users have admin rights, you will have problems. The concept of least privilege means to give only the least amount of access that people need to do their jobs and not an inch more. Not only will you be reducing the quantity of threats, but also lower numbers of privileged users mean less work in oversight and monitoring. If you have 30 system administrators, then you're going to need several full-time personnel to just to review the access logs in a timely manner.

Strong User Management

We've already discussed the key pieces of this earlier in this chapter, but having robust processes around user provisioning and termination really reduces insider access. Insiders sometimes create their own shadow accounts or elevate their privileges in order to commit their crimes. Having strong accountability and monitoring around user rights can nip that in the bud. Watch out, sometimes user rights can slowly add up as they change jobs throughout an organization. If someone leaves a department to go to another, remember least privilege and remove all of their rights, and then add back in what is needed for the new role. I've seen people transfer in and out of sensitive positions but retain their old rights. With accountability and monitoring comes the mandate for unique accounts. There should be no shared accounts for sensitive work. If there needs to be sharing of accounts because of technical limitations, there needs to tight monitoring and oversight on their use. One rule I've used is that every time admins used a generic *root* login on a server, they had to register the event in a help desk ticket so it could be tracked to them individually. Unlogged root accesses were investigated as security incidents when discovered in the audit logs.

Segregation of Duties

In the financial accounting realm, segregation of duties is a powerful tool to limit privileged access. It means to design systems so that the cooperation of two or more people is needed to perform certain tasks. Think of it as the *two keys needed to launch nuclear missiles rule* that you see in movies. It can also mean structuring processes so that one role is designed to act as a control over another. This is why you should set up IT administrative logging to separate from normal IT systems, while also limiting the access of those who do the monitoring over IT systems. Another common segregation of duty control is to separate code development and live systems. The programmers who make changes to source code are not allowed to deploy changes to production systems. Furthermore, system administrators are not allowed to make changes to source code. This provides a check and balance to how production systems function. Both of these forms of segregation of duties are an important part of change control as discussed in Chapter 13, which focuses on administrative controls.

For those working in DevOps environments, segregation of duties regarding deployments and source code can be challenging. In a DevOps environment, developers are empowered to push their own changes into production. Furthermore, IT operations personnel are encouraged to write code. In these cases, you can use automation and logging to take over deployment and change tracking. In DevOps, all code changes should be automatically checked, logged in detail, and have the capability for rapid reversal. Overall, the guidelines for segregation of duties are to segregate requests from approvals and to segregate work operations from work records.

Know Your User

In banking, there is a control called *know your customer* that instructs bankers to verify the identity and intentions of their clients. Regulators are leveraging bankers to spot bribery and money laundering operations. That same principle can work with spotting potential malicious insiders. This does not necessarily mean copious logging of all user actions and alerting on anomalous activity. There are simpler and more direct methods to do this.

One is to encourage and train managers to pay the proper amount of attention to their staff. This means ongoing, weekly one-on-one meetings to track their progress and attitudes. It can also mean having a culture of transparency, where open discussion of issues and concerns are shared. While these two things are often not in the purview of the security department to control, they can be suggested as good management and security techniques to upper management.

In addition, security awareness training should coach employees to report suspicious behavior. The mechanism for reporting should also be designed so that notifications go to multiple persons, spread between groups. In some organizations, I have seen a generic *report_incidents* e-mail address that goes to the entire ISMS committee used. This way the person reporting doesn't risk their message being ignored, deleted, or covered up by a single person. In other organizations, the help-desk ticketing system is used to track incidents.

Filtering

Technical controls that monitor and filter data stores and transmissions can be useful tools to prevent accidental and some malicious copying of confidential data. These tools are often called DLP for data/digital loss/leak prevention (no one seems to agree on what the acronym stands for) and can work with e-mail, file shares, local workstations, and even USB ports. They scan for known confidential data signatures, such as credit card numbers or social security numbers. You can usually program in new signatures based on the unique confidential data types or watermarks used in your organization. When detected, the DLP can block, sound an alarm, or automatically encrypt the data before something unfortunate happens. Like most signature-based technical controls, DLP is not very accurate and can usually be fooled by a skilled attacker. Some DLP solutions also create a lot of false positive alarms as lots of innocent things can look like confidential data. They can also get rather expensive in terms of both software cost and performance drain. As people can make mistakes or worse, act maliciously, a DLP filtering system can help reduce the risk of confidential data exposure.

Processes, Not Individuals

With risks involving people, there is a human tendency to focus on specific individuals. Billy in accounting is somewhat shifty and he's always working late. Maybe he's up to something. Eric the database administrator is always commenting about how the government is invading our privacy and trying to take away our firearms. Tina the web designer is so quiet and never talks to anyone. What is she hiding? However, security professionals should worry more about failed or missing processes, not about specific suspicious individuals. Don't be distracted by your biases and neglect maintaining the controls you have in place. Work on aligning processes and building strong controls, and you will be on the right path to reducing the risk from people.

FURTHER READING

- **Small Business Guide to Background checks**
  https://www.sba.gov/content/pre-employment-background-checks

- **Security Clearance Adjudicative Guidelines**
  https://news.clearancejobs.com/2015/06/10/security-clearance-adjudicative-guidelines/

- **How to check references**
  https://www.manager-tools.com/2013/06/questions-ask-references-check-part-1

- **Center for Information Security Awareness**
  https://www.cfisa.org/

- **SANS: Separation of Duties in Information Technology**
  http://www.sans.edu/research/security-laboratory/article/it-separation-duties

■ ■ ■

CHAPTER 16

Logical Access Control

A very little key will open a very heavy door.

—Charles Dickens, *Hunted Down*

When you mention access control, most people's minds go blank. Those few that understand technology usually think of passwords. When I think of passwords, I think of an organization that I worked with that had arguably the most difficult password policy I had ever encountered in my working life. The policy read: *Passwords are required to be 12 characters, containing one symbol, one number, one lowercase, and one uppercase letter. Passwords must be changed every 45 days and new passwords cannot be related to previously used passwords. Passwords should never be written down or shared.*

The first two requirements were electronically enforced, which meant the third requirement was the one that everyone violated. Since most of us don't have eidetic (or cybernetic) memories, you *had* to write down your password or share it into a password manager. If the risk of password exposure was so high that there needed to be 45-day rotation, then why didn't they use two-factor authentication? Surely, it had to be cheaper than all the lost hours spent recovering passwords or the additional risk of having them written down. However, as misguided as this policy was, there are far common and debilitating mistakes in implementing logical access controls.

While many people associate access control with passwords, logical access controls mean a whole lot more. One of the biggest oversights I see is not considering authorization along with authentication. Authentication is the identity part, while authorization is about what you can do once you've entered the correct password. Too often, once a user gets in, they have excessive authorization to resources. When you reduce their access to what they need (least privilege) and you reduce the risk and with it the reliance on the password. If someone needs extraordinary access, then have her provide higher levels of authentication as needed.

Defining Access Control

We'll dig more into this, but let's get the basics down solid first, beginning with policy.

Sample Logical Access Control Policy

ORGANIZATION will control logical access to IT data and systems based on defined business and security requirements. ORGANIZATION will assign a unique access account to each person who requires access. The management of these access controls will be shared between the IT department and the Security department. The IT department will be responsible for maintaining the access control systems and accounts. The Security department will be responsible for periodically reviewing rights to ensure that only authorized users are listed and the authentication standards are being followed.

© Raymond Pompon 2016
R. Pompon, *IT Security Risk Control Management*, DOI 10.1007/978-1-4842-2140-2_16

The goal is for users to only have access to the IT resources that is required to perform their designated functions and all Users be properly authenticated prior to accessing and using restricted-access ORGANIZATION IT resources.

The Security and the IT department will share responsibility for maintaining authentication standards. These standards will include:

- *Authentication standards for standard users, which describe password usage including password length, password complexity, and password change frequency*

- *Access control standards for standard users including account lockout durations, session timeout, and user management processes*

- *Authentication implementation standards to describe acceptable network authentication protocols such as Active Directory, RADIUS, or Kerberos*

- *Authentication requirements for access to corporate resources*

- *Authentication requirements for administrative or elevated-privilege access control to critical systems*

- *Access control standards for administrative or elevated-privilege users including account lockout durations, session timeout, and user management processes*

- *System administrative access standards defining how system administrators will authenticate and be granted rights for servers and domains*

- *Database administrative access standards defining how database administrators will authenticate and be granted rights for database servers, databases, and database-related utilities*

- *Authentication standards for remote access to ORGANIZATION resources from outside the ORGANIZATION facilities*

- *Authentication standards for service accounts*

- *Forgotten password/lost token access and recovery procedures*

- *Emergency access standards for administrative access when systems are in a failed state*

Authentication

The first piece of logical access control has two components: *identification* (who you appear to be) and *authentication* (prove it). For the most part on IT systems, these two functions are bundled together into authentication. The object identified in authentication is not you, but a data record that exists solely in context to some kind of overall system. The *authenticated object* can be a user account, a software object, a service, or even a network address. All of these authenticatable entities can be subjected to varying levels of access controls. A useful way to look at how to perform authentication is to break it down into something you know, something you have, or something you are.

Something You Know

The most common types of authenticators include passwords, personal identification numbers (PINs), secret questions (what was your mother's maiden name), service shared secrets (long passwords for software), and cryptographic keys. The whole point of something you know is that the authenticator is a secret. That means if it's something guessable or discoverable with a little bit of research, it's not very good. Some of the better systems combine multiple secrets, which is why you see some account reset systems ask you several questions, such as your childhood pet's name and the make of your first car.

The biggest advantage of something you know is that it's cheap to implement. This is why we see passwords and PINs everywhere. No extra hardware needed and the programming work is pretty straightforward.[1] If your organization uses passwords for authentication, and I guarantee it does somewhere, then you need to have some published password standards. The current version of the PCI DSS says that you need a minimum of seven characters containing alpha and numeric characters, rotating every 90 days and preventing any of the last four passwords from being reused. Many organizations have slightly higher standards than this.

Something You Have

Electronic authentication by something you have is as straightforward as sticking a key in a lock. Things you have can include hard/soft one-password tokens, digital certificates, USB dongles, smart cards, Kerberos tickets, cryptographic keys, web cookies and cloud service authenticator keys. If you are somewhat technical, you may have noticed that all of these things are actually shared secrets that only the authentication service can verify. Even ordinary locks and keys rely on a semi-secret pattern (visible in plain sight) cut out of the key, which is why Randall Munroe refers to locks as "shape checkers."[2] This is why there are services available to duplicate a key if you provide them with a photograph of one.

We don't want our IT authentication services to be spoofed by easily duplicated artifacts, so a lot real world authentication tokens (like passports) are forgery-resistant with expensive holograms and watermarks. In the digital realm, cryptography is our anti-counterfeiting tool. Because codes obscured by cryptographic secrets are harder to discover, we encode them with another key that only the authentication service knows. For example, authenticator tokens generate and display a visible code based on a hidden shared secret that changes it periodically.[3]

All of these systems work in a challenge-response fashion, where the authentication service probes the user to respond with the secret from their token or artifact. Sometimes when the artifact is physical, like a smart card, the challenge-response happens locally over a physical computer port. When over the network, the challenge response can be in English ("Enter the code visible on your token") or via software message to the token.

Because of this cryptographic infrastructure, *something you have* also requires overhead for authentication. The same danger also exists for authentication by something known: if the secret gets out,[4] it is easy for attackers to silently impersonate you. There have been a few cases where a breach occurred because a cryptographic authentication key was left in source code or in a script that became publicly available. There are also many attacks, like cookie theft and man-in-the-middle, where attackers intercept and copy an authenticator challenge-response in transit. An additional problem is that theft itself is secret, so the authentication credentials are compromised without the user being aware.

These problems mean you should have standards defined to ensure authentication tokens are protected when being transmitted or stored. The common tool for this is more encryption. There should also be standards for token issuance, rotation, and revocation.

---

[1]http://www.troyhunt.com/2012/05/everything-you-ever-wanted-to-know.html
[2]http://www.dinnerpartydownload.org/randall-munroe/
[3]https://en.wikipedia.org/wiki/One-time_password
[4]https://www.schneier.com/blog/archives/2011/03/rsa_security_in.html

Something You Are

Usually when we talk about *something you are*, we mean *biometrics*. Biometrics is authentication based on a unique human characteristic used to identify you. One of the simplest kinds of biological measurements is the CAPTCHA, which stands for Completely Automated Public Turing test to tell Computers and Humans Apart. This biometric test uses your brain's ability to read squiggly letters to determine if you're a human or software. That's all this biometric determines but it is useful in blocking some automated attacks. The more useful biometrics is unique to each human individual, like fingerprints, facial configurations, iris patterns, and palm geometry. Some biometrics are so broad—such as CAPTCHA or gait recognition—that they work better for identification than other authentication.

For authenticating non-humans, there is a variety of techniques used in access control. For network security, often IP or MAC address can identify a machine. IP address works very well for firewall authentication over the Internet when combined with difficult-to-spoof protocols such as TCP/IP. Software objects can be authenticated based on what they are based on a unique type of checksum called a hash, which is based on the numeric representation of the software object. Done perfectly, a hash is unique to a software object.

One of the biggest challenges with authenticating *something you are* is that many of these factors are things that you cannot easily keep secret, unless you wear gloves and a mask like Spider-Man. It's even harder for non-human objects to hide their uniqueness, as we can see how IP addresses are spoofed when combined with services that use weak protocols for address verification.[5] The implications and issues of this are discussed more in Chapter 17, which covers network security.

Another challenge for biometrics is that you usually need special hardware. Now most mobile phones have built-in cameras and fingerprint sensors, so this is getting easier. Lastly, there are very few standards for trustworthy sharing of biometric information. What often happens is each system that authenticates via biometrics needs an infrastructure to enroll new users, capture the factor, and securely store it (usually as a hash). All of this implies additional infrastructure that must be built.

Multifactor Authentication

You can combine at least two of these things to be multi-factor authentication. A certificate, a fingerprint, or a token by itself is not two-factor authentication. You must combine the factors. This is why tokens and bank cash cards have PINs associated with them and passports have your photograph. The security comes from raising the difficulty of impersonating the user by a compromise of one of the factors. You may duplicate her fingerprint[6] but you still need her password to login. This is why IPsec virtual private networks use a combination of shared secrets (something you know) and IP addresses (something you are). Software objects combine something that you are, like checksum hashes and embedded digital keys (something you have).[7]

Authentication Standards

Standards for authentication are important, but what should they specify? To fully understand the need and the standards definition, you need to delve deeper into the goals and control failure modes of authentication controls. The goal is pretty straightforward: restrict access to only authorized entities that can be identified to some degree of certainty. The more important the resource, the higher the assurance (certainty) required

---

[5]http://www.veracode.com/security/spoofing-attack
[6]http://www.theguardian.com/technology/2014/dec/30/hacker-fakes-german-ministers-fingerprints-using-photos-of-her-hands
[7]https://msdn.microsoft.com/en-us/library/windows/hardware/ff543743%28v=vs.85%29.aspx

around identification. From here, you can see why we would want differing authentication standards for administrative access and scoped systems. Since passwords are vulnerable to phishing and keylogging, they aren't strong enough for access to critical systems or access from high-risk environments (remote access). The industry standard (as of this writing) is username and password authentication for standard access and two-factor authentication for high-value/high-risk access.

What are the failure modes for this control? The simplest is that an attacker guesses the password. Let's make that hard by setting a password standard requiring hard-to-guess passwords. In addition, we can set a standard number of allowed password attempts before locking the account and sounding some kind of alarm.

For something you have authentication, you don't want *that something* to be stolen. When it comes to passwords, keys in scripts, or pinned certificates in software, you really don't want full trust built into a software object in perpetuity. This can also apply to stored password hashes, which can also be stolen off systems. All of these risks can be reduced by authentication rotation. The idea is that if a password hash is stolen, the bad guys will attempt to cryptographically break the hash and guess the password. Some security practitioners mistakenly believe that shorter rotation cycles are always better (like 45 day cycles), but that is not necessarily true.[8] Based on current technology and threat capability, a reasonable rotation scheme for passwords and administrative tokens is around three months. Certificates can rotate at least once a year.

How about the operational and implementation failures? You should have a standard defining the acceptable authentication tools and technologies. This can include specific technologies that you know work in your organization like Windows Active Directory, Soft tokens, Toenail biometric scans, and so forth. Another operational failure mode is how the authentication is first provided to the user. You don't want the helpdesk printing out people's passwords and leaving them face up on the desks. The same goes for password resets in case of lockout. A common attack technique is to phone the helpdesk and impersonate the user to get a password reset. You should have defined procedures for authentication distribution and verification.

Another authorization (not authentication) problem is users leaving the firm and HR failing to inform the IT department. A good control here is to have IT verify that all accounts are active with fresh logins once a month. You can set a threshold (for example, 45 days) that if after which time no activity is seen, the account is locked. This control also takes care of the user who never bothers to login to the system and leaves a dormant account lying around.

When you were doing your business process review, a few more authentication scenarios may have come up; for example, temporary access for vendors needing only to be on the system for a few days or weeks. By definition, these accounts are not going to stick around very long. A procedure can be defined to ensure that the accounts have automatic self-destruct dates added when the account was created.

Sample Authentication Standards and Procedures

Based on the risks and requirements, we have generated the following list of potential standards and procedures:

- *The Security department will publish a list of acceptable authentication systems.*

- *Passwords will be eight characters or longer and must be composed of numbers as well as upper and lower case letters. Passwords should not be re-used or upon changing, be able to be changed back to their own password setting. Passwords are changed at least every 90 days.*

- *After three failed login attempts, the authentication system will be configured to lock the account for thirty minutes and log the event.*

---

[8]https://www.cerias.purdue.edu/site/blog/post/password-change-myths/

- *ORGANIZATION requires two-factor authentication for remote access to critical servers as defined by the Critical Servers Standard*

- *The Security department will be responsible for managing the two-factor authentication system. Two-factor authentication methods will conform to the Federal Financial Institutions Examination Council (FFIEC) guidance for multi-factor methods, such as digital certificates, tokens, or biometrics.*

- *The two-factor authentication system will log and archive authentication successes and failures.*

- *The IT department will verify the user's identity before performing a password reset. A procedure describing this verification will be written.*

- *On a monthly basis, the IT department will scan for accounts with login activity for the past 90 days and disable those inactive accounts until re-authorized by that user calling in to the help desk.*

- *Temporary access procedures will be developed in which IT will create temporary user accounts with automatic expiration dates based on the last day of the temporary access.*

Authorization

Authorization comes after authentication. It is the answer to the question: now that I know who you are, what should I let you do? In the last chapter, you read about the concept of least privilege that describes giving only the least amount of access that people need to do their jobs and not an inch more. Good authorization embodies that concept. Authorization privileges should be based on the trustworthiness of the accessor, verified by authentication, and the sensitivity of the object. This is called *role-based access control*. System administrators strongly authenticated (via two-factor) can modify files, while users lightly authenticated (via password) can just read files. Modern operating systems support this concept with rights, groups, and labels on files/directories.

Role-based Access Control

Authorization implemented in the manner that provides the most amount of control while still allowing users to get work done is called role-based access control. It means looking at specifically what each user needs to do, from where, at what time, and how they connect. For example, Matt takes a credit card order over the phone, so he needs access to the credit card database. However, he only needs write access to the database from 8am to 5pm, Monday through Friday, from his computer on the local area network. We assign processing refunds to Mathilda and give her a different access, but not the ability to enter orders (separation of duties). Take this a step further and don't assign these privileges to Matt and Mathilda directly, assign them to user groups called *Order takers* and *Refunds*, then put their users in those groups. It makes a lot easier to review who has what privileges and to update their rights when things change.

Compartmentalization at this level can be difficult, but worth doing for access to critical systems. The opposite stance, *default permit all*, should be avoided at all cost. Organizing roles and rights can take work, but building hierarchies of access that inherit privileges from the larger groups can make this easier. For the largest groups, like *all users*, you give the most basic privileges like sending jobs to the printer and read-only access to the corporate file shares. Then you add departmental and specific job roles on top of that. Watch out for escalating privileges, where users who change roles frequently and end up with rights to everything. It's important to have periodic reviews of accounts and permissions.

Limit Administrative Access

The biggest target of least privilege and role-based access should be limiting administrative access. The first thing to do is to limit the number of administrators to the lowest number possible. Whenever you can, do not give out blanket full administrative access. Create and split up role-based access accounts for administrators based on what they need to do. For example, create roles based on common tasks like server restarts, applying patches, log checks, and backups. A good way to do this is to have separate user accounts for administrative work and regular work. A sysadmin would have a special account she would use for doing server work. She would then logout and log back in with a lower-authorization user account to read her e-mail or surf the Web.

Another way to limit administrative access is to use internal perimeters and jump workstations. In this configuration, all administrative access must be done over designated *jump workstations*, which are the only systems authorized to access the scoped secure environment. Jump workstations are discussed in more detail in Chapter 17. With this configuration, the actions that administrators can perform are constrained to the tools and network connections on those jump workstations. It also provides a clear authentication wall between the sensitive environment and the rest of the organization. You can also skip putting two-factor authentication on every single host within the sensitive environment if you just make sure that it's on the jump box. Revisiting the scope diagram from Chapter 6, let's expand it to show how this works.

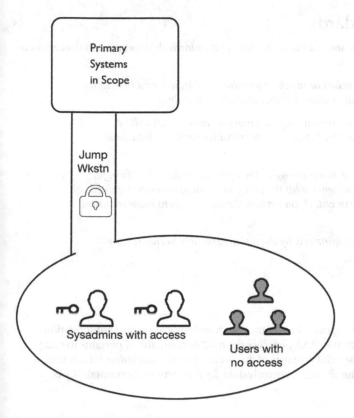

Figure 16-1. Simplified scope barrier

Service Accounts

A subset of administrative access is software service accounts. These are the accounts that are tied to running applications and services on servers. For example, the web server might require a local service account to function. These accounts should be clearly labelled as to their function and have rights restricted to just what is necessary for the service to run. You do not want to use a generic full admin account as service account. You really don't want the web server running off a sysadmin's account, so that when they change jobs and lock out the account, the web server crashes.

Unix operating systems support *chroot jails*,[9] which can automatically configure many of these things for you. If supported by the system, you can also restrict these service accounts to disallow human interactive logins.

System Authorization

Authorization access controls don't just need to apply to users and people. Network firewall rules should also follow least privilege and minimize the services needed to pass through in both directions. Stored authentication tokens in programs can also be restricted using the valet key concept,[10] which limits direct access by clients to services.

Sample Authorization Standards

Based on what we've covered so far, we have some additional security standards that we can add to our access control policy:

- *Administrative access will be limited as much as possible, both in role and in activity. No user will have default admin privileges, either globally or locally.*

- *All Administrative access will be proxied via jump workstations, which will be positioned as the sole systems allowed to administer sensitive services, data, and infrastructure.*

- *Users will be assigned role-based access based on the resources assigned to them for their work. Each department will work with the IT department to develop standards of access for their respective department. Upon leaving the role, access to those resources will be removed.*

- *Access reviews will be conducted quarterly by the resource owners to ensure only authorized persons have access.*

Accountability

Accountability is often discussed as part of logical access control with authentication and authorization. Sometimes the combination is referred to as the "AAA of access control." Accountability pertains to tying actions on the system to a user account. A special property of this is called *non-repudiation*, which means providing assurance, or a guarantee, that the actions were truly done by that person. Accountability is explored in more detail in Chapter 20.

---

[9]http://www.unixwiz.net/techtips/chroot-practices.html
[10]https://msdn.microsoft.com/en-us/library/dn568102.aspx

Access Control Tools

There are many technical tools to assist with access control. In addition to the granular controls and reports available within most modern operating systems, there are many add-on products that can help you manage, track, and enhance access control. One of the most common additional services is two-factor authentication. There are many two-factor systems—with varying levels of cost and compatibility—that can used to bolster standard password authentication.

One of the problems users face is dealing with a variety of authentication systems within a typical enterprise. Vendors began to release *single sign-on* (SSO) tools that would aggregate various authentication systems into a single unified database. A user would just need to login once to the SSO and their credentials would then be sent to other systems as needed. This concept has grown into *federated identity systems*, which are like SSO systems but available outside the organization to other entities in the world. The federated system handles the authentication and the client system manages authorization. Some operating systems began to build in federated identify systems on top of their native credentials.[11]

Another authentication problem is dealing with setting up numerous user accounts and managing them. Some systems can provide self-enrollment capabilities. This is especially useful for secondary authentication systems, like digital certificates, that need to be installed on specific client browsers or devices. For a self-enrollment system, the user visits an internal web page, authenticates with the current system, and then downloads their certificate for installation. Another user self-help tool is an account reset mechanism. Since accounts are normally configured to lock themselves after several failed passwords, users are stuck until they can contact the helpdesk and get unlocked. Some organizations have set up self-reset pages for the user. To prevent abuse, these pages have additional security measures like security questions or even restrictions to only allow the user's supervisor to do the unlocking. In all of these user self-management systems, you want to limit their access to internal networks and log every action that takes place.

FURTHER READING

- **Choosing and Using Security Questions Cheat Sheet**
  https://www.owasp.org/index.php/Choosing_and_Using_Security_Questions_Cheat_Sheet

- **FFIEC Supplement to Authentication in an Internet Banking Environment**
  http://www.ffiec.gov/pdf/Auth-ITS-Final%206-22-11%20(FFIEC%20Formated).pdf

- **NIST: Role-Based Access Controls**
  http://csrc.nist.gov/rbac/ferraiolo-kuhn-92.pdf

- **Passing Passwords**
  https://www.netmeister.org/blog/passing-passwords.html

- **Securing Critical and Service Accounts**
  https://msdn.microsoft.com/en-us/library/cc875826.aspx

- **Identity 2.0 Talk**
  https://www.youtube.com/watch?v=RrpajcAgR1E

---

[11]https://technet.microsoft.com/en-us/library/hh831502.aspx

CHAPTER 17

■ ■ ■

Network Security

People must communicate. They will make mistakes, and we will exploit them.

—James Clapper

Imagine a network worm using a variety of attacks to infect the most popular operating system on the Internet. The author of the worm was so technically skilled that within hours of being launched, it infected one out of ten machines on the Internet. It was called the *Morris worm*[1] after its creator Robert Morris, a computer scientist. The worm hit in 1988, before some people in the security field were even born.

Soon after, network worms plagued the first decade of commercial Internet usage. The nightly news gave the world its first real taste of hacking with stories on worms like Blaster, Lovebug, Code Red, Nimda, and SQL Slammer. What has changed since then? For one, hackers have learned to be stealthier and monetize their malware. Instead of vandalizing the Internet, many worms are honed to fulfill a purpose, usually economic. Many security professionals, including me, began our IT security career doing network defense and battling network worms. Even now, network security has become a core competency of IT security.

Today, a majority IT security attacks still originate over the network. The attacks that don't originate from a network still usually involve a network in some manner. Social engineering attacks are mostly Internet-driven with fake e-mails (phish), booby-trapped sites (watering holes), or fake web sites (pharms). Even some physical security attacks can involve breaking into facilities to plant network spy devices. It seems that every device and application is now Internet aware, where even our household appliances supporting social media accounts.[2]

Understand Networking Technology

This chapter is not going to teach you everything you need to know about network security. Instead, it is going to highlight the major aspects and nuances of the network security issues. Regarding networking technology, there are a few key concepts you should understand, including:

- Network protocols rely on software. All software has bugs. Network attackers can exploit those bugs in unexpected ways to produce malicious results.

    - For example, the ping-of-death exploits a bug in old operating systems such that a single malformed or malicious ping packet crashes the system.[3]

    - Dedicated network devices and appliances also run on software that can have bugs. Those bugs can be exploited as well.[4]

---

[1] http://www.mit.edu/people/eichin/virus/main.html.
[2] https://en.wikipedia.org/wiki/Internet_refrigerator.
[3] https://en.wikipedia.org/wiki/Ping_of_death.
[4] https://github.com/reverse-shell/routersploit.

- There is a difference between the IP protocols of TCP, UDP, and ICMP:

  - TCP connections establish a connection by sending and receiving handshakes and sequence numbers. This makes full TCP connections very difficult to fake. Some denial-of-service (DoS) attacks and network probes try to exploit that handshake sequence.[5]

  - UDP and ICMP network packets are one-way from sender to receiver with no handshake and therefore can be faked.

  - Common network services that use UDP include Domain Name Services (DNS), Simple Network Management Protocol (SNMP), Network Time Protocol (NTP), Trivial File Transfer Protocol (TFTP), and Network File System (NFS). These services can be faked and used in DoS reflection attacks.

  - Most notorious of these weak services are SNMPv1, Telnet, and FTP. These services can be used send files or commands to running systems or file stores. They should never be used over untrusted networks for anything important.

  - ICMP packets have different types with different purposes. Ping (*Echo Request*) and *Echo Response* are two parts of ICMP. ICMP Redirect is another, which means *don't send this packet here, send it over there*. Attackers can use redirects to reroute traffic around security devices or create DoS attacks.

- RFC 1918 addresses are usually used for local area networks.

  - You should never see RFC 1918 addresses on the Internet.

  - Firewalls can network address translate (NAT) between live Internet addresses and RFC 1918 addresses, such as 10.0.0.1 and 192.168.2.3.

These are the highlights of the major topics with network protocols. If you are really interested in doing more work in network security, there is a huge variety of learning material out there. You can start with the "Further Reading" section at the end of this chapter.

Network-based Attacks

The global reach of the Internet provides a vast swamp for anonymous adversaries to strike from and hide in. As everything is always connected, attacks can come at anytime from anywhere. Some network attacks are one-off, with a single attack delivering the final effect such as denial of service or information leakage. Other network attacks are part of a chain that can include self-replicating malware (worms) or create a gateway for additional exploitation. What do these attacks look like? Table 17-1 breaks down the major network attacks and their common impacts.

---

[5]https://en.wikipedia.org/wiki/SYN_flood.

Table 17-1. *Network Attacks and Common Impacts*

Network Attack	Common impacts
Remote exploits	Anything up to full control of impacted host, including remote command execution, remote control, denial of service, information leakage, or installation of self-replicating copies of itself.
Remote password guessing	The same level of authorization granted to the user of the compromised authentication.
Drive-by-downloads	Anything up to full control of impacted host, including remote command execution, remote control, denial of service, information leakage, or installation of self-replicating copies of itself.
Network denial of service	Denial of service. Can be temporary (flooding attack) or long-term (crash the server and/or corrupt the system).
Sniffing	Information leakage. If leakage involves authentication credentials, can lead to the same level of authorization granted to the user of the compromised authentication.
Impersonation	Information leakage. If leakage involves authentication credentials, can lead to the same level of authorization granted to the user of the compromised authentication.
Man-in-the-middle	Alteration of network transmission. Impersonation by adding misleading sites. Information leakage. If leakage involves authentication credentials, can lead to the same level of authorization granted to the user of the compromised authentication.
Exfiltration of data	Information leakage. Can be used for a remote command and control channel of compromised internal hosts.

Remote Exploits

The Morris worm used several remote exploits to gain access to Unix systems. Primarily it used a bug in Sendmail delivered over the Internet on TCP port 25 (Mail) to provide a command shell on the victim machine. Network exploit tools can range from simple Python scripts run at the command line to fully interactive graphical interfaces with point-and-click launchers.

There is a huge range of sophistication and effects from network delivered exploits. Network exploits include things like the ping of death, Heartbleed, and even SQL injection attacks. Most remote exploits embed codes that trigger a software bug and then follow them with some kind of command. Here is the network connection string to a vulnerability on a web server used by the *Code Red virus*:

```
GET /default.ida?NNNNNNNNNNNNNNNNNNNNNNNNNNNNNNNNNNNNNNNNNNNNNNNNNNNNNNNNNN NNNNNNNNNNNNNNNNN
NNNNNNNNNNNNNNNNNNNNNNNNNNNNNNNNNNNNNNNNNNNNNNNNNNNNNNNNNN NNNNNNNNNNNNNNNNNNNNNNNNNNNNNNNNNNNN
NNNNNNNNNNNNNNNNNNNNNNNNNNNNNNNNNNNNNNNNNN NNNNNNNNNNNNNNNNNNNNNNNNNNN%u9090%u6858%ucbd3%u7801%u90
90%u6858%ucbd3%u7801%u9090%u6858%ucbd3%u7801%u9090%u9090%u8190%u00c3%u0003%u8b00%u531b%u53
ff%u0078%u0000%u00=a HTTP/1.0
```

You can see the first part of the network payload is a series of Ns, used to overflow the buffer of a built-in app on the web server. They are followed by some codes representing new commands being given to the system. All the attacker needs to do is connect to the web service (TCP 80), send this string, and boom. Simple remote exploits like these are ideal for network worms since they are fire-and-forget generic attacks. These kinds of attacks aren't limited to servers, anything with a service can be hit, even routers.[6]

Many attackers just wait for new widespread remote exploits to become available so they can quickly weaponize them by adding the exploit onto existing rootkit. Root kits are software packages designed by attackers to secretly control victimized machines.

Some attacks, like SQL Injection, are more sophisticated, because the remote exploit must be customized for the specific service. SQL injection involves delivering a command to a web application that interrupts the normal flow of database operations and injects new commands, such as delete all databases.[7] Because of this customization, these kinds of attacks aren't usually put into worm form, although it has happened once or twice in the past.[8]

Remote Password Guessing

If your organization has any easily reachable login services on the Internet, then you should be on guard for remote password guessing attacks. Network logins can include Terminal servers, Secure Shell (SSH) sites, File Transfer Protocol sites (FTP), Telnet consoles, Virtual Private Network (VPN) logins, and any network service requiring authentication. The tricky thing is that there may be login services available on your Internet perimeter that you do not know about. This can easily happen if network devices are deployed without hardening or disabling administrative services. Most network devices, like routers and switches, have network console services like SSH and Telnet running on their network interfaces by default.

Attackers scan for network logins. When they find them, they try username and passwords from anywhere in the world, day and night. Once they hit the right combination of username and password, it's easy money. To make things easier for them, there are numerous lists of commonly chosen passwords available for them to try. Currently, the top chosen passwords are Password, 123456, 12345678, qwerty, letmein, 111111, and football.

You can find many popular passwords based on previous hacks and public password dumps.[9] There are also easily available default password lists for network devices. If they think you're using a Krypto Router, they can look up the default password for that router (probably *admin* or *password*) and see if it works. There are numerous tools that attackers can use to automatically scan for listening login services and try a list of usernames and passwords. A typical organization with a SSH service on the Internet sees a few of these kinds of scans every minute from all over the Internet.

Drive-by-Download Attacks

Instead of launching attacks at your web services, some attackers booby-trap web sites to infect victims who browse them. First, the attacker finds or creates an exploit that works against a web browser or anything that a web browser may call. These are remote exploits that the victim connects and inadvertently downloads. Since there are many vulnerabilities found in web browsers, web scripting languages, and web animation tools, there is no shortage of exploits to create. The more popular the browser, usually the more browser exploits uncovered and weaponized.[10]

---

[6]http://arstechnica.com/security/2014/02/
bizarre-attack-infects-linksys-routers-with-self-replicating-malware/.
[7]https://xkcd.com/327/.
[8]http://www.darkreading.com/risk/when-mass-sql-injection-worms-evolveagain/d/d-id/1131799.
[9]http://www.passwordrandom.com/most-popular-passwords.
[10]https://www.cvedetails.com/vulnerability-list/vendor_id-26/product_id-9900/Microsoft-Internet-Explorer.html

For this to work, the attacker needs victims to browse to a site with these exploits. To do this, they have a few options. They can host a site themselves and try to drive traffic to it via search engine optimization or by e-mailing enticing links to victims. Attackers can also hack a site and then use these techniques to get people to visit. Attackers could also just hack popular sites that they know their victims would frequent. This is called a *watering hole attack*. For example, if an attacker is looking to compromise a particular defense industry company, they could set up drive-by-download exploits on a web magazine serving that industry. Some attackers sign up for Internet advertising and deliver exploits via banner-ads on legitimate sites. If users are surfing with unpatched browser vulnerabilities, there is no telling where or when they could be hit.

Network Denial of Service

Instead of hacking a site, attackers simply try to knock it down. They can do this with an exploit that crashes the system or a firehose blast of network traffic. Sometimes these kinds of attacks are politically motivated and sometimes they are financially motivated (pay us to stop). In any case, the attacker attempts to send more traffic to the victim than their servers and network connections can handle. The downside for the attacker is that they must maintain the attack the entire time to deny service. Sadly, this is not very hard. Attackers use other previously hacked victims remotely controlled in a huge global network, called a *botnet,* to generate a traffic swarm. Some hackers rent out their botnets for others to use for denial of service.[11] Sometimes people even volunteer their machines to join a DoS attack if they believe in the political cause.[12]

Attackers can also do *reflection attacks* by sending spoofed UDP packets at unsuspecting servers. The sent packets appear to come from the victim, so the return traffic sent by the legitimate unsuspecting server returns en masse to the victim. Also, the attacker's true IP address is never seen by the victim. Instead, the victim sees a burst of reflections from all over the Internet. Here is an example where the attacker spoofs DNS queries from the victim to DNS servers spread around the Internet. Figure 17-1 shows a simplified version of how this works.

---

[11]http://krebsonsecurity.com/category/ddos-for-hire/.
[12]https://en.wikipedia.org/wiki/Low_Orbit_Ion_Cannon.

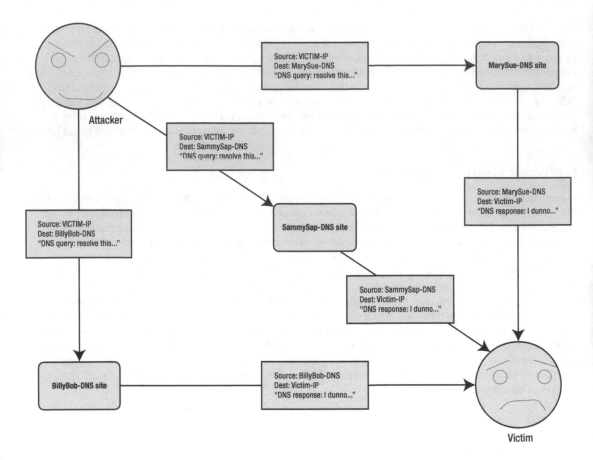

Figure 17-1. *Reflection denial-of-service attack*

Sniffing

Sniffing attacks are eavesdropping or wire-tapping attacks where an attacker listens to all network traffic. Nearly every kind of network interface card supports a *promiscuous mode* where all packets on the transport media are captured instead just the packets addressed to the interface. Sniffing tools can then collect and decode all the traffic. Basic sniffing software tools are built into most operating systems at the administrator level. Here is an example of *tcpdump* on Unix operating systems:

```
$ sudo tcpdump
tcpdump: data link type PKTAP
listening on pktap, link-type PKTAP (Packet Tap), capture size 262144 bytes
19:09:20.732434 IP 192.168.0.14.51750 > www.apress.com.https: Flags [.], ack 50692, win
3925, options [nop,nop,TS val 821382870 ecr 227562921], length 0
19:09:20.732467 IP 192.168.0.14.51747 > www.apress.com.https: Flags [.], ack 44719, win
4010, options [nop,nop,TS val 821382870 ecr 227562921], length 0
19:09:20.732491 IP 192.168.0.14.51750 > www.apress.com.https: Flags [.], ack 53428, win
3839, options [nop,nop,TS val 821382870 ecr 227562921], length 0
```

On networks using hubs, all network conversations are broadcast over every wire, so everything on the local subnet can be sniffed. On switched networks, more work is required. Network switches, which actually segregate network conversations via internal bridges[13] and transmit the conversations to or from the client to their network port. The difference is like having a verbal conversation in a crowded room (network hubs) versus passing private notes amongst each other (network switches). However, many network switches have *span ports* that can be used to copy ongoing connections on that switch to another device. Another way eavesdroppers can gain access to switched conversations to physical tap the local wire by placing a tap in-line somewhere in the connection. This is less relevant within an organization's facility but can happen if an attacker sneaks onsite and plants a tap on a key connection.

A bigger issue is eavesdroppers upstream on the Internet or telecom provider side of the connection listening on Internet conversations going in and out of the organization. This is how some government intelligence agencies spy on organizational traffic.

Wireless network traffic, like hotspots at coffee shops, act like hub networks. Anyone on that wireless network could potentially be eavesdropping on the users of that network. Since wireless networks are nothing but network packets delivered by radio, attackers sometimes set up some distance away with long-range antennas to dip into the conversations.

Another way network traffic is sniffed is at the device level. Local network connections go through a switch and a router or firewall in order to get onto the Internet. Those network devices have the capability to listen and record network conversations. Sniffing is often a common redundant diagnostic feature for these kinds of devices.

Anything that is not encrypted in a network transmission can be decoded by a sniffer. Here is a tcpdump session of logging into an unencrypted web server with the username *globaladmin* and the password *spacepickle*. Note how easy it is to spot in a sniff trace.

```
$ sudo tcpdump -A
tcpdump: data link type PKTAP
listening on pktap, link-type PKTAP (Packet Tap), capture size 262144 bytes
10:02:15.172746 IP 192.168.0.14.51867 > 192.168.0.1.http: Flags [P.], seq 1:417, ack 1, win 4117,
options [nop,nop,TS val 479748387 ecr 9113597], length 416: HTTP: POST /goform/login HTTP/1.1
.......#2.....E...~.@.@..............P..F....$.....&.....
..a#....POST /goform/login HTTP/1.1
Host: 192.168.0.1
Accept: text/html,application/xhtml+xml,application/xml;q=0.9,*/*;q=0.8
Connection: keep-alive
Content-Type: application/x-www-form-urlencoded
Content-Length: 39
loginUsername=globaladmin&loginPassword=spacepickle
10:02:15.182719 IP 192.168.0.1.http > 192.168.0.14.51867: Flags [P.], seq 1:138, ack 417,
win 17376, options [nop,nop,TS val 9113598 ecr 479748387], length 137: HTTP: HTTP/1.0 302
Redirect
```

Malware sometimes installs sniffers on internal servers. These sniffers capture passwords or credit card numbers as they are transmitted around the secure internal network. Attackers can also record volumes of encrypted network traffic and analyze it at their leisure. Some encryption schemes can be broken, given enough captured traffic or time spent deciphering them.[14] Even if an attacker can't break through your network encryption, they can perform traffic analysis and learn what addresses you've visited. Remember that encryption covers the contents of the packet, or envelope, the *to* and *from* addressing information

---

[13]http://ccm.net/contents/307-network-equipment-bridges.
[14]http://null-byte.wonderhowto.com/how-to/hack-wi-fi-cracking-wep-passwords-with-aircrack-ng-0147340/.

has to remain visible for the messages to be delivered. Traffic analysis is a specialized intelligence field that analyzes things like conversation participants (and their popularity in conversations), frequency of communication, and size of communication.

Impersonation

Each host on an Ethernet has a unique fingerprint called a MAC (Media Access Control) address, which manufacturers set. Network software binds these MAC addresses to IP addresses. Hosts on a local network then use Address Resolution Protocol (ARP) to look for the MAC address for a given IP address. If an attacker can spoof a MAC address, they could subvert the ARP process[15] and impersonate that host. These attacks are easy since many network adapters and nearly every operating system supports changing the MAC address. In just one command, I can change the MAC address on my Mac:

```
$ ifconfig en0
en0: flags=8863<UP,BROADCAST,SMART,RUNNING,SIMPLEX,MULTICAST> mtu 1500
 options=27<RXCSUM,TXCSUM,VLAN_MTU,TSO4>
 ether 00:23:32:b3:ce:e6
 inet 192.168.0.14 netmask 0xffffff00 broadcast 192.168.0.255
$ sudo ifconfig en0 ether 00:23:32:b3:ce:e7
$ ifconfig en0
en0: flags=8863<UP,BROADCAST,SMART,RUNNING,SIMPLEX,MULTICAST> mtu 1500
 options=27<RXCSUM,TXCSUM,VLAN_MTU,TSO4>
 ether 00:23:32:b3:ce:e7
 inet 192.168.0.14 netmask 0xffffff00 broadcast 192.168.0.255
```

Sometimes an attacker puts up their own Wi-Fi hotspot with the same name as a local business, and then eavesdrops or hijacks the conversations. Since wireless is just radio, an attacker could also use a much stronger radio signal to overpower a Wi-Fi access point or client. If an attacker has access to the local network, they launch a DoS attack to take a server down and then impersonate it to steal login credentials.

There have even been cases of criminals using stolen or fake SSL or TLS certificates, which are *supposed to be* verifiers of identity.[16] Criminals have also been known to steal entire domain names from registrars for impersonation.

Man-in-the-Middle

If you can sniff a network connection, then you can take it a step further and try to insert yourself into the conversation. Remember that TCP connection streams have handshakes and sequence numbers to track and isolate the connection. If an attacker can sniff those sequence numbers, they can inject themselves into the conversation on both sides. This is called a *man-in-the-middle* attack. Man-in-the-middle attacks can intercept or substitute encryption keys, so attackers can decrypt confidential data. Attackers can also gain access to two-factor authentication in this manner as well.

---

[15]https://en.wikipedia.org/wiki/ARP_spoofing.
[16]http://news.netcraft.com/archives/2014/02/12/fake-ssl-certificates-deployed-across-the-internet.html.

A successful man-in-the-middle attack allows an attacker not only have full access to the conversation but also secretly alter the conversation. One attack is to hijack a victim's web session with their Internet banking system, steal their two-factor authentication while sending the victim an error message. The victim thinks the banking site is down, while the crook cleans out the account. Figure 17-2 illustrates how it looks on a web session.

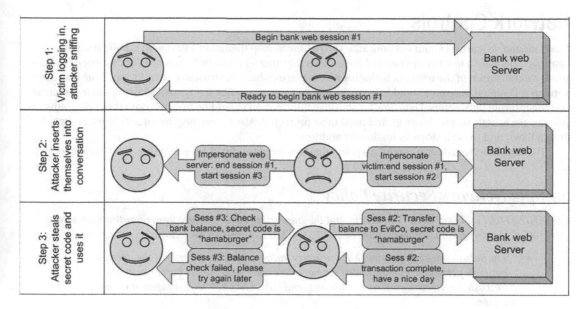

Figure 17-2. *Man-in-the-middle attack*

An attacker can also just sniff and copy the session-ID token out of a web session and then use that token to directly impersonate the user. This isn't a full-blown man-in-the-middle attack; it is called *session hijacking.*[17] It still involves using sniffing or statistical analysis of poorly chosen keys to completely compromise the authentication credentials of the victim.

Some man-in-the-middle attacks originate from an attacker seizing control of the infrastructure involved in the transmission of the information. Sometimes this means taking over routers, a DNS server (to plant false entries pointing to fake sites), or even malware-implanted tools within the network stack on a host.

Exfiltration of Data

Once an attacker has broken into your network, sometimes it's a challenge to maintain a persistent remote control connection and copy all of your data back out. This is called exfiltration and can be accomplished in a variety of ways. Some attackers are brazen and just copy files out via FTP or SSH sessions, if there are no firewalls or network monitors in place to block or alarm for such things. It can be challenging on networks with stringent firewall egress rules (hint: you should have these) so attackers have to get creative.

---

[17]https://www.owasp.org/index.php/Session_hijacking_attack.

Attacker can hide data inside of seemly innocent DNS queries or HTTPS conversations. Who is going to suspect a machine going to a *MyHappyShoppingSite.com*, when in fact, the web request itself contains stolen data and the web site is run by cyber-criminals. Data can be easily encoded or encrypted and then tucked into any kind of communication medium that exits your network. It's very hard to control exfiltration, though that doesn't mean you shouldn't try.

Network Controls

Now that you've learned about network attacks, it's time to stop them. Let's start with administrative controls. There are a few key operational documents that should be recorded for network security. One is a good, clear diagram of the network including all the places where the trusted networks touch the untrusted networks. Detailed diagrams should also include critical networks like the scoped sensitive environments and the Internet perimeters. Data flow for sensitive information should be mapped onto these diagrams, so you can see exactly where things go and need to be protected. All of these help avoid accidents, point out design flaws, and provide documentation for auditors.

The biggest administrative control is a policy that lays the groundwork for everything else. Here's an example:

Sample Network Security Policy

ORGANIZATION will protect its IT networks and the supporting infrastructure from unauthorized access, corruption, or interruption. To accomplish this, ORGANIZATION will do the following:

- *The Security department will have primary authority for the security of the untrusted network perimeter. The untrusted network perimeter refers to the border between untrusted networks, such as the Internet, and ORGANIZATION managed or owned networks.*

  - *The Security department and the IT Department will jointly manage the security of the untrusted network perimeter.*

- *ORGANIZATION will only use these approved network security devices to control access across untrusted network perimeters. Security standards for approved network security devices will be written by the security department.*

- *ORGANIZATION will only make perimeter changes based on business-need and only after a risk analysis and approval process. The IT department will be responsible for making the perimeter changes while the Security Department will be responsible for the risk analysis and approval.*

  - *ORGANIZATION will use a formal process of submission, review, analysis, acceptance, verification, and maintenance to manage proposed changes to the untrusted network perimeter. The Security department must review and perform a risk assessment for all changes to the untrusted network perimeters, either by configuration changes or by the addition of new equipment.*

- *The Security department will be responsible for maintaining a configuration standard describing the protocols, directions, content and business reasons for every network communication crossing the untrusted network perimeter.*

- *The IT department and the Security department will share responsibility of the management of systems placed on the untrusted security perimeter. These systems should be network devices such as Internet routers, network switches and other monitoring devices.*

  - *The IT department will be responsible for maintaining and managing a secure configuration of these devices based on the approved hardening standards. The Security department will be responsible for providing technical risk assessments of these device configurations.*

- *A Demilitarized Zone (DMZ) is a network segregated by security devices such as firewalls. ORGANIZATION will use DMZs to provide defense in depth for critical servers. ORGANIZATION considers DMZs to be semi-trusted domains.*

  - *Network connections from customers and other third parties will terminate in a DMZ.*

- *The Security department will be responsible for periodically assessing the vulnerability and configuration of the untrusted network perimeter. This will take the form of device configuration audits or network vulnerability scans.*

- *Remote access refers to connections to ORGANIZATION owned or managed networks and computers from untrusted networks. ORGANIZATION requires that an approved security device, such as a firewall or a VPN termination device, manage all remote access.*

  - *Remote access connections must use approved cryptographic protocols and approved authentication methods.*

  - *Automated remote access connections will terminate into DMZ networks with additional security inspections in place.*

  - *ORGANIZATION will only permit remote access from approved portable computing devices. Critical systems, such as servers holding sensitive information, will require additional security controls for remote access.*

  - *The IT department and the Security department will maintain an approved standard configuration for remote access, designed to provide adequate security protections for teleworkers.*

- *The IT department is responsible for managing network security to workstations, and may use technical controls such as personal network firewalls and host-based intrusion detection to reduce risk.*

- *ORGANIZATION will not maintain either inbound modem pools or dialup services. No unauthorized connections either to or from ORGANIZATION networks is allowed.*

- *Wireless networking refers to wireless local area networks (WLANs) connected ORGANIZATION owned or managed networks. The Security department will maintain an approved standard for wireless data networking access, designed to provide adequate security protection.*

  - *WLANs will be treated as untrusted network perimeters and therefore be segregated by firewalls.*

  - *WLANs must support approved authentication and cryptographic methods.*

  - *WLANs should support Network intrusion detection and prevention systems.*

- *All communication protocols and messaging systems traversing the ORGANIZATION perimeter will be subject to automated inspection for malware, policy violations, and unauthorized content.*

    - *The IT department and the Security department will share responsibility for managing messaging security. ORGANIZATION will analyze and filter messages to detect and prevent the spread of malware. ORGANIZATION will perform this filtering before the message is delivered to the recipient.*

    - *ORGANIZATION will not allow unencrypted file transfers of confidential data via messaging systems. Users must only use approved encryption methods and hardware/software systems for message security.*

Network Security Standards

In addition to the standards mentioned in the policy, here are few more standards you may want to consider for network security:

- Network security and hardening standards for virtualized networks and default guest images. If you use public cloud systems, you should have an additional set of standards on how those cloud systems should be accessed and configured.

- Detailed network hardening standards for network devices that include things like disabling unused jacks (to prevent unauthorized people from just plugging into your network) and turning off unnecessary UDP network services on the perimeter (to prevent them being used for reflection attacks).

- Standards describing network access control lists used internally or externally.

    - Externally, do you block certain countries by registered country IP address? If so, who determines the list and how is it updated?

    - Can you use internal access control list to ensure that access to scoped networks only occurs from jump hosts? The implementation of jump hosts is discussed in more detail later in this chapter.

    - Can you use access control lists to do least privilege, such as segregating voice and data networks?

- Standards describing administrative access. What services are allowed (SSH but not Telnet)? Which encryption modes are required? Which networks are allowed access and which are not? What are the requirements to segregate out-of-band management networks from the main network? Should administrators have separate authorized accounts for administrative work?

Network Security Procedures

There should be procedures to go with all of these policies and standards. The following are a few to consider:

- Quarterly vulnerability scanning procedures

- Quarterly firewall rule reviews to ensure that temporary rules are removed, bad rules are cleaned up, and only approved rules are in place

- Periodic MAC address inventory sweeps of the network to ensure that no unknown devices have been added to the network

- Periodic wireless network scans to look for rogue wireless access points and cross-connections that aren't firewalled

Firewalls

There was a time long ago when the entire job of the IT security role was managing the firewall. Most of that job entailed explaining to users why their applications failures were not caused by the firewall but by faulty or poorly documented software. Firewalls have gotten more sophisticated and commoditized and so have IT security roles, but users still do blame the firewall occasionally for application failures. *C'est la vie.*

Firewalls are such a critical control that PCI DSS devotes the entire first control objective to firewall management. Firewalls control access between zones of differing levels of trust or as a partition to block the lateral spread of compromise (back to the original definition of physical firewalls). Usually this means keeping the bad people from the Internet out of the internal network, but they can also be used block off access to the scoped environment from the rest of the organization. Over the years, firewall technology has gotten so advanced and cheap that firewall functionality can be found in most internal switching devices.

Firewall technology covers a range of different types of systems. The simplest firewall is a packet filter, which can be easily configured with open source software.[18] Most firewalls also do network address translation (NAT), so that you can use a small number of live Internet addresses to translate to a larger range of internal RFC 1918 addresses. Packet filter firewalls work on a packet-by-packet basis, so they aren't so useful for sophisticated attacks that spoof TCP connections. The next step up is *stateful inspection firewalls* that check that packets and protocols aren't being spoofed. Stateful firewalls also do some limited packet reassembly to try to ascertain what kind of traffic is flowing through them. Some stateful firewalls can do rule matching on the data streams to try to filter out known attacks or alert on suspicious behavior.

The most secure firewalls are the proxy firewalls, which use software listeners to accept connections on one side of the firewall and fully deconstruct connections before rebuilding them on the other side. Proxy firewalls strictly enforce protocol standards, as they aren't just inspecting traffic but rebuilding connections from scratch on the other side. It gives the firewall tremendous control over what is passing through it. This is why you often see proxy firewalls in place in medical, financial, and military networks.

Proxy firewalls come at a cost, as they can be slower and more unforgiving than other firewalls. If a particular software application doesn't fully conform to documented protocol standards and needs to pass through a proxy firewall, it will not work. Cases like these do come up and require firewall engineers to downgrade proxy connections to stateful inspection. Another limitation of proxy firewalls is that the proxy needs to be written to the specification. For example, the protocols for e-mail, domain name services, file transfer, and web traffic are very well known so you can expect intelligent secure proxies to be developed for them. If a new protocol is needed and no proxy is available, then a stateful connection needs to be used.

When looking at firewalls, there are independent organizations that test and certify firewalls. Two organizations to look at are ICSA Lab Certified firewalls[19] and Common Criteria Certified Boundary Protection[20] devices.

---

[18]Netfilter, Linux packet filtering firewall http://www.netfilter.org/
[19]https://www.icsalabs.com/technology-program/firewalls.
[20]https://www.commoncriteriaportal.org/products/#BP.

Firewall Designs

One of the most basic firewall designs is simply to place a firewall between the Internet and the internal network, and be done with it. This may work fine for home networks, but most organizations need to be a little more sophisticated. A DMZ should be used if the organization has any Internet-facing services like the Web and mail servers. A demilitarized zone (DMZ) is a separate network segregated by firewalls. Access in and out of that DMZ is controlled by access control rules so that if one of those exposed Internet-Facing services is hacked, the attackers still won't have access to the internal network. Some even go as far as using different firewall vendors for each end of the DMZ, to try to get as much breadth of control coverage as they can.

Firewalls can also be used to control switch virtual LANs (VLANs) to help implement *least privilege* on the internal network. An ideal design from a network security perspective (but not necessarily a practical design), is a honeycomb of firewalls network segments between all departments and functions. The goal is to move beyond authentication and provide granular network authorization to just the necessary connections. Firewalls can also be used as a gateway between the following:

- Wireless and Wi-Fi networks.
- Remote access gateways
- Database servers and application servers
- Third-party/business partner connections
- Out-of-band management networks like iLO and PDU interfaces
- Internal "Internet of Things" networks like HVAC, door card readers, and voice networks

Firewall Management

When it comes to the firewall rules itself, *least privilege* is your guide. The worst kind of firewall rules are those that allow every host to have full service access to every other host. Not only do these rules defeat the purpose of firewalls but they can also be cited as audit control failure findings. If such a rule is actually deemed necessary, it should be treated as a temporary policy exception and be approved by the ISMS committee.

Organizations are often mindful about the firewall rules allowing connections in from the Internet but forget about the rules going out. Remember the network exfiltration threat. *Egress filtering* is a useful tool that can be implemented on the firewall to limit which machines on the inside network can talk to the Internet. Many servers may never need Internet access, so why give it to them? At the very least, you should limit the protocols that users can access online. There are some organizations that deploy separate web proxy servers that users must web surf through to the Internet. In this way, drive-by-downloads and exfiltration attacks can often be spotted and stopped.

Some firewalls can implement whitelist or blacklist blocks. This means instead of having every single address on the Internet allowed to touch your Internet perimeter, it is limited to a defined set of servers (whitelist) or certain known bad addresses are blocked (blacklist). Subscriptions to the addresses of known addresses with bad reputations are available and can be integrated into some firewalls.

Jump Hosts and Firewalls

Firewalls are powerful but they don't always offer the granular authorization tools that you need. Sometimes you want to apply more control on user or administrator access across a network boundary. Enter the jump host. As discussed in Chapter 6, are sometimes called *bastion hosts*. These are special workstations—virtual or physical—that sit between scope or trust boundaries and manage access. Basically, you build a hardened machine (see Chapter 15 on hardening standards) and allow access through the firewall to it. This machine acts as a secure gateway into the trusted or scoped environment. Technically, you can set this up many ways but commonly people use either SSH-Agent forwarding (often for Linux connectivity) or remote desktop gateway (often for Windows connectivity). Here are two good resources on how to do that.

- **Bastion Host, NAT instances and VPC Peering**
  `http://cloudacademy.com/blog/aws-bastion-host-nat-instances-vpc-peering-security/`

- **RD Gateway Setup**
  `http://docs.aws.amazon.com/quickstart/latest/rd-gateway/setup.html`

IDS/IPS

Intrusion detection systems (IDS) work just like sniffers, but for defense. They are software that either sniffs network traffic or acts as a gateway that traffic passes through. Many intrusion detection systems are integrated into firewall appliances, since the firewall already has direct access to all the Internet traffic. The IDS examines the traffic and pattern matches on known attacks and attack behaviors, sounding an alarm when something is detected. In this way, they work much like antivirus software, with an updating signature list of known attacks.

IDS has also evolved into intrusion prevention systems (IPS), where the system blocks a network stream as soon it detects an attack. IPS must be in a position to block network traffic for them.

Some IDS/IPS support subscriptions to IP address reputation lists, so you can monitor or block connections to known sketchy sites and stop problems that don't have signatures yet.

The key thing to remember about IDS/IPS is they work primarily off lists of known attacks, so they're useful for scraping off the top layer of sewage flowing into your network, but they won't capture everything. They are only as good as their signature lists and those lists usually at least 24 hours behind the latest threat. Some IDS/IPS software packages allow you to write your own signatures, which is handy in emergencies or customizing signatures for your environment.

One big value of an IDS/IPS is since they clear away the Internet background radiation of scans and attacks, you can focus on the really dangerous threats. The second value of an IDS is to give you a network-eye view of what's going on on your network and what threats you might be facing. As you study IDS logs and alerts, you will see probes, port scans, exploit attempts, and all kinds of suspicious behavior. Over time, you'll get an idea about what should be normal for your organization and industry, so that when the threat level changes, you'll have some warning. All of this entails spending time and resources on examining IDS data. There are many tools and visualization systems that can help with this. They all cost something in terms of time or money (or both). The real cost is the expertise and time invested in training or hiring people with strong skills in both network technology as well as network attacks.

When I was a consultant, I used to talk to organizations about IDS deployments. I would ask them if they were currently reviewing their firewall and web logs. When they said no (because they always did), I asked them how they felt about adding another system that would generate more logs for them to ignore. I'll say it bluntly: The value of an IDS/IPS is in the expertise and resources you put into using it. It is not a fire-and-forget control. For some organizations, this is such a burden that they pay an outsourced organization to watch their IDS logs for them and call if they see a real problem.

IDS Deployment

Obviously, you want to have IDS sensors at your Internet perimeter and in front of your sensitive systems. You also should put IDS wherever you see major traffic flows, such as:

- Where users access the Internet, to watch for signs of compromise
- On the scope barrier as discussed in Chapter 6, to watch who's trying to break in there
- Between the DMZ and the inside, to watch for escalating attacks

Some IDS software can be configured with a preloaded HTTPS certification, which automatically performs a man-in-the-middle attack on encrypted web sessions for users. In this way, you can have more visibility into possible threats, such as drive-by-downloads heading down toward user web browsers.

Host-based IDS (HIDS)

Some IDS solutions are software applications that can be loaded on servers or workstations. They listen to incoming and outgoing network conversations from the host, as well as sometimes monitoring what is going on internally on the system as well. Usually a HIDS is configured to transmit its log data to another server so in the event it is compromised, all of the log data is preserved.

Transmission Encryption

Encryption is a good control to counter the threats of sniffing, spoofing, and man-in-the-middle. The encryption most normal people think of is called *symmetric encryption*, where a code key is used to both scramble up a message and descramble it. This is called *encrypting plaintext data into ciphertext data*. Since you use the same code key to encode as you to decode, you need to keep this code key a secret.

The problem arises if you have to exchange code keys over an untrusted network without meeting in person. Here's an old riddle: a prince is fighting a civil war. He needs to send a message to his one trusted Duke in a nearby castle, but there are traitors everywhere in his kingdom. He commissions a special iron box from his master blacksmith, DiffieHellman. This box has a big iron rings on the lid and case to affix locks onto. He puts his message in it, and then locks it with a padlock that only he has the key to (see Figure 17-3).

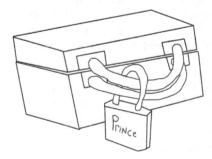

Figure 17-3. *DiffieHellman's Iron Box with the Prince's lock*

He summons his fastest rider, Squire Internet. He doesn't really trust Squire Internet, but he has no choice. He gives the locked chest to the Squire and tells him to take it to the Duke. Upon receiving the box, the Duke smiles, as he knows what to do. He snaps a second lock onto the chest ring, one that only the Duke has the key to open (see Figure 17-4).

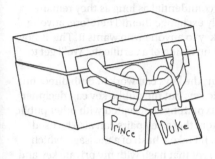

***Figure 17-4.** The box with both the Prince's and the Duke's lock*

He hands the box back to Squire Internet and tells him to return it to the Prince. The Squire shrugs and rides back to the castle. Upon receiving the Squire, the Prince unlocks his padlock and tells the Squire to ride the box back to the Duke (see Figure 17-5).

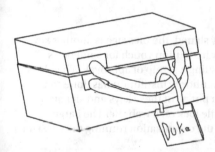

***Figure 17-5.** The box with just the Duke's lock*

Upon receiving the box a second time, the Duke can open his lock, safely knowing that no one but the Prince ever had access to the message.

This method works well for solving riddles and as an analogy for public key cryptography. Instead of a single shared secret key between two individuals, public key cryptography uses two pairs of keys for each participant. The key pair consists of a private key and a public key. The public and private keys are mathematically derived to be related to each other, but it is unfeasible to figure the private key from the public.[21]

---

[21]http://www.emc.com/emc-plus/rsa-labs/standards-initiatives/what-is-a-one-way-function.htm.

In the Prince/Duke example, the public key functions as the lock and the private key unlocks the lock. Each participant has a public key that other participant can use to encrypt, but not decrypt, messages. So when setting up a communications channel over an untrusted network, like the Internet, participants sends their private key to the other. They can then use each other's public keys to send messages that only the other can read. Usually, these messages are the code keys, called symmetric keys, which are used to both encrypt and decrypt messages. These symmetric keys only keep data confidential as long as they remain secret to outsiders, but public key cryptography gives us a way to safely exchange them. Therefore, anyone wanting to receive encrypted information just publishes their public key to anyone who wants it. This is how secure HTTPS web servers work, with their public key being wrapped up inside of a certificate. We'll get to what that means in a minute.

Our analogy breaks down a bit because in *public key cryptography*, the keys can work in both directions. Not only can the private key decrypt things enciphered with the public key, but the public key can decipher things encrypted with the private key. However, public keys can't decrypt things encrypted with other public keys. It only works within the pair. This gives us a useful new application: these key pairs can also be used to verify their counterpart. This is where digital signatures come from. If I take a hash of a message, which you may recall is a mathematical fingerprint of the file, and then I encrypt that hash with my private key and the other person's public key. Now I send out that encrypted hash as a digital signature with the original message. Someone who gets my message can take their own hash of the received message. If they have my public key, they decrypt the signature with my public key and compare the hashes. If the hashes match, then they know (a) the file hasn't been altered and (b) it had to come from me since only I have the private key. Viola, the file is authentic.

Web Encryption

Now take it one more step. What if instead of a message being digitally signed, the message is another key, a third person's key. This is how you can have a large trusted authority institution vouch for someone's public key. They can choose to digital sign someone's key as way of issuing a stamp of approval. What does that stamp approval mean? Well, it could mean that the large trusted authority institution has done some legwork to verify there the person's name matches their key. Now, you put all of these keys and signatures into a standardized format and you have HTTPS certificate, aka the little lock on a web site. The Large Trusted Authority Institution is the *certificate authority*, which is who the organization running the web site has paid to sign their key.

So now when you visit a web site, you get two things from the certificate: a key to start the encryption for talking to the web site and a method of verifying that the web site is legitimately who it claims to be. Certificates also include validity dates, because you do want to rotate your keys every couple of years or so. Web certificates also include the domain name of the server they're verifying, which is the mechanism for establishing legitimacy of the site. You really don't want some random cable modem web site to be capable of claiming to be *PugetRegionalBank.com*.

If you've been paying attention, you may notice something is missing here. How does your browser verify the certificate authority's signature without having access to its public key? Moreover, if I don't have their key, how do I get it in a manner that I trust? Doesn't another certificate authority have to sign it? This could go on forever. Yes, and this is why the folks who write browser software just include a big bunch of certificate authority keys that are *pre-trusted* by your browser. These are called *trusted root certificates* and you can view them in your browser settings. Don't be too shocked by how many are in there. Some of the more privacy-minded security professionals go in and remove many of these certificates to limit who they trust by default. Not a bad idea, but it can be a lot of work to maintain and not exactly user friendly.

Whenever a browser has a problem with a certificate, it displays a message warning the user. We talked about how confusing this can be to non-techies. Here's a breakdown of what the messages are and what they mean:

- *Expired*: This certificate used to be trustworthy but that was a long time ago (or yesterday), expiration date has passed.

- *Mismatch*: Domain name and certificate don't match.

- *Revoked*: This certificate is no longer trustworthy, be very worried.

- *Untrusted*: This certificate is not in my root list (includes self-signed).

Note that in each case, the actual transmitted data is still encrypted, but the certificate message questions the identity of the opposite end.

Virtual Private Networks

Another major use of network encryption (and public key cryptography) is with *Virtual Private Networks* or VPNs. A VPN encapsulates or tunnels network traffic inside an encrypted connection to the other end of the VPN tunnel. Users on the VPN appear to have a direct link to the things on the other side of the tunnel. To everyone else, all they see is an encrypted network stream passing back and forth. This means VPNs ideal for connecting remote sites and untrusted networks to your organization without the cost or hassle of wiring up direct lines.

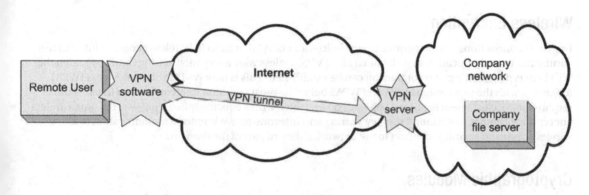

Figure 17-6. *A VPN tunnel over the Internet*

Both sides of the VPN connection must be running compatible software and have the same encryption settings. The VPN software can run locally on a computer as a VPN client or within a server as a VPN gateway. VPN software is available in almost every commercial firewall and most of them are compatible with each other. Many VPNs also have firewall capability within the tunnel itself, which is very useful. Remember *least privilege*. Give connections just the access they need and no more. You can use firewall access control rules to manage access by destination host and allowed service through the tunnel. Some VPN solutions can even allow IDS scanning of tunnel traffic, which is a nice extra control to have on those remote connections.

One downside of VPNs is that they are completely dependent on a network to flow over. If you are using VPNs over the Internet to link up your remote offices, a denial-of-service attack or Internet outage means a loss of the VPN. Organizations that really put Internet providers or telco companies in their significant threat list run VPNs over their leased lines to remote sites. This significantly reduces the risk of eavesdropping from the telecommunication providers or national government intelligence agencies.

VPNs come in a variety of flavors, but the most common contemporary types are IPsec and SSL, although almost any persistent communication channel can be used for a VPN (e.g., SSH). IPsec VPNs are based on IPv6 and are pretty much the standard for network-to-network connections. They can require some work to set up, as there are half a dozen settings to make sure match on both sides of the tunnel. IPsec VPNs also require several different network services (protocols and ports), which can make them hard to run from behind firewalls. SSL VPNs are web-based and actually now use TLS encryption since SSL has been deprecated. SSL VPNs are lightweight and work over the web HTTPS service. They are often used as remote access connections for road warriors who need the flexibility and ease of use. With remote access VPNs, you can usually tie whatever authentication systems you have in your organization to the remote connection. Since they are accessing your network from parts unknown, stronger authentication standards should apply. Using two-factor authentication for VPN connections into scoped networks is prudent and required for PCI DSS.

Console Encryption

Administrative credentials should also be protected by encryption, so standards should specify the use of HTTPS, Secure Shell (SSH), and Remote Desktop Protocol (RDP) for all admin work. All of these services are encrypted by default, but you should specify in a standard what levels of encryption should be used. Both RDP and HTTPS support TLS encryption with certificates, which can be self-signed or externally purchased.[22] SSH encryption can also be configured from relatively weak to strong.[23] Remember what you learned about access control in Chapter 16 and specify stronger authentication for administrative access, especially if admins are logging from the Internet.

Wireless Encryption

For Wi-Fi connections, there are quite a few choices for encryption as well. Wireless access points can use certificates as authentication as well, much like a VPN. Unless your encryption settings and key match the Wi-Fi encryption settings, no connection can be established. This is how Wi-Fi Protected Access (WPA) functions, with the two versions WPA and WPA2 being the most common implementation in use. Both require the wireless client to enter a pre-shared key, which works effectively like a password. Some wireless encryption schemes can handoff this key sharing and integrate native Windows authentication to allow wireless clients to seamless connect to the network if they're part of the domain.

Cryptographic Modules

Some organizations opt to acquire cryptographic modules to do their encryption. Instead of setting up servers, software, and configuring interfaces, they use cryptographic modules for ease of use. These are hardware or virtual image appliances with pre-configured cryptographic software and an interface to do the encryption. There are many commercial cryptographic modules and most are certified to NIST standards to be acceptable for certain classes of government work.

---

[22]https://technet.microsoft.com/en-us/magazine/ff458357.aspx.
[23]https://www.digitalocean.com/community/tutorials/understanding-the-ssh-encryption-and-connection-process.

Acceptable Encryption Methods

Cryptographic methods are always changing. Sometimes flaws in implementations or algorithms are found. Sometimes new technology and techniques find ways to decipher encryption schemes without the keys. Some encryption schemes work well for some kind of applications and not for others. This means that you should have published encryption standards specifying acceptable algorithms, key lengths, and appropriate usages. You should revisit the standard at least yearly, and update appropriately.

As a note on this, anyone foolish enough to think they can write their own encryption algorithm without thorough outside review should remember the assume breach concept as well as Schneier's Law, which states: "Anyone, from the most clueless amateur to the best cryptographer, can create an algorithm that he himself can't break."[24]

FURTHER READING

- **TCP in detail**
  http://home.mira.net/~marcop/tcpip_detail.htm

- **Fallacies of distributed computing**
  https://en.wikipedia.org/wiki/Fallacies_of_distributed_computing

- **Distributed Denial-of-Service (DDoS) Attacks/Tools**
  https://staff.washington.edu/dittrich/misc/ddos/

- **Exfiltration and remote commands**
  http://www.advancedpentest.com/help-beacon

- **The Basics of Cryptography**
  http://www.pgpi.org/doc/pgpintro/

- **NIST Guideline for Using Cryptographic Standards in the Federal Government: Cryptographic Mechanisms**
  http://csrc.nist.gov/publications/drafts/800-175/sp800-175b_draft.pdf

---

[24]https://www.schneier.com/crypto-gram/archives/1998/1015.html#cipherdesign.

CHAPTER 18

■ ■ ■

More Technical Controls

Nothing in this world can take the place of persistence. Talent will not; nothing is more common than unsuccessful men with talent. Genius will not; unrewarded genius is almost a proverb. Education will not; the world is full of educated derelicts. Persistence and determination alone are omnipotent.

—Calvin Coolidge

This chapter covers several other major technical services that require security controls. Once again, you may notice that the emphasis for effective security is on good basic practices like simplicity in design, security standards, and maintenance. As always, I urge you to think about what you need to accomplish with respect to risk reduction before you start implementing technical solutions or start buying tools. Fix the problems you need to fix and make sure that your operations team can maintain them and you have sufficient time and expertise to review their output.

Internet Services Security

Services that you directly exposed to the Internet are definitely at high risk to attack. Sometimes network worms and amateur hackers target them simply because they are there for anyone to use. Unfortunately, these are also the common services that most organizations insist be open on the Internet for business reasons.

The security policy for these services is pretty straightforward and simple:

> *To minimize unauthorized access, modification, or downtime to Internet-visible applications, ORGANIZATION will maintain and follow secure application development, secure configuration, and ongoing maintenance processes.*

The standard and the specifics controls in place can get more complicated.

Web Services

The most commonly exploited Internet service is the Web. Building upon the chapter on Network Security, I am going to go into more detail on securing a web site. First off, like any other critical service, you need to define a hardening standard for web servers, probably even broken out by type of web server and purpose. You should also have a standard for the HTTPS or secure web, which defines the acceptable forms of cryptography and certificates to use. Static web sites are rare these days, so you should expect to deal with web application services and server-side scripting languages. Dynamic web services are notorious for having vulnerabilities, so these sites should be subject to at least monthly vulnerability reviews and persistent patching.

© Raymond Pompon 2016

R. Pompon, *IT Security Risk Control Management*, DOI 10.1007/978-1-4842-2140-2_18

Web Stack

Web sites that actually do things, like process transactions, are usually deployed in stacks. At the front end facing the Internet, you have the web server. Behind that, a web application server does the heavy lifting of the processing and business logic. Finally, behind that you have a database or storage solution of some sort to hold all the data. In a three-tier setup, this can be deployed as shown in Figure 18-1.

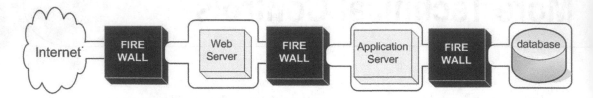

Figure 18-1. *A typical three-tier architecture for web sites*

In this figure, I have placed firewalls to segregate each tier into its own subnet. You should define the standard for firewall access rules to allow only the necessary traffic between tiers. From the Internet to the web tier, you should allow only web traffic. From the web tier to the application tier, you should allow only the application data connections, preferably originating from the application server to the web server as a destination. That method protects against a compromise of the web server granting an attacker access to the application server. From the application tier, only allow a database connection. You can also add intrusion detection, load balancing, and network encryption controls on all of these barriers as well. Because each tier has their own unique traffic type passing into them, you can use specialized firewall rules to do things like dampen denial-of-service attacks or filter out specific web application attacks.

Web Application Attacks

Web application attacks, like software security, are about manipulating vulnerabilities in custom software. Web applications are often specific to the organization and the service they're offering, making the application unique and complex. This means that no generic vulnerability scan of the web service can give you an adequate picture of potential security problems. There are specialized tools and specialized testers who can perform this kind of testing. Lists of web application scanning tools are located at the following two web pages:

- `https://www.owasp.org/index.php/Category:Vulnerability_Scanning_Tools`

- `http://sectools.org/tag/web-scanners/`

Web application security can also use specialized defensive tools, such as web application firewalls. These are firewalls, which are specifically designed to analyze and block web application attacks. They go beyond standard firewalls in that you can program them to match the unique application requirements of your web site. Some can also take data feeds from web application vulnerability scanners and do *virtual patches* by blocking previously uncovered but yet unpatched web vulnerabilities. The downside is that web application firewalls are complex and require customization to work well. A free, open source, web application firewall that you can explore is Mod Security at `https://www.modsecurity.org`.

Like software security, web application security is a huge specialization, which I do not have space to cover here. These are two good resources:

- **Web Application Security Consortium**
  `http://www.webappsec.org/`

- **Open Web Application Security Project**
  `https://www.owasp.org/`

E-mail Security

E-mail is a vital resource that every organization uses to some degree or another. E-mail is also a conduit for a variety of security problems including malware infiltration, confidential data leakage, and inappropriate usage. Users should have already been advised about what e-mail actions are appropriate as part of the published acceptable usage standards. You can use controls like *digital leak prevention* to scan for confidential data sent out via e-mail. In addition, it's common to have both antivirus and anti-spam filters for incoming messages. First, a good basic e-mail policy to set the goals:

Sample E-mail policy

The IT and Security Department will share responsibility for managing messaging security. To achieve this, the ORGANIZATION will:

- *Use e-mail filters to help prevent the spread of malware*

- *Use approved encryption methods and hardware/software systems for sending confidential data in e-mail*

- *Warn users that e-mail entering or leaving the ORGANIZATION will be subject to automated inspection for malware, policy violations, and unauthorized content*

As you can see, this calls out for some standards, such as what should be filtered as well as how e-mail should be encrypted.

Spam Prevention

Unsolicited e-mail is more than just an annoyance, since a lot of it includes scams, malware, and phishing attempts. A good spam solution reduces all unsolicited e-mail, reducing the likelihood of security attacks via e-mail. Like these other topics, e-mail filtering is large field of study and I am going to touch on some of the important points. A common defense against spam is *reputation blacklisting*. These are downloadable lists, called Real-time Blackhole Lists (RBL), which contain the source addresses and characteristics of known spammers. The most famous is the Spamhaus Project at https://www.spamhaus.org. You can configure mail filtering systems or your firewalls to constantly update themselves with these lists to block e-mail from these known bad addresses. Blacklists aren't a perfect solution but they are good for knocking down a good percentage of the spam.

Another popular technique is to do an analysis of the e-mail itself, looking at known keywords present in spam and common mail header formats. Some systems—like the open source Spam Assassin[1]—use multiple techniques combined with machine learning to figure out what real e-mail to your organization looks like and what is spam. Then the analysis engine scores the e-mail on the likelihood of spam, and you can set a threshold for what will be rejected.

One thing you do not want to have happen is to have your e-mail server used to spew spam at other people. Not only does that make you *part of the problem*, but it also quickly lands your organization on a Real-time Blackhole List. When that happens, other organizations start blocking all e-mail from your organization. Besides being infected by spam-relaying malware, another way this can happen is if your mail server is configured as an *open mail relay*. This happens when a mail server on the Internet allows anyone to send e-mail through it. Your organization's mail server should only allow e-mail to be sent by your users or to your users. Some mail server software configurations allow open relay by default, so checking for this and locking it down should be part of your server-hardening procedures. Some malware payloads also create

---

[1]http://spamassassin.apache.org/

spam relays, which means spam e-mail originates from your IP address and possibly land your organization on a *blackhole list*. It's prudent to use the firewall to block outbound e-mail from your internal network except from the authorized e-mail servers. However, some malware-infected hosts send their spam through the authorized mail server. This is why some organizations spam-filter outgoing e-mail as well.

Attachment Filtering

A lot of malware can flow in through e-mail attachments. There are days when it seems like I get twice as many malware e-mail attachments than legitimate ones. At the very least, you want to have e-mail antivirus software running to block known malware attachments. With thousands of new malware attacks being created every day, you should take it a step further and block mail attachments. The safest response is to block all attachments and force users to transfer files in another manner, but this isn't usually feasible in most organizations. So where do you begin with attachment blocking? First, you should begin with a standard defining what you will block, and then communicate that standard to your users. A simple message like this: *To help keep our organization secure, we have implemented a policy to remove any mail attachment that potentially can hide malware. If any mail attachment is on the following list, it will be blocked from entering or leaving our network. Please make your senders are aware of this restriction. If you have any questions or problems, please contact the IT help desk. Thank you.*

What do you block? The most dangerous attachments are known executables and the system configuration-altering extensions. There is very little reason for users to send these kinds of files to each other, so they are a safe bet to block. A list to start with could include the following: ASF, BAS, BAT, BIN, CMD, COM, CPL, CRT, DLL, DOS, DRV, EXE, HTA, INF, INI, INS, ISP, JAR, JS, JSE, LIB, LNK, MSC, MSI, MSP, MST, OBJ, OCX, OS2, OVL, PIF, PRG, REG, SCR, SCT, SH, SHB, SHS, SYS, VB, VBE, VBS, VXD, WS, WSC, WSF, WSH.

Attached media files, such as movies and sound clips, are also often blocked. They could contain exploits that attack the user's media players on their workstation, so there is a malware risk. They could also contain subject matter that is inappropriate or a violation of copyright. Third, these files are often large and consume network bandwidth and storage resources. Users rarely need to e-mail large files to each other, so these are commonly blocked as well. A good list of extensions for media includes the following: ASX, MP4, MPEG, PCD, WAV, WMD, WMV.

Another category to block is documents. Some documents, like Microsoft Word or Excel files are commonly e-mailed, but could contain confidential information. Perhaps if your organization has a secure file transfer solution, then you could block all document attachments. Another risk from documents is that they could contain macros, which can also contain macro viruses. Lastly, some documents can contain exploits that take over the viewer programs with malware. Here are some file extensions associated with documents: ADE, ADP, ASD, DOC, DOT, FXP, HLP, MDB, MDE, PPT, PPS, XLS, XLT.

One way attackers sneak malware attachments into organizations is to compress the files. In the e-mail, users are instructed to uncompress and open the attachments. It's convoluted but it has been known to work.[2] Some antivirus solutions look inside compressed files and remove known infections or tagged file extensions. Attackers have responded by compressing the files with passwords and putting the password in the e-mail instructions. Therefore, some antivirus solutions block all compressed files with passwords. Here are some extensions associated with compression: 7Z, CAB, CHM, DMG, ISO, GZ, RAR, TAR, TGZ, ZIP.

Some attackers embed malicious JavaScript code within HTML-formatted e-mail. These are not attachments but embedded within the text of the e-mail itself.

---

[2]http://www.hoax-slayer.net/fake-order-status-emails-contain-locky-malware/

Mail Verification

With all this spamming, malware attachments, and phishing going on, it can be a challenge for mail software to pass on every legitimate e-mail. Many spam-filtering solutions use a wide variety of techniques to score the validity of incoming e-mail as spam-like, using many techniques to verify the legitimacy of the sender. However, every now and then real e-mails are misidentified and blocked. A positive thing your organization can do to boost their legitimacy score is to use mail verification identifiers. The two methods used for this are Sender Policy Framework (SPF) and DomainKeys Identified Mail (DKIM) signatures. Both work with your Domain Name Server (DNS).

SPF involves adding an extra DNS record that lists which of your domain's mail servers are the legitimate senders. Mail servers receiving e-mail from your organization's domain can do DNS lookups on the incoming IP addresses to verify that the e-mail hasn't been faked. This kind of verification is good to use for organizations that frequently e-mail notifications to their customers. You can learn more about SPF at http://tools.ietf.org/html/rfc4408.

DKIM signatures are similar to SPF in that it involves the DNS records to verify that the sending mail server is legitimate. DKIM takes SPF a step further and adds a digital signature. The digital signature is carried in the e-mail itself and the DNS record provides the key to verify the signature. This extra step provides further evidence that an e-mail is legitimate. You can learn more about DKIM signatures at http://tools.ietf.org/html/rfc4871.

The problem with SPF and DKIM is that they are not universally adopted. Even if you were to spend the time and resources to implement them, there is a percentage of your e-mail receivers who never bother to check. However, many large organizations who have added e-mail verification have seen a reduction in fake e-mail.[3]

DNS Security

Domain Name Services are one of the most critical services for an organization. You need to publish accurate DNS records for anyone to send you e-mail or access any of your Internet services. You need to correctly resolve the DNS addresses of others in order to send anyone e-mail or access any of their sites. Back in the days of yore, DNS didn't exist and everyone on the network had to use IP addresses to talk to one another. I still remember having a note taped to my monitor with the IP addresses of the University servers I needed for my work. DNS is powerful and scalable, but it was never designed to be secure. DNS queries run on the UDP protocol, which is easily spoofed. DNS servers themselves are just simple software with no special security features. Because of their importance, there are number of specific threats to DNS servers:

- *Denial-of-service attacks*. Attackers try to shut down or block access to your DNS server, thereby cutting off customers from all of your Internet-visible services. It's a single weak spot that can take down an entire domain worth of services.

- *Poisoning attacks*. Attackers try to insert fake DNS records into your server to misdirect or trick customers. Sometimes this can be done by taking over the DNS server directly. Other times attackers can use DNS software vulnerabilities to introduce false records.

- *Harvesting attacks*. An attacker probes the DNS server for overly descriptive records that could provide inside information on the organization's architecture. For example, some poorly implemented DNS servers could be serving DNS both externally to the Internet as well as internally to the users. Those servers could leak information about addresses and names of the internal servers, which could aid attackers in technical or social engineering attacks.

---

[3]https://security.googleblog.com/2013/12/internet-wide-efforts-to-fight-email.html

If you are running your own domain servers, then you need to harden them against attack. A good guide on this is the *NIST Secure Domain Name System (DNS) Deployment Guide* (`http://dx.doi.org/10.6028/NIST.SP.800-81-2`).

DNSSEC

Since trusting Domain Name System servers and the records they provide is critical to the operation of the Internet, there is an enhanced DNS security service. Called the DNS Security Extensions, or DNSSEC, it is an additional protocol run on the DNS server that provides digital signature verification to DNS records. Anyone querying a DNS server with the DNSSEC extensions running is able to verify any requests against the authoritative DNS server for the domain. DNSSEC has not yet been widely adopted, but it is slowly catching on. More information is available at `http://www.dnssec.net/practical-documents`.

Encrypting Data at Rest

Data encryption is seen as the perfect security solution for data at rest. However a significant portion of security breaches are because of application attacks, especially web application attacks. Application attacks often give the attacker direct access to the encryption keys (because they are stored in disk or in memory) and therefore, open access to the stored data regardless of how strong it was encrypted. So when thinking about encryption, consider the specific threat you are trying to block. Let's look at the threats in Table 18-1.

Table 18-1. *Encryption's Viability Against Threats*

Threat	Will Encryption help?
Stolen server or hard drive	Yes. Without encryption key, the drive is a brick
Insiders at cloud company	Yes. Without encryption key, insiders download scrambled data.
Insiders at your organization	No. Sysadmins have the key or access to a system with the key.
Accidental data leakage	Maybe. Persons who have accidents are likely to have unencrypted data.
Hackers breaking into the web site	Maybe. If hackers can control software, they can get the key.
Account take-over attacks	No. Possession of privileged user's account means possession of the key.
Government disclosure	No. Governments usually have the resources to break or backdoor most encryption. They can also put you under duress until you give up the keys.[4]

When looking at the risks solved by encryption, the thing to look at is who has the decryption keys. An ideal system would entail that only the data owner had access to the decryption key, but that wouldn't be very useful for large-scale data processing or collaborative work. You need to work on the data and it's hard to work on data if it's encrypted. In the end, most encryption systems require you to trust at least two entities: the system administrators and the software they're running on. You can apply controls to both to reduce risk, but the thing to remember is that encryption by itself is never a complete solution.

Lastly, if you're under PCI DSS, you have no choice. You must use storage encryption for credit card data.

---

[4]`https://nakedsecurity.sophos.com/2016/04/28/suspect-who-wont-decrypt-hard-drives-jailed-indefinitely/`

Why Is Encryption Hard to Do?

You may have heard that encryption is expensive to implement and expensive to maintain. That's true, but why? Let's begin with Auguste Kerckhoffs and his principle: *A cryptosystem should be secure even if everything about the system, except the key, is public knowledge.*

This means you should not rely on hidden knowledge, other than the key, to protect the data. After all, the software used in most encryption systems is freely available to all. The algorithm and the implementation of that algorithm must be mathematically strong enough to resist decoding. Not a trivial task. On top of that, the implementation is usually where you first can get into trouble. A poorly implemented cryptographic system is hard to distinguish from a correctly implemented one. Indeed, if you look at the major cryptographic failures in the past decade, they have nearly all been because of faulty implementation. Implementation failures have included a poorly chosen random seed, choosing the wrong encryption mode, repeated keys, and sending of plaintext along with encrypted text. However, the output from these failed implementations look just as indecipherable as working implementation until scrutinized very carefully.

Even when a cryptographic system is implemented correctly, technological progress can render a scheme obsolete. Faster processors and shortcuts in calculations (often due to implementation flaws) have led to failures of encryption to protect secrets. When this happens, encryption needs to be updated or replaced. After that, all of the data that was previously encrypted must be decrypted with the old busted implementation and re-encrypted with the new hotness. This is not a trivial task. It doesn't help that for the average organization that when this happens is out of their control.

The next thing that makes encryption expensive is key management. Remember that ownership of the key can make or break the security of your encryption. What is involved in key management?

- *Key length*: Keys are numbers and they should be long enough to be unguessable. In general, the longer the key, the better. However, the longer the key, the more computational work the system needs to do in order to encrypt or decrypt something. You need to balance key length with performance.

- *Key creation*: Selection of a key should be completely random, but computer generated random number systems are imperfect. In fact, random number generator systems should be tested as safe for use in cryptography.[5]

- *Key storage*: Keys need to be kept somewhere, unless you are going to memorize several hundred digits. Cryptographic key stores are often protected by... wait for it... more encryption. So you have a master key that unlocks all the other keys. The master key is usually tied to a strong authenticator, which you absolutely need to keep secure. Some implementations can *split* the master key between several entities, like requiring of two keys to launch the nukes. This is great for segregation of duties but you can see how this gets complicated.

- *Key backup*: Naturally, you want to back up your key in case it gets damaged or lost in a fire. Like normal backups, you want to keep it well protected and away from where it normally lives.

- *Key distribution*: Once a key is chosen, how does it get sent from key storage to where the encryption is happening? Again, you can use transmission encryption like good old HTTPS. Just make sure that the connection is strongly authenticated on both ends so no one can *man-in-the-middle* you and steal the key.

---

[5]https://en.wikipedia.org/wiki/Cryptographically_secure_pseudorandom_number_generator

- *Key rotation*: Keys should be rotated every now and then. The more a key is used, the higher the likelihood it could be guessed and broken. All things being equal, the usual key rotation period is about a year. Key rotation means choosing a new key, decrypting everything with the old key, and re-encrypting with the new key. Then you need retain the old key in some secure manner for a while because you probably have backups that were encrypted with the old key floating around.

- *Key inventory*: Now that you have all of these keys, perhaps even different keys for different systems, that are all expiring at certain times, you need to keep track of them all. Therefore, you need a key inventory system.

Luckily, there are encryption appliances that do all of this key management for you and present you with a friendly web interface. However, they do come with cost and require you maintain schedules and procedures to manage them.

This finally brings us to encryption policy and standards.

Storage Crypto Policy and Standards

In Chapter 17, we explored encryption standards describing acceptable algorithms and their usages. All you need to do is make sure that you have standards that cover storage encryption as well. This means defining what types of encryption should be used in the following scenarios:

- Disk/virtual disk

- Individual file

- Database

- Within an application

- E-mail

You also need to lay out procedures and schedules to do all of your key management. Don't forget to assign responsibility for all those duties and ensure that records of the activities are being kept.

Tokenization

A close cousin to encryption is *tokenization*, which refers to substituting a specific secret data element with a token that stands in for it. Think about when you used to go to the video game arcade. You'd put a buck in the money changing machine and you'd get out four game center tokens. These tokens work on all the games in the arcade but are worthless elsewhere. You can't change your token back into a real quarter. Each token stands in for 25 cents but only in the arcade. You have to use them there. Tokenization does the same thing to your confidential data and the arcade is your data center, making the tokens useless if stolen.

So how does it really work? Let's take the common example of credit card processing. Suppose you have a large application that collects, processes, and stores transactions that includes credit card numbers. We'll call his application *Legacy*. It'd cost a ton of money to recode Legacy to use encryption. Unfortunately, Legacy connections and processes go everywhere in the organization, so any scope of protection is far wider than you'd like it to be. In fact, most of the places where Legacy is used don't actually require a real credit card number; it simply gets dragged along with all the other customer records. So now, you have a huge scope to protect for no other reason than a limitation of existing technology. Enter tokenization.

As soon as a credit card is entered by a customer, it is sent to a secure separated encrypted system. This secure system is locked down with extremely limited access. It can do payment processing but only under strict conditions in specific defined ways. After the number is saved, it generates a unique token number that looks just like a credit card number.[6]

This is the number that is stored in Legacy in the credit card data field instead of the number the customer entered. It is the token. Whenever a normal user calls up a customer record anywhere in the Legacy system, all they see is the token. It looks real, so the Legacy system can store and track it, but it is useless for payment processing. Whenever someone really needs to activate a credit card payment charge or chargeback, a secure call is made to the secure encrypted system, which uses the real credit card number for the payment. Since this system is locked down, it's difficult for a someone to execute fraud on the card and it doesn't ever need to share the real number with anyone inside the organization.

With tokenization, you have now limited your scope to just the secure system. You didn't have to make expensive and drastic changes to the Legacy application for encryption either.

Malware Controls

Malware is probably topping your risk list and for good reason. With the surge of ransomware attacks, malware has jumped back into the headlines. One of the first controls that IT professionals become familiar with is antivirus software. It forms the third corner in the trinity of classic controls along with passwords and firewalls. Just like every other classic control, antivirus software has been in an arms race against the cyber-criminals. To manage a critical control like antivirus, we should start with a good policy:

Anti-Malware Policy and Standards

The IT and Security Department will be responsible for maintaining security controls to hinder the spread of malware within ORGANIZATION systems and networks. The ORGANIZATION will use antivirus software on all systems commonly affected by viruses.

The Security Department will maintain standards for the following:

- *Approved Antivirus software for workstations*

- *Approved Antivirus software for servers*

- *Approved Antivirus software settings and signature update frequency*

- *Antivirus software alerting and logging*

The Security Department will be responsible for ensuring compliance to the approved antivirus software standards.

Malware Defense in Depth

As you can see from the policy, antivirus software needs to be running anywhere it can be feasible run. While we know antivirus software is far from perfect and can't stop every infection, it's far better to have it running than not. While some may believe that antivirus is a no-maintenance control that is fire-and-forget, it is not. You need to make sure that the antivirus software is fully running, has the latest signatures, and is upgraded to the newer versions. I know many corporate antivirus suites claim that their software does all of these things automatically. It's been my experience that there are failures with

---

[6]https://www.rosettacode.org/wiki/Luhn_test_of_credit_card_numbers

running, updating, or upgrading in about 3% to 4 % of the machines in an organization. So you need to have procedures to periodically verify. In addition to always watching files and memory on the protected machine, the antivirus software should also be configured to do periodic full scans. This can sometimes pick up things from a new signature update that were previously missed.

Because of the prevalence of malware and the capability of the threat, antivirus software is a key control. That means you should have additional controls in place in case it fails. One possible additional control is network antivirus filtering. This is an intrusion prevention network control that runs either on the firewall or in line to filter traffic coming in and out of the Internet. It's not easy to catch the malware in-flight without slowing down the user experience too much, but these filters add a powerful extra control. This is also why additional internal firewalls are useful to prevent lateral spread.

When considering anti-malware controls, don't forget the basics. We've already talked about patching and hardening under vulnerability management. They are absolute essentials when stopping malware from getting a beachhead on your network. Some malware tries to shutdown antivirus software and disable logging, which makes patching even more essential. If the malware can't break into a machine, it can't affect other running programs. Newer operating systems are also much resistant to malware than older ones.

There are now specialized controls that go beyond antivirus software. Some of them add additional protection to the operating system, like Microsoft's Enhanced Mitigation Experience Toolkit (EMET).[7]

Another new control is *application whitelisting*, which are software agents that only allow a pre-determined list of applications to run on computers. You can think of traditional antivirus software as blacklisting, with the signature being the list of malware not allowed to run. As you can imagine, whitelists do require configuration to define what users are allowed to run. Differing solutions offer different approaches to managing these whitelists, from crowd-sourced reputation scoring to user prompting that the newer Macintosh OS X systems do.

In the end, you need to assume breach. You will never stop all malware from getting into your organization. In the normal course of business, with user mistakes and prevalent software, someone will be infected. This means you need to think about detection, containment, and response in the event of an infection. Good logging of antivirus software and user Internet activity can help in this. This is explored more in Chapter 20, which focuses on response controls.

Building Custom Controls

There are times when find that there is no technical control that fits your risks and assets adequately. When acquiring new controls, it's pragmatic to choose controls that can serve multiple purposes over a single purpose. Everyone has limited budgets and you can never know what is coming at you next, so it's helpful to have tools that you can adapt as needed. Sometimes the best controls aren't security tools but generic IT solutions. I've gotten a lot of value out of generic automation systems for collecting logs, sniffing out malware, and tracking down data leaks. However, if you have the talent and the resources, you can build your own technical controls.

When setting out to build your own controls, first you need to remember that whatever you do will be imperfect and somewhat slapped together. Unless you're a security tools company, you're unlikely to build a robust and comprehensive tool that is easy to maintain. That means you shouldn't rely on it too heavily. Most of the custom controls that I've built and used were detective and response controls. It's rare and risky to build and rely on your own preventative controls.

---

[7]https://microsoft.com/emet/

Custom controls can be as simple as scripts that sweep through Active Directory looking for suspicious entries. Computing technology is best at managing and ordering existing pre-formatted data so many useful custom tools scrape and parse the output of other security controls. Friends of mine built a vulnerability management risk-scoring engine called VulnPryer (https://github.com/SCH-CISM/VulnPryer) that helps sort vulnerability scanner data. I've built more than a few custom tools that analyze security log data to spot targeted attacks and suspicious insider activity. If you look around, sometimes you can find an existing open source project or tool that you can enhance or adapt to work better in your environment.

Whatever you come up with, it's a good idea to write up what you've done and talk about it. There might be others in the security community who could benefit from or be inspired by your work. We defenders can use all the innovation we can get.

FURTHER READING

- **Importance of Web Application Security**
  http://blog.jeremiahgrossman.com/2009/08/overcoming-objections-to-application.html

- **NIST Guidelines on Electronic Mail Security**
  http://csrc.nist.gov/publications/nistpubs/800-45-version2/SP800-45v2.pdf

- **Malicious documents**
  https://zeltser.com/analyzing-malicious-documents/

- **OWASP Cryptographic Storage Cheat Sheet**
  https://www.owasp.org/index.php/Cryptographic_Storage_Cheat_Sheet

- **NIST Special Publication 800-175B, Guideline for Using Cryptographic Standards in the Federal Government: Cryptographic Mechanisms**
  http://csrc.nist.gov/publications/drafts/800-175/sp800-175b_draft.pdf

CHAPTER 19

■ ■ ■

Physical Security Controls

One of the problems with offices is that you can get into them because by design you have to actually go to work.

—Chris Nickerson

The interesting thing about physical security is that some security folks write it off as *not my problem*. We too can be victims of the *Someone Else's Problem* effect. In 2016, the California Attorney General reported that 22% of all reported breaches came from physical theft and loss. Physical security problems were second only to malware. As much as we IT security geeks would like to distance ourselves from physical security problems, it's something we need to address.

The good news is that comparatively speaking, physical security is easier to get a handle on than most other IT security domains. This is because of two big reasons. The first is that physical security is a thing that human beings can tangibly examine and test, as opposed invisible and multifaceted world of technology. The second is that we humans have been dealing with physical security challenges as far back as we've been human. It's a mostly solved problem, we just need to apply the appropriate controls and make sure that they remain working.

Getting a Handle on Physical Security

As with applying any control, the first thing you should think about is the risk to scoped assets. When you look at the assets, the primary ones in your scope are likely going to be the data center, server rooms, wiring closets, and portable media. You use the majority of your physical security controls to protect those. From there, you move out and look at the surrounding office areas with their laptops, workstations, and open network connections. Finally, you can move your attention to the outer physical perimeter: the office suite, the floor, the building, or the campus.

Many organizations have multiple office locations, sometimes in different countries, which can make securing the premises a challenge. This is where scope comes into play again. Maybe you don't need to protect all of your offices because you only have data centers in scope for a handful of them. You may have locations based on the logistics or business needs, but the physical security is weak. For example, shared offices within another organization or open buildings with a lot of temporary workers. These are the kinds of places where you want to pull back scope to exclude them, and then build a perimeter to protect the rest of the organization. In effect, you treat these out-of-scope zones as untrustworthy or as *the outside*. This is just like the scope barriers in the electronic world, but now in the physical. This could mean having different key and visitor access requirements when people move from an untrustworthy area into a scoped protected one. It's at this perimeter entrance where you can place additional surveillance cameras. Perhaps you have controls for both, just stronger controls in the scoped areas. Sometimes you can have several levels of increasingly controlled zones as you move closer to the core scoped assets. Think of the difference in physical security layers in a bank: between the bank lobby, behind the teller line, and finally the bank vault. The scoped area should have less foot traffic than the un-scoped, so additional controls shouldn't be much of a hassle.

© Raymond Pompon 2016

R. Pompon, *IT Security Risk Control Management*, DOI 10.1007/978-1-4842-2140-2_19

Physical Risk Assessments

When you look at physical security risks and where to put controls, you should carefully examine the existing practices. How do people enter and exit the facility? If you walk the process yourself, you can review yourself and spot where things might break down. How do visitors enter the facility? Does someone have to do something to let them into the facility (unlock a door), or is the visitor supposed to *check in* at a desk as they pass down a hall into the rest of the office? I call this the *honor system of physical security*, because only the rule-abiding visitors check-in; the scofflaws blaze by into the facility, often unnoticed if the entry is busy. Are strangers challenged once inside the building and wandering around?

When looking at door locks, remember that these are controls based on technology and technology is complex and can fail. Table 19-1 shows some technological vulnerabilities with physical security that you should be aware of.

Table 19-1. *Physical Controls and How They Can Be Defeated*

Physical Control	Can Be Defeated By
One-way fire exits	Tape over the lock bolt, door propped open with a small wad of paper
One-way entrance doors that unlock via Infrared beam on the inside	Sliding a stick under the door and tripping the sensor[1]
Keyed entrance locks	Lock-picks, bump keys[2], forcing the lock cylinder
Proximity card reader door locks	RFID duplicator[3]
Combination code door locks	Nearby hidden camera placed by attacker to record code

Beyond doors, you have walls. When looking at physical security, consider the strength and coverage all *six walls* of a room. This means don't forget the floor and ceiling. Many server rooms and data centers have drop ceilings and raised floors that may not fully block access from areas beyond the secured perimeter. I have also seen secured areas where the doors are heavy and thick, but the walls are just drywall nailed on to the studs. If a wall is weak enough to be easily broken through, then make sure that it's in a high-visibility area so that at least attackers call attention to themselves. This is also the reason why outside walls should be clear of vegetation and hiding places for would-be burglars and snoops.

Speaking of visibility, be sure to consider the security of your scoped facilities after hours. While some places have guards or personnel on site 24/7, other places become abandoned after business hours. What would happen if an intruder attempted a break-in after dark? Would any alarms be raised? Another question to ask is when the last person leaves, do they have a checklist to follow to make sure that all the entrances and windows are actually locked (remember the tape-on-the-door-lock trick) and the burglar alarm is armed?

Physical Security Policy

Before getting into the details of the physical security controls, you should set the ground rules with a physical security policy. From this policy, you can see the controls, standards, and training that is needed.

---

[1]http://thedailywtf.com/articles/Insecurity_Doors
[2]https://www.nachi.org/inspectors-bump-keys.htm
[3]http://www.eweek.com/security/hacking-rfid-tags-is-easier-than-you-think-black-hat

Sample Physical Security Policy

ORGANIZATION will protect its facilities, offices, equipment, and media from unauthorized physical access, tampering, or damage. The Security department, the IT department, and the Office Manager will share responsibility for managing the physical security of ORGANIZATION's facilities, offices, computing systems, and media. To help meet this goal, the ORGANIZATION will:

- *Control access to its offices, server rooms, and wiring closets with self-locking entrances.*

- *All authorized employees and contractors of ORGANIZATION will wear photo-id badges.*

- *The rooms containing IT equipment, network wiring, or media will be designated as secure facilities and must use keyed entrance locks.*

- *Secure facilities will be physically segregated within ORGANIZATION and require high-level of keyed access to enter.*

- *ORGANIZATION will deploy detection tools such as card access logs, video surveillance cameras, and alarms to control access to secure facilities.*

- *The IT department will have the responsibility for controlling visitors into secure facilities and tracking the visitor's name, organization, and reason for visiting.*

- *Visitors in the secure facilities will be escorted and supervised at all times.*

- *Visitor escorts will prohibit visitors in the secure facilities from bringing or removing media or IT equipment without inspection or approval.*

- *The front desk reception will have the responsibility for authorizing visitor access into the facilities, assigning visitor badges, verifying, and tracking visitor information including name, organization, and reason for visiting.*

- *ORGANIZATION employees or on-site contractors will be instructed and trained to supervise visitors and report unsupervised visitors.*

- *ORGANIZATION will use physical and IT security controls to ensure the protection of portable computing devices and media. These controls can include laptop encryption, laptop cable locks, and media safes.*

- *ORGANIZATION will track and monitor portable media containing confidential information and properly dispose of them when no longer needed.*

- *Co-location and Cloud service providers engaged by ORGANIZATION to manage IT systems used by ORGANIZATION will adhere to these standards.*

- *Co-location service providers engaged by ORGANIZATION will use an authorized access list to the facilities. Service provider will track formal authorizations from ORGANIZATION for changes to the access list.*

- *The IT and Security department will share responsibility for managing co-location facility access and ensure that only authorized individuals are on the access list.*

Personnel Security

An anthropologist named Robin Dunbar proposed that a human can only comfortably maintain a relationship with around 150 people.[4] This seems like a good limit to the members of an organization where you begin to lose track of who's authorized to be onsite. At a few hundred personnel, employees can no longer recognize other employees and you have the danger of unauthorized personnel wandering around the corridors of your office. Therefore, for larger organizations, it is prudent to have all authorized personnel wear badges. These badges should be difficult to duplicate and recognizable at a distance. Badges can also include a photo of the bearer to help identify the badge holder. Badges aren't a perfect control because a determined attacker can just counterfeit one; but badges are still useful in spotting opportunistic intruders.

Visitor Security

Staff should have guidance on how to handle visitors and strangers wishing to enter the facility. These visitor procedures should be included in the security awareness training that all staff receive. They should be instructed not to let strangers into the office or let them tailgate behind authorized persons unlocking doors. Visitors should remain outside or in a controlled waiting area until the purpose of their visit can be determined. For example, if Mary Sue is coming to visit Bobby Joe, she should remain in the lobby until Bobby Joe comes out to meet her and escort to where they plan to meet. Under no circumstances should visitors or unaccompanied strangers be allowed to roam around looking for someone's office or meeting room. In more secure environments, visitors should be formally signed into a register with their name, affiliation, and purpose of visit. Their identity can be verified with government photo-id and they can be issued a temporary visitor badge. Visitor badges can be printed with the valid date. Some sophisticated badges are chemically treated to slowly change color over the day to indicate they are invalid.

Staff should also be trained to challenge unrecognized or unbadged strangers found inside the facilities. This *challenge* can be as simple as telling staff to approach the person and say, "I don't recognize you. Can I help you with something?" If the staff person feels uncomfortable or senses danger, they should disengage and report the stranger to the office manager or the security department immediately. When escorting visitors or strangers, staff should be instructed not to take their eyes off them until someone has taken the handoff or they've exited the secure area.

Training

Naturally, some people will find all of these procedures a hassle or awkward to do. Since you're creating policies and procedures and planning to be audited, you should either make the procedures representative of the culture of the environment. If you don't, you will have to work persistently to ensure that they are enforced.

One way to train people is to conduct random drills. Have a colleague wander around the office without a badge to see if he is stopped by staff. If so, have the "fake stranger" escorted to the security department, where you reward the staff person with a free coffee card or some other prize. Publish overall results so that employees know that this is going on, but don't shame individuals. You can also engage people's self-interest with training by telling them that part of the purpose of these procedures is to cut down on office thefts. There are occasional purse-and-phone thieves who wander through offices, stealing whatever they see lying around, which is usually people's personal belongings. This tends to get people's attention more than protecting the corporate assets.

---

[4]https://en.wikipedia.org/wiki/Dunbar's_number

Security in the Offices

As stated in the sample policy, the best way to handle the front door is lock it all the time and require someone come up and open it for visitors. Always locked doors imply that authorized personnel have keys to let themselves in. Having keys means you need to keep track of who has what keys. People also need to be trained to report lost keys in a timely manner. This is where electronic key cards are handy, as you can quickly invalidate a lost or stolen key without having to call a locksmith. Always locked doors should also have auto-closers on them and door prop alarms, especially for doors that are low traffic or in low visibility areas.

Clean Desk Policies

Even with all the visitor policies and locked doors, one should always assume breach. Attackers could get in via social engineering and mistakenly allowed access through deception. Given that, how do you prevent confidential information from walking out the door? This is where a clean desk policy comes in. As the name says, the ideal policy is for all desks to be clean of all papers and drawers locked when someone is not there. Not only is this the most secure way but it is also the easiest to audit. If you told people to remove only the papers with confidential information from their desk, how could you ever verify this without reading every single paper you find? We are in the fourth decade of the so-called "paperless office," so maybe this is a realistic goal in your organization. This also means that you need to ensure that all staff has access to locking drawers and cabinets, and that someone has the master key in case of emergencies. Be aware that the clean desk can apply to more than papers, as things like laptops, portable drives, and mobile devices should also be put away when someone leaves the desk.

Similarly, computer screens that could display confidential information need to be positioned so that they are not easily read from outside windows or by visitors. There are special privacy screen overlays available, which prevent shoulder surfers from seeing anything but a blur. Only someone sitting directly behind a monitor can see clearly. Staff should also be instructed to clean off white-boards and dispose of meeting materials in conference rooms when done. Not only is this secure, but it also looks much more professional.

Obvious security mistakes like taping password notes to monitors or walking away from a logged in session should be discouraged through training and reminders from security personnel. One training practice is to leave *parking tickets* for offenders and small prizes for good behavior on random office checks.

Devices like paper shredders or shred bins should be made available so that staff has a simple and easy way of doing the right thing with confidential documents. As a perk, some organizations even allow employees to bring confidential documents from home in to be shredded, as long as it's reasonable.

Screen Saver Lockouts

In event that people forget to log out of their systems and leave for the day, most modern operating systems offer an automated screenlock after a certain amount of inactivity on the computer. The industry standard is 10 or 15 minutes[5] for a password-protected screen-obscuring screen saver to activate on an unattended system. Users should be encouraged to log-off fully at the end of the day.

---

[5]PCI DSS 3.2 control objective 8.1.8 states that "If a session has been idle for more than 15 minutes, require the user to re-authenticate to re-activate the terminal or session."

Network Access Controls

To prevent attackers plugging unauthorized devices into the organization's network, there is a network security system called Network Access Control (NAC). The NAC system authenticates and tracks every authorized device on the network. When a new device is detected, the NAC system automatically shunts their connection, usually via VLAN, to a network of limited access until their validity can be established. These systems are very handy to prevent the office visitor who plugs their laptop in and infects the whole network with malware they didn't know they had. The downside is that NAC systems are not simple or cheap to implement, but they may be worth deploying in some environments that need that level of control.

Secured Facilities Controls

Secure facilities, like server rooms, need to have stronger security controls than the general office environment. They should have their own locked door that requires a different key than the main office door. This may sound obvious but I have seen server rooms in offices separately only by a fabric curtain. Secured facilities should also have their own visitor sign-in procedures with rules regarding what equipment can be allowed in or out of the room. You do not want random vendors sticking their USB drives, possibly full of malware, directly into your servers.

Access to secure facilities should be based on least privilege and extremely limited. There should be a formal procedure that tracks changes to the access list and list should be subject to periodic review. Photography within secure facilities should be prohibited and the secure facilities should be kept out of public building directory listings. It's likely that despite all of this, building maintenance personnel may have access to the room anyway. Be sure to work with your landlord to ensure that they only enter the room when accompanied by organizational staff, unless it's an extreme emergency.

Racks and Cages

Within the room, the ideal would be having all racks and cages also locked just in case someone does make into the room. This isn't always feasible, but you can look at locking the racks and cages with your most sensitive equipment and connections. As with the door locks, the keys to the racks should be tracked and reviewed. Since there are no door prop alarms on racks on cages, you need to drill staff about leaving doors unlocked and unattended. These are examples of things that auditors double-check and write up a finding about.

Cameras

In addition to all the locks and visitor procedures, a video surveillance camera recording all entries and exits into the secure facilities is also prudent and a PCI DSS audit requirement. A good place to position your camera is inside the secure facility facing the door. This way when the door opens, you can get a full body picture of whoever is entering. Motion sensors can also trigger video recording and e-mail an alarm. Remember that video surveillance is technology and thus prone to occasional failures and glitches. Assign someone to review the camera and footage on a periodic basis to make sure that it is capturing what you think it should capture. You need to retain your video logs for at least 90 days.

Alarms

Secure facilities can also have alarms. Some surveillance camera systems can have schedules so that they alarm when detecting motion during certain times. You can also install door prop alarms. If you have alarms, make sure that you have assigned responsibility and procedures to respond to them. An unattended e-mail box full of motion sensor alarms is not doing anyone any good.

Guards

If you have the resources, then you can have physical guards patrolling your facilities. Sometimes the building management company already has guards that you can leverage as part of your security program. You should make sure that you have a good working relationship with the guards and that they understand your security requirements and goals. This is especially true if the guards are not hired directly by your organization. Reviewing the guards and building management security capabilities should be part of your risk assessment. In addition, if the guards are external to your organization, then you need to review their security and general processes as described in Chapter 23, which focuses on third-party security. Lastly, you need to make sure that the guards know what to do and who to contact if an incident occurs. Supplying them with your phone number is insufficient; they should have an escalating call list of numbers to contact.

Environmental Controls

Since computers don't react well to heat or water, it's common to have environmental controls in server rooms. These include heating ventilation and air conditioning (HVAC) systems to control temperature and humidity. These HVAC controls should be tied to alarms, so that if there is a problem in the middle of the night, someone is alerted immediately (instead of waiting until the morning shift discovers a room of overheated and ruined equipment).

Media and Portable Media Controls

It's a safe bet to assume that anything small enough to be carried off, will be. This includes print outs, laptops, mobile phones, backup tapes, flash drives, isolinear optical chips, hard drives, floppy disks, and workstations. There are numerous cases of major breaches being attributed to the loss or theft of these kinds of devices. Sometimes these devices are mistakenly thrown away without the information being rendered unreadable. All of these kinds of mishaps are so easy to prevent, yet so devastating, that it is likely that you will look negligent and/or stupid if it happens to you. So don't let it happen.

When it comes to managing media with confidential data, the first thing to do is know what you have. This means assigning responsibility for keeping an inventory to track things like backup tapes and external drives. A security standard defining the protection requirements for this media should be published as well as procedures for media handling. Minimum physical security standards for off-site transport and storage of backup tapes need to be developed, as this is where many accidents occur. Procedures for handling drives and systems sent out for repair should also be established. You do not want a critical server full of credit card numbers shipped off to the local computer repair shop without first removing the drive or ensuring proper security at the repair depot. One idea is to color code the media and systems that contains scoped data, so that it is physically easy to spot when drives or equipment are taken out of the secure facilities (see Chapter 23 for a discussion on ensuring security at external repair depots).

Media Destruction

When it comes time to get rid of equipment and media, the data needs to be rendered completely unreadable. Dumpster diving by attackers looking for accidentally thrown away confidential information is a real threat. Furthermore, you do not want classified information sitting around on old laptops donated to charity. There are data-erasure software applications that can erase and write zeros to make it very difficult to recover data from a disk. Even more secure are media-shredding companies that physically turn a hard drive into metal splinters and provide you with a certificate of destruction. Some even come on-site to do the destruction to ensure that the sensitive data never left the premises.

Laptop Controls

As thousands of laptop computers are stolen each day[6], users should be educated on how to protect their portable devices. This can be part of the security awareness training and should include basic tips like:

- Don't leave laptops unattended in a vehicle, especially in plain view.

- Don't leave your laptop unattended in public places like coffee shops.

- Be vigilant at airport security checkpoints; keep an eye on your laptop when it emerges from the X-ray machine.

- Don't check your laptop in with your luggage when flying; keep it with you.

- Carry your laptop in a nondescript bag.

- If your laptop is lost, report it to the security department and the police immediately.

In addition, you can have laptop security standards that include engraving or affixing tags to the laptops to assist in their recovery. There are laptop anti-theft software agents that can track or remote wipe laptops or mobile phones when reported stolen. One of the best controls is laptop encryption. In fact, any media or device containing confidential information that can crooks can carry away should be encrypted.

Convergence of IT and Physical Security Controls

A large number of modern physical security controls are network-ready, which means they can generate meaningful log data as well as allow remote administration. This includes door locks, surveillance cameras, motion sensors, and temperature sensors. Some organizations keep these systems segregated in order to prevent an IT attack from escalating into physical penetration. However, other organizations are converging their physical and IT security controls to gain greater prevention, detection, and response capabilities. For example, key card logs can be cross-referenced with user logins. This could trigger an alert when the system sees user login to a machine in a building that never saw a key card entry login. Either the user tailgated in off someone else's card or that's not him. Some converged systems can take this a step further and not allowing a network login to occur until a user has physically carded into the building. Convergence can also provide security administrators with a single interface to manage user access. It can be very powerful to have a single interface to review (and revoke) all user permissions.

FURTHER READING

- **American Society for Industrial Security (ASIS)**
  https://www.asisonline.org/

- **Hackers love Lockpicking**
  https://hackaday.com/tag/lockpicking/

- **Physical and IT Security Convergence: The Basics**
  http://www.csoonline.com/article/2117824/strategic-planning-erm/
  physical-and-it-security-convergence--the-basics.html

---

[6]https://en.wikipedia.org/wiki/Laptop_theft

CHAPTER 20

■ ■ ■

Response Controls

A good plan, violently executed now, is better than a perfect plan next week.

—General George S. Patton, Jr.

How you react when things go wrong is a huge factor in how much damage an incident does to your organization. If you run around like your hair is on fire, things will not go so well. When we are busy or stressed, we make bad decisions. There is panic, confusion, and indecision. Who is in charge? What do we do? Who do we call? This kind of disorder can magnify impacts and turn a bad situation into a disaster. However, if you remember the assume breach principle, then you know incidents are inevitable and you can be ready. What do you need to do to be ready? It involves three principles: preparation, planning, and practice.

When preparing for incidents, there were two kinds of controls that can be used: detective controls, which is primarily about event logging, and corrective controls, which is primarily about backups and failover systems. When planning, we need to look at business continuity plans, when defining how the organization can keep running after disasters and outages, and security incident responses to contain and remedy breaches. Lastly, we try to learn from these events and practice for future incidents.

Logging

An important part of response is responding to the right thing. This means knowing what is actually going on. This is where logging comes in. With comprehensive logging and regular log review routines, it's possible to catch a breach attempt in progress before catastrophic damage occurs. Even if you don't have an active incident occurring, logs can give you an idea about what is going on inside your organization. Let's begin with the logging policy, which will give you a good idea of what logging is all about.

© Raymond Pompon 2016
R. Pompon, *IT Security Risk Control Management*, DOI 10.1007/978-1-4842-2140-2_20

Sample Logging Policy

ORGANIZATION will monitor and review critical systems for signs of unauthorized access as well as to ensure that controls and systems are properly functioning within expected parameters.

The IT and the Security department will share responsibility for configuring and maintaining event logging for all critical systems and security devices. The Security department will have sole responsibility for maintaining and protecting security event logs from unauthorized erasure or modification. Access to logs will be limited to those with specific needs.

- *Systems will be configured such that all system clocks will be synchronized to a trusted time source*

- *Systems will be configured to record the following types of events:*

  - *Login/authentication successes and failures*

  - *Process or service execution successes and failures*

  - *Major system faults and errors*

  - *Administrator actions and configuration changes*

  - *Creation and deletion of system services and objects*

  - *Creation and deletion of security services and objects*

  - *Access, modification, and restart of logging*

  - *Antivirus alerts and events*

- *Each log record will include the following details:*

  - *Date/time of event*

  - *User ID of who initiated event*

  - *Type of event*

  - *Source or origination of event (network address or subsystem)*

  - *Name of affected data, system component, or resource objects*

Confidential data should not be stored in event log data. If for unavoidable technical or business reasons, confidential data is stored in a log, then ORGANIZATION will use additional controls to protect either the confidential data elements or the entire log file.

The IT Department is responsible for regularly reviewing all logs for critical systems.

The Security department is responsible for regularly reviewing all security device logs for systems like firewalls, intrusion detection system (IDS), and two-factor authentication servers.

Log history will be retained for at least one year, with a minimum of three months of searchable online availability.

Log files will be backed up to a centralized log server or media that is difficult to alter.

What You Must Log

While some of the items in the policy are self-evident, there are others that are worth exploring in more detail. One of them is what should be logged. In an ideal world, you'd log every device capable of logging and keep the data forever. While storage space is relatively cheap, it's usually not feasible to store, organize, and review that much data. I've worked with systems where nearly a quarter of the internal network bandwidth was consumed by data streams from security devices to the log servers. You need to prioritize what you need to record.

The first things to consider are which controls should be generating logs and how should it be captured. Nearly every security device and service on the market now has the capability of generating logs. Since your technical security controls are your primary means of defense, they will be one of your best sources of information when something is going on. You will want as much data as possible from them. This means firewalls, intrusion detection/prevention systems, virtual private network devices, antivirus software, and authentication servers.

In that same vein, you want to capture any security-related events generated by the systems maintaining your infrastructure. Nearly every infrastructure system, including cloud-based services, can generate logs about their status. You absolutely want to capture the events related to security. Sometimes those are clearly categorized by the system and sometimes you have to explicitly select them. When selecting for security events, you want information on adding/changing users, modifying user privileges, stopping/starting services, adding/changing access rules, excessive login failures, and modifications to the logging system itself. Infrastructure systems can include anything from storage systems, domain controllers, file servers, network devices, and virtualization platforms. Many public cloud service providers provide detailed logging feeds on usage and management of their system. Be sure to capture the security related events there as well.

Any systems in scope, including the systems managing the scope barriers, should also be logging. This includes accounting servers, web servers, database servers, e-commerce servers, and mail servers. These servers should also log any access attempts, failure or success, to the software and data that is in scope. If someone logs in and views the credit card data, you want that event logged. If a system administrator modifies the software running the e-commerce site, you want that logged as well. If someone tries to login and fails repeatedly, you definitely want to capture that. In some regulatory environments, like HIPAA, all accesses to health records (for example) must be logged and auditable.

Lastly, every server and workstation should be set up to do a minimal set of logging as well, even if those logs aren't sent off-box for collection and analysis. You want the same level of logging, capturing security and administrative events on those boxes. On workstations and servers, it's really useful to track software installs and local logins. All of this can prove valuable during an incident.

Logging systems differ, but most should offer the same basic capabilities. You should be able to record the user-id or IP address of what triggered the event, the type of event (which will vary based on the system), whether the event failed or succeeded, where the event come from (the source address or which subsystem), which subsystems or data was affected by the event, and the date/time of the event.

When looking at the time/date of the event, make sure that all of your systems are set up to do clock synchronization to a trusted, reliable master time source. Without clock sync, system clocks will slowly drift away from the actual time. During an incident, you do not want to realize that one system is 9 seconds fast, while another is set to the wrong time zone and 12 seconds behind. It can turn into a real mess and slow down a critical investigation when every minute counts. Use clock sync and verify that it is working periodically. Establishing an accurate timeline of events across multiple disparate devices is much easier if they are all using the same time source.

Look at Your Logs

Capturing logs is great. Looking at them is better. You do not want to be in the middle of an incident when you realize that you haven't been capturing proper log data from key systems. More subtly, if you haven't been studying your logs, it's hard to spot abnormal behavior and discern attacker actions from normal user actions. The gold standard is by checking your logs so often that you spot an incident in progress and are able to stop if before the damage goes too far. To keep everyone on track, assign the responsibility for log review, set a schedule, and have that person follow a procedure for log review. Part of that log review procedure should be to generate records of the log review and their findings. This serves several purposes. One, filling out the paper work forces them to do the actual log review. Second, this log about your logs provides you with some history and intelligence to review in case you need to look back after an event occurred. Third, auditors will ask you for these records as proof that someone is doing log review. Fourth, they provide proof to everyone else that IT security is doing their job. Security is mostly invisible and when we succeed, nothing happens. Having a record showing how hard we work to make nothing happen is a wonderful tool during budget season. By the way, you don't actually have to use paper. Many security analysts just open a help desk ticket and record their log review events and findings there.

If you can manage it, there are some great logging-review software packages out there. Some of them are commercial and some are open source, but all require a lot of set up and customization. Every organization's infrastructure is unique and their logging needs vary, so setting up a reliable and useful system to review logs can take some time. Some systems allow you to set alerts and triggers, which watches the logs for you and sends you an e-mail or raise an alarm when something happens. Here are some things to set triggers on:

- Security changes
- Root logins (sysadmins should use named accounts)
- After-hours access (if atypical for your organization)
- Access control list and other security policy changes
- Disabling/restarting of services
- Changes to the local logging system
- Account lockouts for system or service accounts

All of these can be indications that a security incident is happening. They could also be administrators doing their jobs, but those actions should be traceable in the change control system. Remember that for any alert to be useful, it has to be actionable. It makes no sense to receive hundreds of alerts every day if all you do is file them away and forget them. That's logging, not alerting.

You need triggers and alarms on any changes to the logging system. If the logs consume all the disk space, you need to get on that. It may be that you are under large-scale-but-below-the-radar attack, so no large event triggered but millions of small ones did. This can also happen during a port scan or a brute force attack. In any case, you don't want logging to stop because your disk is full. You also want an alert if the logs suddenly stop coming or are cleared. Attackers will try to shut down or tamper with logging to cover their tracks. Sometimes the only sign you'll see of an intrusion is logging being silenced.

What Are You Looking For?

An answer is only as good as the question, so what questions are you asking of your logging system? Here are some of questions I want to know the answers to:

Has Someone Successfully Broken In?

Which boxes of mine have been breached? Who did it? How did they do it? How far did they get/going? What are they after? What data did they access? What software did they plant? What users did they add? How sure can I be about all of these answers?

Has Someone Singled Me out for Special Attention?

If you're on the Internet, you're under attack right now. It's mostly harmless junk bouncing off your firewalls and filters. Is someone poking at me and only me (or my industry)? Do they know my weaknesses? What do they know about my organization and its people? Is this part of some kind of campaign against my organization? Can I tell who they are and what they want? When combined with external intelligence sources, I can look for what else have they done that I haven't noticed yet?

What Is Going on My Scoped Systems?

Is someone doing something to those systems without authorization? Do active changes match up to change control tickets? Are patches and hardening being put in place in a timely manner? Are all the security controls on those systems working properly? Did someone add a new system to my scoped environment and not tell me? Often interpreting these kinds of logs requires some technical and local environment expertise. A software install or change will look different depending on the operating system, environment, and usage patterns of the system.

How Is Everything Going on that Internet Thing?

What is the state of the state? Are there more probes today than yesterday? If so, why? Is there a new vulnerability out there that I don't know about? Are users surfing to strange and scary places more than usual? What parts of my infrastructure are getting the most attention? What kinds of malware, spam, and phishing are coming into our network? What services are getting lots of attention from attackers right now?

What Have I Seen Today that I've Never Seen Before?

I see a lot of stuff in my logs, but what's appeared today that was never there before? I couldn't get through a security book without mentioning the great Marcus Ranum. He said, "By definition, something we have never seen before is anomalous" and he even created a simple little log tool to look for it.[1] Maybe the new thing is just a new technology or service on the Internet that we're just noticing for the first time. No big deal. Maybe a sysadmin made a change and we didn't get the memo. Good to know. Or maybe something wicked this way comes. It's an easy check to build into your logging review process and always seems reveal interesting bits of information.

Protecting Your Logs

As I mentioned before, attackers go after logging systems to cover their tracks by erasing or altering log data. With the threat of insiders, those attackers can include your own system administrators. Some systems, especially the scoped business servers, put confidential data into the logs as well. So you need to protect your logs. It's best to have the logs sent away from the log source to a protected server, and then encrypted and digitally signed as they're saved. The first part is pretty easy, because most systems have the native capability to send logs over the network to some kind of a repository. The most common format for this is syslog with the data being captured in structured text.

The log repository should be secured, even from the IT department and possibly even secure from tampering by the security team as well. This is where digital signatures of hashes of the log data can be used. Encrypting the logs is best, but if you can't, then lock down the log repository server as best you can. Two-factor access and segregating it from the other systems is a good start.

---

[1]http://www.ranum.com/security/computer_security/code/.

Backup and Failover

When talking about responding to problems and disasters, our oldest and best control is backup. Although the backup process is usually owned by the IT department, the security team has a stake in its success or failure. When something bad happens, be it man-made or natural, everyone is going to turn to the backups to get things going again. Backups need to be reliable and available when a problem strikes. Not having a good backup when you need it is one of those things that make you look negligent or stupid.

Keep Backups Offsite and Safe

Backups should be stored securely and some distance away from the systems. If a flood takes out the city where the office resides, you don't want the backup tapes to be in a nearby building. Ideally, you should look at your risk analysis and check the area of effect of the more likely natural disasters when planning an offsite storage system. For example, in Seattle, I try to get my backups out of the fault zone of any major earthquakes. I don't want my tapes buried in the rubble along with my data center.

If backups are being sent offsite, how do they get there? The old-fashioned way means a courier driving tapes around. Remember how lost tapes can lead to data breaches, so the tapes should be encrypted. If the tapes are encrypted, then you need to have access to the decryption key in the event you need to rebuild somewhere else. Obviously, you don't want the key to travel with the same courier as the tapes. You also want to make sure that you have a device and software not in the same location as the potential disaster that can read the tape if you have to rebuild at a new location.

If you are sending your backups offsite the new-fashioned way, then you need lots of network bandwidth. Modern offsite backup entails copying your data to a remote archive over private lines or Internet encrypted links. In some cases, backups require so much bandwidth that they can take huge amounts of time to transfer offsite. Also, watch out for data restores. If you have to rebuild at a new location, make sure that there is sufficient bandwidth to pull down your backup files in time to meet requirements. If you have the resources, you can stand up a remote failover data center and stream backups to that site, so they're immediately available in the event of an emergency.

What to Back Up

In addition to backing up key data, there should be backups of the software and configuration of supporting systems. The goal with backup is to be able to rebuild from scratch, which means starting with brand new servers (bare metal) and building from there. Your recovery procedures need to be written with that assumption in mind. A good place to begin is to enumerate and evaluate the business process that needs restoration, as the technical requirements will flow from there.

When responding to security incidents, you may need to take key systems offline for analysis. New systems should be able to be put in their place to keep the business up and running. The last thing you want to do in an incident is get into a fight with a business head about whether to keep a compromised system up in the middle of an investigation. Make you plan to be able to replace things as needed and quickly.

Lastly, I once had a boss who didn't consider any back up to be *real* until it was tested. I've worked in other places where they've worked on faith that all their backups were going to work perfectly without testing. Being a man who lives by assume breach, you can guess that I prefer my old boss's philosophy. Test your backups by attempting to restore from them. Also, you should also have some idea how long it takes to restore a system from backup. I once worked 74 hours straight when I was a sysadmin because I was restoring a failed file server before the users came back to work on a Monday morning. The restore function on our backup library would fail after transferring data for a few hours, so I couldn't run the complete restore in one shot. I had to babysit the tape drive and coax it through byte by byte, hour after hour. It was a very long weekend. Test your full restore procedures.

Backup Policy

Here is a basic backup policy. In addition to this, you should have standards describing what should be backed up and when, as well as written procedures for backup and restoration of data as well as backup media management.

The IT Department will be responsible for performing adequate data backup for ORGANIZATION corporate resources, hosted production environments and the supporting infrastructure.

The IT Department will be responsible for maintaining documented operational processes for backup, restoration, and media handling.

The IT Department will be responsible for documenting a schedule and processes for data archiving, media rotation and proper media destruction.

Failover Systems

The IT department should also be responsible for building failover and redundant systems as necessary. This includes systems capable of taking over for failed or overloaded storage, bandwidth, or compute and memory. Sometimes these devices sit cold, requiring some effort and time to be brought online when needed. Sometimes they can be hot and ready to accept data at a moment's notice. Some are already in line as part of a load-balanced solution, where workloads are spread evenly amongst them. In larger more mature environments, entire secondary data centers and sites are available to mirror or take over in the event of a problem in the main location.

Failover and high-availability is a diverse topic and one I'm just skimming here. Where you need to be concerned is what failover capacity is available for which systems. You will be working with the IT team on the disaster and business continuity response plans, so you need to know what capabilities are in place. Even if you don't do any disaster work, there are security incidents that effectively act like disasters and take down systems. A denial-of-service attack or virulent malware infection can easily overwhelm a data center. It would be good to know what your options are for failover and restoration in that event.

Business Continuity Planning

Business continuity is an area of specialization connected to IT security but not necessarily part of it. In smaller organizations, the head of IT security is also responsible for business continuity. In larger organizations, they are separate functions that still work together. It's not uncommon to meet business continuity professionals who may have different training, certifications, and backgrounds than IT security professionals. Nonetheless, business continuity often falls within security and some its functions are audited in a security audit as well.

This chapter provides an overview of a business continuity plan, but it is not complete. There are many excellent guides to building a business continuity plan. A great one is the National Fire Protection Association's *Standard on Disaster/Emergency Management and Business Continuity Programs*, which is available at www.nfpa.org/assets/files/AboutTheCodes/1600/1600-13-PDF.pdf.

One of the key elements of a business continuity plan is the business impact analysis. It gives you the set of risks that you need to respond to with the plan. Chapter 4 already covered everything you need to know (and more) to create a useful and comprehensive business impact analysis. In fact, if you used failure mode effect analysis, you already have specific disaster scenarios that you can construct response plans against.

Next is a policy defining the business continuity plan.

Sample Business Continuity Policy

ORGANIZATION will create, maintain, communicate, and test business continuity processes to mitigate unplanned interruptions and outages of critical system processes and networks.

Department heads will be responsible for writing and testing disaster recovery plans for their business units to maintain or restore critical functions in the event of a disaster. The security department will be responsible for providing information on potential disasters. The business units will be responsible for identifying critical business functions and defining alternative work procedures in the event of a loss of IT resources, facilities, or personnel.

The Head of IT will be responsible for technical operational responsibilities and duties related to maintaining or restoring systems in the event of a disaster. The Head of IT will designate and ensure adequate resources to support primary, secondary, and emergency roles for critical functions to ensure consistent and reliable coverage.

The IT Department and the Security department will share responsibility for maintaining a general disaster recovery plan for critical ORGANIZATION infrastructure and corporate resources.

Disaster Recovery plans will include the following information: locations, personnel, business processes, technical system inventory, impact analysis, recovery site information, disaster declaration procedure, recovery roles and responsibilities, recovery training plan and schedule, applicable service level agreements, contracts, and other records.

The ORGANIZATION will securely store the business continuity plan in a secure offsite location so that it can be easily located by authorized personnel in the event of a disaster.

During disasters, the ORGANIZATION will strive to maintain the same security objectives it has defined during recovery operations.

The business continuity plan and disaster recovery plans will be reviewed at least annually and updated to reflect changes and new requirements in ORGANIZATION.

Expectations for Recovery

Regarding disasters that can take down entire business functions within an organization, what is the expectation from upper management? In the absence of information, management is likely to expect that everyone is just *taking care of this*, and things failover if something happens. Since this is likely not the case, it is someone's responsibility (probably yours) to inform them of the current recovery capability of the organization and the business impact implications.

From here, you can find out what management expects you to recover from and how fast. If they expect things to be running perfectly in the face of category five storms and massive denial of service attacks, then you need to explain what resources are needed. Is there any point where management will throw their hands up and say after a large-scale disaster, company survival is up to the will of the gods? I have heard both responses. You can also factor in regulatory and customer contract requirements, as there are often business continuity service levels that need to be met. Find out what is expected before you begin the long and tedious process of building response plans.

When talking about business continuity and disaster recovery expectations, two key terms often come up—RTO and RPO, which are covered next.

RTO, or *recovery time objective*, is the amount of time it takes for a system to come back online after a disaster takes it down. This is the running stopwatch on the recovery or failover efforts. It is the goal that you work from when building your plan. Different services and business functions can have different RTOs depending on need and resources available. Not meeting an RTO usually has consequences, especially if they are part of customer contractual requirements. Usually, the lower the RTO, the higher the cost to implement.

RPO, or *recovery point objective*, defines how much data you can afford to lose. Since backups are never going to be instantaneous, it is likely that when your IT systems go down, you will lose some data. Some RPOs are measured in minutes and some in days. It all depends on the criticality of data and resources available. For RPOs measured in minutes, usually data replication systems are needed to copy live data to back up systems as soon as possible. Like RTO, the lower the RPO, the higher the cost. In many cases, the price goes up logarithmically as you approach lower and lower objectives.

Also, the business owners should also set expectations as to when they expect systems to be failed over and when they should be restored. IT should be given explicit information as to when a disaster is declared and when failover mode is triggered. Expectations as to when to restore from backup should also be defined. In some cases, this expectation can take the form of a particular person (or persons) making a formal disaster declaration.

Disaster Recovery Planning

So far, I've talked about business continuity and disaster recovery but not specifying the terms. Disaster recovery is a subset of business continuity. Business continuity is about the entire business response process to ensure that an organization keeps chugging along in the face of a disaster. Disaster recovery refers to the specific response plans for specific systems or business units. The business continuity plan is the big picture and the disaster recovery plan is the technical detailed procedures. Usually the bulk of disaster recovery efforts happen with the IT systems, since IT systems run nearly all of our organizations now.

As you can see in the policy, the design and execution of IT disaster recovery is owned by the IT department. They are in the best position to set up data backup, failover systems, redundant links, as well as test them. One element often overlooked in disaster recovery plans is *key personnel continuity*. What happens when a pandemic hits and the one database administrator who knows how to run everything is sick with the Ebola Gulf-A virus? An effective disaster recovery plan includes contingency plans for personnel. This may include hiring and training backup personnel or having contractors ready to go to take over functions. Ensuring personnel are safe and can work effectively during a disaster event is also an important factor.

Staging and having an assured source of equipment in the event of a major disaster should figure in a recovery plan. Even if you already have a replacement agreement with your suppliers, you do not want to find out during an emergency that you are not the highest priority for the limited available hardware.

One thing to remember is that unless your organization runs or has critical regional resources or assets, it's likely that you will receive lower priority (or no) support from government emergency response in the event of large regional disaster. I have heard the fire chief tell me that in the event of a large earthquake, he will drive his fire engines right by my collapsed building and wave as he heads to the nearby school. And that's the way that it should be. So in a disaster, you can expect to be on your own for some time. Plan accordingly, with food and shelter in place capability. It'd also be helpful if some of your staff had some Red Cross training.

Business Continuity Plan

Overall, the business continuity plan is a big document. Also, if the building burns down, it doesn't help if the plan burns with it. The plan needs to be available so that personnel can use it during a disaster. Also, it's likely the plan contains confidential details about the organization and potential security weaknesses. This means the plan shouldn't just be posted on a web site for all to peruse. It needs to be available and protected.

The business continuity plan should include responses for each of your identified risk scenarios as they affect the various business units. Sometimes the disaster recovery plans for each of these units are stored in the main plan and other times they can be found as separate accompanying documents. The most important thing is to have complete coverage of response plans and that the plans are relevant and understandable. Other key elements that the plan should include are:

- Coordination and role definitions telling who's in charge of what, and their designated backups

- Activation instructions which detail how is a disaster declared and by whom.

- Notification defining how people will be called, checked on, and organized
- Plans detailing what to do if people aren't available and where to get additional help
- Priorities to tell which recoveries go first, in what order and what does it look like
- How things go back to normal from disaster mode and how services fail back

How Security Is Maintained During the Disaster

During a disaster when you're executing on the disaster recovery plans, what is the status of all of your security controls? It's not likely that just because your organization is in trouble that the bad guys are going to lay off. In fact, they may be more inclined to attack since they know things are in chaos and you're operating out of a recovery site. Sometimes they may even cause the disaster event to move your organization to a more vulnerable state. They might expect your recovery site and failover systems to have a lower level of security than usual. Personnel usually engaged with monitoring controls and locking down systems will be unavailable or otherwise engaged. This is a new risk that you need to raise with the ISMS committee and management.

Is it acceptable for security to be downgraded during an emergency event? If not, you need to identify resources and plans can be made to ensure that things stay locked down. This is a reason why secondary sites are often identical in all aspects, including the same controls as primary sites. If this is not feasible, you can look at focusing your efforts on the key systems that are recovered. Maybe you do not bring up all services in a disaster so you can ensure that the ones that are up remain strong against attack.

Incident Response Planning

A security incident is what you've been working hard to avoid, but they are also inevitable. Your goal is to catch them early, with complete information, and contain the damage. A security incident can be as small as a user surfing pornographic web sites or as large as a group of cyber-criminals downloading your entire payment card database. Both kinds of incidents require a response, and the organization will look to you for leadership. That is why it is crucial for you to be the one who remains calm while pointing to an existing incident response plan and offering confident and reassuring advice on how to weather the storm. While it is also important that you be brought into the crisis as soon as possible, a good incident response plan should work without your direct involvement. The entire organization should be aware that any security problems or policy violations are to be relayed to the security team immediately so the plan can be activated. The best way to get that ball rolling is to have a policy.

Incident Response Policy

ORGANIZATION will maintain and communicate security incident management processes to ensure that timely reporting, tracking, and analysis of unauthorized access, modification of critical systems and data. All ORGANIZATION employees and contractors are required to report security incidents to the Security department.

Security incidents can include: Unauthorized exposure of confidential data, Unauthorized access to systems or data, Unauthorized modification or shutdown of a security device, Loss of system or media containing ORGANIZATION data, Malware infections, Unauthorized or unexplained access to systems or data, Denial of Service, Threatening behavior, or Violation of acceptable usage policies.

The Security department is responsible for maintaining and communicating an incident response plan that describe the response procedures, recovery procedures, evidence collection processes, technical responsibilities, law enforcement contact plans, and communication strategies.

If the breach involves data not owned by ORGANIZATION but entrusted to ORGANIZATION, then upon confirmation of the breach the ORGANIZATION will notify the affected parties as quickly as possible based on advice from legal counsel and law enforcement.

Executive Management and the Public Relations department will be responsible for contacting the affected third-party data owners and facilitating ongoing communication with them.

If a data breach involves internal data such as employee records, then Executive Management in conjunction with the Human Resource department will facilitate notification.

The Security department is responsible for facilitating a post-incident process to uncover lessons learned from the incident. Furthermore, the Security department is responsible for recommending modifications to the incident response plan and the security policy according to lessons learned.

Incident Response Plan

This chapter isn't going to cover how to write a complete incident response plan, but you definitely need to write one. It needs to be specific and customized to your organization, its compliance requirements, and the culture. There are many guidelines to base your plan on. Here are three good resources:

- **Expectations for Computer Security Incident Response**
  http://www.rfc-base.org/rfc-2350.html

- **Handbook for Computer Security Incident Response Teams**
  http://resources.sei.cmu.edu/asset_files/Handbook/2003_002_001_14102.pdf

- **How to create an incident response plan**
  http://www.cert.org/incident-management/products-services/creating-a-csirt.cfm

Let's go over some of the important pieces of an effective incident response plan. These are the high-level steps:

1. Detect.
2. Contain.
3. Eradicate.
4. Recover.
5. Post mortem.

A Team Effort

Security incidents can have huge impacts that vary greatly based on how you respond. Therefore, security incidents are an *all hands on deck* situation where you do not want to be working alone. In fact, a Super Friends–approach works best where you bring together the best and most powerful heroes of your organization to meet the challenge. Having pre-existing relationships with law enforcement will speed this process along as well. These individuals need to be ready to answer the call at any time, so a designated secondary should be identified as well. Table 20-1 shows some incident response team common roles and their responsibilities.

Table 20-1. *Roles During a Security Incident*

Role	Individual	Duties
Lead incident handler	CSO	In charge of the incident response team, directs other team members and responsible for executing the plan
Incident recorder	Varies but could be another security team member	Keeps track of time line of events, information known so far, pending tasks and questions. Like secretary and project assistant since incident handler is busy
Executive representative	C-level officer	Makes executive decisions regarding incident, provides authority to the team
Legal representative	Legal counsel	Provides legal advice regarding incident
IT operations coordinator	Head of IT	Provides, coordinates, and leads technical resources in response efforts
HR representative	Head of HR	Facilities employee communications, provides advice on internal personnel issues
Customer communications representative	Head of public relations or head of customer-facing business unit	Facilitates and helps craft two-way communication with customers regarding incident

Within these roles and responsibilities, the team should meet on a regular basis, usually quarterly, to work out the specifics of these roles. There are certain things that you want to have already decided before an incident happens, such as the following:

- Who has the authority to take a system offline? This includes live, customer-serving systems that could affect service level agreements or ongoing revenue.

- Who will notify law enforcement and work with them?

- How do we respond to ransom/blackmail demands from criminals?

- Who will handle communication with customers (minor and major), third parties, business partners, vendors, and suppliers?

- What message will we post publicly in the event of breach? Who and how can customers contact us for questions?

- What message will we post internally in the event of breach? Who and how can employees contact us for questions?

- How do we go about doing an immediate termination? What do we need to do if there is to be legal action? If so, is the legal action going to be civil or criminal or both? Will the terminated person need to sign something?

Communication Strategies

A number of the items to work out beforehand include communication plans. This also means you need to have all those critical outside contacts detailed within the plan. This includes names, organizations, and full contact information. You should have escalation paths worked out as well, so that if you can't reach someone, you can go upstream to get help. The key contacts you want to have are:

- Law enforcement contacts for several agencies, federal and local

- Legal advice (if you need outside counsel), specializing in computer intrusions

- Key vendors, including all of your ISPs, co-location providers, hosting companies, and cloud service providers

- Security vendor contacts, in case signatures or controls need to be updated or patched

- Key customer and third parties

- Forensic investigators (either in-house or external)

Beyond who you are contacting, the message is also important. You do not want to be bickering with the team about the details of a notification to all of your customers in the heat of crisis. In major breaches, this initial notification is what hits the news. Regardless of the actual response, this is what outside analysts discuss regarding how competently the company is handling the crisis. You surely don't want to go off half-cocked and send out a poorly worded message that you have to later take back. Have the team work on canned response messages for the major incident scenarios ahead of time. They can be customized as needed when the time comes. Messages would include things like:

- "Sorry, we've had a breach and here's what we're doing about it..."

- "Hackers are attacking our site so we're going offline for a bit but we'll be back..."

- "All employees - we've had an incident and we're working on it. In the meantime, everyone log off the system now..."

- "All employees - we've had an incident but it's over. Now, change your password..."

The legal implications regarding reporting breaches to customers is described in a few pages.

Procedures for Common Scenarios

Your previously completed risk analysis and knowledge of what attacks are affecting your industry should give you a rough idea of the major threat scenarios that could affect your organization. Put that information to good use by preparing general response plans to guide the team if the incident happens. These plans can include checklists and scripts for IT responders, data gathering goals and procedures, key individuals to contact, systems/services to activate or deactivate. You can even include instructions for critical controls to use during an incident. Table 20-2 shows some common general scenarios to get you started:

Table 20-2. *Sample Incident Scenarios*

Scenario	Checklists for
Denial of service	Working with internet service providers, activating anti-DDOS firewall tools, contacting customers, contacting law enforcement
Malware infection	Gathering samples, performing rapid assessments, containing malware, determining if a system is clean or infected, obtaining new antivirus signatures and rolling them out, contacting users
Insider unauthorized access	Collecting log data and evidence, Analyzing systems for data storage, shutting down external links to contain exfiltration, disabling a user, working with HR and legal
Inappropriate usage	Collecting log data and evidence from browsers and firewalls, disabling a user, working with HR and legal

Gathering Data

Knowing what data was accessed by intruders figures prominently in your notification response plan. According to most breach disclosure laws,[2] you are required to notify the affected parties if you have evidence that their information has been exposed to unauthorized individuals. If you cannot determine what data was leaked and what wasn't, you may need to notify based on the assumption that all it was leaked. This is why logging is so critical to response. So knowing that only 50 people had their credit cards stolen is a different response than assuming that a hundred thousand cards were leaked.

When IT admins are taking systems offline or seizing laptops, they need to be very careful not to destroy or corrupt potential evidence. Even if you later choose not to go to court, you should still capture as much pristine evidence as you can. You never know when a later lawsuit or related incident may occur. Seizing, handling, and analyzing digital evidence is a discipline all of its own. It's also a discipline where a wrong move can cause an entire legal response to be invalidated or even backfire. There is insufficient information in this chapter to teach anyone how to do this properly. This is the case where if you don't know what you're doing, you should hire or contract with an expert.

That said, the basic idea is to leave the system and data as untouched as possible. This means taking physical possession of the system or copying the data to read-only media (burn it to DVD). This evidence needs to be tracked (time/date stamped, who has custody) and locked up where no one can tamper with it. If you absolutely need to do analysis before expertise is available, you can work off copies from the original. Unless you are qualified or absolutely must capture the current state of memory, avoid doing forensics on the live affected machine.

---

[2]http://www.ncsl.org/research/telecommunications-and-information-technology/security-breach-notification-laws.aspx.

Hunting and Fixing

Part of your response plans should include how systems and data can be protected during an incident. The plan should have information on how to move or segregate data stores from the active infected network. This may mean new internal firewall rules, temporary user rights revocations, and disconnecting systems from the network. The plan needs to include how to restore affected systems to their last known good state. Proper communication from the incident response team to the responders in the field is also crucial. Information about the incident should be passed along so that those in the field can properly defend systems as needed. Remember the Northwest Hospital malware infection, where systems were taken offline, cleaned, and then placed back on the wire—only to be reinfected.

A formal method for communicating this information has been developed called *indicator of compromise*, or IOC. An IOC is usually a signature of an intrusion that technical personnel can use to scan systems. Most IOCs are for malware and exploit-driven intrusions and can be shared amongst defenders online. For example, an IOC may be a digital hash of the malware, attacker source IP address, malicious domains, malware filenames, or known artifacts found on compromised systems. If the incident analysts can determine an IOC for an ongoing incident, these can be used to scan to see how many machines are infected. Depending on how detailed your available logs are, and how far back they go, you can also use IOCs to determine when an attack began and how it spread throughout the organization.

Legal Reporting Requirements

If your organization is in possession of other people's personal information, then you likely have legal obligations to provide notification in a timely manner. If you are a service provider in a business-to-business (B2B) arrangement, you may be in possession of personal information not shared directly with you, but with your partner/client. This means you probably have contractual obligations with those customers to notify them so that they can work directly with their end consumers.

Having complete information is critical when you need to do the notification. Most breach disclosure laws have definitions that tie disclosure to a "reasonable belief" that "personal information" was "acquired by an unauthorized person." Unfortunately, attackers work diligently to hide their actions, making the determination of the extent and timeline for a breach difficult. Nevertheless, you are on the hook for notification. When you are working with your legal team and law enforcement on how and when to notify, there is some key information you need to have:

- **Exact data elements that have been compromised**
  Does the data constitute PII? Customers also want to know what was leaked.

- **Exact format of the data**
  Is it encrypted, obfuscated, de-identified, or obscured in an odd format?

- **Likely identity and motivation of the attacker**
  Will the information be used for fraud?

- **How the data was compromised**
  Was it copied, viewed, modified, or physically lost?

- **How the incident has been mitigated**
  Do we expect more breaches or are we sure it's all over? How sure? Why?

Remember that combinations of what is considered personal information creates the obligation to notify. That includes names in combination with social security numbers, government ID numbers, financial and credit card numbers, and passwords.

All in all, it's in everyone's best interest to act like a responsible victim and be as transparent and clear as possible. Being transparent doesn't mean starting a publicity campaign with incorrect or insufficient information. It means sharing what you know and don't know with the right persons. Sometimes the right persons are law enforcement and regulators, not the general public.

A good general guideline is available from the California Office of the Attorney General at `https://oag.ca.gov/sites/all/files/agweb/pdfs/privacy/recom_breach_prac.pdf`.

Working with Law Enforcement

Many security incidents do involve the violation of the law, which means you can contact the police for help. In some cases, law enforcement involvement can override notification timeline requirements as going public could jeopardize an ongoing investigation. Law enforcement can sometimes offer useful incident response advice as they may have responded to similar cases and have an idea about outcomes and magnitudes.

One thing that you need to do before contacting law enforcement is get permission from organizational leadership. Unless you personally are the victim of a cyber-crime, you should not be speaking on behalf of your organization without authorization. The executive leadership represents the organization and is the best one to decide whether to report and when. Although there are some crimes, like child pornography, where the lack of reporting itself is a crime.

Sadly, some executives are reluctant to report cyber-crimes for fear of bad publicity. Some even wonder if law enforcement can do anything to help the company once the damage has been done. In some cases, they can. If a perpetrator is successfully prosecuted, reparations can be identified as part of the judgement. Successful prosecutions also open the way for civil damage lawsuits as well. Reporting cyber-crimes also works to make the whole Internet community safer as well. Even if law enforcement can't prosecute on your organization's particular incident, they will keep your information for a later investigation. There have been quite a few major cases where the perpetrator was not identified until years later. When that happens, your case can figure into the overall damages and sentence for the criminal. If nothing else, reporting cyber-crime helps law enforcement build threat intelligence and encourage future investigations and community warnings. Conversely, cyber-crime being allowed to flourish without consequences creates an incentive for epidemics of new attacks, like the ransomware epidemic.

There are many different law enforcement agencies that you can work with, depending on the crime. By being active in security communities like Infragard, you can establish law enforcement relationships beforehand. This helps speed up their response during an incident as you already know and trust each other. In general, the FBI is the primary agency to contact. They can redirect you to various other agencies as needed depending on the nature of the crime.

Human Side of Incident Response

This is a hard job and lot of what's tough about it, they don't teach you in a book. Incident response can get ugly, especially when dealing with insiders. As a responder, you may end up having to dig through people's browser history, e-mail boxes, and chat logs. You may learn things about people you know that will make you see them in a new light. You may discover that people you thought were trustworthy have a dark side or unethical motivations. Even if the data you uncover doesn't lead you to a malicious incident, you may still find shameful or personal secrets. It's up to your professional integrity and discretion to keep these matters to yourself or limit the scope of your investigation.

Another difficult aspect of incident response is that as its consequence, people can get fired, get sued, or even go to prison. The things they did may become public because of legal action and there may be personal repercussions for them. It is normal for you to feel guilt for feeling that you were the cause of these consequences, even though you know you weren't. It helps to talk to someone about it. This can be other security professionals, friends or family, or even a mental health professional. Sometimes it's better to feel a little bad about the fate of wrongdoers than it is to be indifferent or rejoice in their misfortune.

After Action Analysis

When things go wrong and you've finally made it through to the other side, the last thing people want to do is rehash the events. However, reviewing the event and how the teams reacted is a vital learning opportunity. In some ways, examining what went wrong also gives the organization a sense of closure and if in the case of a control failure, the confidence that things won't repeat themselves. Any major outage or security incident should be followed up by after action analysis. More mature organizations also do analysis after *near miss* events where the disaster or incident didn't really occur but came very close. Those too can yield a lot of valuable data.

The response team, whether it's the business continuity team or the incident response team, should all be present for after action analysis. It should be a brainstorming session, where you are looking for causes and effects, not assigning blame. Remember that by definition, whatever caused the interruption event was beyond your organization's normal capability to respond. Also don't forget the assume breach principle. People are going to be pushed to their limit, technology isn't going to work right, and communications are going to break down. You know that there are people out there who have made a career out of breaking security systems. When you examine things carefully, you're likely to find much of the real causes are systems failures that run much deeper than a particular individual, team, or technology.

Root Cause Analysis

The goal of getting to the real cause of the incident is to fix whatever went wrong so it doesn't happen again. It's likely that the true cause might go much deeper than something as simple as "there was a blackout."

One straightforward but effective technique is called the 5 Whys. You simply start at the beginning of the event and walk backward asking why something happened. You do this at least five times but you can go deeper. As you can see from this example, there are number of interesting things that turn up that are ripe for fixing.

- The web farm crashed.... Why?

- The load balancers started flip-flopping.... Why?

- The high-availability connection had an error. Both systems thought the other was down.... Why?

- The cable connecting the units got crimped.... Why?

- Someone was in the server room and closed the cage door on the cable.... Why?

But don't stop now, let's keep going.

6. The cabling in the back of the racks is a huge rat's nest.... Why?

7. Everyone ignores cable management.... Why?

8. We're busy and cable management isn't high priority.... Why?

So here we're getting closer to the bigger problem. What other IT hygiene and maintenance tasks are being skipped over in favor of more expedient work? If the response committee's report can convince management, perhaps some lower-level resources (like interns) could help IT? Or maybe management is willing to accept the risk of future outages based on the current workload? In any case, you've uncovered a bigger potential problem that can go into your future risk analysis reports.

Another type of root cause analysis is the Ishikawa Fishbone, which looks at the interactions of many different possible causes. You draw an effect diagram with spokes for different possible cause categories such as people, processes, technology, information, and environment. You can learn more about it at http://asq.org/learn-about-quality/cause-analysis-tools/overview/fishbone.html.

Executive Summary

Once the analysis is complete, the results should be written up. Not only do stakeholders and customers often require these reports, auditors like to see them as well. Naturally, you should use this report to justify future control and process improvements or lacking that, identify new risks. The report should include the following:

- Executive summary with a few paragraphs at most describing the event and the response

- A list of strengths listing what went right, worked well, and was effective

- An analysis of response metrics, such as:

  - Time to detect

  - Time to respond once detected

  - Time to containment (if applicable)

  - Time to recovery (vs. RTO)

  - Recovery coverage (vs. RPO)

  - Time to resume

- Areas for improvement

- Recommendations for next steps

Here are a few sample after action reports for some major disasters.

- **Hurricane Sandy FEMA After-Action Report**
  https://www.fema.gov/media-library/assets/documents/33772

- **Fukushima After Action Report**
  http://iaea.org/newscenter/focus/fukushima/missionsummary010611.pdf

- **Denial of Service After Action Report**
  https://blog.cloudflare.com/todays-outage-post-mortem-82515/

Practicing

You already have heard that how an organization responds to an incident or disaster is crucial factor in its outcome. If response is so important, then it's a good idea to practice. Not only does this shake out the bugs in the plan, but it also gives the team the chance to work together and gel. In some regulatory environments, like HIPAA, testing your incident response plan is required.

There are many IT professionals and executives who don't understand the assume breach concept and may resist training exercises. Their expectation is that a breach will never happen because the security team will keep them safe. Explain to them that preparation for a breach is part of your defense. Having strong incident response can make the difference between a minor problem and a major breach. This work is vital as any other work you do to defend the organization. It only takes a few hours once a year (or more), and it can be fun[3].

---

[3]http://www.csmonitor.com/USA/Military/2012/1031/No-prank-On-Halloween-US-military-forces-train-for-zombie-apocalypse.

There are lots of different exercises and tests that can be done to practice response plans. Some can involve just the response committee, some can include just key stakeholders, and some can engage the entire organization. Practice runs can include:

- **Walk through**
  Everyone involved in a response scenario simply reads their steps out loud from the plan describing the details they would take. This is a good exercise for a new plan and/or a new team.

- **Tabletop exercise**
  Much like the role-playing games that I enjoyed in college, this is a *dice and paper* simulation of an event scenario. A moderator creates and runs a session, describing events and changing conditions and the participants reacts and verbalizes their responses. The moderator can even assign probability to the success of certain actions, using dice to determine the outcomes. These can even be held in remote conference sessions to make it easier for all participants to attend.

- **Simulations**
  This is a functional run through of a scenario complete with participants doing as much real work in response as they can. Failover to remote locations may actually be tested. If a response plan says that someone needs to call an engineer and have her run a program, then an actual phone call is made to that engineer and a simulated program is run. Even fake news stories and panicked distress calls can be made to the response center to fully immerse people. I've participated in regional disaster simulations where some participants were *irradiated* and were escorted out of the practice room for decontamination (made to wait in a nearby conference room).

The first place you should look for response scenarios is your risk analysis. The top risk scenarios identified are excellent candidates for practice as by definition, they're likely to affect your organization the most. As the saying goes, never let a good crisis go to waste. Scenarios can also come from past disasters, incidents, and near misses. You have the after action report data to help you define the scenario. It's also a chance to assure everyone that if it happens again, you're ready.

Like actual incidents, you should write practice exercise after action reports as well. Stakeholders and auditors will be looking for them, and following up on the suggested next steps. How often should you do these practices? At least once a year is standard, but you can do more if you need it. The saying goes, "Amateurs practice until they get it right. Professionals practice until they can't get it wrong."

FURTHER READING

- **NIST Special Publication 800-92 - Guide to Computer Security Log Management**
  http://csrc.nist.gov/publications/nistpubs/800-92/SP800-92.pdf

- **Association of Contingency Planners**
  https://www.acp-international.com

- **Community Supported Indicators of Compromise**
  https://www.iocbucket.com

- **NIST Special Publication 800-84 - Guide to Test, Training, and Exercise Programs for IT Plans and Capabilities**
  http://csrc.nist.gov/publications/nistpubs/800-84/SP800-84.pdf

- **Specific IOC structured data formats and protocols**
  https://www.us-cert.gov/Information-Sharing-Specifications-Cybersecurity

PART IV

Being Audited

CHAPTER 21

■■■

Starting the Audit

Once you have all of your controls in place and running smoothly, you can think about auditing them. A successful audit is the closest thing you'll get to proof that your organization is secure. Which audit should you consider? You probably won't get to choose as most audits are thrust upon us. If you're lucky, you'll only have to deal with one audit instead of several overlapping ones. All of the processes and controls discussed in this book are applicable to SSAE 16, ISO 27001, PCI DSS, and other major audit requirements. So where do you begin?

Getting Ready for Audit

The first thing to do is review everything you've done, with a careful eye toward how you've defined scope. Remember that an auditor may challenge the decisions you've made regarding scope, so be prepared to defend your choices. Concerning process and controls, how much has been documented? Not just policies, standards, and procedures but do you have records based on these processes running? To an auditor, if an activity wasn't documented with a paper trail then the activity may not have been done. It's also important that all of your processes are being followed by everyone who is supposed to be following them. Publishing documents is insufficient. The controls must be used.

You need to make sure that everything was completed, from start to finish, and been running for a while. This book presented things in conceptual order, not necessarily chronological. Read, understand, and implement the whole thing before paying money for an audit. Here is a checklist for implementing a security program:

1. Analyses
   a. Asset analysis
   b. Risk analysis
   c. Impact analysis
   d. Threat analysis
      - Natural threats
      - Adversarial threats
   e. Control analysis (Existing controls)
   f. Compliance analysis
      - Identify specific required controls and assets per compliance regime.

© Raymond Pompon 2016
R. Pompon, *IT Security Risk Control Management*, DOI 10.1007/978-1-4842-2140-2_21

2. Define scope.

3. Build Governance model

   a. Obtain management endorsement.

   b. Set up ISMS Steering committee.

   c. Select members.

   d. Create charter.

   e. Review analyses.

   f. Perform risk management.

      i. Define risk acceptance criteria.

      ii. Accept risks.

      iii. Eliminate risks.

      iv. Transfer risks.

      v. Mitigate risks.

   g. Control risks.

   h. Develop risk treatment list.

      i. If pursuing ISO 27001, write SoA matching controls to risks and compliance requirements.

4. Write key security policies.

   a. Organizational security policy

   b. Acceptable usage policy

5. Design controls.

   a. Design controls based on risk treatment list.

   b. Develop control policy, standards, and procedures.

   c. Develop tools to monitor control effectiveness and coverage.

6. Develop control implementation projects.

7. User training

   a. Security awareness training

   b. Policy roll out and training

   c. Control process training

8. Roll out controls.

   a. Implement control projects.

   b. Collect records of controls in action.

   c. Monitor control effectiveness.

9. Assess program for audit.

   a. Review all work so far against specific compliance requirements.

10. Select and hire audit firm.

11. Begin audit.

The first eight steps have been covered so far. Now you need to assess your security program against the audit requirements you're going to face. This means you need to obtain the latest guide for the audits you need to pass. Here is where you can find some of them:

- **SSAE 16 SOC 1,2,3**
  http://www.aicpa.org/Publications/AccountingAuditing/KeyTopics/
  Pages/ServiceOrganizations.aspx

- **PCI DSS**
  https://www.pcisecuritystandards.org/document_library

- **ISO 27001**
  http://shop.bsigroup.com/ProductDetail/?pid=000000000030282638

These URLS may have moved around a bit between the writing of this book and when you're reading it. However, it should be easy to find audit guides to any major audit program directly from the certifying body. Be aware that some of audit guides cost money, but definitely worth the investment before your spend thousands of dollars and hours of work on auditors and consultants. These guides are designed to help you map your processes and controls to the requirements. This is where you roll up your sleeves and do a gap analysis. Some organizations hire a consultant to do this work for them as well. This is an option, but it still is a good idea for the security team to have a clear idea of the audit criteria they are expected to meet.

After this review, you may need to go back and tweak some processes and add a few controls. Once you are satisfied that you are doing what is described in the audit guide, you can move on to hiring an auditor.

Picking an Auditor

Most of the time, but not always, you can choose your own auditor. Audits and auditors are supposed to be standardized and interchangeable. When you get into the details, this is not really the case. Sometimes this means that the quality of that testing varies. Since quality is a relative term, it can mean speed of testing, cost of testing, depth of testing, thoroughness of testing, or appropriateness of testing. There are a few things to look for in an auditor to make sure that they're a good fit for your organization's needs.

The first big factor is experience with testing in your industry or vertical. If your organization is a string of boutique retail stores, you may not want a PCI DSS auditor from the e-commerce world. You want someone familiar with the processes, threats, and issues that are prevalent in your industry. You don't want to have to explain business processes and unique regulatory pressures either. In fact, you'd want the auditor to have a good idea of what is common practice for you organization and the common pitfalls. Since we are talking about IT security, what kind of technical expertise do they have in the areas of technology your organization uses? When choosing, you want to make sure that the audit engagement team has at least a dozen or so audits worth of experience in a business sector like yours. Ask them for references from other organizations.

Another major factor is how they perform the audit. While their certifying body dictates the audit workflow, each firm has its own particular methods that may or may not work well for your organization. Are they local to your region or will they fly folks in? Will they have dedicated technical experts in your office doing the testing (expensive but quick) or will there be junior team members doing the legwork supervised by the experts (cheaper but slower). Will they gather and analyze data on site or will it be shipped off to the auditor's offices for analysis? Do they offer additional complimentary audit services, like can they do both PCI DSS and SSAE 16? Do they offer vulnerability and penetration testing services? How fast can they turn around a report? All of these may mean something to you or not, it depends on your needs and resources.

One factor that may be important is the auditor's reputation and name recognition. Organizations who want prestige from their completed audits want an auditor with a strong reputation. Big names from trusted firms can look good with customers, partners, and regulators. Would you rather hand a customer a report from a large internationally recognized audit firm or Jasper's Audit Emporium? However, the big names are not the cheapest, fastest, or most flexible either. It's a good example of defensive decision making,[1] but it can be worth it. If you just need to check a box and get off the hook for compliance reasons, then maybe a smaller relatively unknown firm is the way to go.

We're All on the Same Side

When you're hiring an audit firm, it's in everyone's best interest for you to pass. The firm doesn't want to issue a report full of so many findings that your organization is shown to be non-compliant and they never get hired again. This may be a different story with regulators or externally hired auditors, but in general, hired audit firms want to pass you. This doesn't mean they'll overlook things on purpose or bend the rules. These auditors can be sued or decertified for not upholding the standard they're charged with testing. In general, I've seen that the larger firms with big name recognition are stricter than the smaller ones. Larger firms have more cut and dried audit methodologies and less time on engagements to be flexible on the interpretations of the rules. They also may have a larger chain of experts needed to sign off on understand an audit finding.

I say all of this because I actually prefer the more strict and formal audit firms. It's not because I enjoy torturing my organization and myself. I want the most exacting and demanding audit possible. Remember the goal of the audit is to expose through transparency any potential problem with a security program. Anything less than thorough sets you up for failure with another auditor or an attacker. Assume breach can apply to many things and you never know who will audit you after this firm leaves. I want to set a high bar on my program in case there's future trouble involving regulators, customers, business partners, or even the courts. I want my organization to be as compliant as possible because it means we have a better reputation and are carrying less liability. Lastly, a good tough audit keeps everyone inside my organization honest. It supports my efforts to reduce risk to have solid controls and fewer mistakes in processes. All things being equal, if you have to choose between an easy audit or a tough one, I say aim high.

What Happens During Audit

In general, audits all follow the same workflow. After engaging with an auditor, they discuss your compliance requirements and work to ensure your business objectives are met as well. They may even suggest a different audit or audit approach based on your needs and the regulatory environment. They dive deep into how your organization functions, both in process and in technology. For this, you should be providing them with high-level network diagrams, physical locations, organization charts, business process service models, and a list of the major technologies in use. Even though they are evaluating you for an audit, any audit firm you hire is still there to make sure that your needs are served. So do you best to be open and clear on how your organization functions and what you hope to get out of the audit.

The auditor should then do a high-level review of your scope, security program, and controls. This is not an audit but just a quick skim of the project so they can gauge how much time and effort are required to complete the audit. Based on this, the auditor may suggest doing a pre-assessment. A pre-assessment is

---

[1]https://en.wikipedia.org/wiki/Defensive_medicine.

a light version of the audit that doesn't count. It's a gap assessment that can uncover design or operational problems that you don't want coming up later during the real audit. These do take time and effort to complete, so pre-assessments aren't usually offered for free and can delay the start of the audit. However, if this is your first real audit, I recommend doing it. Once the actual audit begins, any problem that the auditor uncovers is written up as findings in the final report. Pre-assessments are also useful as an independent expert opinion can demonstrate to upper management the need for more time or resources to mature the security program without the impact of an audit finding.

Once the audit is ready to begin, the last thing to finalize is the audit period. Some audits, like SSAE 16 Type 1, are just a single point in time, so this isn't a concern. For most others, there is a defined range of time being reviewed. For example, if your audit period is January 1st until December 31st, then any control activity during that time is fair game for auditor review. This is true even if the auditors haven't shown up until March or April. The auditors review your records going all the way back to the beginning of the period to confirm that controls were running at that time. For this reason, there can be some wiggle room on the start period of the audit. If the pre-assessment turned up numerous problems, then an audit period may be pushed to start later, after all things are corrected. You may not have the flexibility to do this for contractually mandated audits, like PCI DSS, but for SSAE 16 and ISO 27001k, you can.

Scope Review

As you've seen earlier, scope establishes the context for the entire audit. Therefore, the audit team begins by examining your scope in meticulous detail. They need information on the relevant scoped physical locations, networks, servers, and personnel defined by the scope. This review may include investigating the following:

- Detailed network diagrams, perhaps even down to the cable and individual IP address level.

- Inventory and configuration of critical systems that store, process, receive, and transmit scoped data.

- Scoped data record format.

- How scoped data is identified and tracked within the environment, in and out of scope

- All the people involved in scoped data and systems, including engineers, support technicians, developers, and managers.

- All of the relevant processes that interact with scoped data, systems, and data flows.

Lastly, the auditors look carefully at where and how the scope barriers operate. Warning, the auditor may change your scope if the integrity and effectiveness of your boundaries is insufficient.

Control Review

After confirming your scope, the auditors now dive through all the control objectives and the controls supporting them. For each control, they need to verify it's in place and designed adequately. Depending on the type of audit, they then check that the control is functioning as designed over the period of time being audited.

Auditors usually do their request for evidence with a formal checklist or *pull list* based on their earlier discussions and analysis. This checklist includes requests for the following:

- Documents, which are numbered and tracked by the auditor, including:
  - Policies, standards, checklists, procedures
  - Logs, meeting minutes, system records, e-mails, helpdesk tickets
  - Reports and output from systems and third parties

- Requests for meetings with individuals, usually identified by role. The individual sessions consist of the following:
  - *Walk-throughs* in which the audit team asks an individual to describe how specific controls and processes are performed. During the walk-through, the auditors likely ask the individual to provide follow-up evidence such as screen-shots, configuration dumps, help desk tickets, or completed checklists. The auditor may even shadow people as they run procedures to get a hands-on idea on how something functions.
  - *Interviews* in which the auditors ask questions about how processes, controls, or risks are done. The answers are compared to your policies and standards to see how things match. Auditors may also ask individuals to explain how certain processes or technical function to get a better idea on the details.
  - *Follow up discussions* with managers or security personnel regarding questions or discrepancies uncovered so far.

Audit Evidence Gathering

As you can see, auditors rely on a variety of methods to gather evidence. Not just individual attestations, but records and configuration snapshots. The variety and diversity of evidence helps solidify their assurance that you are doing what you claim. When there are large bodies of records and controls to examine, the auditor may use sampling to select a percentage of the records for examination.

The selection is based on statistical sampling methods, the criticality of control, and ease of collection. There are many methods for the auditor to select samples, from random selection designed to statistically ensure significant coverage. There may even be some variation in sampling methods from audit type and audit firm, but their chosen methods need to be approved by the certifying body. When sampling, if the auditor uncovers evidence of control failures, they may request additional records to give them a better idea of the size of the problem. This is where you hope the failures turn out to be a one-time failure (but still be noted as a finding) and not an endemic design weakness.

How does the audit evidence-gathering process actually look? Next are some examples for various control audit scenarios.

Control Being Audited Is Background Checks

1. Auditor asks HR for a list of all employees hired during the audit period so far.

2. HR produces a list.

3. Auditor randomly selects a percentage of new hires from the list.

4. Auditor then submits the selected names to HR with a request for background check records for those individuals.

5. HR either produces the records or schedules a walk-through session in the HR offices to review the records with the auditor.

Control Being Audited Is Scope Control Barriers

1. Auditor asks for detailed network diagram of scoped environment.

2. Network engineer provides diagram.

3. Auditor reviews diagram and notes the use of a firewall and several network switches used to manage the scoped environment.

4. Auditor requests a full configuration report from the firewall and switches.

5. Auditor brings in experts to parse these reports and verifies they match diagram description.

6. Auditor requests a walk-through with a network engineer to explain configuration on firewall and shows live settings.

7. Auditor requests a walk-through with a system administrator to demonstrate functionality of scope barrier by trying to make an authorized connection from an out-scope-machine to a scoped machine.

Control Being Audited Is Antivirus Software

1. Auditor has a walk-through with a system administrator on the antivirus console.

2. Auditor asks for screenshots of system inventory and antivirus settings.

3. Auditor selects a percentage of hosts from the system inventory.

4. Auditor asks for a walk-through for each of these hosts and review local host antivirus settings to check version and signature settings.

Control Being Audited Is Change Control

1. Auditor asks for a list of all authorized changes since the period began.

2. Auditor asks for a list of all authorized change approvers during the period.

3. Auditor randomly selects a list of authorized changes and requests the records associated with those changes.

4. Auditor compares change records and lists them against change control procedures and standards.

5. If this is a key control (like for SSAE 16 SOC 2), then auditor also requests a walk-through of an active change being performed by a system administrator.

Roles During an Audit

During the audit process, it's a good idea to have a clear idea of the roles and responsibilities of each party. Sometimes the audit firm spells this out for you at the start of the engagement, other times it's not so clear. Therefore, so you know, next we'll go over everyone's general roles.

The Auditor's Role

The auditor's duty is to evaluate your scoped assets against the compliance standard for the agreed upon period. Anything else is extraneous. Things you did before the period or after don't count. Things out of the scope aren't part of the audit either.

Auditors are almost always restricted from auditing their own work, depending on the certifying body. This means that the auditor can't design controls or provide security advice regarding what they're auditing. Some audit firms spin off separate consulting divisions with different management structures in order to provide additional services. In general, the consulting advice you may get from an auditor is during the pre-assessment regarding how other audited customers may have solved your particular problem.

Auditors are responsible for keeping you informed on their progress. They publish a project schedule and give you updates as they progress. They report findings and observations in a timely manner, so that you don't get a huge wave of information at the end. If it is a short or small audit, you may not get much until the end. In general, they let you know if they find something as soon as they've confirmed it.

Auditors can also pass on observations, which are like light findings that don't show up in the actual audit report. They are more suggestions and potential problems that the auditor feels you should be aware of, so that you can nip an issue in the bud.

Auditors are also bound to keep everything confidential except the contents of the final report. Sometimes even the audit report has access restrictions baked into it. For example, SSAE 16 SOC 1 and SOC 2 audit reports state that the contents of the report are solely for the use by the audited organization and organizations that rely on the scoped services. Only SSAE 16 SOC 3 reports are designed to be posted on the Internet for anyone to see. SOC 1 reports are designed for use as part of financial audits. Auditors looking at financial reporting integrity for Sarbanes-Oxley compliance are not allowed to rely on SSAE 16 SOC 2 or SOC 3 reports for their assurance work.

The Audited Organization's Role

The audited organization has many responsibilities as well. An important one is designating a primary contact to coordinate all the audit activity. This person, perhaps you, is responsible for scheduling the auditor's visits, arranging office space, scheduling interviews, and procuring documents for the auditors. It is also the audited organization's responsibility to be open and forthcoming about their environment and controls. Not only should you be transparent and honest when answering questions, but you should also keep the auditor up to date about major changes or problems in the organization that could affect the audit.

As part of the audit contract, you may be required to disclose any suspected deception by staff that could affect the audit. If you lie during an audit, the least bad thing that could happen is that the entire audit is invalidated with the audit firm getting to keep the audit fees.

Third-Party Roles

If part of your scope or controls extend to a third party outside of your organization, they too need to be covered in the audit. The best solution is for the third party to have already undergone an audit against the same compliance requirements as you. This way your auditor can simply review the third party's report and check off the coverage for the outsourced pieces. Many service providers obtain audits for a variety of compliance regimes for this reason. If they haven't had an audit, then they too need to be audited. You, your auditor, or another audit firm needs to provide assurance that the security at that third party is adequately addressed. This topic is covered in more detail in Chapter 23, which focuses on third-party security.

Specific Audits

Moving beyond the general audit overview, let's explore the specific audits covered in this book.

SSAE 16 Audits

SSAE 16 audits are certified by the AICPA and must be done by CPA firms. This can make them a little more expensive and formal than other audits, but they are also more recognized in mature industries.

Remember that there are six different permutations of SSAE 16 audits, but regarding the workflow of the audit, the biggest difference is between the Type 1 and Type 2 audits. The Type 1 audit is a design audit. Type 2 is an operational effectiveness audit and it includes the Type 1 activities. The Type 1 audit involves a review of the controls and scope, but no examination of the operation of the controls. This the auditors focus on document gathering and design walk-throughs. There is no pulling of records of control operation or checks of running processes. It is just a snapshot of the control architecture. You usually see type 1 reports in the first year of an organization's SSAE 16 audit experience. After that, organizations do Type 2 audits.

Type 1

Where Type 1 audits can get interesting is for SOC 1 engagements. For SOC 2 and SOC 3, the control objectives and controls are supplied from the AICPA based on the *service principles* chosen. However, with SSAE 16 SOC 1 audits, the audited organization is responsible for designing their own control objectives and control stack. The design of the control objectives must effectively mitigate the risk of unauthorized changes affecting the integrity of the organization's financial reporting system. Usually the control objectives are straightforward, covering the major types of security like logical, physical, operational, and so forth. The auditors can easily check the objectives and may even have wording changes to meet up closer to generally accepted standards in the SSAE 16 world. The second piece of design the audited organization must do is select the controls to support the control objective. Chapter 12, which was on control design, is a big help here. The controls need to cover risk and should include defense in depth in case a key control fails. The auditors go over these controls and your scoped processes to make sure that the design is adequate.

Type 2

Type 2 audits usually cover a period of six to twelve months, although three-month periods are not impossible. The auditor visits several times during the period to examine running controls and do their testing. They may also spread out their visits between physical locations, based on their sampling methods, to make sure that they have a good handle of what's going on with the scoped systems. The overall goal is to look at the operational effectiveness of the running controls. It won't matter if the controls are inefficient, costly, or laborious. All they care about is how well they mitigate the risk to the control objectives. Their findings and feedback is in the context of the control objectives.

SOC 1

For SOC 1, the scope of the audit is focused on the one or more products and services used by a customer and their reliance on the control design and operation. The customer in this case can be internal or external; it really depends on how they rely on these controls to ensure accurate financial reporting and disclosure. As stated by the AICPA: "These reports are important components of user entities' evaluation of their internal controls over financial reporting for purposes of comply with laws and regulations such as the Sarbanes-Oxley Act and the user entities' auditors as they plan and perform audits of the user entities' financial statements."[2]

---

[2]https://www.aicpa.org/InterestAreas/FRC/AssuranceAdvisoryServices/Pages/AICPASOC1Report.aspx.

SOC 2/3

You do not design control objectives for SOC 2 or SOC 3 audits, you select from up to five service principles. Each principle has its own control objectives and associated controls. In summary, they are as follows:

- *Security Service Principle*: Controls covering governance, security awareness, risk management, control monitoring, operations and change management.

- *Availability Service Principle*: Controls covering capacity management, data backup, and system recovery.

- *Confidentiality Service Principle*: Controls covering system acquisition, system disposal, system boundary protection, third-party confidentiality, service providers, and user awareness of confidentiality.

- *Processing Integrity Principle*: Controls covering management of processing errors, system input integrity, data processing accuracy, data storage, output accuracy, and modification protection.

- *Privacy Principle*: Privacy policies, privacy notices, privacy consent processes, data collection processes, data usage and storage limitations, internal access controls, third-party disclosures, IT security controls, data quality, compliance monitoring. These controls go beyond IT security and are not covered in this book.

SSAE 16 Reports

SSAE 16 reports are structured into five major sections, as follows:

Section 1

This is the description of scope and the auditor's opinion. *Unqualified* means the control objectives were met. *Qualified* means everything is good *except* certain named control objectives were not achieved. A qualified report is not good, but not the end of the world. This is the first section of the audit report.

Section 2

This is the audited organization's formal assertion that they didn't lie or withhold information to the auditors, that their controls were designed to meet the risks, and their controls were consistently used throughout the period.

Section 3

The audited organization's description of the control environment. This is a large narrative describing the organization, the scoped environment, and how all the controls function. The fun part is that the auditors don't write this section, you do. The auditors review it for accuracy and completeness, but the audited organization needs to draft it.

Section 4

After the auditor's opinion, this section is the second most important. This section is a big matrix detailing the actual audit tests performed and the results. Findings and control failures are detailed here. Forget a background check for a new hire? It is noted here. The audited organization can include a *management response* providing explanation or remediation descriptions regarding the finding. For example, the response may say, "New hire background check was missed because of an HR transition to a new system. Management added a new second review process to ensure that future checks are always performed." Some of the recipients of your audit report will dissect this part of the report and ask you to further explain things. In a Type 1 report, this section would just be a listing of the controls and control principles/objectives.

Section 5

This is an optional section where an audited organization can include a few pages to clarify the report. This section usually includes descriptions of other controls and services outside the scope (which means they aren't verified by audit), descriptions of future plans (next year, we'll be adding new controls), or even descriptions of services that customers may want to purchase. The auditor officially expresses no opinion on this section, so when reading someone else's report, you can view this section as non-essential.

ISO 27001 Audits

ISO 27001 audits can only be done by companies certified to perform them. They are not as expensive as SSAE 16 audits, but the supply of ISO auditors is somewhat smaller than other auditors, especially within the United States.

The ISO 27001 audit is against an ISO management standard that encompasses how an organization has designed and runs its security program. It looks at the IT security governance structure, including the leadership, policy, and roles. It also delves into the processes, ensuring they properly align to the Plan-Do-Check-Act methodology. The review of planning phase involves the processes around risk, compliance, and asset assessment, as well as the risk treatment process. The review of the Do phase incorporates the specific control testing. The review of the Check phase is around control monitoring and internal audit processes. Lastly, the Act review looks at how the security governance team works to improve and update the security program to meet changing needs and ineffective controls. Chapter 7, on governance, covers the ISO 27001 standard for security governance—the ISMS, or information security management system.

The controls used in an ISO 27001 audit are based on the defined risk treatment plan and the statement of applicability (SoA). If you remember, the SoA is a document that shows the link between the chosen controls and the risks and compliance requirements. The SoA also must include a review of all 114 controls detailed in ISO 27002, which break down into the major areas of security policy, security governance, remote access, human resource security, asset management, data classification, access control, cryptography, physical security, operational security, communication security, system acquisition and development, third party supplier security, incident management, business continuity security, and compliance.

An ISO 27001 audit consists of two major phases, an offsite document review, and the onsite process review.

Document Review

This is the first stage of an ISO 27001 audit. It is done off site, as it is easy to review documents without incurring travel and lodging expenses. The audited organization provides the auditor all the relevant documentation related to the ISMS, including the risk assessment, the risk treatment plan, the SoA and all the documentation regarding IT security governance. Much like the SSAE 16 Type-1 design review, the auditor looks at the coverage and completeness of the security program. Does the risk assessment look reasonable and does it adequately cover the scope? Is the risk treatment plan acceptable and the chosen controls appropriate for the risks and assets involved? Are all the controls in ISO 27002 adequately addressed in the SoA? Does the governance model align with ISO standards?

Governance is a big focus of this review, as it is the heart of ISO 27001. The auditor is looking for policies, standards, procedures, and records for scope, policy objectives, asset inventories, risk assessment standards, risk treatment planning, security roles and job descriptions, and reviews of control operations.

Once the auditor feels the documents represent a satisfactory IT security program design, they inform their customer and proceed to scheduling an onsite visit.

Onsite Review

Like the SSAE 16 Type 2 audit, this inspection is about making sure all the documentation you supplied is being used. The auditor examines process and control activity with walk-throughs and interviews. They also look at records and configuration details for technical controls. Sites are visited as well, to examine physical security and the processes in action. Systems can be selected and reviewed against published standards. The auditor can also use logs and help desk tickets to track adherence to procedures.

The ISO 27001 auditor also focuses on the monitoring and correction (check/act) phases of IT security governance. This means the auditor looks at the internal auditor function, making sure they are independent and have been reviewing the security program. The auditor will want assurance that the internal auditor's reports are being reviewed and acted upon by the ISMS committee. This means that a brand new security program cannot be submitted for ISO 27001 audit. The program has to be running for at least a few months, so that controls and processes can go into operation, be internally audited, and management can respond to that feedback. Internal audit is covered more in Chapter 22.

Findings in the ISO 27001 world are called *non-conformities*, and they always include a direct reference to the specific section of the ISO 27001 standard documentation. This makes remediation and analysis easier, as you can go right to the standard and see what is needed.

Surveillance Audits

After passing your ISO 27001 audit, the certification is good for three years. During that three-year period, the auditors return each year for a *surveillance* audit, which is a smaller version of the first audit. This is to ensure that your practices and controls are still in place.

PCI DSS Audit

The PCI DSS audit is the most constrained and because of that, the most simple (but not easy) of these audits. Per the Payment Card Industry Security Standards Council: "PCI DSS applies to all entities involved in payment card processing-including merchants, processors, acquirers, issuers, and service providers. PCI DSS also applies to all other entities that store, process or transmit cardholder data (CHD) and/or sensitive authentication data (SAD)."[3]

If you store or process more than six million payment card transactions per year, you are considered a Level 1 merchant. For Level 1 merchants and anyone who has experienced a PCI DSS breach, these audits must be done by certified qualified security assessors (QSA); visit the PCI DSS web site at https://www.pcisecuritystandards.org/assessors_and_solutions/qualified_security_assessors.

---

[3]https://www.pcisecuritystandards.org/documents/PCI_DSS_v3-2.pdf.

Organizations with lower annual payment card transaction counts can submit their Self-Assessment Questionnaire (SAQ). There are many different types of SAQs broken out by type of organization and their role in the payment card transaction. The PCI standards organization has a good document called "Understanding the SAQs for PCI DSS," which is available at https://www.pcisecuritystandards.org/document_library?category=saqs#results.

The PCI DSS is one of the most technically prescriptive of all the audit compliance regimes. The audit therefore focuses a lot on technical controls, especially the vulnerability scanning and penetration testing. These scans must be done by an approved scanning vendor (ASV), listed online at https://www.pcisecuritystandards.org/assessors_and_solutions/approved_scanning_vendors.

Vulnerabilities found during scanning or penetration testing must be remediated if rated higher than medium, or 4.0 on the CVSS score range.

The QSA also looks very closely at the technical controls segregating the scoped environment from the rest of the world. PCI DSS refers to the scoped environment as the *cardholder data environment* (CDE). As for the controls themselves, the PCI DSS includes the testing procedures directly in the standard, so you know exactly what should be done.

After the review of controls, the QSA produces an Initial Report on Compliance, or IROC. If there are gaps, your organization has a few months to fix things before the auditor returns for retesting. When everything is clean, you receive a final Report on Compliance (ROC), which is your audit report. It contains an executive summary, a scope description, details on the CDE and organization, quarterly ASV scan results, and findings and observations by the QSA. Details on the format of this report are available right on the PCI DSS web site as the Report on Compliance (ROC) Reporting Template for auditors at https://www.pcisecuritystandards.org/document_library.

Disagreeing with Auditors

There may be times when you disagree with an auditor's findings. Changing an auditor's mind can be tough and you will often lose. The real trick is to politely disagree and explain your perspective on the finding without antagonizing the auditor. I like to see my role as a defense attorney trying to make sure that I receive justice for my client. I need to be firm with my client's case, but I do not want to usurp the judge's authority and sink my entire case. It takes a gentle but firm touch to voice a dissenting opinion with an auditor. This can be especially difficult since the auditor expects push back and likely hears complaints all the time. Stick to the facts, the audit standard, and use logic. Let's break down some types of findings in Table 21-1.

Table 21-1. *Audit Findings and Responses*

Finding	Likely Reason	Your Response
This control was excluded and therefore there is a finding	Some controls are always applicable in some audit requirements, some are not	If the control is not required by the audit, explain how the risk it mitigates is negligible or covered by another control elsewhere.
This automated control failed and that's a finding	Control did not function as described	Although it is still our fault that this control failed because of a manufacturer's bug, we have other controls that address this risk (defense in depth). Although these controls aren't as fast or robust as the automated control, they still address the risk during the short duration of this failure.

As you can see, the strategy is to focus not on the control but on the risk. Some auditors focus too much on controls and don't consider risk in their evaluations. Your response is to drive the conversation to the heart of the problem and go over the specific risks, matching them to the control and the potential impacts. When discussing risk, make sure that you discuss both likelihood and business impact.

FURTHER READING

- **The DevOps Audit Defense Toolkit**
  http://itrevolution.com/devops-and-auditors-the-devops-audit-defense-toolkit/

- **BIP 0072:2013: Are you ready for an ISMS audit based on ISO/IEC 27001?**
  http://shop.bsigroup.com/ProductDetail/?pid=000000000030282638

CHAPTER 22

■■■

Internal Audit

A corollary to *assume breach* is to assume control failure. In the words of many a CIO, if you don't check it then it wasn't done. Anyone who has managed operations or service vendors knows that some IT workers have a different definition of *done* than you. Given time and exposure to the real world, things drift from their modeled description. Policies don't match what people are doing. Project status updates are inflated. Network diagrams aren't current or complete. Log data isn't captured or if it is, the data slumbers unanalyzed somewhere. People leave the organization but their accounts remain active. Implementation projects get paused mid-implementation because of operational emergencies, but they are never resumed. Maintenance slips and patching doesn't complete. I'm not pessimistic—this just happens in a large, busy IT organization. However, if a control isn't working as described by policy, then you need to find it and fix before the auditors or attackers spot them. That is what internal audit is about.

The Role of Internal Audit

Internal audit is a role in your organization with the same kind of duties as the external auditor but they are on staff and embedded in the security program permanently. In larger organizations, internal audit is handled by its own distinct department and it often covers multiple audit compliance systems. If you are pursuing an ISO 27001 audit, then the internal audit role is a mandatory function. For other audit requirements, it is not necessarily required but it is still a useful and powerful role to have. There are two major requirements that internal auditors must meet: independence and competence.

Internal Auditor Independence

Since internal audit is about questioning the design and effectiveness of the entire security program, the internal auditor must be free to express an honest opinion without fear of backlash. Any conflict of interest between the security team, the IT operational team, and the internal auditor will produce a chilling effect on the quality of reporting. If the auditor finds a mismatch between goal and reality, it must be disclosed completely and candidly to management. This means the segregation of duties concept is required for this role.

The internal audit must not report to IT or even the security team. This auditor should report to the management, which is to say, the same executive (or higher) that the chief security officer role reports to. If the security team is under the chief operating officer, then internal audit should be a direct report as well. I have also seen internal audit report to the CEO or an entirely different wing of the organization. For example, internal audit could be attached to the financial department, which may already have an internal audit function for accounting. Figure 22-1 shows a sample organization chart illustrating this.

© Raymond Pompon 2016
R. Pompon, *IT Security Risk Control Management*, DOI 10.1007/978-1-4842-2140-2_22

Figure 22-1. *Sample org chart with internal audit*

There have been cases where an internal auditor attached to the IT department was fired because they uncovered fraud. Unfortunately, this lack of independence within internal audit was not uncovered until the subsequent criminal investigation after much damage was done.

Internal Auditor Competence

Just as important as auditor independence is that the auditor understands the technology requirements and the compliance requirements to be met. In the best case of an untrained internal audit team, they may miss control failures and potential threats. In the worst case, the auditor could be misled or steered away from potential problems by those being audited. If you don't know what exactly to look for regarding technology and security, it's easy to be confused or mistaken about how something functions. The lapse will be worse if you have a malicious insider actively working to cover up a mistake or crime. You also don't want a situation where internal audit has consistently given a security control a passing grade only to have an external auditor find significant fault in it.

To assist with this problem, there are internal auditor training classes. The ISO training institutions offer multi-day ISO 27001 internal audit training, which can be found by running that phrase through your favorite search engine. Some organizations send their PCI DSS internal auditors to full QSA training to ensure that they are fully qualified in the standard. In the financial accounting world, there is the Institute for Internal Auditors,[1] which offers training and certification in the general practice of the internal process auditing. However, those auditors should also undergo additional training to ensure that they understand the technology and specific compliance requirements that they will audit against. In most cases, internal auditors are not formally beholden to a certifying standards body, so their training and certification have a different weight than a true independent auditor.

Beyond the specific technical skills, auditors also need to be competent in acquiring, interpreting, analyzing, and reporting the data. They need to have an attitude of *professional skepticism* and question everything they are told. Even machine-produced results should be examined to ensure that they are telling the whole story. A useful skill for internal auditors is how to test for internal fraud. There is training and certification in this area from the Association for Certified Fraud Examiners.[2] An auditor with technical, compliance, and fraud skills is a triply valuable individual to have on staff.

---

[1]https://na.theiia.org
[2]http://www.acfe.com/AIF/

How Small Can the Role Go?

Larger organizations can afford the resources to dedicate employees to internal audit but smaller ones may not. This doesn't mean you give up on this vital function. Internal audit is a role, not necessarily a job title. All the audit needs is independence and capability. I've seen smaller organizations create part-time internal auditors out of external consultants, internal financial auditors (with additional training), and benched personnel between projects. If you aren't looking to hit ISO 27001 certification, you can even push the limit of segregation of duties and have members of the security team do internal audit duties as well. Internal non-dedicated auditors can still provide the benefit from redundancy and cross-checks for other team members.

To Heal, Not to Punish

Internal audit exists to make the organization's security program stronger. I have seen some organizations where the segregation of duties has gone too far. A healthy rivalry between internal audit and IT security is tolerable and in some cases, worth encouraging. However, you should avoid cultures where internal audit is out to *get* the IT team. Internal auditors should never set out to trap or trick people into failing audit. Even if this isn't the intention, this perception can be damaging to morale and create performance impacts. This only fosters an adversarial relationship where both parties end up deceiving and withholding information from each other, and ultimately impedes the organization's security program.

The goal is to have everyone working together toward an evolving security program with the best controls for current risks that the organization can afford. Consider the stance between a *culture of negative error* and a *culture of safety*. Negative error cultures are defensive where employees work to avoid getting in trouble or being blamed for mistakes. Negative error cultures focus on exclusively managing to the letter of the law and nothing beyond. They stifle speaking up about problems as mistakes are seen as personal failings and not systemic issues. Defensive decision-making flourishes, where choices are made based on minimizing culpability.

A culture of safety is about prevention, transparency, and continuous improvement. In a safety culture, everyone functions in some way like an internal auditor, looking out for mistakes and deficiencies in order to promote the greater goal of safety. Problems and findings are not blamestormed, but analyzed to uncover the organizational processes and design issues that led to them. In a culture of safety, reminders and reviews from internal auditors are valued and heeded, rather than feared and avoided.

Check Before the Auditors Check

The internal auditor's job is to fix things before there are severe impacts or external audit findings. They should walk through the entire stack of controls to ensure that everything functions as described in policy. This means getting up to their elbows in firewall rules, user accounts, change control tickets, and security policy decisions.

Usually, lots of *cruft*, or leftover obsolete and unnecessary things, are found during these checks, such as the following:

- Confidential data stored and forgotten on systems that should have been removed or encrypted

- Systems that should have been decommissioned but still left online

- Expired licenses and subscriptions for operational and security systems

- Live user accounts for individuals who had left the organization

- Zombie service accounts still active but no longer needed

- Excessive management overrides of internal controls for policies that don't fit

- Unrecorded (and therefore unauthorized) changes to key systems under change control

- Half-installed controls from rushed projects or distracted implementation teams

- Missing patches, hardening, or control installs

- Missing root cause analyses from incidents

- Firewall rules that are no longer needed, but have not been decommissioned

All of these things are the typical meat and potatoes of an internal auditor's review. Any one of these things can lead to a security incident or audit finding.

The Internal Audit Process

Just like an external audit, the internal audit process should involve both a document review and personnel interviews. Overall, the internal audit plan should look a lot like an external audit plan, but spread out over a longer period. External auditors are usually onsite a few weeks at most per year, internal auditors should take full advantage of the fact that they live onsite. A schedule should be set up for the internal auditor to sample each control and process area over the audit period (usually a year), circling back to key controls on a regular basis. The key controls should be checked at least quarterly are user management, authorized changes, access control less and data backup functionality. Whatever the audit schedule is, it should not be published outside of internal audit too far in advance. To the audited parts of the organization, the audits should be somewhat unpredictable.

Like external auditors, the internal audit plan involves a *pull list* of key records to examine in each control area. Executive management should ensure full cooperation with internal auditors. Refusing to comply in a timely and transparent manner with internal audit should be considered an audit finding itself.

Measuring a Control

Control measurement isn't just limited to internal audit, as the security team will also be involved in tracking the progress of their program. Because of their role, internal auditors are in a good position to take and track control metrics. Over the period, internal auditors verify and inspect every process and control in the organization related to security.

This measuring process necessitates that the controls and processes be designed so that they produce observable artifacts on the functionality. Firewalls should be capable of creating logs and configuration reports. Meetings should have minutes and agendas. User access requests should have paper trails and authorization tickets. The auditor saying applies here as well: if it isn't documented, it does not exist. The failure to produce verifiable proof from an active control or process is an audit finding.

However, it still may fall upon the internal auditor to devise their own tests and checks for controls and processes. The goal is to find a measure that yields good information on the intent of the thing being measured. If a control is implemented based on a policy to reduce a particular type of risk, then there should be a way to measure the implementation against policy and test its risk-reduction capability. Sometimes this is easy and sometimes it is a challenge. Let's look at some ideas for doing this in Table 22-1.

Table 22-1. *Controls and How to Measure Them*

Control or Process	Possible Check
Asset inventory	Last time done. Random sample spot-check of live assets against inventory list.
Risk analysis	Last time done. Review of risk assumptions. Review of compliance analysis. Review of threat analysis. Review of impact analysis.
Scope	Review of scope perimeter. Review of scope perimeter controls. Check scoped assets. Check operational processes. Look for scope data leakage. Review business processes for impacts to scope.
Security training	Review training attendance records. Last update of training material. Training topic coverage and relevance to risks and compliance. Review training test results. Review past security incidents related to training topics.
Security Policy	Review user policy sign-off records. Last policy update. Policy coverage and relevance to risks and compliance.
Standards and Policies	Coverage of documents to requirements. Completeness of documents. Last updated.
Security department	Review of security team job descriptions. Last security training attended. Certifications completed.
IT department	Review of IT job descriptions. Last IT operational training attended. Review segregation of duties.
General controls	Review key controls for defense in depth. Check control deployment. Review control operational records. Review Control maintenance records.
Change control	Look for unauthorized changes done. Review unauthorized changes detected. Scan change control records for documentation completeness.
Authentication	Reconcile UserIDs to current HR records. Check authentication implemented vs standard across systems. Check password settings to standard. Check two-factor inventory.
Authorization	Review authorization settings per UserID and groups looking for excessive or obsolete rights.
Firewalls	Review firewall configurations. Review firewall rule documentation records. Check for software updates. Review maintenance records. Check the number of administrators on the firewall. Review firewall change logs. Check firewall configuration vs published standards.
Intrusion Detection/ Prevention	Review signature update dates. Review maintenance records. Review records of alert responses and analysis. Check coverage of system on critical net flows. Check log retention.
Network devices	Review VLAN configurations on critical segregations. Check configured administrators per device. Review change-logging records. Check actual configuration vs. published standard.
Vulnerability scans	Check that it was done at least quarterly. Review depth and breadth of scan. Verify competence of scanner operator. Review scan settings to ensure updated. Ensure that results were reviewed. Ensure that remediation was done.

(continued)

Table 22-1. (*continued*)

Control or Process	Possible Check
Penetration tests	Check that it was done at least annually. Review depth and breadth of test. Verify that competence of tester. Ensure that results were reviewed. Ensure that remediation was done.
Internet-visible applications	Check that application security was reviewed. Review last security scan done. Check actual hardening vs. published standards. Ensure that DMZ and network segregation are in use. Check last code update.
Network encryption	Check actual configuration vs. published standard. Review last update of standards. Review last vulnerability scan. Review configuration documentation. Check software updates. Review maintenance records. Check admins per device. Review change logging. Ensure that encryption has not gone obsolete.
Storage encryption	Check actual configuration vs. published standard. Check coverage of encryption across devices. Check last update of standards. Review configuration documentation. Check change logging.
Crypto key management	Actual configuration vs. published standard. Key management records. Admins per system. Key inventory. Ensure that encryption has not gone obsolete.
Physical perimeter security	Check key/card key inventory vs. current employees. Ensure that PIN codes are being properly rotated on schedule. Verify proper locks function on doors (closets. cages. rooms). Check automatic door closing mechanisms. Ensure that co-location facility list is current.
Visitor security	Review visitor log record. Spot-check the usage of badges. Review retention of logs. Spot-check for unescorted visitors.
Cameras	Check coverage and visibility of cameras. Ensure that cameras are properly recording. Review retention of video log to standard.
Physical security	Check for unsecured confidential data sitting out unprotected. Check media inventory vs. actual media. Ensure that assets are locked up. Check that media is properly labeled. Review disposal records. Ensure that shred bins are being used. Spot-check recycle bins for confidential documents not shredded.
Business continuity	Ensure that continuity tests are being done regularly. Check last update on plan. Check coverage of plan vs. possible outages. Review plan for training records. Check plan relevance to current environment. Check root cause analysis reports vs. known outages. Review call trees and notification mechanisms.
Incident response	Review record of past incidents. Review last update on plan. Check plan training. Check plan relevance to current environment. Review post-mortems to known incidents. Review call trees and notification mechanisms.
Third-party security	Check security reviews vs. actual third parties. Check when last completed for each. Review depth and breadth of review. Check that connections are documented. Review third-party perimeter standards vs. actual implementation.

Findings and non-conformities should mean a frequent and often revisit of the activity until assurance is given that no additional findings will turn up. Even then, controls that had findings should be given higher priority thereafter in future internal audits.

ISO Standard for Measurement

For more ideas on how to measure control effectiveness, consider looking at ISO 27004. This standard provides details on how to measure the effectiveness of an information security management system. If you are implementing and auditing against ISO 27001, I strongly suggest that you investigate this standard. Even if you're not, the standard includes detailed instructions on how to build indicators and metrics for IT security controls. You can find out more about it at http://www.iso.org/iso/catalogue_detail?csnumber=42106.

Publish to Management

As part of the internal audit cycle, auditors need to provide reports to management. An audit is useless if there are no adjustments based on the findings. Management is responsible for reading and acting upon the results in order to improve the security program. In ISO 27001, this is a major requirement of the ISMS process. This also means that internal auditors need to report their findings in a timely and understandable manner. The internal audit report should look like an informal, shorter version of an external audit report. It should have the following elements:

- Executive summary
- Specific compliance requirements being tested (PCI DSS v3.1 Requirement 1 – Firewall, etc.)
- Methodology and time/date of testing
- Audit tests performed and results
- Participants (name, job, role)
- Specific controls tested and results
- Recommended corrective actions (if any)

Regarding executive summaries, they should be written with an executive in mind. Remember the chapter on talking to the suits and keep the writing clear, factual, and to the point. Don't fluff up the summary with the specifics of the internal audit process, those can be reported later in the main report. The summary should just contain what was tested, the findings uncovered, and an opinion on how an external audit of this area would play out. The goal is that summary is actionable, so that a decision can be made.

Keep Records

Since the internal audit function can be subject to external audit, there should be proper documentation and record keeping. These records should include the following:

- Description of internal audit team and roles
- Schedule of audits (past and present)
- Internal audit methodology (it should align with organizational priorities, risks, and asset values)

- Audit reports to management including details on findings
- Management's documented response for corrective actions
- Internal audit's follow up on corrective actions

Since these audits may contain confidential information regarding controls and organizational processes, the reports should be classified as confidential and access controlled.

FURTHER READING

- **Internal Auditor training**
  http://www.irca.org/en-gb/Training/IRCA-Certified-Training/

- **ISO 19011:2011: Guidelines for auditing management systems**
  http://www.iso.org/iso/home/store/catalogue_tc/catalogue_detail.
  htm?csnumber=50675

- **ISACA: Internal Audit's Contribution to the Effectiveness of Information Security**
  http://www.isaca.org/Journal/archives/2014/Volume-2/Pages/Internal-
  Audits-Contribution-to-the-Effectiveness-of-Information-Security-
  Part-1.aspx

- **Security Metrics**
  http://www.securitymetrics.org/

CHAPTER 23

■ ■ ■

Third-Party Security

Doveryai no proveryai. (Trust, but verify.)

> —Russian proverb used by President Ronald Regan during arms
> control negotiations with Russian President Mikhail Gorbachev in the 1980s.

Every organization is dependent on other organizations outside of itself. It's unlikely that your organization writes all of its own software, builds its own hardware, owns the buildings it occupies, and is an internet service provider. Your security is dependent on many of these things but if they are produced outside of your organization, your control is limited. Previous chapters touched on risk and controls for third parties, but what happens when those third parties are critical to your scoped environment and audit? You need to manage the security where the third party touches your scoped environments. Before you manage, you need to measure. To measure the security of an outside organization, you need to use everything you've learned about being audited and apply it to someone else. Even if you pay someone else to audit the third party, you still need to define the scope, requirements, and testing, and interpret the results.

Which Third Parties Are Relevant?

The third parties we're concerned about are the ones where their actions or inactions can affect the security of your scoped environment. You probably won't include the company that supplies the water cooler bottles, unless they have their own keys to a secure facility. A good indicator is the criticality of dependence. If you are relying on the services from an outside organization, they fall into scope. The following are some of the third parties that IT security programs often have to deal with:

- Building management and janitorial
- Co-location facility
- Cloud-services providers
- Contracted IT workers
- Internet Service Providers
- Off-site backup services
- Shredding services
- Software packages and vendors that touch scoped systems
- Managed security service providers

R. Pompon, *IT Security Risk Control Management*, DOI 10.1007/978-1-4842-2140-2_23

In large, dispersed organizations, even other divisions of the same company could be treated like third parties. It all depends on the level of control that you can wield over the entity. If a company department is outside the authority of the security program but still has connections into the scoped environment, then you need to treat them as a third party. For example, if your scoped environment resides within the e-commerce division of a large manufacturer. All of the activity and management of e-commerce are run within the e-commerce division except human resources. A parent company in a city far away handles all HR activity, even for your division. The VP running the e-commerce division has no direct authority over HR back at headquarters. Since hiring and background checks is in scope, you need to set up some kind of third-party arrangement to ensure that HR does things according to the standards required by the e-commerce security program. Another good example is a government entity, where some critical functions are provided from another government entity outside its realm of authority.

Customers and business partners can also qualify as third parties. Depending on your business model, there are instances where a customer may need network access to an internal scoped environment. This creates a touchy situation where you need to measure and apply controls to a customer that you don't want to irritate. In some cases, you have scope by association. If you share information with a business partner, you need to consider who they share that information and how.

Analysis of Third Parties

As with everything in security, you need to understand what risk to what assets before you apply controls. The challenge with a third party is that you do not have direct access to all the information you may need to assess risk accurately. The depth of your assessment should be based on the potential impact from a third-party security failure. Whatever process, service, or asset can be affected by the third party needs to be investigated. Third parties with direct access to scoped systems and data is a high priority and requires very thorough analysis and testing to ensure that you're seeing a satisfactory representation. These analyses should be done upon first contracting/connecting with the third party and repeated and at least annually, depending on changes to their environment.

Risk Analysis

The question of what to test at a third-party provider is probably the easiest thing to answer. It should flow directly from your current control objectives and audit requirements. Since your controls and requirements come from a risk analysis, it makes sense that the third parties should mirror your control objectives as well. One of the things you can request is a risk analysis related to the contracted services done by the third party. A good sign of a healthy security program is relevant and complete risk analysis, so this in and of itself would be a good indicator of their maturity.

In the absence of a risk analysis from a third party, you need to do one yourself. All things being equal, there are probably a handful of relevant general risk scenarios to consider with the third party. Not all of these may be applicable with all of your third parties, and there may be additional scenarios, but here is a good starting list of risks to consider:

- Rogue insider at the third party steals or leaks your data

- Outage of contracted service

- Malware in third-party network leading to leakage or outage of your data

- Lost media or portable device containing your data

- Internet-facing service at third party hacked leading to leakage or outage of your data

- Unauthorized physical access to third-party facilities leading to leakage or outage of your data

- Any of these risks occurring at another third party being used by your third party (fourth party)

You can present this list of risk scenarios to the third party and ask them how they manage these risks. This is can be a time-intensive approach that requires more interpretation and analysis, but it yields far more useful information about their security and trustworthiness.

Control Gap Analysis Approach

The more common approach in third-party analysis is skip the risk analysis and jump right into a gap analysis against the controls that should be in place. This approach is simpler but makes assumptions about the typical risks and appropriate defenses required. You could use your current control set as a master list to check against. To save time and energy, especially if you have many third parties to investigate, you could boil things down to key controls that you feel might be important. Here is a simple list of likely key controls to check:

- Data encryption on portable media and computers

- Change control on contracted services/applications

- Security policy and security planning

- Regular vulnerability assessments

- Background checks on personnel

- Application security analysis if providing or developing apps for you

- Anti-malware strategy (beyond just antivirus software)

- Access controls

Instead of general controls covering large risks to services, you could also do control gap analysis on the specific services being offered by the third party. Table 23-1 is a list of controls broken out by service.

Table 23-1. *Third Parties and Controls to Examine*

Third Party	Controls to Investigate
Building management and janitorial	People controls especially background checks
Co-location facility	Physical controls, operational controls, people controls
Cloud-services providers	Pretty much all controls except application controls
Contracted IT workers	HR controls especially background checks, security training
Internet service providers	Response controls, especially business continuity
Off-site backup services	Physical controls, operational controls, people controls
Shredding services	Physical controls, operational controls, people controls
Major software vendors	Software development controls, vulnerability testing
Managed security service providers	All controls

You could trim some of the specific controls back but only after conferring with the third party and hearing their explanation as to why that particular control would be not applicable. It's better to ask for more and then drop what you don't think is important. It is a waste of everyone's time if you are going to delve into detailed examinations of controls and processes that are wholly irrelevant to your scoped requirements. For example, I'm not going to investigate the software development controls of my shredding service provider.

Getting Answers

Now that you have an idea about what to ask, how do you go about getting answers from the third party? The simplest and most common way is to send the question list to the third party and give them a deadline to respond. This is called a *self-assessment*, which relies on the third party attesting to the truth of their answers. To bind them tighter to truthful answers, you can include a formal attestation statement at the end of the questionnaire for an executive to sign. You can deliver these questions electronically via e-mailed spreadsheet or document. Some organizations use web-based survey tools and have third parties login and answer.

The next level of assurance is to require the third party to submit documentation along with their answers. Just like your auditors, you can ask them to provide screen-shots and administrative control documentation as proof of existing controls. Along with this, it is not unheard of to ask for actual output from scans and completed checklists.

The highest level of third-party review is to send a team on-site to their offices and conduct a direct assessment of their security program. This should be planned just like an audit, with an agenda, a pull-list of requested information, and interviews with selected roles. It is the most informative, since you can directly examine the risks and controls at the third party. It is also the most resource intensive, especially if the third party is distant from your organization. Many financial institutions use this kind of assessment for their key vendors because of the high risk involved in banking and bank transactions. Some organizations also hire consultants or auditors to go on-site for them and perform assessments.

Reading Their Audit Reports

Because many IT service providers have customers who are under compliance requirements, they obtain their own independent audits of the relevant parts of their service. As discussed in Chapter 1, a report from a reputable auditor is a good indicator about the confidence an organization places in their IT security program. External audits are expensive and force an organization to have a formal security program.

If the audit report is scoped correctly and covers the right services, then your risk assessment work is much easier. In fact, since many IT service providers are under intense scrutiny from their customers, they often end up covering many different compliance requirements with comprehensive audits. Providers can also leverage economies of scale and have superior security programs than what your organization could afford. Don't discount a third party as being insecure by default.

When receiving third-party audit reports, be sure to read them carefully. Remember which parts of the audit report to examine. You need to look at the scope to make sure that what was audited matches the services relevant to your organization's usage. You cannot make any assumptions about the state of things out of scope; they are unknown and must be tested to be validated.

You should also look at the date of testing. All audit reports, by definition, are out of date the second they are published. Audit reports only point backward in time. So you still have to use your judgment to determine if all the audited controls they have in place remain in place in the future. For this reason, audit reports are perishable with a shelf life of less than a year. Any report older than that should not be considered viable for risk analysis. For dynamic organizations, such as fast-growing startups, the report's shelf life would be shorter.

Analyzing It All

Once you've gathered data about the third party, you need to analyze it and render an opinion to management on the risk of using the third party. Based on this analysis, the organization can choose to stop using the third party (eliminate the risk), continue as before (accept the risk), or manage the risk (apply additional controls). Keep that in mind when doing the analysis. It's likely that your organization needs to manage the risk either directly or indirectly (by requiring the third party to add controls), so management's next questions after receiving your analysis will be about controls and scope changes.

In addition to the maturity and the effectiveness of their controls, you can also get sense of the overall strength of their security program. You can learn this not only from the answers, but also by *how* they answered you. Are they responsive, complete, and transparent in their answers? Or do you get the sense they are reactive and struggling to fit inappropriate controls to meet risks? Do their security personnel understand security concepts like least privilege and assume breach? Or are they attempting to meet the letter of the compliance law? When challenged, are they open to your questions or do they react defensively with statements like, "Everyone else accepts this. You should too." Evasion, defensiveness, preparedness, speed, and reluctance to answer are all warning flags that their program may not meet your needs. The question to consider is this: How is the third party answering the questions? A prepared organization may pull answers from a frequently asked question list. An unprepared organization may generate new material—perhaps not even based on the truth and awareness, but on aspiration and what they think you want to hear.

Concerning the controls and risks as a whole, if you find many problems, you should consider if there is evidence that the problems are any of the following:

- *A matter of maturity.* They know where they're going; they're just not there yet.

- *Design problems.* They know where they're going, but it's the wrong place.

- *Organizational problems.* They are completely reactive to security problems and have no consistent plan.

As you might guess, some of these problems are more manageable than others. Sometimes these kinds of conclusions are difficult to make, especially if you're new to audit and third-party review. I mention them as considerations so you have some idea of the analysis techniques of seasoned security professionals.

Controlling Third-Party Risk

Like controlling all other risk, when we talk about controlling the risk for third parties, we focus our controls on reducing the likelihood or the impact of possible undesired actions. You can reduce the likelihood by requiring the third parties to have their own security controls in place. This is probably both the most effective in terms of outcome and the most difficult to do since you do not exert direct control over their security. Sometimes a third party asks you to incur some of the costs of additional controls that you are requiring of them

If adding controls at the third party isn't feasible, you can also apply your own controls directly upon certain kinds of third parties. For example, you could require all on site contractors to be background checked by your HR department and attend your organization's security training.

Another type of control to apply is to limit damage from a third party. You can do this by reducing the scope of their access. You can look at limiting their time exposure and/or asset exposure to your organization. For example, contractors can only access our VPN during business hours and can only connect to these three machines. Sometimes this is difficult, depending on the nature of the work that the third party is doing. That leaves trying to contain an impact with internal barriers and rapid detection controls. If building janitorial personnel need full access to your office, then lock the server cages and put up surveillance cameras. As we move into looking at controls, let's start with some policy.

Sample Policy for Third-Party Management

To ensure that all contractors and vendors who have access to critical systems and data will support ORGANIZATION security objectives, ORGANIZATION will maintain a formal Third Party Management Process that will:

- *Contractually require these third parties comply with ORGANIZATION security policies and documented processes. These contractual requirements will include provisions for the third party to:*

  - *Acknowledge their responsibility for the security of ORGANIZATION data they possess*

  - *Acknowledge their duty to quickly notify ORGANIZATION in the event of a breach of privacy or IT security*

  - *Provide proof of the third-party security controls with either an independent audit report such as SSAE-16 SOC 2 or ISO 27001 or agreement to be audited by ORGANIZATION or its representative at least annually*

- *Furthermore, ORGANIZATION will perform a risk analysis of all third parties with access or influence on critical systems.*

  - *This risk analysis will be the responsibility of the Security department and will be completed before the third party is granted access to critical systems.*

  - *Based on this risk analysis, the security department will propose controls and changes to ORGANIZATION management reduce the risk to acceptable levels.*

  - *This risk assessment and controls review process will be repeated annually for all third parties with access to critical systems.*

- *The IT and Security department will work together on a software security standard that will be used to evaluate acquisitions of Commercial Off The Shelf software (COTS) as well as custom software used for collection, processing, and storage of sensitive data.*

- *Documentation regarding the third-party risk analysis and the specific process controls and checks that are used to ensure compliance with the third-party security requirements, including preferences for independent audit such as SSAE 16 SOC 2 or ISO 27001*

Be cautious requiring employees of a third-party organization to sign your security policies. With individual contractors directly hired by your organization, requiring individuals to sign carries some enforceable obligation, such as terminating their individual contract. With an organization, your policy statements should be agreed upon between organizations. It is then the responsibility of the third party to ensure that their representatives fulfill the policy objectives. Often in most organizations, only a select set of individuals are empowered to legally agree to terms on behalf of the organization. You could be creating a false sense of security and a potential legal hassle by trying to get the guy who empties your trash can to sign your acceptable usage agreement.

Software Procurement

The third-party security policy defines the need for a security standard for software acquisitions. What should be in this standard? The first thing is to make sure that any software you use on scoped systems can support your existing controls. That last thing you want is building compensating controls for a new piece of software that won't pass audit. If you require two-factor access into the scoped environment (and in many cases you should), then any systems you install should be able to either do or integrate two-factor authentication. Similarly, look at your requirements for authorization, hardening, encryption, backup, and logging.

If it's a large and important application, then your standard can call out a requirement to perform a vulnerability scan against a demo or proof-of-concept version. This should be done before software acquisition. When deployed, the application is subject to the normal vulnerability scanning you do already. Similarly, your standard can include requirements around support, vulnerability notification, and timely delivery of patches. You should test web-based applications against the OWASP top ten vulnerabilities,[1] especially if they are Internet facing.

For custom software, application security testing and/or secure code scanning should be a requirement. If serious vulnerabilities are found, the third party should be obligated to fix them in a reasonable time. You can put these requirements into a software development contract, which is described in the next section.

Acquired systems that fall into scope for PCI DSS need to meet the Payment Application Data Security Standard (PA-DSS)[2] for software and the PIN Transaction Security (PTS) Standard[3] for point of sale devices.

Security Service Agreements

The problem with outsourcing is that you're giving up control to the third party. You have no direct levers or methods to ensure that security practices are being followed. If you can't apply technical controls on a third party, then you can use legal controls like a security service agreement. These agreements can include outsourcing contracts, IT service agreements, and *Memorandums of Understanding* (MOU). In general, all of these agreements are legal documents, which are tied to technology and third-party services performed for your organization.

These agreements can stipulate what security controls you require to have in place with the third party with some kind of penalty for non-conformance. Ultimately, the agreement is leverage for future legal action if something goes wrong. The agreement itself spells out what is expected, and therefore, what is considered negligent.

MOUs are agreements for other divisions of a large dispersed organization. It may not make sense to have an actual legal agreement between the divisions, but an internal formal agreement between departments can help clarify responsibilities and expectations for both sides. In some ways, the MOU acts like an acceptable usage agreement between departments in an organization. The MOU can also spell out service level agreements regarding security, which you can use to assign responsibility if something goes wrong.

You are likely not an attorney, which means you wouldn't be ultimately responsible for writing the final version of a security service agreement. However, in most cases of using a third party, there is already a legal agreement being developed. If the third party is providing IT services, then there is probably a section of the agreement spelling out the technical specifications. Your need to work with your legal team to ensure that there are adequate security provisions in the agreement, either in their own section or within the technical specification, or both. The review of those contracts should be considered a required administrative control that you could put into policy.

---

[1]https://www.owasp.org/index.php/Category:OWASP_Top_Ten_Project.
[2]https://www.pcisecuritystandards.org/assessors_and_solutions/vpa_agreement.
[3]https://www.pcisecuritystandards.org/assessors_and_solutions/pin_transaction_devices.

Contents of the Agreement

What should be in this agreement? The goal is to make sure that all of your relevant identified security objectives and risks are covered. You can go down your list and make a list of how it applies to the third party. From there, you can consider how you want the third party to cover that risk and what you want to happen if the risk occurred. Here are some ideas of what can go in there:

- *Data classification.* Begin at the beginning and define the data types that should be protected by the third party. This can include credit card account numbers, personally identifiable information, and documents labeled "confidential."

- *Non-disclosure.* Not just restrictions on sharing your data (which should be there), but what the third party can talk about outside the relationship. Can they share information about your organization and its internal processes? Are they allowed to talk about what they do for your organization?

- *Data locale.* Where can your data be moved within the third party? Can it be moved outside the country? Can they use a cloud service provider to store your data? Make sure that they get your organization's permission before doing any of these things.

- *Required controls.* Define exactly what controls you want the third party to use to protect your stuff. This is often a long list, so it's better to include it as an attachment to the agreement describing your security requirements. The goal is to be detailed enough to ensure that things are done to your requirements. For example, saying you want *background checks* isn't enough. For the third party, that may be interpreted as just calling their previous employer. Describe your background check criteria in detail.

- *Right to audit.* Hold them to the same standard you need to meet for the relevant services. This means that the third party needs to provide an annual independent audit report for a specified compliance requirement or agree to be audited by you or your representative. Who pays for the audit is often another negotiating point in these kinds of discussions.

- *Data ownership.* Make sure that your organization retains ownership of all data provided to the third party and that you can get access to that data even if there are financial or contractual disputes. The third party should not be using your data for anything other than what is required to perform the agreed upon services. Is metadata being collected about your organization's usage of services? How is being used and shared? Is there a privacy policy?

- *Data handling in the event of legal action.* If the third party is sold or in bankruptcy, ownership and access to your data should still clearly belong to your organization. If a government authority requests access to your data while at the third party, you should be notified promptly.

- *Data handling upon termination.* When you are done working with this third party, all of your data should be returned or destroyed.

- *Remote access and interconnections.* Define which systems will be connected, who will be using them, what data will be moving in each direction, which security controls need to be set up on the connection (authentication, authorization, logging), and what the acceptable usage of the connection (no vulnerability scanning into your network without permission, no malware transfers). There should also be least privilege applied, no traffic allowed over the connection except what is part of the contracted obligation.

- *Code protection.* If code is being developed by the third party for your organization, it should be protected from malware, loss, bankruptcy (with source code escrow), leakage, and malicious insider back doors. As the one most able to control these things, the third party should guarantee the code is protected from these threats.

- *Vulnerabilities.* If severe bugs and security vulnerabilities are discovered in developed software, the third party should provide patches and mitigations in a timely manner (30 days). There should be a defined vulnerability reporting and support resolution process.

- *Breach and incident notification.* Define breach (unauthorized access or alteration of your data) and the notification and remediation requirements for the third party. Who is going to pay for the damages both to your organization and your organization's customers? How quickly should you be notified if the third party confirms an incident?

- *Penalties.* What happens if any of these provisions are violated? One common response is the entitlement to *injunctive relief,* which means your organization can take this agreement to court and force the third party to stop whatever they're doing (like sharing your data with marketers). Another response is financial penalties like the refund of payment for services or payment for damages. Lastly, there is termination of the entire agreement and therefore, relationship with the third party.

Technical Controls

Where third parties have access to your environments, technical controls can be very powerful in managing that risk. Technical controls are very useful when third parties are electronically connecting to your organization. This connection can be ad hoc, such as occasional remote access to perform contracted services, or it could be continuous via a network-to-network link. Technical controls can provide the verification of the access agreement.

Authentication and Authorization

Any users coming into your network should be authenticated and their access limited based on least privilege. This is even more important for users who don't belong to your organization. If feasible, two-factor authentication should be used for third-party access. If this is access is infrequent or limited to a few occasions, then third-party users can be *electronically escorted*. This means having a system administrator use screen-sharing remote control tools to relinquish keyboard/mouse control. This way all of the third-party actions can be tracked in real time by a knowledgeable person. This is ideal for vendors and consultants who need quick temporary access for remote technical support. For even tighter control, the remote third party could be in read-only screen-share and instruct your people what buttons to press.

All authentication access attempts and failures should be logged and those logs reviewed along with everything else on a regular basis.

Network Controls

Chapter 17, which discussed network security, had a security policy that stated, "Network connections from customers and other third parties will terminate in a DMZ." These are sometimes called *extranet* connections and should be firewalled and managed. These connections usually originate from a dedicated leased-line or a site-to-site VPN. Regardless, access control rules should be applied to the incoming connection to limit the connections from specified source addresses to specified destination addresses on specified network ports.

There are some situations where a vendor needs to put equipment directly onto your network. These are devices inside your perimeter that you do not have administrative control over. You can segregate these devices onto their own subnets or VLANs and manage access in both directions via a network access control list.

If you are allowing third-party network traffic into your network, you should monitor it. All of your network security monitoring tools can apply, including intrusion detection/prevention, network antivirus scanning, and digital leak prevention sniffing.

Vulnerability and Risk Monitoring

For third parties that have possession of sensitive data or direct links into your organization's networks, you should ensure that vulnerability scanning of their network is done on a regular basis. You should require that the third party not be the one doing the scanning. Either they can contract with an independent scanning vendor and provide you with a report, or you can do the scanning yourself. These scans should be done at least quarterly and include an annual independent penetration test.

In addition to scanning for technical vulnerabilities, there are services that monitor third parties' risk footprint on the Internet. They scan for the third party's IP addresses and domains on various reputation lists as well as perform periodic configuration hygiene tests against the third party's perimeter. Based on that information, they issue a rating on the estimated security strength of the third party. Here are three such companies who do this:

- **MarkIt**
  http://www.markit.com/product/ky3p

- **BitSight**
  https://www.bitsighttech.com

- **Security Scorecard**
  https://securityscorecard.com

Document Your Work

Like everything else, you should document this work. The standards, scheduling of testing, and the records of the third-party risk analysis are all part of your due diligence in keeping your organization safe. Roles and responsibilities for third-party tasks such as onsite reviews and reviewing scan results should also be documented. Third-party network connections should be diagramed with data-flows and controls noted. Lastly, a master registry of all relevant third parties with their services and risks defined should be kept and updated. All of these documents are important to external auditors.

FURTHER READING

- **ICT Procurement Security Guide for Electronic Communications Service Providers**
  https://www.enisa.europa.eu/publications/security-guide-for-ict-procurement/at_download/fullReport

- **CSA Security, Trust & Assurance Registry**
  https://cloudsecurityalliance.org/star/

- **Shared Assessments: Tools and methods for third-party assurance**
  https://sharedassessments.org

- **PCI DSS Third-party Security Assurance**
  https://www.pcisecuritystandards.org/document_library

CHAPTER 24

■■■

Post Audit Improvement

Everything flows and nothing abides. Everything gives way and nothing stays fixed.

—Heraclitus

So now you're done. Your security program is up and running, you've made it through your audit, and everyone is happy. Take a vacation and rest. You can forget about security, forever. Yeah, you know I'm kidding. As long as there are threats in the world, the security team can never close their eyes.

Now that you've seen how your security architecture has stood up against adversity and auditors, it's time to tackle the final step of the *Plan-Do-Check-Act Cycle*. This is when the ISMS committee tweaks and augments the program. However, you needn't wait until after the audit for this. There's nothing wrong with making changes to running processes in the middle of an audit or business cycle, it can just be a little more work on the paperwork side as controls transition from one state to another. In reality, the end of an audit is just an illusion, as most organizations run back-to-back audit periods. One audit period ends at midnight on December 31st and the next one starts at 12:01 a.m. on January 1st. Like security, the auditing truly never ends.

Nevertheless, people often use the end of an audit or a business year as a natural break point to reevaluate and adjust. Whenever you do it, you need to take a hard look at your program at least once a year. Over time, your IT security program must evolve and adapt, or it will fall into the trap of Fort Pulaski and be blindsided by new technology and new threats. You may also find that many controls aren't working as well as you had hoped and process improvements could save money or provide new advantages. Security is an iterative process. The security program you built may end up looking radically different in a few years. There is never a single right solution and there are plenty of wrong ones.

Reviewing Everything

Before you make any big decisions, it's a good idea to look at everything in perspective. We often have a strong bias to look at only the failures. We naturally focus on audit findings, security incidents, and outages. When security is working perfectly, nothing happens and business runs as usual. Aberrations and failures stick out like smoke plumes across a golden meadowland. There will be plenty of analysis of those problems, but don't forget what didn't happen and why it didn't happen.

Reviewing What Worked

The best evidence of your success is your passing audit report. Every control without auditor comment or finding counts as a win. These are the processes that are working and have a good chance of continuing to work in the near future. These are the positive examples that you can build upon for other controls, or that you can expand as needed. Not every control survives unaltered over time, but at least you know something

© Raymond Pompon 2016
R. Pompon, *IT Security Risk Control Management*, DOI 10.1007/978-1-4842-2140-2_24

worked this time. Some technologies may work better in your organization than others. Sometimes the success comes from the design; sometimes it comes from the people involved; and sometimes it's the process used. If the team was particularly successful in implementation or operation, consider spreading their expertise by having them train, mentor, lead, or document their lessons learned.

Near misses are when you almost had an audit finding or a serious security incident, but made it through with minimal impact. It's likely you've had a few of those over the audit period. This could be a failed control that a secondary control caught, a security policy violation reported before it caused any damage, or a malware infection that was stopped mid-install because of a particular technological tool. These are also good things to examine, replicate, expand, or share throughout the enterprise.

Similarly, you should look at averted and potential attacks. This can come from log analysis work looking for attacks thwarted by timely patches, malware blocked by filters, and firewall blocks. You are looking for potential new threats or rising attack trends. Sometimes these kinds of successes are better looked at in aggregate with statistics, so let's get down to numbers.

Chapter 12 talked about the quality of controls. Control quality breaks down into *control coverage* (assets covered) and *control effectiveness* (risk stopping power). Here's a list of the ways that you can measure control quality:

- *Asset management effectiveness and coverage*: Actual inventory vs. inventory records (do an annual hand count).

- *Vulnerability scan coverage*: Scanned hosts vs. actual hosts; last scan date.

- *Vulnerability management effectiveness*: Percentage of critical systems with no high/medium vulnerabilities.

- *Vulnerability management effectiveness*: Vulnerabilities exploited in pen-test and/or hacks.

- *Vulnerability management coverage*: Percentage of servers meeting hardening standard.

- *Vulnerability management effectiveness*: Average time to close vulnerabilities (break down by severity, server type, etc.).

- *Disaster recovery coverage*: Percentage of critical systems with recovery plan/tested recovery plan.

- *Scope containment*: Pieces of scoped data found outside of scope.

- *Incident response effectiveness*: Amount of time to detect; amount of time to respond vs. goals.

- *Access control effectiveness*: Number of unauthorized users found.

- *Change control coverage*: Number of authorized changes vs. changes.

- *Documentation coverage for a control*: Policy, standard, procedures in place per control.

This is just a small list of ideas. You should deploy metrics and measures alongside the controls so that you can collect and review them at this time. Over time, you can see how a control matures and becomes more effective (or not). These are the kinds of statistics that are useful when you need to do executive presentations (here's what we did this past year), customer demonstrations (here's how we protect you), and budget justifications (here's how we spent your money; we'd like some more).

Reviewing What Didn't Work

Now the bad news. You need to look at where the wheels came off. Like successes, there are many rich sources of problems to review. If you really want to improve and future-proof your security program, then you should broaden your idea of what went wrong to include those aforementioned *near misses*, audit observations, and anywhere you fell short of expectations. The purpose isn't to flog people for blame, but to look for weakening seals and rusty gears. Here's a list of things to examine:

- Audit findings (control failures, control objective failures)
- Auditor observations
- Security incidents
- Security policy issues such as including violations, policy exceptions, and difficult enforcements/reminders
- Unplanned outages and service failures
- Vulnerability scan and penetration test results
- Scoped information leakages
- Scope changes without analysis and approval
- Deadline violations, such as not patching within policy required period

It can be useful to keep a standardized register of all of these things. You should already be keeping your security incidents in a register, but you can add in these other things and create a summary timeline for analysis. The ISMS committee will want to review things at a higher level rather than rehash every detail. Table 24-1 shows an example of how to do this.

Table 24-1. *Sample Security Incident Register*

Date	Relevant Process	Incident	Impact
Feb	HR termination	Employee left firm— IT did not remove account	Internal audit finding
Apr	Backup	Service outage—backups failed	No restore capability for 3 days
May	Log review	IDS logs not reviewed for two days	Audit finding
May	Vuln scanning	Quarterly vuln scan 1 month late	Audit control failure in report
June	IT	Lost laptop at airport	Cost of laptop $1,000
July	HR onboarding	New-hire checklist records lost/not filled out	Audit finding
Sep	Access controls	Two-termed users not removed after two months	Internal audit finding
Nov	Change controls	Change control ticket missing approval	Audit finding
Dec	Access controls	Two servers had wrong password length settings	Audit finding
Dec	HR training	Two employees did not attend training	Audit finding

You can even take this a step further and use a formal incident framework like the Vocabulary for Event Recording and Incident Sharing (VERIS)[1] to track and analyze incidents.

Analyzing the Data

All control failures are not alike, and more importantly, they are often just the tip of the iceberg. You should treat every major audit finding and control failure as a symptom of a larger problem. Sure, dumb luck is going to turn against you every now and then, but your controls should be resilient enough to withstand random misfortunes. Remember, there are people out there working relentlessly on creating bad luck for their victims. There are many reasons why a control might have failed. Here are some ideas and examples:

- Failure to follow defined process... Why?
    - The importance of the process was not communicated well by management.
    - The documentation was unclear, insufficient, unavailable, and not used.
    - The training was insufficient; people weren't trained.
    - Missing resources (didn't have the people to do this).
    - The process was not practical, was incomplete, and/or was too difficult.
- Technological failures... Why?
    - Lack of needed maintenance
        - Too much maintenance needed for our resources
    - Lack of needed oversight on technology
        - Too much oversight needed to work technology
        - Too complicated to operate, which yielded poor performance
    - Improperly deployed/installed
        - Insufficient training/documentation
        - Difficult to deploy/install
        - Does not provide feedback on status
    - Software bug/component failure
    - Missing feature
    - Misunderstood feature
- Insufficient Design... Why?
    - No applicable control to cover this risk adequately
    - Process/attacker bypassed existing controls
    - Missing needed actions/steps/inputs
    - Did not provide adequate feedback on effectiveness

---

[1]http://veriscommunity.net

In addition to the possible causes, how the problem unfolded is also relevant. Was it a singular occurrence (or short bursts of occurrences)? Or does the problem occur every now and then? How was the problem detected? Do all the relevant processes and controls have sufficient mechanisms to provide feedback on their status? Did the maintenance needs of a control or process change unexpectedly or silently? How well did the organization recover from the incident, including both time to recover and effort to recover. All of this information can be useful in doing a root cause analysis (as described in Chapter 20).

There is a saying: *No matter how it looks at first, it's always a people problem.* You should look at how your organization's personnel acted before, during, and after the problem. Did they need help but not ask for it? Were they prevented from asking for help or providing a warning by internal culture, a lack of awareness, or no clear channel to communicate? When uncertainty or external pressure ramps up, people often retreat into their documented roles and make defensive decisions. If the process doesn't call out for doing something, no matter how rational, employees may not deviate or speak up for fear of retribution. This can be a process design issue but also an education issue. The organization and the people involved need to understand the reason for the process and work toward the common goal.

Looking for Systematic Issues

When doing this analysis, look for what permitted the problem to happen and offer a solution at the right layer. Designs and systems can have different *shearing layers*,[2] which means that they age and function at different rates. These layers can include organizational culture, physical facilities, IT infrastructure, ongoing IT projects, user behavior, and business process. All of these layers interact and change at different rates. Often, technological layers go obsolete faster than the people process.

Sometimes the problem is conceptual. The control design itself doesn't match the reality of the process it's protecting. This could be because of the activity's bad model, a control that doesn't fit the process (a common problem with off-the-shelf technology), or a system that has grown so complex that it no longer works well.

Sometimes the problem is resource constraints. This goes beyond having enough people or money. It can mean that the people involved do not have the skill set or correct mental framework to understand the process that they need to navigate. It could mean that the technology is being pushed past its limit, both in terms of load or feature set. There could be policy constraints, which goes beyond the current published policies but could also involve issues with cultural issues, regulatory mismatches, or informal processes baked into the culture.

Look for Things that Aren't Broken yet, but Will Be

Beyond looking for existing problems, you should also be on guard for emerging problems. You need to keep an eye on processes that are slowly growing or requiring more resources. Without high-level oversight and intervention, some solutions can encroach on other useful work and become more trouble than they're worth.

A likely suspect for potential future problems is persistent *temporary* solutions and work-arounds. These are the *good enough* solutions that someone slapped on until a better solution could be found. They worked well enough and people got busy, so the temporary solution is still there, years later. What began as a state of exception has become persistent, embedded, and worst of all, expanding. You do not want these duct tape solutions to become part of the permanent infrastructure.

You should review all major security policies as well. Although policies are supposed to be high-level and not very specific, it is possible that they have drifted from the original goals. Policies need to reflect the current practices and needs of the organization. If a policy goes slowly out of alignment, there could be control failures or wasted resources.

---

[2]https://en.wikipedia.org/wiki/Shearing_layers

Lastly, you should ensure that the security critical analyses are updated for the new period. This includes asset analysis, threat analysis, impact analysis, and compliance analysis. All of these analyses should converge into your updated risk analysis. Your chosen risk analysis framework should have processes to ensure regularly updates. Like policy, if the risk analysis has not kept abreast of the organization's environment, there could be serious problems.

Making Changes

The final part of the ISMS PDCA process is doing corrective action on the IT security program for processes that aren't meeting goals. Now that you've collected data and done your analysis, it's time to consider changes.

Look Before You Leap

Before you start making changes, you should first consider whether the change is worth it. You don't have to solve every problem at once. If a control is mostly working, be sure to brainstorm on if the change will make things better or worse. Remember the thresholds of risk acceptance; your controls may work fine up to a point and any more work comes with a diminishing return. Consider the problem of lost laptops. Let's say that you lost three this year, but because of your controls, they were all encrypted. You could do more security awareness training and add laptop-tracking controls. Perhaps this will drive down the number of lost laptops—but at what cost? Also, don't forget to consider the opportunity costs. The money you spend on new controls is also the same money that the organization could use to further its mission.

Just like your original proposed controls, every control change or new control should include a business case describing the intended benefits and both the direct and indirect costs. When making a change to running control, you should enumerate your assumptions about the change being made and the impacts. If feasible, you can do trials and testing on the new control or process to check the results. Don't forget the possibility of unintended consequences and how the organization itself may react to the change. Remember that there may be some lag time before the effects (both positive and negative) of changes become apparent. In addition to risk and control cost, you can use the confidence in the effectiveness of the change to prioritize your efforts.

Improving the Controls

When looking to improve your controls, look at the trade-off from administrative controls vs. technical controls. A control could be more effective if you replaced it with a technical control, or perhaps the opposite. Don't limit yourself to just expanding and tweaking an existing process. Sometimes the best way forward is to redesign a control from scratch. There are other, simpler changes that you can try to improve things, such as additional training, reassigning responsibility of the control, adding new verification steps, or modifying the frequency of human interactions.

Over time, your controls need to get stronger and your analyses more thorough. Your adversaries will only be improving their attack technology and methods, so you need to keep improving too. Most successful organizations are constantly growing, so your security program needs to consider this as well. Can your security program stretch and manage twice its current load? Large-scale expansion is a good group exercise for the ISMS committee to consider. The exercise may also uncover new ideas to improve control in stopping power, coverage, and the cost to run and deploy.

For SSAE 16 SOC 1 audits, you can also look at redesigning entire control objectives. It's not unheard of to move controls around between objectives to strengthen coverage and build more defense in depth. Similarly, you may have used a single control to support two different objectives; for example, security policy for both access control and human resource security. If an audit finds problems with that control, its failure endangers two different control objectives. It may be efficient to share controls between objectives, but if that control has problems, you could risk having twice the audit findings.

Speaking of audit findings, those findings should definitely feed into the work of the internal audit team. Anything that the auditor finds needs to be checked and rechecked for a long while. Sometimes audit findings and observations aren't around control failures but on the accompanying records and proof. Record management for running controls should also be improved, with internal audits that keep an eye on things.

Ideas for Improvement

How do you specifically improve or fix a control or process? Here are some ideas to consider for your improvement plans:

- Additional training and testing on that training
- Create and require the use of checklists
- Automate all or part of the process
- Split up a complex process step into substeps
- Add additional supervision, monitoring, or oversight
- Add an end-of-process review

Another improvement idea to enforce attention to detail on critical but tedious tasks is to create mechanisms for *deliberate actions*. For example, if you need someone to do daily log review, require him to fill out a short blank form with a summary of what was in the logs. This goes beyond just checking the box that he viewed the alerts and charts, but moves him to absorb, think, and explain the data. In high-stress, low-tolerance jobs like piloting an aircraft or ship, deliberate action is enforced through the use of verbalization of actions being performed; for example, the helmsman who says "I intend to make right full rudder in 3-2-1..." before he turns. The idea isn't just to communicate to everyone what is going on, but force the operator to be specific and careful in his or her intentions and actions.

Bridge Letters

For SSAE 16 Type 2 audits, it is possible to have gaps between audit periods. Some firms align their audit periods based on their fiscal year and not the calendar year. For example, an audit may begin on June 1st and run for twelve months until next year. However, some external parties will want an audit based on a calendar year, so there is a gap in audit coverage until the next report is issued. Similarly, some firms do only six- or nine-month SSAE 16 Type 2 audits for cost reasons, also leaving gaps in coverage. In these cases, the audited party can issue a formal attestation, called a *bridge letter,* to cover the gap. This letter defines the coverage gap and attests that the organization has not made any *material changes* to the controls in place. It's not as good as an audit, but if sandwiched between two good audit reports, it's usually sufficient.

Rolling out a Change Plan

Once you've decided what is going to be changed, you need to build a prioritized project plan. In addition to having the ISMS committee budget resources and assign responsibility for the project work, they should also consider time-lines, feedback and progress milestones. When you change or replace controls, you want to have controls overlapping so that the risk and compliance needs are fully covered. More risky, but more common, is a direct transition at a particular time. From this date forward, we will be using the new process to do background checks and retire the old one. If you can get control overlap, then you have the opportunity to analyze the feedback and adjust the new control before dropping the old one.

We Can Never Stop Trying to Improve

For the organization, the executive team, and yourself, the goal is *no unpleasant surprises*. You don't want to be surprised by a risk that you hadn't thought about, an asset sitting unprotected in danger, a control failure that you hadn't anticipated, or an audit report full of findings. If you work hard and grind away at your assessments and control work, then you are doing the best that you can to reduce unforeseen calamities.

In the end, nothing that is functional can also be impregnable. The Internet age has moved into a time of cyber cold war. Our organizations are being covertly targeted and attacked by governments, industrial spies, and political groups. Large-scale industrial espionage, denial of service, ransomware, and revenge hacking are becoming normal. A security program that can meet these challenges requires relentless attention to detail and a deep commitment to reevaluating your assumptions. You need to do your best—and then push to be better—every day. In the end, what you protect needs to feel like an extension of you. You need to know it, feel it, and defend it as if it's where you live.

What I have described in this book is by no means the final word for building or maintaining a security program. Every organization is different and unique. I challenge you to build things better than what I've described here. This is only the beginning. The rest is up to you. Never give up. The world needs your good work.

FURTHER READING

- **Dancing with Systems, the Donella Meadows Institute**
  http://www.donellameadows.org/archives/dancing-with-systems/

- **Marcus Ranum's Computer Security**
  http://www.ranum.com/security/computer_security/

- **Engineers and Existentialists, by Richard Thieme**
  http://www.thiemeworks.com/engineers-and-existentialists-how-critical-infrastructure-protection-turns-security-professionals-into-philosophers/

Index

© Raymond Pompon 2016
R. Pompon, *IT Security Risk Control Management*, DOI 10.1007/978-1-4842-2140-2

Get the eBook for only $5!

Why limit yourself?

Now you can take the weightless companion with you wherever you go and access your content on your PC, phone, tablet, or reader.

Since you've purchased this print book, we're happy to offer you the eBook in all 3 formats for just $5.

Convenient and fully searchable, the PDF version enables you to easily find and copy code—or perform examples by quickly toggling between instructions and applications. The MOBI format is ideal for your Kindle, while the ePUB can be utilized on a variety of mobile devices.

To learn more, go to www.apress.com/companion or contact support@apress.com.

Printed in the United States
By Bookmasters

Printed in the United States
By Bookmasters